LYING
About
HITLER

Also by Richard J. Evans

Death in Hamburg (1987)
In Hitler's Shadow (1989)
Ritual of Retribution (1996)
In Defense of History (1999)

LYING
About
HITLER

*History, Holocaust,
and the David Irving Trial*

RICHARD J.
EVANS

BASIC
BOOKS

A MEMBER OF THE PERSEUS BOOK GROUP

Copyright © 2001 by Richard J. Evans
Published by Basic Books, 2002.
A Member of the Perseus Books Group

Designed by Jim Buchanan of Bookcomp Inc.

Library of Congress Cataloging-in-Publication Data
Evans, Richard J.
  Lying about Hitler : history, Holocaust, and the David Irving trial / Richard
Evans.
    p. cm.
  Includes bibliographical references and index.
    ISBN 0-465-02152-2 (hc) ; 0-465-02153-0 (pbk.)
      1. Irving, David John Cawdell 1938—Trials, litigation, etc. 2. Lipstadt, Debo-
rah E.—Trials, litigation, etc. 3. Penguin (Firm)—Trials, litigation, etc. 4. Trials
(Libel)—England—London. 5. Holocaust denial literature—Great Britain. I.
Title.
KD379.5.I78 E95 2001
940.53'18—dc21

00-140130

This book is dedicated to the survivors
of Nazi genocide, murder and violence,
and to the memory of the millions who
did not survive

CONTENTS

ABBREVIATIONS

BA	Bundesarchiv
BBC	British Broadcasting Corporation
BDC	Berlin Document Center
Der Prozess	*Der Prozess gegen die Hauptkriegsverbrecher vor dem Internationalen Militärgerichtshof Nürnberg* (Nuremberg, 1949)
GTB	Goebbels Tagebücher (Elke Fröhlich [ed.], *Die Tagebücher von Joseph Goebbels* [Munich, 1994–98])
IfZ	Institut für Zeitgeschichte
IMT	*The Trial of the Major War Criminals before the International Military Tribunal, Nurenberg, 14 November 1945–6 April 1946* (Nuremberg, 1946)
JHR	*Journal of Historical Review*
KGB	Commitee for State Security
LICA	Ligue Internationale Contre L'Antisemitisme
ND	Nuremberg Document
NSDAP	Nationalsozialistische Deutsche Arbeiterpartei
PRO	Public Record Office, London
RAF	Royal Air Force
SA	Sturmabteilung (Brownshirts)
SD	Sicherheitsdienst
SOPADE	Sozialdemokratische Partei Deutschlands
SS	Schutzstaffel
TS	Transcript (High Court of Justice, Queen's Bench Division, 1996/I/No. 113, transcribed from the stenographic notes of Harry Counsell & Company)
VfZG	*Vierteljahrshefte für Zeitgeschichte*

PREFACE

This book is about how we can tell the difference between truth and lies in history. It uses as an example the libel case brought before the High Court in London in the spring of 2000 by David Irving against Deborah Lipstadt and her publisher, Penguin Books. It concentrates on the issue of the falsification of the historical record which Lipstadt accused Irving of having committed and which was the subject of the investigations that I was asked to present to the court as an expert witness. The first chapter explains how I became involved in the case, sets out the background, and provides a context. The next four chapters present the results of my investigations. Chapter 6 is an account of the trial itself, explaining how Irving dealt with the findings presented in my report. The final chapter looks at the aftermath of the trial and discusses some of the wider issues it raised. All of this, I hope, will provide concrete illustrations of the general questions of problems of historical objectivity and historical knowledge that I raised in my earlier book, *In Defense of History*, published in England in 1997 and in the USA two years later.

This is not, therefore, intended to be a rounded or comprehensive account of the whole case. Others will be attempting that. Some of the aspects of the case that received a great deal of media attention at the time, such as the debate over the mass gassing facilities at the Auschwitz concentration camp or the nature and extent of Irving's connections with the German far right, are also the subject of other books, by the experts who dealt with them in court, and they are only alluded to in this book briefly, if at all. The central issue in the following pages, as I believe it was in the case as a whole, is the falsification and manipulation of the historical record that Lipstadt alleged Irving had committed. Although discussion of this issue took up more time during the trial than anything else, it was barely mentioned in press reports of the proceedings, and as a result the general impression of the trial purveyed by the international news media was a rather distorted one, since they devoted the lion's share of their attention to Irving's racism and antisemitism. One of the aims of this book is to set the record straight in this respect.

Inevitably, even within this limited compass, my treatment of these issues cannot hope to be comprehensive. In chapters 2, 3, 4, and 5 I offer a series of significant examples. Much has had to be omitted for the sake of clarity and readability and to keep this book to a reasonable length. The original expert report that forms the basis for these central chapters was 740 pages long, and in many places it was more suited for a court of law than for a reader with a more general interest in these matters. However, the most important issues treated in the report and upheld in the corresponding parts of the judgment are included, even if only in a slimmed-down form.

Aside from the usual archival and printed sources, this book rests in particular on materials compiled for the trial. These consist in the first place of David Irving's published books and articles and the documents that entered the public domain through the process of Discovery in the court case, and their citation in court in the expert reports, the defense statements, and the judgment. They include consecutively numbered videotapes and audiocassettes of Irving's speeches, various numbered sequences of documents in separate collections, and numbered folders belonging to the original Discovery list and the supplementary Discovery lists. In addition, a series of documents was submitted to the court during the trial by both sides in the case.

All of this material was initially collected and collated by Mishcon de Reya, the solicitors for the second defendant. The verbatim record of the trial was made available from stenographic notes supplied on a daily basis by Harry Counsel and Company, Clifford's Inn, Fetter Lane, London EC4. Basic legal documents included Irving's Writ and Statement of Claim, the Defense of the Second Defendant (i.e., Deborah Lipstadt), Irving's Reply to the Defense of the Second Defendant, and the defense's Restatement of Case. The court was also supplied with copies of the Opening and Closing Statements by both parties; in both cases, the typed version of the Closing Statement was considerably longer than the version read out in court. The defense also issued written questions to Irving, and Irving issued written questions to me, to which I supplied lengthy written responses. The researchers and experts supplied the court with a large quantity of photocopied original documents from German archives, and Irving also presented a number of similar documents to the court. Irving's website coverage of the trial and additional relevant material were also downloaded on a regular basis. All of this material is referenced in the notes at the appropriate junctures.

It was Anthony Julius who asked me to become involved in the Irving case, and thus provided the opportunity to write this book. My thanks go to him, to James Libson, Laura Tyler, Pippa Marshall, and all the team at Mishcon de Reya for all the hard work they put in to obtaining, collecting, and sorting much of the material for the report on which a large part of this book is based. Richard Rampton QC was a source of sage advice, and his acute questioning forced me rethink a number of issues. I am extremely grateful to both him and Heather Rogers, junior defense counsel in the case, for their efforts to lend legal and conceptual precision to many of the more academic points originally put forward in my report, and for clarifying the issues in their own meticulous compilations of the documentary evidence.

My special thanks go to Thomas Skelton-Robinson and Nik Wachsmann, my research assistants, without whose invaluable detective work the report could not have been written, and to Tobias Jersak, who helped root out a number of errors in it before the trial began. Christopher Browning, Hajo Funke, Peter Longerich, and Robert Jan Van Pelt, the other defense witnesses, were a pleasure to work with and helped elucidate a great deal both about Irving and about the subjects with which he dealt. Martin and Susie Gilbert lent moral support while I was in the witness box and my colleagues at Cambridge tolerated my frequent absences in London with good humor and forbearance. Deborah Lipstadt's amazing cheerfulness throughout her whole ordeal was an inspiration and helped convince me it was all worth it.

Don Fehr, Felicity Tucker, Jim Buchanan, and the editorial and production teams at Basic Books smoothed the path from floppy disk to bound copy. Nik Wachsmann, James Libson, and Richard Rampton again put me in their debt, as did Kristin Semmens, by reading through the final version of the typescript at short notice and suggesting many improvements. My thanks to all of them, and once more especially to Christine Corton, who, with our sons Matthew and Nicholas, provided sanity at home after the stress and strangeness of the daily proceedings in the High Court, and enabled me to complete both the report and the book in good time. As for the dedication, there could really be no other.

Richard J. Evans
Cambridge, October 2000

CHAPTER ONE

History on Trial

I

What is historical objectivity? How do we know when a historian is telling the truth? Aren't all historians, in the end, only giving their own opinions about the past? Don't they just select whatever facts they need to support their own interpretations and leave the rest in the archives? Aren't the archives full of preselected material anyway? Can we really say that anything historians present to us about the past is true? Aren't there, rather, many different truths, according to your political beliefs and personal perspectives? Questions such as these have been preoccupying historians for a long time. In recent years, they have become, if anything, more urgent and more perplexing than ever. Debate about them has repeatedly gravitated toward the Nazi extermination of the Jews during the Second World War. If we could not know for sure about anything that happened in the past, then how could we know about this most painful of all topics in modern history?[1]

Just such a question has been posed, and answered in the negative, by a group of individuals, based mainly in the United States, who are certainly far removed in intellectual terms from postmodernist hyper-relativism, but who have asserted in a variety of publications that indeed there is no real evidence to support the conventional picture of the Nazi persecution of the Jews. There is a thin but seemingly continuous line of writing since the Second World War that has sought to deny the existence of the gas chambers at Auschwitz and other extermination camps, to minimize the number of Jews killed by the Nazis until it becomes equivalent to that of the Germans killed by the Allies, to explain away the killings as incidental by-products of a vicious war rather than the result of central planning in Berlin, and to claim that the evidence for the extermination, the gas chambers, and all the rest of it had mostly been concocted after the war.

A number of scholars have devoted some attention to this strange and disturbing stream of thought. The most important of their works is *Denying the Holocaust: The Growing Assault on Truth and Memory*, by the American historian Deborah Lipstadt. Published in 1993, this book gave an extended factual account of the deniers' publications and activities since the Second World War and identified them as closely connected with neo-fascist, far-right, and antisemitic political extremists in Europe and the United States. Whether or not Lipstadt was correct to claim that these people posed a serious threat to historical knowledge and memory was debatable. But the evidence she presented for the existence of the phenomenon and for its far-right connections seemed convincing enough. Lipstadt argued that denial of the Holocaust was in most cases antisemitic and tied to an anti-Jewish political agenda in the present. The denial of history was the product of political bias and political extremism, which had no place in the world of serious historical scholarship.

Yet how unbiased was Lipstadt herself? There was no doubt about her commitment to Jewish causes. Born in 1947 in New York of a German-Jewish immigrant father who was descended from a prominent family of rabbis, she had been brought up in what she described as a "traditional Jewish home," she had studied at the Hebrew University of Jerusalem for two years, and been present in Israel during the 1967 Arab-Israeli war. She had studied modern Jewish history, the Third Reich, and the Holocaust at university, and taught courses on the history of the Holocaust at a variety of institutions, including the University of Washington and the University of California at Los Angeles, before joining the staff of Emory University in Atlanta, Georgia, in 1993, where she held an endowed chair and was setting up a new Institute for Jewish Studies. She was also a member of the United States Holocaust Memorial Council—a presidential appointment—and had acted as a consultant to the United States Holocaust Memorial Museum while it was being built.

Aside from these academic credentials and activities, Lipstadt was also a member of the United States Department of State Advisory Committee on Religious Freedom Abroad. In 1972 she had visited the Soviet

Union and inspected sites of major Nazi killings of Jews such as Babi Yar. This was a period when controversy was being aroused by the Soviet authorities' refusal to allow Soviet Jews to emigrate to Israel, and there was a good deal of subtle and sometimes not so subtle antisemitism on the part of the authorities. Lending her Jewish prayerbook to an elderly Jewish woman in a synagogue in Czernowitz, Lipstadt was denounced to the authorities and arrested by the KGB for distributing religious items, strip-searched, held in prison for a day, questioned, and deported. After this, she had continued for some years to work hard for Soviet Jews while they were being persecuted.

Combined with her many discussions with camp survivors in Israel, she reported, this experience had led her to study the history of anti-semitism and, in particular, the Holocaust. Remembering the Holocaust was crucial in the perpetuation of Jewish tradition, but also in teaching lessons about the need to fight prejudice and persecution of many kinds in the world today. However, Lipstadt insisted, whatever her political and religious beliefs, she was convinced that the history of the Holocaust had to be researched to the highest possible scholarly standards and taught in a straightforwardly factual manner. She denied any wish to impose her views about the lessons of the Holocaust on her students. After the pub-lication of her book, Lipstadt left no doubt that her work on Holocaust denial had led some of the deniers to engage in "a highly personal and, at times, almost vile campaign against me." She had been vilified on the Internet, accused of fascist behavior, and phoned up by deniers and depicted by them in "an ugly and sometimes demeaning fashion." They had also left notes in her home mailbox. This had not stopped her from working in the field. Her book *Denying the Holocaust* was an academic project, but it had also taken on a broader significance.[2]

Lipstadt's book, when taken together with her previous work, made it clear that her main interest was in reactions to the extermination of Europe's Jews by the Nazis rather than in the extermination itself. After completing her work on Holocaust denial, she planned a book called *America Remembers the Holocaust: From the Newsreels to Schindler's List*. She had never written about German history and had never been in a German archive. Indeed, as far as I could tell, she did not even read German. She was really a specialist in the history of the United States since the Second World War. Yet it was easy enough for her to include in *Denying the Holocaust* refutations of some of the principal arguments of the deniers on the basis of well-known secondary literature about the extermination. Given the main focus of her work, which was on denial as a political and intellectual phenomenon, that was surely all that was required.

Nevertheless, her book did not pull its punches when it came to convicting deniers of massive falsification of historical evidence, manipulation of facts, and denial of the truth. One of those whom she discussed in this context was the British writer David Irving, who certainly did read German, had spent years in the archives researching the German side in the Second World War, and was the author of some thirty books on historical subjects. Some of them had gone through many reprints and a number of different editions. The great majority of them were about the Second World War, and in particular about Nazi Germany and its leaders. Before he was thirty, he had already begun researching and writing on twentieth-century history, publishing his first book, *The Destruction of Dresden*, in 1963, when he was only twenty-five.

Irving had also written *The Mare's Nest*, a study of German secret weapons in the Second World War, published in 1964, and a book about the German atomic bomb, *The Virus House*, published in 1967. In the same year, Irving published two more books, *The Destruction of Convoy PQ17, and Accident—The Death of General Sikorski*. Despite their somewhat specialized titles, these books in many cases aroused widespread controversy and made Irving into a well-known figure. *The Destruction of Dresden* created a storm by alleging that the bombing of Dresden by Allied airplanes early in 1945 caused many more deaths than had previously been thought. *The Destruction of Convoy PQ 17* aroused serious objections on the part of a British naval officer criticized by Irving in his book. *Accident* generated considerable outrage by its suggestion that the Polish exile leader in the Second World War, General Sikorski, had been assassinated on the orders of Winston Churchill. By the end of the 1960s, Irving had already made a name for himself as an extremely controversial writer about the Second World War.

With the publication of his massive study of *Hitler's War* in 1977, Irving stirred up fresh debate. In this book, he argued that far from ordering it himself, Hitler had not known about the extermination of the Jews

until late in 1943, and both before and after that had done his best to mitigate the worst antisemitic excesses of his subordinates. Irving heightened the controversy by publicly offering a financial reward to anyone
who could come up with a document proving him wrong. The furor completely overshadowed his publication of a biography of the German general Erwin Rommel in the same year, under the title *The Trail of the Fox*.
The following year, Irving brought out a 'prequel' to his book on Hitler
and the Second World War, entitled *The War Path*. In 1981 he published
two more books—*The War Between the Generals*, devoted to exposing
differences of opinion among the commanders of Hitler's army during
the Second World War; and *Uprising!*, arguing, to quote Irving himself,
"that the Uprising of 1956 in Hungary was primarily an anti-Jewish uprising," because the communist regime was run by Jews.[3]

The stream of books continued with *Churchill's War* in 1987, *Rudolf
Hess: The Missing Years* published in the same year, a biography of Hermann Göring (1989), and most recently a book on *Goebbels: Mastermind
of the 'Third Reich'* (1996). And while he was producing new work, he
also published revised and amended editions of some of his earlier books,
most notably, in 1991, *Hitler's War*, which also incorporated a new
version of *The War Path*, and in 1996 *Nuremberg: The Last Battle*, an
updated version of a previously published book, reissued to mark the fiftieth anniversary of the Nuremberg War Crimes Trials.

Despite all this, Irving had never held a post in a university history
department or any other academic institution. He did not even have a
degree. He had started a science degree at London University but never
finished it. "I am an untrained historian," he had confessed in 1986. "History was the only subject I flunked when I was at school."[4] Several
decades on from his self-confessedly disastrous schoolboy encounter
with the subject, however, Irving clearly laid great stress on the fact that
the catalogue of his work demonstrated that he had now become a 'reputable historian':[5]

> As an independent historian, I am proud that I cannot be threatened
> with the loss of my job, or my pension, or my future. Other histori-
> ans around the world sneer and write letters to the newspapers about
> 'David Irving, the so-called historian', and they demand, "Why does
> he call himself a Historian anyway? Where did he study History?
> Where did he get his Degree? What, No Degree in History, then why

does he call himself a Historian?" My answer to them, Was Pliny a
historian or not? Was Tacitus? Did he get a degree in some university? Thucydides? Did he get a degree? And yet we unashamedly call
them historians—we call them historians because they wrote history
which has done (*recte*: gone) down the ages as accepted true history.[6]

This was true. Irving could not be dismissed just because he lacked formal qualifications.

Irving was clearly incensed by a reference to him on page 180 of Lipstadt's book as "discredited." Lipstadt also alleged in her book that Irving
was "one of the most dangerous spokespersons for Holocaust denial.
Familiar with historical evidence," she wrote, "he bends it until it con-
forms with his ideological leanings and political agenda." According to
Lipstadt, Irving had "neofascist" and "denial connections," for example,
with the so-called Institute for Historical Review in California. More
important, Lipstadt charged that Holocaust deniers like Irving "misstate,
misquote, falsify statistics, and falsely attribute conclusions to reliable
sources. They rely on books that directly contradict their arguments,
quoting in a manner that completely distorts the authors' objectives." Irving himself, she claimed, was "an ardent admirer of the Nazi leader," who
"declared that Hitler repeatedly reached out to help the Jews" (p. 161).
Scholars had "accused him of distorting evidence and manipulating documents to serve his own purposes . . . of skewing documents and misrepresenting data in order to reach historically untenable conclusions,
particularly those that exonerate Hitler." "On some level," Lipstadt concluded, "Irving seems to conceive himself as carrying on Hitler's legacy."[7]

These were serious charges. Historians do not usually answer such
criticisms by firing off writs. Instead, they normally rebut them in print.
Irving, however, was no stranger to the courts. He wrote to Lipstadt's
English publisher Penguin Books in November 1995 demanding the
withdrawal of Lipstadt's book from circulation, alleging defamation and
threatening to sue. Lipstadt responded, pointing out that her book mentioned Irving only on six out of more than three hundred pages. The publisher refused to withdraw; and Irving issued his defamation writ in September 1996.[8] By December 1997, the legal process of mounting a
defense against the writ was well under way, and a date for the proceedings to be held before the High Court in London was due to be fixed.

II

It was at this point that I became involved in the case on the initiative of Anthony Julius, of the London firm of solicitors Mishcon de Reya. I had never met him in person, but of course I knew of him through his high media profile as the solicitor who had won a record settlement for Princess Diana in her divorce from the Prince of Wales. Julius was not just a fashionable and successful lawyer. He was also well known as a writer and intellectual, although in the field of English literature rather than history. He was the author of a scholarly if controversial study of T. S. Eliot and antisemitism, and he wrote frequent book reviews for the Sunday papers. Julius was representing Deborah Lipstadt. When he phoned me toward the end of 1997, it was to ask if I would be willing to act as an expert witness for the defense.

Later, in his cramped and book-lined Holborn office, Julius explained to me in more detail what would be involved. The first duty of an expert witness, he said, was to the court. That is, the evidence had to be as truthful and objective as possible. Expert witnesses were not there to plead a case. They were there to help the court in technical and specialized matters. They had to give their own opinion, irrespective of which side had engaged them. They had to swear a solemn oath to tell the truth and could be prosecuted for perjury if they did not. On the other hand, they were usually commissioned by one side or the other in the belief that what they said would support the case being put rather than undermine it. At the end of the day, it was up to the lawyers whether or not they used the reports they had commissioned. I would be paid by the hour, not by results. So the money would have no influence on what I wrote or said. If I did agree to write an expert report, however, and it was accepted by the lawyers, then I could expect it to be presented to the court and I would have to attend the trial to be cross-examined on it by the plaintiff.

Why me? I asked. There were a number of reasons, Julius said. First, I was a specialist in modern German history. A copy of my most recent book in this field, *Rituals of Retribution*, was on his bookshelf. It was a large-scale study of capital punishment in Germany from the seventeenth century to the abolition of the death penalty in East Germany in 1987. Like much of my other work, it rested on unpublished manuscript documents in a range of German archives. So it was clear that I had a good command of the German language. I could read the obsolete German script in which many documents were written until the end of the Second World War. And I was familiar with the documentary basis on which a lot of modern German history was written. I had also for many years taught a document-based undergraduate course on Nazi Germany for the history degree at Birkbeck College in London University and before that in my previous post at the University of East Anglia. Clearly, the trial was going to turn to a considerable extent on the interpretation of Nazi documents, so expertise of this kind was crucial; and it was expertise that the court itself could not be expected to possess. Second, a couple of months earlier, I had published a short book entitled *In Defense of History*, which had dealt with such vexed questions as objectivity and bias in historical writing, the nature of historical research, the difference between truth and fiction, and the possibility of obtaining accurate knowledge about the past. These in a way, Anthony Julius explained, were the central issues in the case that Irving was bringing against Lipstadt.

What Anthony Julius wanted me to do was to advise the court on whether Lipstadt's charges were justified. I was in a good position to do so not only because of my previous writings, but also because I had no personal connection with either of the two main protagonists in the case. Indeed, I had never actually seen either of them in the flesh. Irving was a famously combative figure, but he had never had occasion to cross swords with me. As I left Anthony Julius's office, I tried to put together what was known about Irving's reputation. Irving insisted that his works on the Second World War had a high standing and claimed in his libel suit that Lipstadt's allegations had caused "damage to his reputation" in his "calling as an historian."[9] Yet as I began to plow through the reviews of Irving's books written by a wide range of historians and journalists over the years, the case he made for his high reputation among academic reviewers began to crumble. Academic historians with a *general* knowledge of modern history had indeed mostly been quite generous to Irving, even where they had found reason to criticize him or disagree with his views. Paul Addison, for example, an expert on British history in the Second World War, had concluded that while Irving was "usually a Colossus of research, he is often a schoolboy in judgment."[10] Reviewing *The*

War Path in 1978, R. Hinton Thomas, professor of German at Birmingham University, whose knowledge of the social and political context of twentieth-century German literature was both deep and broad, dismissed the book as "unoriginal" and its "claims to novelty" as "ill-based."[11] "Much of Irving's argument," wrote Sir Martin Gilbert, official biographer of Churchill, about *Hitler's War* in 1977, "is based on speculation." But he also praised the book as "a scholarly work, the fruit of a decade of wide researches."[12] The military historian Sir Michael Howard, subsequently Regius Professor of Modern History at Oxford, praised on the other hand the "very considerable merits" of *The War Path*, and declared that Irving was "at his best as a professional historian demanding documentary proof for popularly-held beliefs."[13]

In similar fashion, the eminent American specialist on modern Germany, Gordon A. Craig, reviewing Irving's *Goebbels* in the *New York Review of Books* in 1996, seemed at first glance full of praise for Irving's work:

> Silencing Mr Irving would be a high price to pay for freedom from the annoyance that he causes us. The fact is that he knows more about National Socialism than most professional scholars in his field, and students of the years 1933–1945 owe more than they are always willing to admit to his energy as a researcher. . . . *Hitler's War* . . . remains the best study we have of the German side of the Second World War, and, as such, indispensable for all students of that conflict. . . . It is always difficult for the non-historian to remember that there is nothing absolute about historical truth. What we consider as such is only an estimation, based upon what the best available evidence tells us. It must constantly be tested against new information and new interpretations that appear, however implausible they may be, or it will lose its vitality and degenerate into dogma or shibboleth. Such people as David Irving, then, have a indispensable part in the historical enterprise, and we dare not disregard their views.[14]

Yet even reviewers who had praised "the depth of Irving's research and his intelligence" found "too many avoidable mistakes . . . passages quoted without attribution and important statements not tagged to the listed sources."[15] John Charmley, a right-wing historian at the University of East Anglia, wrote that he "admires Mr. Irving's assiduity, energy, and courage." He continued: "Mr. Irving's sources, unlike the conclusions which he draws from them, are usually sound." But he also noted: "Mr. Irving is cited only when his sources have been checked and found reliable."[16]

Historians with firsthand research experience and expertise in Irving's field were more critical still. An early, prominent instance of criticism from such a quarter came with Hugh Trevor-Roper's review of *Hitler's War* in 1977. Trevor-Roper had worked in British Intelligence during the war and had been charged with heading an official mission to find out the true facts about the death of Hitler. The result of his researches, published in 1947 as *The Last Days of Hitler*, immediately established him as a leading authority on Nazi Germany and especially on Irving's home territory of Hitler and his immediate personal entourage. Reviewing *Hitler's War*, Trevor-Roper paid the by now customary tribute to Irving's ingenuity and persistence as a researcher. "No praise," he wrote, "can be too high for his indefatigable scholarly industry." But this was immediately followed by devastating criticism of Irving's method. Trevor-Roper continued:

> When a historian relies mainly on primary sources, which we cannot easily check, he challenges our confidence and forces us to ask critical questions. How reliable is his historical method? How sound is his judgment? We ask these questions particularly of any man who, like Mr. Irving, makes a virtue—almost a profession—of using arcane sources to affront established opinions.

Trevor-Roper made it clear he found Irving's method and judgment defective: "He may read his manuscript diaries correctly. But we can never be quite sure, and when he is most original, we are likely to be least sure." Irving's work, he concluded, had a "consistent bias."[17]

The same view was taken by Martin Broszat, director of the *Institut für Zeitgeschichte* (Institute for Contemporary History) in Munich when Irving published *Hitler's War*. One of the world's leading historians of Nazi Germany, Broszat began his critique of *Hitler's War* by casting scorn on Irving's much-vaunted list of archival discoveries. The evidence Irving had gathered from the reminiscences of Hitler's entourage might provide more exact detail of what went on at Hitler's wartime headquarters, he wrote, and it might convey something of the atmosphere of the place, but it did little to enlarge our knowledge of the important military and political decisions that Hitler took, and so did not live up to the claims Irving made for it. Broszat went much further, however, and included the allegation, backed up by detailed examples, that Irving had manipulated and misinterpreted original documents in order to prove his arguments.[18] Equally critical was the American Charles W. Sydnor Jr., who at the time of writing his review had just completed a lengthy study, *Soldiers of Destruction: The SS Death's Head Division, 1933–1945*, published by Princeton University Press. Sydnor's thirty-page demolition of Irving's book was one of the few reviews of any of Irving's books for which the reviewer had manifestly undertaken a substantial amount of original research.[19] Sydnor considered Irving's boast to have outdone all other Hitler scholars in the depth and thoroughness of his research to be "pretentious twaddle." He accused Irving of innumerable inaccuracies, distortions, manipulations, and mistranslations in his treatment of the documents.[20]

Peter Hoffmann, the world's leading authority on the conservative resistance to Hitler and the individuals and groups behind the bomb plot of 20 July 1944, and a profound student of the German archival record of the wartime years, was equally critical of Irving's biography of Hermann Göring, published in 1988:

> Mr. Irving's constant references to archives, diaries and letters, and the overwhelming amount of detail in his work, suggest objectivity. In fact they put up a screen behind which a very different agenda is transacted. . . . Mr. Irving is a great obfuscator. . . . Distortions affect every important aspect of this book to the point of obfuscation. . . . It is unfortunate that Mr. Irving wastes his extraordinary talents as a researcher and writer on trivializing the greatest crimes in German history, on manipulating historical sources and on highlighting the theatrics of the Nazi era.

Hoffmann commented that while the 1977 edition of *Hitler's War* had "usefully provoked historians by raising the question of the smoking gun" (whether an order could be found from Hitler to perpetrate a holocaust against the Jews), twenty-two years on, so much research had been carried out in this area by historians that although he repeated it in *Göring*, "it is no longer possible to regard Mr. Irving's thesis as a useful provocation."[21]

John Lukács, an American historian who had written extensively on the Second World War, declared in a review of one of Irving's books in 1981 that "Mr Irving's factual errors are beyond belief." He renewed his criticisms of Irving years later in a general survey of historical writings on Hitler."[22] "Few reviewers and critics of Irving's books," Lukács complained, not without some justification, "have bothered to examine them carefully enough." *Hitler's War* contained "many errors in names and dates; more important, unverifiable and unconvincing assertions abound." There were references to archives "without dates, places, or file or page numbers." "Many of the archival references in Irving's footnotes . . . were inaccurate and did not prove or even refer to the pertinent statements in Irving's text." Lukács found many instances of Irving's "manipulations, attributing at least false meanings to some documents or, in other instances, printing references to irrelevant ones." Often "a single document, or fragment of a document, was enough for Irving to build a very questionable thesis on its contents or on the lack of such." "While some of Irving's 'finds' cannot be disregarded," Lukács went on, "their interpretation . . . is, more often than not, compromised and even badly flawed." He convicted Irving of "frequent 'twisting' of documentary sources" and urged "considerable caution" in their use by other historians.[23]

Similar conclusions were reached by Professor David Cannadine, currently director of the Institute of Historical Research at London University, when he came to consider the first volume of Irving's biography of Sir Winston Churchill.[24] Cannadine noted that the publishers to whom the book had originally been contracted (Michael Joseph in London and Doubleday in New York) had turned the manuscript down and it had been published by an unknown Australian company. "It has received almost no attention from historians or reviewers," and, Cannadine added, "It is easy to see why." Irving's method was full of "excesses, inconsistencies and omissions." Irving, he charged, "seems completely unaware of recent work done on the subject." "It is not merely," he observed, "that the arguments in this book are so perversely tendentious and irresponsibly sensationalist. It is also that it is written in a tone which is at best casually journalistic and at worst quite exceptionally offensive. The text is littered with errors from beginning to end."[25] In Cannadine's judgment, too, therefore, Irving's work was deeply flawed.

"Perversely tendentious," "'twisting' of documentary sources," "manipulating historical sources," "pretentious twaddle": these were unusually harsh criticisms emerging from the wider chorus of praise for Irving's energy and persistence as a researcher. Clearly, Lipstadt was far from being the first critic of Irving's work to accuse him of bending the documentary record to suit his arguments. For many years, professional historians had seemed to regard him as an assiduous collector of original documentation, although there was some dispute over quite how important all of it was. But when it came to Irving's interpretation of the documents, several eminent specialists were harsh, even savage, in their criticisms. Nor was this all. Irving's writings had repeatedly landed him in trouble with the law. He had been sued for libel by a retired naval officer who considered Irving's charge of cowardice against him in *The Destruction of Convoy PQ 17* to be defamatory, and had been forced with his publishers to pay damages of £40,000, later confirmed by the House of Lords. The award, made in 1970, was very large for the time, and included £25,000 in exemplary damages, which can only be awarded when it has been shown that the defendant is guilty of a deliberate 'tort' or wrong committed with the object of making money. His allegation in the introduction to the German edition of *Hitler's War* that the *Diary of Anne Frank* was a forgery had led to his publisher being forced to pay damages. In 1968 he had been sued for libel by Jillian Page, author of a newspaper article about him, as a result of his allegation that the article had been the result of her "fertile brain." Irving had apologized in the High Court and paid costs on condition that Page agreed to withdraw the action. Similarly he had also been obliged to pay costs in an unsuccessful libel action against Colin Smythe, publisher of a book (*The Assassination of Winston Churchill*) attacking Irving's views on the death of General Sikorski.[26]

During the 1960s, 1970s, and 1980s, Irving's books had been published by a variety of mainstream publishing houses, including Penguin Books, who had brought out a paperback edition of the early version of *Hitler's War* and its companion volume on the years 1933–39, *The War Path*; Macmillan, under whose imprint later editions of *Hitler's War* had appeared up to about 1992; Hodder and Stoughton, who had published the original hardback; HarperCollins, whose paperback imprint Grafton Books had published an edition of Irving's Göring biography in 1991; and Corgi paperbacks, who had produced more than one of the various editions of *The Destruction of Dresden*. Since the late 1980s, however, Irving had ceased to be published by major houses, but instead had brought out all his books under his own imprint, Focal Point. "If I write a bad book," he said, perhaps rather surprisingly, in 1986, "or if I write two or three bad books, with boobs in it which the newspapers pick out, which I'm ashamed to admit are probably right, then of course the time comes when publishers turn their back on me."[27]

Moreover, while he had run into the law at various points in his career, most notably in his arrest and deportation from Austria in 1983, his difficulties in this respect had increased noticeably during the 1990s, with his conviction for insulting the memory of the dead in Germany in 1991 and his banning from entry into that country, into Canada, and into Australia, all in 1992–93. One would not have expected a reputable historian to have run into such trouble, and indeed it was impossible to think of any historian of any standing at all who had been subjected to so many adverse legal judgments, or who had initiated so many libel actions himself. Irving's reputation as a historian, never entirely secure, seemed to have plummeted during the 1990s. In an interview with the American journalist Ron Rosenbaum in the mid-1990s, Irving himself had admitted as much, confessing that his reputation among historians was "down to its uppers," though adding that it "hasn't yet worn through to the street."[28]

Yet, because of his early reputation as a formidable historian, and because of his "articulate, plausible demeanor," as the journalist Sarah Lyall pointed out, "Mr. Irving has confounded efforts to write him off as a harmless crackpot."[29] Jenny Booth, indeed, writing in *The Scotsman*, thought that Irving "was still seen as a substantial scholar in England and the US."[30] The right-wing historian Andrew Roberts noted that "several distinguished historians, all of whom asked not to be named, told me how much they admired Irving's tenacity in uncovering new material from Nazi sources."[31]

Yet such admiration was almost always highly qualified. Wolfgang Benz, director of Berlin's Centre for the Study of Antisemitism, echoed the more dismissive tone of most German assessments of Irving's reputation: "Irving," he told an interviewer, "is overpraised as a writer for the general public. He has delivered details from the perspective of the key-hole—from conversations with courtiers and chauffeurs—and thereby mobilized the last knowledge that could be brought to light from Hitler's entourage. But nothing really new." The Irving of the early years had been an outsider who was to some extent to be taken seriously, Benz concluded, but he had subsequently radicalized his political views and could no longer be treated as a serious historian.[32]

III

A picture emerged, therefore, of a man who had left no stone unturned in his search for new documentation about Hitler and his role in the Third Reich, but whose use of that documentation raised many objections in the minds of those who knew the field well. Their criticisms raised real issues of objectivity, bias, and political motivation in the study of history that went far beyond the work of Irving himself. Yet Irving clearly insisted that his work was unimpeachably objective, describing himself as "an expert historian on the 'Third Reich'; I have spent thirty years now working in the archives in London, in Washington, in Moscow—in short, around the world. (If I) express an opinion it's probably a reasonable (*sic*) accurate opinion which I have arrived at, over a period of years."[33] In researching Hitler, he claimed to have

> adopted strict criteria in selecting my source material. I have burrowed deep into the contemporary writings of his closest personal staff, seeking clues to the real truth in diaries and private letters written to wives and friends. For the few autobiographical works I have used I have preferred to rely on their original manuscripts rather than the printed texts, as in the early postwar years apprehensive publishers (especially the "licensed" ones in Germany) made drastic changes in them. . . . But historians are quite incorrigible, and will quote any apparently primary source no matter how convincingly its pedigree is exposed.[34]

Irving argued in the introduction to the 1991 edition of *Hitler's War* that other historians had been almost uniformly "idle" in their attitude to the sources and that therefore everyone else's work on Hitler was unreliable.[35]

He listed a whole variety of diaries and other sources on which he claimed previous historians had relied, and which he himself had exposed as falsifications. All these falsifications, he argued, were to the disadvantage of Hitler. Yet his "idle predecessors" in writing about Hitler had failed to detect them.[36] "Each successive biographer" of Hitler, he declared in 1977, "has repeated or engrossed the legends created by his predecessors, or at best consulted only the most readily available works of reference themselves."[37] They had never bothered to visit the surviving relatives of leading Nazis to search for additional material. And they never troubled to consult the most basic documentation. In a debate held in 1978 in the German town of Aschaffenburg, Irving attacked establishment historians for allegedly simply copying out of each other's books, while he was the only Hitler specialist who actually consulted the original sources.[38]

Historians were inveterately lazy. "A lot of us, when we see something in handwriting, well, we hurriedly flip to another folder where it's all neatly typed out. . . . But I've trained myself to take the line of most resistance and I go for the handwriting."[39] Most historians, he averred, only quoted each other when it came to Hitler's alleged part in the extermination of the Jews. "For thirty years our knowledge of Hitler's part in the atrocity had rested on inter-historian incest."[40] Thus Irving contemptuously almost never cited, discussed, or used the work of other historians in his own books. Irving was evidently very proud of his personal collection of thousands of documents and index cards on the history of the Third Reich. He pointed out that he was "well known for providing every assistance to and answering the queries of his colleagues, regardless of their attitude to his works," and that he had made his research materials generally available for historical study at the German Federal Archives and at the Institute of Contemporary History in Munich.[41] Irving's self-assessment spurred Neal Ascherson, normally a sober-minded journalist, to pen some remarkably purple prose. Irving's reputation as a collector of documents was unparalleled:

This is a shadowy underworld, hidden beneath the clean, bright places where scholars write books. Down in the cellar of Third

Reich studies, con men and SS veterans, obsessive journalists and forgers and real historians stumble about in echoes of fantastic rumour. And here Irving is a dark prince: His special gift is finding papers which others don't even know how to look for.[42]

This was an unduly romantic view, however, which accepted too much of Irving's own assiduously propagated self-image at face-value. Whatever Ascherson might have thought, historians did not always work in 'clean, bright places' like the British Library or the German Federal Archives in Koblenz, any more than Irving has avoided such places in his own search for documents. Many historians had surely shared experiences like my own, when I discovered major collections of documents in attics in two different German cities in the course of researching for my doctorate, and had to endure difficult conditions in going through them. Almost all historians have come across sources untouched by any other historian since they had been filed away by those who compiled them. Irving had no monopoly on such research. Historians have always been obliged to get their hands dirty.

There were hundreds of historians—German, British, American, Israeli, Swiss, French, Dutch, Canadian and so on—who had researched the subjects with which Irving concerned himself.[43] The major documentary collections had been generally available to historians for decades. Already in the immediate aftermath of the war, Allied war crimes prosecutors had sifted through tons of captured German documents to prepare their indictments in the Nuremberg Trials. Many of these had been printed in the published record of the trials. The eventual return of the original documents, many times more voluminous than the printed selection, to the German Federal Archives, had provided the stimulus for a massive new research effort, spearheaded by Munich's *Institut für Zeitgeschichte* (Institute for Contemporary History). Since then, vast new masses of documents, both official and private in provenance, had become available to scholars in a variety of public state archives in Germany and other countries. This was not an area of history like, say, the fifth century, when historians had to make do with sparse and obscure source material to reconstruct what happened. Historians of the Third Reich and the Second World War were more in danger of drowning in a sea of sources.

Moreover, perhaps because he had not gone through such training himself, Irving seemed not to realize that the training of a professional historian in Germany, Britain, the United States, and elsewhere had long been based on the Ph.D., which required proof of mastery of all the necessary techniques of archival research and historical investigation based on original documents. From the 1960s onwards, generations of Ph.D. students from many countries had descended upon the German archives and the microfilmed editions of captured German documents available in the National Archives in Washington, D.C., the Imperial War Museum, and elsewhere, and produced a mass of published research into the history of Germany under Nazism and during the Second World War that, four decades later, was almost overwhelming. The techniques of documentary investigation in which Irving presented himself as the master were in fact a normal part of the stock-in-trade of every trainee professional historian. Of course, Irving had discovered new documents and obtained new evidence, for example, by interviewing surviving eyewitnesses of the time. But this was true of a vast number of other historians too. The difference was that professional historians did not make such a fetish of it. Irving's attitude toward new sources seemed more like that of a journalist pulling off a scoop than a professional historian just doing his job. New discoveries in this field were quite normal. Such was the vastness of the documentary legacy left by Nazi Germany—twelve years in the life of a major, modern industrial state—that much of the archival record still remained to be worked through at the beginning of the twenty-first century.

Historians also had to rely on each other's work. There was nothing wrong with this, where the work relied on conformed to the accepted canons of scholarly research and rested on thorough, transparent, and unbiased investigation of the primary sources. So vast was the material with which historians dealt, so numerous were the subjects they covered, so consuming of time, energy, and financial resources was the whole process of historical research, that it would be completely impossible for new historical discoveries and insights to be generated if every historian had to go back to the original sources for everything he or she wanted to say. This need to rely on each other's work had nothing to do with copying or plagiarism: on the contrary, the conventions of scholarship ensured that footnotes and other references were used in scholarly historical work to pinpoint precisely where the historian had obtained information, and to allow the reader to check up on this if so desired.

Irving's refusal to consult the work of other historians was disturbing, therefore. More disturbing still, however, was an incident I recalled from Robert Harris's (nonfiction) book *Selling Hitler*. In 1983—the fiftieth anniversary of Hitler's appointment as Reich chancellor—the respected German weekly *Stern* serialized extracts from what its reporters claimed were diaries written by Hitler and recently made available from East German sources. Hugh Trevor-Roper (Lord Dacre), acting for Times Newspapers, declared them to be authentic after a hasty perusal of the manuscripts in a Swiss bank vault. As a result, serialization of an English translation began in *The Sunday Times*. Confronted with doubts about the diaries' authenticity from a number of historians, *Stern* organized a press conference on 25 April.

Irving had come into contact with the diaries through August Priesack, an old Nazi who had been one of the first to be approached by the forger in his quest for authentication. Irving himself had purchased some eight hundred pages of Hitler documents that emanated from the same forger in October 1982 and had been on the verge of selling them to Macmillan when he had begun to have doubts. Priesack's collection of Nazi memorabilia was full of obvious forgeries. This made it overwhelmingly likely that the 'diaries' were forgeries too. Funded by rival newspapers who wished to preserve their circulation in the face of a threatened *Sunday Times* scoop, Irving appeared in person at the *Stern* press conference and denounced them as fakes. "I know the collection from which these diaries come," he shouted across the crowded floor. "It is an old collection, full of forgeries. I have some here." Within a short time he had been proved right. The diaries were quickly shown by tests carried out by the German Federal Archives on the ink and paper to be postwar products. Their author, Konrad Kujau, was eventually sent to prison for his offense.[44]

Irving subsequently portrayed his role in this affair as evidence of his unrivaled expertise on the original source material for Hitler and the Third Reich.[45] Thus while eminent academics had authenticated them, he proved his superior knowledge of the original documents by recognizing them for what they were—a crude fake. Yet, one reason why the forgery got as far as being printed as authentic in the national press was the fact that eminent academics had not been allowed near them. There were those who had, like the American historian Gerhard Weinberg and the Stuttgart expert on Hitler, Eberhard Jäckel, expressed grave suspicions almost from the very start. Even Hugh Trevor-Roper had changed his mind about them immediately after he had sent off his article authenticating them to the *Sunday Times,* and had used the *Stern* press conference, much to the discomfiture of the organizers, to give voice to his newfound skepticism.[46]

Moreover, what Irving subsequently conveniently forgot to mention was that a couple of days after the press conference, he had changed his mind. According to Robert Harris, he did this because he was uncomfortable at being aligned with majority, respectable historical opinion, because he was impressed by the sheer size of the diaries—sixty volumes—which seemed almost beyond the capacity of any one individual to forge, and because, having finally seen the diaries for himself, they looked more convincing than he had expected. "Finally," added Harris, "there was the fact that the diaries did not contain any evidence to suggest that Hitler was aware of the Holocaust." Indeed, all the way through, they seemed to give a favorable impression of Hitler. Whereas most historians held Hitler responsible for the antisemitic pogrom of the *Reichskristallnacht* in November 1938, for example, the diaries showed him ordering a stop to it as soon as he found out about it. Whereas most historians thought the flight of Rudolf Hess to Scotland in 1941 the act of a madman, the diaries revealed him to have been acting on Hitler's orders in pursuit of a genuine peace mission. On point after point, the diaries seemed to endorse Irving's rose-colored view of the Führer.[47]

Soon Irving was on the front page of *The Times* declaring his belief in the diaries' authenticity. When forensic tests shortly afterwards revealed them definitively as fakes, Irving issued a statement accepting the finding but drawing attention to the fact that he had been the first person to unmask them as forged. "Yes," said a reporter from *The Times* when this was read to him, "and the last person to declare them authentic."[48] According to Harris, therefore, Irving's documentary expertise was by no means as flawless or unbiased as he liked people to think it was. He seemed troublingly inclined to apply it in a way that all too obviously suited his own particular interests and ideas.

During the 1990s, Irving described himself as waging an "International Campaign for Real History." "My version of Real History," he conceded in 1992, "may be *wrong* History!"—and he continued:

> I am not so arrogant as to say "thou shalt have no other version of history but mine." . . . Nobody has the right to stand up and say, only my version of history is right: all other versions are wrong: and nobody has the right to propagate alternative versions. . . . And that's what I say about my book Hitler's War; it may be right, it may be wrong! But is certainly a magisterial work . . . a book which makes my rivals livid with envy and rage.[49]

Yet Irving claimed on so many occasions that he had discovered the objective truth about Nazi Germany, and the professional historians had not done so, that his concession that he might be wrong could not really be taken seriously, unless it was taken to apply only to minor matters of detail. Asked in 1993 whether he was a partisan historian, he replied:

> Every historian has to be selective: If I write a biography about Adolf Hitler, then the archives have got about ten tons of documents on Adolf Hitler, and you have to select which documents you present. And if you're a Jewish historian, you present the facts one way, because they have an agenda to present. I don't have any kind of political agenda, and really, it's rather defamatory for people to suggest that I do have an agenda. The agenda I have, I suppose, is, all right, I admit it, I like seeing the other historians with egg on their face. And they're getting a lot of egg on their face now, because I'm challenging them to produce the evidence for what they've been saying for fifty years.[50]

Irving did not appear to believe that other historians could rise to this challenge. Rather, he believed that there was an international campaign orchestrated by the "Jewish community" ("our traditional enemies") in many countries to stop him from telling the truth. "My duty as an historian," he told the Munich court that rejected his appeal against conviction for denying the Holocaust on 5 May 1992, "is to establish the truth."[51] "Our traditional enemies refuse to debate me," he told an audience in Canada on 1 November 1992; "they can't debate me." Describing his continuing International Campaign for Real History, he went on:

> It is the word real that frightens my opponents, because they have got away with it now for the last fifty years, with their Madison-avenue, their Hollywood versions of history, their television versions of history. Real history is what we find in the archives, and it frightens my opponents because it takes the planks out from beneath their feet.[52]

Irving actually was saying that in crucial respects all other versions of the history of the Second World War apart from his own were wrong, because they were not based on "what we find in the archives." Only 'Real History', history as he practiced it, was correct.

It was scarcely surprising, therefore, that he objected to Lipstadt's charges of falsification. Lipstadt's book had only sold two thousand copies in the United Kingdom up to the moment of the trial, so it had hardly done very widespread damage to Irving's reputation or even, indeed, given significant publicity to his work.[53] This was I thought one reason why Irving tried to widen the case by arguing that Lipstadt was part of conspiracy to suppress his work and deny him access to major publishing outlets. He alleged in support of his writ that she had "pursued a sustained malicious vigorous well-funded and reckless world-wide campaign of personal defamation" against him. Irving claimed from the outset that the central issue in the trial was freedom of speech—his freedom of speech, that is, not Deborah Lipstadt's. Orchestrated by the Board of Deputies of British Jews, individuals and organizations in many countries, he suggested, had conspired to have his books rejected by mainstream publishers, his speeches cancelled, his entry permits denied. He had been expelled from Canada and fined in Germany. He and his family had been subjected to threats and abuse. All of this he put down to the fact that he was telling the truth about Hitler, the Germans, and the gas chambers, and the Jews wanted to stop him from being heard. They were the ones who had lied about the past, and they were too cowardly to defend their lies in open debate.

Despite complaints about losing his livelihood because of the refusal of reputable publishers to print his books, Irving could not resist boasting about the "astonishingly good economics" of producing them himself under his Focal Point imprint and distributing them by the simple means of taking them to bookshops in a lorry. "I get the author's cut, the publisher's cut and the distributor's cut," he bragged. In addition he offered his books for sale through the Internet and via the so-called Institute for Historical Review.[54] Still, he may well have been right to argue that he could have sold far more had he continued to publish his work through major publishing houses as he had done in the 1970s and 1980s.

Such claims led a number of commentators to voice a certain sympathy with Irving's predicament. Thus Anne Sebba, in *The Times Higher Education Supplement*, expressed the fear before the trial that it would lead to some kind of censorship. "Legitimate scholars must be allowed to speak and write the truth as they see it without fear of personal attack. To stifle free-ranging debate is good neither for academics nor for the rest of us."[55] But who was trying to stifle free-ranging debate here? Wasn't it Irving who was trying to silence his critics by bringing a libel suit against one of their number? An astonishing number of commentators seemed to forget this rather basic point as they sharpened their pens in defense of free speech. Some even appeared to think that it was Irving himself who was on trial. John Mason, writing in the *Financial Times*, thought that the issues raised by the case included "when are the ideas of historians or academics so appalling (that) their work should be forever banned?" and "whether, or where, one limits free speech."[56] "Old-fashioned liberals," proclaimed Martin Mears sympathetically in the legal pages of *The Times*, "uphold his right to express any view no matter how odious"; and he went on for three half-columns to deliver a thundering justification of freedom of expression, as if it was the defense in the case that threatened it and not Irving.[57] "It would be sad," added the journalist Peter Millar, who had accompanied Irving on his trip to Moscow in 1992 to get a copy of the Goebbels diaries, "if we allowed political correctness to condemn Irving for thinking (or even saying) the unsayable."[58] Many people, including distinguished colleagues in the historical profession, seemed to think I was appearing for Irving when I told them I was acting in the trial as an expert witness for the defense. *The Guardian* newspaper slipped on one occasion and referred to Irving's side as "the defence."[59] An American commentator appeared to believe that Deborah Lipstadt was attempting to put David Irving in prison.[60]

A number of commentators seemed to think that it was Lipstadt's publisher, Penguin Books, who were pursuing Irving and not the other way round. "Penguin," according to Irving's collaborator on a book in the 1960s, the retired Stevenson Professor of International History at the London School of Economics, Donald Cameron Watt, "was certainly out for blood."[61] That it was he who was being hunted, not Lipstadt or Penguin, was Irving's own line, here taken over lock, stock, and barrel by Watt. "They are out to ruin me," Irving said: "They want to take my work from me, my reputation and my home."[62] Irving reminded reporters that he had offered to settle the case out of court for a payment of £500 and an apology from the publishers.[63] Yet the offer, made 11 September 1998, included the demand that Penguin withdraw the book and issue a full apology. It was only in his second offer of settlement, on 14 October 1999, that he dropped these other conditions also extended to Lipstadt.

Penguin Books were not "out for blood," as Cameron Watt claimed. For what were they supposed to do in the face of a libel suit that threatened them with huge expenses, the withdrawal of one of their books, and the prevention of the publication by them or anyone else of any work containing the least breath of criticism of Irving and his fellow Holocaust deniers? No responsible publisher could afford to back down, least of all the publisher who had risked so much in defending previous publications such as *Lady Chatterley's Lover* and *The Satanic Verses* from censorship or worse. Any publisher would have the moral duty to stand by an author in the face of such a threat. And no publisher who ratted on its authors in such circumstances could hope for much sympathy from the literary world in the future. So this was not just a moral stand on Penguin's part, it was a commercial decision too.[64]

In any case, Penguin's withdrawal would still have left Lipstadt in the firing line. Irving was never likely to make an acceptable offer of settlement to Deborah Lipstadt. For she, rather than her publisher, was the real object of his venom, and there was no way he was going to settle with her. For Irving, Lipstadt was the pointed end of the conspiracy he believed had been working for years to destroy his reputation. Penguin, by contrast, were his former publishers, against whom he had no specific grudge to pay off, either real or imagined. "They wanted a scrap," Irving told Michael Horsnell of *The Times*, "so I gave them one. I had to take action."[65] The 'they' were not Penguin, of course, but the Jewish organizations whom Irving termed the "traditional enemies of truth."

Some commentators therefore placed the responsibility for the action not on Penguin's shoulders but on Deborah Lipstadt's. Stuart Nicolson, writing in *The Scotsman*, noted that Irving had become "the ultimate hate figure" to people like Lipstadt, who reviled him "as a malign force intent on wiping the horrors of Auschwitz and other death camps from the pages of history."[66] Jonathan Freedland, author of some of the most thoughtful reflections on the trial, claimed in *The Guardian* that Irving

> could have been ignored. The decision to take him on instead, at enormous cost, is typical of a strong current in contemporary Holocaust thinking: the desire to defeat "revisionism" once and for all. The sentiment is keenest in America. Indeed, it's telling that it was US Jewry which wanted to do battle with Irving in a London court: British Jews were wary of handing him a free platform. But the Americans prevailed, as they nearly always do when it comes to the Shoah.[67]

Freedland was not the only commentator who thought this way. Jürgen Krönig, the London correspondent of the respected German weekly *Die Zeit*, wrote: "The fact that things came to trial is in the end the consequence of the determination above all of Jewish-American groups to wrestle down the deniers of the Holocaust and their 'revisionism.'" Lipstadt's book itself was part of this "offensive procedure," according to Krönig, who noted that Lipstadt had added more material on Irving to the first draft of her manuscript when Yehuda Bauer, of the Yad Vashem Institute in Israel, had pointed out to her that it had neglected the man he regarded as the principal representative of Holocaust denial in Western Europe. If the Israeli and American Jewish communities had ignored the Holocaust deniers rather than gone on the offensive against them, Krönig suggested, then the trial would never have begun.[68]

Perhaps the most trenchant expression of this point of view came from the British historian John P. Fox, writing in the *Independent on Sunday* on 30 January 2000. Fox attacked what he called "Jewish racism" which, he thought, was one of "the political and cultural purposes which lay behind the American and Israeli Jewish 'management' of the Holocaust over the past 40 years." "The Holocaust," Fox alleged, was an "emotional catch-all term" which he had "long argued" should be abandoned in favor of a more neutral description of the Nazi persecution and extermination of the Jews. Fox thought that belief in the uniqueness and preeminence of Jewish suffering as symbolized by the term 'Holocaust' had "become the touchstone, in certain areas and respects, of free speech and intellectual honesty" for "whether some historians or writers are deemed acceptable for entry into the fold of the chosen," whatever that might be. Rejection of the idea of uniqueness meant "you are excluded and damned to hell in your profession," which he regarded as "nothing less than intellectual fascism." The claim that he had long argued for the abandonment of the term 'Holocaust' was surprising in view of the fact that Fox had been the founder of the *British Journal of Holocaust Education* and continued to edit it until 1995. Evidently, however, he had changed his views since then, for Irving announced his intention of calling him as a witness on behalf of his case against Lipstadt, and he seemed to be willing to appear, although in the end he never testified.

Even some Jews took this line, or at least a more moderate version of it. The German-Jewish historian Julius Schoeps agreed with an interviewer, Ulrike Herrmann, who put to him the claim that "this trial happened in the end because there was an attempt at an offensive strike against Irving and his denial of the Holocaust." This Schoeps believed was a problematical tactic, since it allowed the court to become a public forum for Holocaust denial, and what he saw as the defense's aim of shutting Irving up had failed. Instead, he had once more found a worldwide audience. In the end, thought Schoeps, it would have been better to have ignored him.[69] So too did others, and there was at least one observer who considered that the whole trial would provide nothing but free propaganda for Irving.[70] For the first time in many years, he would be at the center of things, addressing not a tiny huddle of neo-Nazis but a worldwide audience.[71] Other German commentators shared this view.[72] But they were writing, of course, in a country where the central facts of the Nazi extermination of the Jews were legally defined as indisputable and where Holocaust denial was a criminal offense. Things were, and are, very different in Britain. Lipstadt and her publisher were not letting the genie out of the bottle when they decided to defend the action. It was out already.

After plowing through a lot of this journalism, I had to pinch myself to recall that it was Irving who had launched the court case; Irving who was attempting to silence his critics; Irving who wanted a book withdrawn from circulation and pulped, its author and publisher ordered to pay him damages and costs, and undertakings given that the criticisms they made of his work should never be repeated. Defending yourself in these circumstances is a necessity, not a matter of choice. "Short of apologising on bended knee to a Nazi sympathiser," as Jonathan Freedland wrote in *The Guardian*, "Lipstadt had no choice but to defend herself in court."[73] Who, in the end, was advocating censorship here: the people like Lipstadt, who automatically assumed that it was legitimate to write freely about such matters, or the London correspondent of *Die Zeit*, who evidently thought that people should keep silent about them? The view that the writ could somehow have been ignored was untenable, whatever Lipstadt's own political convictions or those of her American supporters might have been: a writ is a writ, and it will not go away just because those on whom it is served refuse to respond to it.

Moreover, Irving had other libel actions in progress, or threatened, at the same time. Most particularly, he was suing the journalist Gitta Sereny and *The Observer* newspaper for an article alleging in terms not dissimilar to those employed by Lipstadt that he falsified the historical record. Irving's use of the British libel laws to deter criticism of his work was made clear by his reaction to criticisms of his work, already mentioned, in John Lukács's book *The Hitler of History*, first published in the United States. On 25 October 1997 Irving wrote to Lukács's American publishers telling them that he considered the book "libellous" and adding: "A major British Sunday newspaper was obliged to pay me very substantial damages for similar libels eighteen months ago." He followed this up on 28 October 1997 with a letter to Lukács's British agents asking them if they would "in their own interests, inform any prospective British publisher of the risks attendant on publishing this work in an unamended form. . . . I put you, and through your agency any such publisher, herewith on notice that I shall immediately commence libel proceedings against any publisher who is foolish enough to repeat these libels within the jurisdictions of our courts." Among the statements by Lukács that Irving declared defamatory were his claims in the book that "almost all of Irving's references . . . must be considered with caution," his accusation that (in Irving's words) Irving was "an apologist, rehabilitator, and unrepentant admirer of Adolf Hitler," and that his books engaged in "twisting and manipulating documentary evidence . . . falsifying citations and references . . . inventing historical sources or printing non-existent archival numbers, and . . . making up quotations."[74] Up to the point when the trial began, Lukács's book had not been published in Britain, although he was a well-known author, the topic was eminently marketable, and several of his previous works had found British publishers.

IV

The English law of defamation is uniquely loaded in favor of the plaintiff. As Anthony Julius explained, all that the plaintiff had to do was to show that the defendant had published statements that on the face of it were damaging to his or her reputation or honor. Unlike in American law, where the First Amendment to the US Constitution guaranteed freedom of speech, no further burden of proof was placed upon the plaintiff. In the United States, a plaintiff who was a public figure—a very broad category—had to show both falsity and malice on the part of the author of the objectionable statements. In English law, however, such statements could be made in good faith, and unless the defendant succeeded in establishing a positive defense, they could still be deemed libelous. There were generally only three possible lines of defense. The first was to dispute the meaning of the statements to which the defendant objected. The second was to admit their meaning but deny that they were defamatory, or in other words to deny that they damaged the plaintiff's reputation. Neither of these lines seemed open to the defense in this particular case. Lipstadt's clear and unambiguous prose left no room for doubt on the first score, and although Irving's reputation wasn't quite as unsullied as he claimed it to be, still, sufficient numbers of historians and, more important perhaps, ordinary book-buying readers considered him to be a serious writer about Hitler and the Second World War, whatever their reservations about some aspects of his work, that a blanket statement that he falsified the historical record was bound to have an adverse effect on his standing. Moreover, Irving was able to rely on the presumption in English law that he was entitled to a good reputation unless and until the defense proved otherwise.

A third line of defense remained. This was to claim justification, or in other words to prove that the statements in Lipstadt's book were true. That the entire burden of doing this rested on the defense was what, in effect, stacked the cards in favor of the plaintiff. For the law assumed that defamatory statements were lies unless proven otherwise. Proving that Lipstadt was telling the truth was going to be a difficult, complicated, and time-consuming business. The strategy that Julius and his team, backed by Penguin's solicitors Davenport Lyons, unfolded was three-pronged. First, it involved commissioning professional historians to provide expert reports to the court presenting the evidence for the gassing facilities at Auschwitz, for the mass murder itself, for the existence of a co-ordinated Nazi policy to exterminate the Jews, and for the involvement of Hitler in this operation. Regrettable though it was, there was clearly something to be said for ensuring that most of them were not Jewish, since Irving would undoubtedly try to make something out of it if they were. Assembling a range of experts from various countries—Britain, the United States, Germany, and Holland—would also indicate the international dimensions of recent and current research on modern German history and the Nazi period, and further counter any suggestion that such research was mainly carried out by one particular ethnic group or nationality.

We obtained the agreement of Robert Jan Van Pelt, author of a standard work on Auschwitz, to deliver a report on the evidence for the existence and use of gassing facilities at the camp. Christopher Browning, an eminent specialist in the history of the extermination and the policies that led to it, agreed to write a report on the evidence for the extermination of the Jews on a wider scale. Peter Longerich, a German, formerly of the Munich Institute for Contemporary History and now teaching at Royal Holloway College in the University of London, who had just completed a massively documented overview of the making of Nazi policies toward the Jews between 1933 and 1945, was commissioned to provide reports on the evidence for Hitler's antisemitism and the systematic nature of the killings. In all cases the emphasis was to be on the original documentation of various kinds that provided the basis for historical knowledge. Where necessary, the experts were to deal at length with criticisms leveled at the authenticity or reliability of such accounts, although in the end this only proved to be necessary in the case of Auschwitz. The overall purpose of these reports was not to show what had actually happened, though in the end there was no doubt that they went a long way toward doing precisely that. The purpose, rather, was to put before the court the evidence which any fair-minded, objective commentator would have to take into account in writing about these issues. This evidence in turn provided the basis for the defense's argument that Irving was neither objective nor fair-minded in his treatment of these issues.

The second prong of the three-pronged defense was to commission experts to document Irving's political views and his connections with far-right, neo-fascist, and extremist political organizations. This was important because Lipstadt had referred to these in her book and alleged that Irving distorted historical evidence, as Irving put it in his "Statement of Claim," "essentially in order (to) serve his own reprehensible purposes ideological leanings and/or political agenda." Reports were duly commissioned from experts on the far right in Britain, Germany, and the United States, although in the end only the German report, by Hajo Funke, professor of politics at the Free University of Berlin, was formally presented to the court.

This left the third prong of the defense, and this is where I came in. What Julius and his team wanted me to do was to go through Irving's work, or at least a sample of it large enough to be representative, and write a report on whether or not Lipstadt's allegation that he falsified the historical record was justified. Clearly the lawyers expected that the answer contained in the report would be in the affirmative. But as I told them early on, there was no guarantee. I was not familiar with Irving's work. Apart from what I already knew from reading critics like Sydnor or Broszat, I had little idea of what I would find.

There was certainly no lack of material on which to base my report. First and most important were Irving's published books, thirty or more of them, a number of them available in numerous editions. Many if not most of them could easily be consulted both in English and in German in different versions in libraries in Britain and Germany, although some proved rather hard to track down. I was startled to find that the 1991 edition of *Hitler's War* could only be read at the desk in the Rare Books Room of the British Library reserved for literature deemed by the library to be pornographic. Second, Irving had also published a smaller number of articles, most of them edited versions of speeches, mainly in *The Journal of Historical Review*, which were also available for public inspection in institutions such as the Wiener Library. Third, Irving maintained an extensive website on the Internet (http://fpp.co.uk) which posted the edited texts of various of his speeches, together with a large quantity of other material revealing of his views on the history of the Third Reich.

But there was clearly more that was not generally available at all. This was where the legal process checked in. As Irving remarked in 1991,

> The first thing that happens in a libel action is this: only a few weeks after you've served a writ on a gentleman there comes a very expensive stage for both parties known as Discovery. The word 'Discovery' written with a capital 'D', just like the word 'Holocaust' written with a capital 'H'. Only this time the word is on my side. Because Discovery is an ugly phase, for plaintiff and defendant, when you face each other across a lawyer's table, at the choosing of the Plaintiff, and you say, "I want to see your documents and you can see mine." And at that stage usually all the defendants crack up and cop out.[75]

In the present case, however, the defense did not "cop out," and Irving was obliged to disclose an enormous mass of material in addition to the list of documents he initially agreed to supply. In a series of interim actions, Anthony Julius went to a High Court official known as the Master of the Queen's Bench, whose task it was to deal with the case until the trial judge took over at the beginning of the formal public proceedings, and applied for Court Orders to force Irving to disclose all the material in his possession that was relevant to the defense case. Irving kept a vast private archive of his speeches, letters, and other documents. Clearly all of this was relevant to questions such as Irving's contacts with neo-fascists and political extremists and could be highly revealing of his private views on history and politics as well as those expressed before public and—even more important—closed meetings of his supporters. It might well be the case that, for example, he was relatively scrupulous in his treatment of his historical evidence in his books, but far less so in his speeches and interviews.

These Discovery actions were successful. As a result I gained access, as did the other expert witnesses, to many videotapes and audiocassettes of Irving's speeches, tens of thousands of pages of documents, his complete private diaries, thousands of letters, and a great deal of other material, including the notes he had taken while collecting historical documents, preparing drafts of his books, and interviewing surviving members of Hitler's entourage. As all of this piled up in the lawyers' offices, it soon became apparent that the amount of material available was too vast for me to master in the relatively short space of time I had available before the deadline for submitting the reports, especially given my other commitments such as my regular academic work.

I was fortunate therefore that the lawyers agreed that I could use the research assistance of two of my Ph.D. students, Nikolaus Wachsmann, who subsequently became a Junior Research Fellow at Downing College, Cambridge, and Thomas Skelton-Robinson, who moved from London in 1998 to research for a Ph.D. at Churchill College, Cambridge. Both had first-class honors degrees in History (from the London School of Economics and from Glasgow University respectively), both had a first-rate command of German, and both had a good knowledge of twentieth-century German history. Nik had been working for some time on state prisons and penitentiaries in the Weimar Republic and the Third Reich and had already made himself familiar with many German archives; Thomas had recently started research on the West German government's policy toward the student movement in the late 1960s. Both of them agreed to put aside their research for a few months to work on the Irving material. Neither of them, probably, realized at the outset just how time-consuming it was to be, nor quite how important their work was to prove.

The two researchers compiled transcripts of the salient parts of the audiocassettes and videotapes and went through this and the other material supplied by Irving during the process of Discovery, taking extensive notes. Meanwhile I set to work going through Irving's major books, above all *Hitler's War* in its 1977 and 1991 editions, and the biographies of Göring and Goebbels. During the period January 1998 to April 1999, we met frequently, exchanged notes and drafts, and discussed what to do next. At various points, too, Nik and Thomas undertook research in German archives and libraries and we engaged in a considerable amount of correspondence. German archivists were enormously helpful, often faxing vital documents at very short notice; we also obtained material from Moscow, from Washington, and, during the trial itself, from Israel, where the government was persuaded to release the lengthy autobiography that Adolf Eichmann wrote before his execution there in 1961.

Before we started work, few historians had actually gone to the trouble of subjecting any of Irving's publications to a detailed analysis by taking his historical statements and claims and tracing them back to the original and other sources on which he claimed they rest. Doing so was an extremely time-consuming exercise, and most historians had better things to do with their time. Historians assumed that the work of fellow-historians, or those who purported to be fellow-historians, was reliable in its footnoting, in its translations and summaries of documents, and in its treatment of the evidence at a basic level. They might make mistakes and errors of fact, but they did not generally deliberately manipulate and distort documents, suppress evidence that ran counter to their interpretations, wilfully mistranslate documents in a foreign language, consciously use unreliable or discredited testimony when it suited their purpose, falsify historical statistics, or apply one standard of criticism to sources that undermined their views and another to those that supported them. These were the kinds of things that Lipstadt claimed Irving had done. But she had not mentioned any specific examples. So we had to start from scratch. Since what was stake was a general allegation, or series of allegations, it was not necessary to confine ourselves either to the works Lipstadt had read by Irving—which were understandably few, given the very marginal position that Irving's work occupied in her analysis—or to what Irving had said or written before the publication of Lipstadt's book in Britain in 1994. The whole of his *oeuvre* was at our disposal.

Deciding on these matters was by no means an easy task. It raised very large questions of historical epistemology as well as demanding the minute examination of very small pieces of empirical evidence. For historians often disagreed with one another, and scholarly disagreements often involved accusations of misreading or neglecting sources, or stretching interpretations beyond what the evidence seemed to allow. How was it going to be possible to distinguish between interpretation and fantasy, argument and tendentiousness, imaginative readings of the sources and outright manipulations of them, minor errors of fact and deliberate distortions of the documents, or the accidental omission of relevant material and the deliberate suppression of inconvenient evidence?

This task was, in a sense, made easier by Irving's repeated insistence that he was not putting forward an argument for debate, but simply telling the truth. His philosophy of history was revealed in a press conference held in Brisbane, Australia, on 20 March 1986:

JOURNALIST: It could be argued, couldn't it, that history is always subjective, and your view of history too.

IRVING: Oh yes. Look at the life of Rommel here, the life of Rommel, *The Trail of the Fox*. In writing that, I used two thousand letters that he wrote to his wife over his entire life. . . . Well, two thousand letters, that manuscript was probably six hundred pages long when it was finally (completed), you're doing a lot of condensing, you're condensing an entire man's life into six hundred pages of typescript, and that process of condensing it is the nice way of saying, "but of course you're selecting, you're selecting how to present this man." And that is undoubtedly a subjective operation. And this is why I hope that the readers look at the overall image presented of David Irving by the media and they think to themselves: "Well, on balance we can probably trust him better than we can trust Professor Hillgruber, or Professor Jacobsen, or any of the other historians who write on the same kind of period."[76]

JOURNALIST: Surely the same argument that you're putting up against the bulk of historians could be levelled at you.

IRVING: Ah, but then, you see, but this is the difference: they can't prove their points, they can't prove their points. I can prove all my points because I've got all the documents and the evidence on my side, but they can't find even one page of evidence to attack me, and that is why they're beginning to rant and rave instead.[77]

In other words, Irving admitted a degree of aesthetic subjectivity in condensing and organizing his material, but conceded none at all in formulating his arguments (or, as he would put it, proving his points). Yet this still left a good deal of room for him to maneuver. In particular, even if we identified numerous factual errors in his work, deciding whether these were the result of mere carelessness, on the one hand, or deliberate falsification on the other, was obviously going to be no easy matter. For how exactly could you prove that someone had deliberately falsified the historical record? Wasn't it all a matter of interpretation anyway?

Precisely such issues were what made the case so fascinating for me. It raised in an acute and at the same time practical form many of the problems with which I had been wrestling in my book *In Defense of History*. For both myself and my researchers, the intellectual principles at stake were the most important ones as we began our work. It was not a political trial. In many ways Lipstadt seemed as politically committed to her cause as Irving was to his. Yet in the end, political commitment should not interfere with historical research and writing. Certainly there were many historians who had strong views on a variety of political issues. It was not realistic to demand that they keep their politics out of their work. The real test of a serious historian was the extent to which he or she was willing or able to subordinate political belief to the demands of historical research. Documents and other kinds of historical evidence often threw up things that fitted uncomfortably with one's political beliefs. Both Lipstadt and Irving insisted that they were objective historians. Discovering whether or not Lipstadt's accusation that Irving falsified the record in the interests of his political beliefs became a test case of whether it was possible to pinpoint someone actually doing this and show with chapter and verse how such distortion occurred.

Others, however, saw the trial as being about far more than the issue of falsification, serious though that was. What was at stake, thought *The Times* of London, was "whether one of the blackest chapters of 20th-century history actually happened, or is a figment of imaginative and politically motivated Jewry."[78] It was this belief that led a large number of commentators to describe the trial as "one of the most far-reaching court cases ever heard on the Holocaust."[79] Efraim Zuroff, director of the Israel office of the Simon Wiesenthal Centre in Jerusalem, spoke for many when he said before the trial: "it's almost inevitable that the major

focus of the case will be the crimes of the Holocaust and whether they
took place and how they're interpreted. . . . Any victory for Irving is a loss
for historical justice and a blow to the memory of the Holocaust."[80]

For many German observers, this all made the trial difficult to understand. Ralf Sottscheck, writing in the Berlin *Tageszeitung*, thought that
the English libel law did indeed make it necessary "to prove that the
Holocaust took place."[81] And this was precisely the problem. In Germany
itself, the historical reality of the Holocaust was anchored in law as legally
indisputable, like the fact that the earth was round, and Irving had long
been known by commentators as "the most prominent whitewasher of
the Nazis in the world," as Jost Nolte put it at the beginning of the trial.
Like many Central European commentators, Nolte confessed himself
baffled by the fact that the matter had come to trial at all. "How does one
react," he asked, "if someone claims the sheep ate the wolf, or a Jewish
beggar attacked a German shepherd dog? With counter-proofs? With
arguments? Hardly. One is more likely to call in a psychiatrist."[82] For this
reason, many German and Austrian observers simply found the whole
case "bizarre," "nonsensical." and "absurd."[83] "It is," wrote Caroline
Fetscher, "as if a quack was challenging the most prominent doctors in
the international medical profession. Absurd. Here in London an obsessive charlatan is forcing a parade of top researchers to take part in a duel
that he will win one way or another, either as a martyr or as a successful
plaintiff."[84] "Really," wrote Werner Birkenmaier in the *Stuttgarter
Zeitung*, "this trial is a farce. All the world knows that six million Jews
were murdered, and yet we still have to debate this fact in front of a
court."[85]

Walter Reich, former director of the United States Holocaust Memorial Museum, even feared that alarmists who proclaimed that the case
constituted "nothing less than a trial of the truth of the Holocaust," might
give the verdict more weight than it deserved. "If the plaintiff wins, the
alarmists will have created the very sort of damage that they are trying to
prevent—doubt among the ill-informed about whether the Holocaust
happened." He took issue with Deborah Lipstadt's claim that if she had
not contested the lawsuit, Irving's "definition of the Holocaust would
have become the standard definition recognized by the High Court in
London." This indeed might have been something of an exaggeration on

Lipstadt's part. On the other hand, there was something to it as well. For if Irving did win, the way would be open for him and those who agreed with him to sue anyone who claimed that their version of events rested on the falsification and manipulation of evidence, or suggested that they were not engaged in legitimate and bona fide historical research. To this extent, a judgment in Irving's favor would indeed legitimate his denial of the Holocaust, if that turned out to be what he was engaged in.

While a finding for Irving, Reich thought, "might say something about the nature of British libel law, it would say nothing at all about the reality of the Holocaust." Strictly speaking, of course, this was true; but Reich did not consider the consequences for free debate and discussion about the Holocaust, and in particular about how it was researched and written about, in the event of an Irving victory. These could be very serious indeed.[86] Quite apart from anything else, a victory for the plaintiff would have meant a confirmation of all the abuse that Irving had heaped upon the historical profession over the years.[87] So much more was involved than simply deciding on the issue of falsification, important though this was.

Was the Holocaust on trial, then? David Cesarani argued that the idea that "history was on trial" was a "common misconception" about the case. The factuality of the Holocaust was never at issue. "The outcome of the trial," wrote Cesarani, "will not alter events from 1933 to 1945."[88] Indeed, Judge Charles Gray, who presided over the trial itself, made the central issue very clear from the outset. "What was at issue—it can't be said too often—was Irving's methodology and historiography, not what happened back in the 40s," he said. The distinction between whether the evidence was that the Holocaust had happened, and whether the Holocaust had actually happened in reality, was a real one.[89] This view was echoed by others involved in the case, including Anthony Julius himself.[90] Irving also repeatedly drew everyone's attention to the fact that what was at issue in the action was what went on within the four walls of his own study, not what went on in East-Central Europe during the Second World War.[91]

Yet in the end the distinction proved almost impossible to maintain.[92] In reality the trial was about both issues.[93] If the evidence for the gas chambers, the 6 million dead, and other aspects of the Holocaust was overwhelming, indisputable, then surely this did amount to proving, insofar as historians could prove anything, that it had actually happened. In a more general way, too, the trial had a direct bearing on how the Holocaust would be regarded and how it was debated and discussed in public. The most perceptive reporters were fully aware of what was at stake in this connection. Neal Ascherson, writing in the *Süddeutsche Zeitung* at the end of the third week of the trial, pointed out: "Should Irving win this case, then the damages would be the least evil. Much worse would be the fact that his credibility as a historian would be salvaged by such a judgment; his version of the Holocaust and his interpretation of Hitler would suddenly count as plausible."[94] "If he wins," Ian Burrell of *The Independent* noted, irrespective of the particular instance of Irving himself, "the door will have been opened for revisionists to rewrite any event in history without a requirement to consider evidence that does not suit them and without fear that they will be publicly denounced for their distortion."[95]

All these implications emerged only gradually, as preparations for the trial went ahead and then the public proceedings themselves got under way. In a sense, they did not concern those of us who were involved in researching and writing the expert reports. What we had to concentrate on were the specific allegations that were at the heart of the legal action. In the case of Lipstadt's charge against Irving of falsifying the evidence, this demanded some form of selectivity. The sheer mass of material was simply too great to go through in the time available before the report had to be submitted to the High Court in July 1999. It seemed clear that Irving's work had to be scrutinized with a view to reaching an opinion on whether or not he was a Holocaust denier, a claim by Lipstadt that Irving vehemently rejected. And as far as the issue of falsification was concerned, it seemed sensible to link this to another of Lipstadt's allegations—that Irving was an admirer of Adolf Hitler—and go through all the instances where Irving claimed to have documentary evidence that Hitler was a friend of the Jews and did his best to stop them being persecuted and killed—if, indeed, that was what he argued.

Finally, as a kind of control exercise, just to see if this particular argument was some kind of aberration from a normally scrupulous handling of the evidence on Irving's part, we decided to look at his account of the Allied bombing of Dresden in February 1945, in a book that had established his reputation and probably been more successful than any other he had written. All this still left open the larger issues of principle raised by the allegation of falsification. How this would emerge from the detailed scrutiny of Irving's sources remained to be seen. After eighteen months' hard work, I finally completed my report at the end of July 1999. It is time to turn to what I discovered about Irving's way of dealing with the evidence and his manner of writing about the past.

CHAPTER TWO

Hitler and the Jews, 1924–1939

I

Deborah Lipstadt described Irving as an admirer of Hitler and an apologist for many of his deeds. How plausible was this view? Irving presented himself in his writings and speeches as a man who had discovered the objective truth about Hitler and the Nazis, rescuing it from the myths and legends perpetrated by historians, politicians, and others by refusing to believe what other historians wrote and by going back to the original sources instead. "I saw myself as a stone-cleaner," he wrote in the introduction to his book *Hitler's War* in 1977, "less concerned with architectural appraisal than with scrubbing years of grime and discoloration from the façade of a silent and forbidding monument."[1] Hitler, Irving argued, had been caricatured by posterity, beginning with the Nuremberg War Crimes Trials, where everybody tried to shift the blame to him. "These caricatures have bedeviled the writing of modern history ever since." Irving portrayed himself as a man who had achieved the feat of demolishing these caricatures and restoring a true picture of Hitler and Nazism by massive, indefatigable research into primary sources, and by a scrupulously critical attitude to the documents.

Reading his various prefaces and programmatic statements, however, I soon realized that there was more to it than this. In the preface to the first edition of *Hitler's War*, Irving wrote that "this book views the situation as far as possible through Hitler's eyes, from behind his desk." This almost inevitably led to an unusually positive view of Hitler's aims and career:

> Adolf Hitler was a patriot—he tried from start to finish to restore the earlier unity, greatness and splendour of Germany. After he had come to power in 1933, he carried out the programme whose real-

isation he had promised since 1922: he restored faith in the central government; he rebuilt the German economy; he removed unemployment; he rebuilt the disarmed German armed forces, and then he used this newly-won strength to attain Germany's sovereignty once more, and he became involved in his adventure of winning living-space in the East. He had no kind of evil intentions against Britain and its Empire, quite the opposite. . . . Hitler's foreign policy was led by the wish for secure boundaries and the necessity of an extension to the east. . . . The forces which drove Germany into the war did not sit in Berlin.[2]

I did not think that these claims were in any way substantiated by Irving. The work I knew by specialists on these subjects indicated, rather, that Hitler did not restore the German economy in any normal sense, but rapidly distorted it through his extreme prioritization of rearmament; his intentions toward Britain and its empire were far from benign; and his "adventure of winning living-space in the East" was a war of genocidal extermination against the Poles and other peoples who had lived there, justified by an ideology of racial supremacy: there is no evidence that Germany and the Germans actually needed 'living-space' in the East.[3]

This identification of Irving with his subject had not gone unnoticed by others. Reviewing *Hitler's War* in 1977, Hugh Trevor-Roper found a "consistent bias" in favor of Hitler and against his opponents. This was, he thought, in part the consequence of Irving's decision to describe the war from the point of view of Hitler and his court. But it went further than this. Given the nature of the sources, which reflected the standards and assumptions of Hitler's entourage, Trevor-Roper concluded that it was unsurprising that Hitler's view should prevail in Irving's book. "Hitler's popularity and radiating charm is constantly stressed: no man, we are told, possessed 'The affection of the German people' as completely as he did, in the summer of 1944, just before the attempt to assassinate him." "Mr. Irving's sympathies," Trevor-Roper concluded, "can hardly be doubted"; and in his view they were consistently in favor of Hitler and the Nazis.[4]

The journalist Robert Harris, in his meticulous and often hilarious account of the 'Hitler diaries' affair—his last work of nonfiction before he turned to writing the political thrillers that I so often enjoyed reading on plane journeys—concurred in this judgment. Harris's description of *Hitler's War* went further than Trevor-Roper's in pointing to the identification of the author with his subject:

> Irving's aim was to rewrite the history of the war "as far as possible through Hitler's eyes, from behind his desk." This made for a gripping book, but one which was, by its nature, unbalanced. However "objectively" he might piece together the unpublished recollections of Hitler's subordinates, they were still the words of men and women who admired their ruler. And confined to Hitler's daily routine, the biography had a curiously unreal quality: the death camps, the atrocities, the sufferings of millions of people which were the result of Hitler's war were not to be found in *Hitler's War* as it was reconstructed by David Irving.

Interviewing Irving about the 'Hitler diaries,' Harris noted, perhaps a little mischievously, some even more alarming aspects of the identification of author and subject than were readily apparent from the book:

> Irving admitted that in writing *Hitler's War* he had "identified" with the Führer . . . "I don't drink," he would say, "Adolf didn't drink you know.". . . In 1981, at the age of forty-one, he had founded his own right-wing political group, built around his own belief in his "destiny" as a future British leader. With his black hair slanting across his forehead, and a dark cleft, shadowed like a moustache between the bottom of his nose and the top of his upper lip, there were times, in the right light, when Irving looked alarmingly like the subject of his notorious biography.

Harris was perhaps indulging in a little journalistic license here. But the fundamental point that he was making about *Hitler's War* seemed convincing, and shared by others too.[5] Irving's book, he noted, aimed to humanize Hitler, to make him, as the book's introduction claimed, "an ordinary, walking, talking human."[6]

Reviewing *Hitler's War* in 1979, the American historian Charles W. Sydnor Jr. found that Irving portrayed Hitler not as a monster but as "a fair-minded statesman of considerable chivalry." Irving's Hitler, moreover, was "a man capable of genuine warmth and maudlin sentimental-ity."[7] The American historian John Lukács, reviewing Irving's work in the course of a general and often highly critical survey of historical writ-ing on Hitler over the past few decades, commented in 1998 that *Hitler's War* was a "partial rehabilitation of Hitler" and "revealed for the first time (that is, to careful readers) [Irving's] admiration of Hitler."[8] Similarly, the late Martin Broszat, perhaps the most influen-tial of the German historians who worked on Hitler's Third Reich in the 1970s and 1980s, noted that there was an obvious contradiction between Irving's self-confessed desire to look at events from behind Hitler's desk, and his claim to take an objective view of events. "Irving," he continued, "does not remain silent about individual actions of killing and annihilation which go back to Hitler, but portrays them in an excul-patory and often erroneous way." The whole book, Broszat charged, was dominated by a perspective narrowed by partisanship in favor of Hitler.[9]

Attentive and knowledgeable reviewers, therefore, had often con-sidered Irving to be an admirer of Hitler. The terms in which Irving por-trayed Hitler in his books, writings, and speeches confirmed this view. Irving himself made no secret about how he saw his role:

> Every time I've written a biography, you find you become close to the character you're writing about because you're his ambassador then. You're his ambassador to the afterlife. Or to the next genera-tion. And if you do your job conscientiously, then you bend over backward to do it. . . . I don't think it should lead you to adopt an unobjective position.[10]

Irving was more expansive to an audience of historians and fellow publicists in 1978, when he explained how fate had anointed him Hitler's historian:

> Basically Hitler himself determined who should be his biographer. I know that since I found Hitler's ear, nose, and throat doctor in Krefeld in early 1970, the man who treated Hitler after the assassination attempt of 20 July 1944, Dr. Erwin Giesing. I called on him in his practice. He had no time at that moment and I had to wait for half

an hour for him. Already in the waiting room he gave me a file to read, about 500 typed pages. Can you imagine how one feels when one reads the diary of the doctor who treated Hitler after the assassination attempt? It begins on 23 July 1944. I ask him, why are you giving this to me, Herr Dr. Giesing? He answers me, read page 387. It's about a conversation between Hitler and Giesing. . . . Hitler said, . . . Perhaps an Englishman will also come one day who wants to write an objective biography of me. It has to be an Englishman of the next generation. Because a representative of the present generation cannot write the truth about me and certainly won't want to either. It has to be an Englishman who knows the archives and who has mastered the German language. And that is why you are getting the diaries Mr. Irving, the doctor said.[11]

Irving, it seemed to me from this remarkable passage, saw himself in the end not as a neutral, objective historian but as Hitler's representative in the world after his death, as the historian chosen, as it were, by the Führer himself.

In a very real sense, indeed, he evidently conceived of himself as carrying on Hitler's legacy, just as Lipstadt claimed in her book. Speaking to an audience in Calgary, Canada, in 1991, he revealed that he had once been described as a "self-confessed moderate fascist," and added: "I strongly object to that word 'moderate.'" As with many apparently flippant remarks, this seemed to me to have a kernel of truth in it; after all, he had not objected to the word *fascist*. More strikingly still, in an interview for the television program *This Week*, in 1991, Irving said: "I think Adolf Hitler made a lot of mistakes. He surrounded himself with people of very very poor quality. He was a rotten judge of character. These are the mistakes that you have to avoid replicating."[12] *You* in this context could only really be understood as referring to Irving himself.

Whatever mistakes he thought Hitler had made, I soon had no doubt that basically Irving's attitude toward him was one of admiration. At a press conference in Brisbane in 1986, a journalist asked him, "Do you admire Hitler?" Irving replied:

Erm, yeah, certain aspects. What a tricky question; you see now, I thought I had you. You're asking a question which, really, however you answer it, you're going to be in deep water, because there are certain aspects of his life that everybody admires. The fact that he had risen from nobody. You see she's writing it down. He'd risen from nobody, and he'd risen from nobody and become the admired and respected leader of two great nations, Germany and Austria. That after a very, very hard and difficult fight in 1933, just five years later he got 49 million Germans to vote for him, which was 99.8 per cent of the electorate. . . . I think that from 1938 onwards he began to go off the rails, in the moral sense. He became too big for his boots, and assumed that he was the law. And that is a very common defect.[13]

This criticism was not a serious one, however. Irving failed to mention that in the 1938 vote there was massive intimidation of the electorate. Democratic societies do not produce 'yes' votes of 99.8 percent.[14] Irving's own writings about Hitler's conduct during the war did not suggest that he thought Hitler went off the rails. Finally, however much Irving might have sought to relativize his own admiration for Hitler by arguing that others shared it, his claim that "everybody admires" aspects of Hitler's life was in my experience demonstrably untrue.

At the same press conference, another journalist asked him: "Wouldn't it be fair to say that the historical perspective that we're given here in the West is that Churchill was the person to be looked up to and Hitler was the rogue. Are you saying that that situation is really quite the reverse?" Irving replied: "Quite the reverse." In a debate chaired by David Frost on BBC1 television in June 1977, Irving put the same point in another way. Asked whether he thought Hitler was evil, he replied: "He was as evil as Churchill, as evil as Roosevelt, as evil as Truman."[15]

Irving had always seemed particularly sensitive to the charge that Hitler was antisemitic. "Hitler," he claimed at one point, "used his anti-semitism as a political platform from which to seize power in 1933, but that after that he lost interest in it except for occasional flights of public oratory; while Dr. Goebbels and other lesser Nazis continued to ride that horse to the hounds, to the mounting irritation of their Führer Adolf Hitler who no longer needed antisemitism."[16] Even before 1933, Irving argued, Hitler's antisemitism was only tactical, and in practice he was not personally ill-disposed toward the Jews. In a discussion on BBC1 television in 1977, he said that once Hitler had become Reich chancellor, "he became a statesman and then a soldier . . . And the Jewish problem was

a nuisance to him, an embarrassment."[17] Irving summed up his views on
Hitler and the Jews when he said in 1983 that "probably the biggest
friend the Jews had in the 'Third Reich,' certainly when the war broke
out, was Adolf Hitler. He was the one who was doing everything he could
to prevent things nasty happening to them."[18]

When I looked through his writings and speeches, I could not help
but conclude that Irving certainly had a strongly held bias in favor of
Hitler. But did this amount to a distortion of the historical record? Wasn't
it just a point of view like any other, even if it was a repulsive one? Irving
did not seem to think so. He claimed that he was doing no more than
reflecting accurately what was in the documentary evidence. In the introduction to the 1991 edition of *Hitler's War*, Irving declared: "Every document actually linking Hitler with the treatment of the Jews invariably
takes the form of an embargo." In 1983, Irving said: "There is a *whole
chain* of evidence from 1938 right through to October 1943, possibly even
later, indicating that Hitler was completely in the dark about anything that
may have been going on" with respect to mass killings of Jews. "So far," he
boasted triumphantly, *"I haven't been disproved."*[19] Similarly, in his written submission to the High Court, Irving argued that when the documents
were subjected to rigid historical criteria as to their authenticity, the reasons for their existence, and the vantage point of their author, "a relatively
slim dossier of evidence resulted which portrayed Hitler intervening in
every instance to mitigate or lessen wrongdoing against the Jews. . . . There
were few, if any, documents of comparable quality—documents which
met the same criteria—giving the opposite sense."[20]

What did these documents look like, then? Did Irving give an accurate account of their contents? Or did he knowingly and wilfully distort
them? The first link in Irving's much-vaunted chain of documents related
to an incident early in Hitler's political career. In 1924, Hitler stood trial
before a Bavarian court for his leadership of a failed attempt the previous year to seize power in Munich as a prelude to a march on Berlin—
the infamous 'beer hall putsch' of 9 November 1923.[21] During the
putsch, according to Irving, Hitler disciplined a Nazi squad for having
looted a Jewish delicatessen:

> Meanwhile, Hitler acted to maintain order. Learning that one Nazi
> squad had ransacked a kosher grocery store during the night, he sent

for the ex-army lieutenant who had led the raid. "We took off our Nazi insignia first!" expostulated the officer—to no avail, as Hitler dismissed him from the party on the spot. "I shall see that no other nationalist unit allows you to join either!" Göring goggled at this exchange, as did a police sergeant who testified to it at the Hitler trial a few weeks later.[22]

Irving cited this incident again in his 1991 edition of *Hitler's War*,[23] and also in his written submission to the court.[24]

Where did Irving get this information? It was far from easy to find out. In his *Göring*, he only told the reader that his narrative "is knitted together from the eyewitness evidence at the trial."[25] The only way for me to examine Irving's account was to read through the entire record of the Hitler trial, searching for the original source of his depiction of the events in question. Fortunately, the complete trial transcript of 1924 was available in a scholarly edition. The evidence to which he referred was in the court record for 4 March 1924, when a former police officer, *Oberwachtmeister* Hofmann, said:

> Apart from this, I want to mention a previous incident because acts of violence which individuals have committed have always been ascribed to him. I once went along to Hitler when I was still in the force and said to him: this and that have happened again. Some elements had attacked the Israelite delicatessen. "That gives a bad impression of the party, and it's rather embarrassing for us in the police that such a thing should have to happen." By chance the leader of the group, a young, wartime army lieutenant, was there. Called on to speak, this man said: "I took off the party badge." Hitler said: "By doing this you admitted that you did not belong to the party at the moment when you committed that act. You are expelled with immediate effect from the party with your whole team and I will take care that you don't get admitted to any nationalist fighting squad again." Hitler always condemned these acts of violence and the individual excesses which occurred.[26]

When I checked this testimony against the account given by Irving and quoted above, a number of discrepancies emerged.

To begin with, Irving had simply invented the assertion that "Göring

goggled at this exchange" between Hitler and the Nazi activist. Göring
was not mentioned in Hofmann's testimony as having been present at all.
Irving was also wrong to say that the police officer "goggled" at the
exchange. Irving invented this passage to give the impression that Hitler
must have expressed his views in an exceptionally forceful way. I could
find no warrant in the document for such a description. Moreover, the
brownshirt leader was not summoned by Hitler, he was present "by
chance" when Hitler was told about the incident. Irving cast Hitler in a
more favorable light than the document actually allowed. He was also
wrong to claim that the incident took place on the night of the failed
putsch. It was clear from Hofmann's testimony that the incident had
taken place at some unspecified time earlier than the putsch, about which
Hofmann had been giving evidence up to that point.

That was not all, however. For Irving failed to make the obvious
inference from what Hofmann claimed Hitler did on this occasion: that
Hitler disciplined the brownshirts because they had taken off their party
insignia and therefore laid themselves open to the charge that they were
engaging in a criminal rather than a political act. This could have caused
serious damage to the party's reputation by associating it with common
thieves. Had the brownshirts kept their party badges on, Hitler might
well have had no objection to their action. Nowhere did Hofmann imply
that Hitler's primary motive was to protect the Jews. Nowhere did Irving
imply that Hitler's primary motive was to protect the party's name.

More important still, Irving failed to mention the fact that Hofmann's
evidence in any case was highly suspect. Hofmann was a fully paid-up
member of the Nazi Party, which, it seemed, he had joined in 1921. As a
Nazi supporter in the police service until he left the force on 1 January
1924, he had organized a fast-track system for issuing visas to foreign Nazi
sympathizers. Hitler made him head of the political section of the
NSDAP's intelligence unit. Hofmann actually participated in the putsch
of 8 and 9 November 1923. According to his own testimony, he accompanied Hitler much of that night.[27] Hofmann also seemed to have visited
Hitler in prison while he was awaiting trial.[28] I had no difficulty in discovering this from readily available published documentation, including
the stenographic record of the trial itself. All these facts cast serious
doubts on the reliability of Hofmann's testimony at Hitler's trial. Hofmann was a long-standing Nazi supporter and party official who tried

hard to present Hitler in a favorable light as a law-abiding citizen. This tactic was even recognized by the lenient court in 1924, which did not take his evidence on oath because it regarded him as biased. At the end of his evidence, the presiding judge complimented the ex-policeman on the fact "that you are speaking out on behalf of your leader."[29]

The most important feature of these discrepancies, it seemed to me, was that Irving must have known the basic facts about the police witness and his testimony because he had read the transcript of Hofmann's evidence. His failure to mention these facts could not be accidental in view of his intention to use the testimony in support of his position that Hitler was a friend of the Jews. So Irving must have deliberately concealed these salient facts about Hofmann and his evidence, and he made it more difficult for others to discover his deception by failing to provide a proper footnote reference to the document in which it was revealed.

II

If Hitler was not really antisemitic, then how did Irving explain the hostility shown to the Jews by the Nazis? Goebbels, he wrote in 1996,

> would highlight every malfeasance of the criminal *demi-monde* and identify it as Jewish. In the closing years of the Weimar republic, he was unfortunately not always wrong. In 1930 Jews would be convicted in forty-two of 210 known narcotics smuggling cases; in 1932 sixty-nine of the 272 known international narcotics dealers were Jewish. Jews were arrested in over sixty percent of the cases concerning the running of illegal gambling dens; 193 of the 411 pickpockets arrested in 1932 were Jews. In 1932 no fewer than thirty-one thousand cases of fraud, mainly insurance swindles, would be committed by Jews.[30]

Where did he get these convincing-looking crime statistics? Irving gave the following detailed footnote reference for his claims:

> Interpol figures, in Deutsche Nachrichten-Büro (hereafter DNB), Jul 20, 1935; and see Kurt Daluege, 'Judenfrage als Grundsatz,' in *Angriff*, Aug 3, 1935 (Hauptamt Ordnungspolizei files, BA file R.

19/406); on the criminal demi-monde of 1920s Berlin, see Paul
Weiglin, *Unverwüstliches Berlin. Bilderbuch der Reichshauptstadt
seit 1919* (Zürich, 1955) and Walther Kiaulehn, *Berlin: Schicksal
einer Weltstadt* (Munich, 1958).[31]

On checking out these references, which were, typically for Irving,
without specific page numbers, I eventually managed to establish that
while there were indeed sections in Kiaulehn's and Weiglin's books that
dealt with the Berlin criminal underworld, not a single reference could
be found in either of the books to back up Irving's claim that Jews dominated the crime scene in the 1920s.[32]

The Interpol figures, as quoted in the *Deutsches Nachrichtenbüro,*
sounded very authoritative. However, when I looked at this document
more closely, it turned out to be nothing more than a piece of Nazi propaganda. The *Deutsches Nachrichtenbüro* (DNB) was not an independent news agency, but a mouthpiece of the Nazi leadership. From its creation in December 1933, it had been controlled directly by Goebbels'
Propaganda Ministry. It was subject to the same controls and directions
as any other part of the Nazi news media.[33] Moreover, the article of 20
July 1935 in the DNB did not report any Interpol figures, as Irving
claimed. It consisted instead of a transcript of a press conference by Kurt
Daluege on the Jews and criminality.[34] Daluege was anything but an
objective source. He was a committed Nazi, who had joined the NSDAP
as early as 1926 and entered the SS in 1930. In September 1934, he was
awarded the rank of *SS-Obergruppenführer* and in April 1935 he was
promoted to *Generalleutnant der Landespolizei.*It was in this capacity
that he gave his press conference on 20 July 1935.[35]

Daluege's conference was a blatant propaganda exercise, designed to
justify the brutal Nazi persecution of German Jews. Daluege complained
that while the 'Jew-subservient' (*judenhörigen*) sections of the world
press reported the alleged persecution of Jews in Germany, none of these
journalists went to the trouble to discover the reasons

> that compel the German people to take up its defensive struggle
> against Jewish arrogance and against Jewish criminality. I am in a
> position to supply to all those who out there in the world make them-
> selves out to be so concerned about the allegedly endangered posi-

tion of the German Jews material which will make their mood more reflective.

Daluege went on to present figures detailing the alleged participation of Jews in criminal activities in Germany. The implication was clear: it was not Germany that posed a danger to the Jews, it was the Jews who threatened Germany:

> When one reflects on the fact that according to the latest statistical investigations there are 7.6 Jews per 1,000 Germans, and that the Jew is at the top of the figures with 80 per cent in particular types of crime and in others again at least a quarter of all convictions, one can be really happy that the German people has been freed from a large part of this evil. We want to deal all the more energetically with the other part, which now as before is mounting its thieving raids against the property and the health of our people.[36]

This antisemitic propaganda by a fanatical Nazi was utterly useless as a statistical source for the participation of German Jews in the Weimar Republic in criminal activities. The official figures from the Weimar period were readily available. I checked them. They did not indicate that Jewish criminality was particularly widespread. For instance, in 1925, only one in a hundred among all inmates in Prussian penitentiaries (*Zuchthäuser*) was Jewish.[37]

My research revealed similar things about the final source cited by Irving for his claims about the dominance of Jews in the criminal underworld, Daluege's article of 3 August 1935 in the Nazi propaganda organ *Der Angriff*. In this article, Daluege merely defended the material he had presented at the press conference on 20 July 1935:

> If a section of the foreign press is trying to portray the official statistical material on the criminality of the Jew as an attempt to justify the legal measures which are to be expected against the increasing presumptiousness of the Jews, that is either malicious, or at least a lack of understanding for the standpoint of the German people in the Jewish question.[38]

As a supposedly objective source, Daluege's article was just as worthless as his preceding press conference of 20 July 1935.

Not only did Irving present Daluege's propaganda as an objective source; he even failed to cite Daluege's figures correctly. For instance, in the original text of the press conference, Daluege claimed that in 1933, there were a total of 31,000 fraud cases recorded in Berlin. By 1934, there were only 18,000 such cases, reflecting in his view the impact of the Nazi regime in reducing this type of criminality since it had come to power the previous year. According to Daluege, "a considerable part, if not the largest (part)" of these perpetrators in 1934 were still Jewish. In Irving's text, this passage was rendered in the following way: "In 1932, no fewer than thirty-one thousand cases of fraud, mainly insurance swindles, would be committed by Jews." This did not correspond to Daluege's original text. Daluege's figure of 31,000 fraud cases referred to 1933, not 1932. And not even Daluege claimed, as Irving did, that *all* of these 31,000 fraud cases involved Jews. Daluege nowhere claimed that these fraud cases were mainly insurance swindles, as Irving did. It would have been easy for Irving to have verified his account against other sources. But since he did not, I did. The official German Criminal Statistics for the year 1932 recorded a total of *74* persons, Jewish and non-Jewish, convicted of insurance fraud (paragraph 265 of the German Criminal Code) *in the whole of Germany*— a far cry from Irving's claim that the 31,000 fraud cases mostly involving insurance swindles had been committed by Jews.[39]

III

So far, therefore, I had discovered that Irving's treatment of the documents was highly misleading, to say the least. I had also uncovered evidence that he falsified statistics in his version of Daluege's crime figures. Were these small, relatively rare mistakes in his work? Or were they part of a pattern? Further investigation was clearly necessary. Another link in Irving's chain of proof that Hitler defended the Jews was provided by a whole complex of documents relating to the nationwide outburst of anti-Jewish violence on 9–10 November 1938, dubbed by the acerbic popular humor common Berlin as the *Reichskristallnacht* or 'Reich night of broken glass.' All over Germany, gangs of Nazi and brownshirt thugs burned down synagogues, smashed the windows of Jewish-owned shops and trashed the contents, and broke into Jewish houses and apartments, vandalizing them and beating up their inhabitants, in what Goebbels described as a spontaneous outburst of disapproval of the shooting of a German diplomat in Paris, vom Rath, by a young Polish Jew, Herschel Grynszpan, on 7 November. Who was responsible for this appalling outburst of mass violence, destruction, and murder? In his various accounts of the events, David Irving blamed it entirely on Goebbels. He claimed that Hitler did not approve of the pogrom, did not know about it until it was well under way, and tried to stop it when he found out about it, much later that night. On what documentation did Irving base his claims?

The first key document was an entry in Joseph Goebbels' diary, describing what went on in Munich, where Hitler and all the leading Nazis were gathered to celebrate the anniversary of the attempted putsch in the city on 9 November 1923, fifteen years before. Goebbels was a compulsive diarist, and his voluminous private record of events had long been available in parts. A comprehensive edition of the available texts had been published by the Munich Institute for Contemporary History, and a full version on glass microfiche plates had been discovered by the Institute's editor of the diaries in the former KGB Special Archive in Moscow in early 1992. On pages 273–74 of his book *Goebbels: Mastermind of the 'Third Reich,'* Irving wrote:

> Events that evening, November 9, are crucial to the history of what followed. As Goebbels and Hitler set out to attend the Nazi reception in the old city hall, they learned that the police were intervening against anti-Jewish demonstrators in Munich. Hitler remarked that the police should not crack down too harshly under the circumstances. 'Colossal activity,' the Goebbels diary entry reports, then claims: "I brief the Führer on the affair. He decides: Allow the demonstrations to continue. Hold back the police. The Jews must be given a taste of the public anger for a change.'

This seemed solid enough as a source. There was no doubt about the authenticity of the diaries, and we could easily check the relevant passage in the printed version, published in a German news magazine shortly after the diaries' discovery in Moscow.

Yet far from being a faithful account of the German original, Irving's

version was full of mistakes. An accurate translation of this passage would
be as follows:

> Big demonstrations against the Jews in Kassel and Dessau, syna-
> gogues set on fire and businesses demolished. The death of the Ger-
> man diplomat vom Rath is reported in the afternoon. But now the
> goose is cooked. I go to the Party reception in the Old Town Hall.
> Colossal activity. I brief the Führer about the matter. He orders: let
> the demonstrations go on. Withdraw the police. The Jews must for
> once feel the people's fury. That is right.

In his summary of this diary entry, Irving gave the entirely false impression that the context had been provided by some "anti-Jewish demonstrators" in Munich. In truth, the context for Hitler's decision, as the diary
made clear, was the serious destruction of Jewish property in Kassel and
Dessau.

Irving also failed to note that the phrase *colossal activity* referred to
the meeting in the Town Hall (basically it just meant there were a lot of
people there) and not to the alleged demonstrations in Munich. "Hold
back the police" was absolutely wrong as a translation of the German original, *Polizei zurückziehen*: its proper translation was: "withdraw the
police." "The Jews must be given a taste of the public anger for a change"
was also erroneous as a translation of the last sentence in the diary's original text. Nowhere did the words *taste* or *for a change* occur. The cumulative effect of these mistranslations and omissions was to give the
impression that Hitler merely ordered the local police not to intervene
against some unspecified anti-Jewish demonstrators in Munich. But what
Goebbels really recorded Hitler as saying was that police forces should
be withdrawn in the case of "demonstrations" against Jews, so that the
Jews would feel the "people's fury," as expressed in the destruction of
Jewish property which had already occurred in Kassel and Dessau.

It was not difficult for me to confirm Hitler's involvement in the decision-making process by turning to another contemporary source, the
investigation of the Supreme Nazi Party Court into the pogrom, published as part of the printed documentary accompaniment to the Nuremberg War Crimes Trials and available in many major reference libraries
and specialist collections such as the Wiener Library in London, where I

consulted them. While Hitler, unexpectedly, went home after his dinner discussion with Goebbels, Goebbels went on to deliver a speech to the Nazi officials assembled in the Old Town Hall. He told them about the anti-Jewish actions in Hesse and Anhalt, and added: "On his briefing, the Führer had decided that demonstrations of this kind were neither to be prepared or organized by the Party, but insofar as they arose spontaneously, they were not to be opposed." The Nazi Party's own Supreme Party Court later found that all party officials present apparently understood Goebbels to mean that "the Party should not appear to the outside world as the originator of the demonstrations, but should in reality organize them and carry them out." It added that it was customary to read out of such a command more than the actual words that had been put into it, "just as, in the interest of the Party, it is also in many cases the custom of the person issuing the command—precisely in cases of illegal political demonstrations—not to say everything and just to hint at what he wants to achieve with the order."[40] Yet this key part of Goebbels' speech on 9 November 1938 was entirely omitted from *Goebbels: Mastermind of the 'Third Reich.'* Only by suppressing the information could Irving later claim that the Party Supreme Court inquiry left little doubt about Goebbels' "sole personal guilt."[41]

In order to dissociate Hitler further from the pogrom, Irving also had to deal with two telexes sent out on the night of 9–10 November 1938 by the police leadership in Germany, telling police units all over the Reich how to conduct themselves. The texts of these telexes were also readily available. They were included in the German-language version of the Nuremberg Trial Documents, also held among other places in the Wiener Library. The first telex was sent at 11:55 P.M. on 9 November 1938 by Heydrich's subordinate Heinrich Müller, head of Section II of the Security Police. Müller warned German police officials:

> Actions against Jews, in particular against their synagogues, will very shortly take place across the whole of Germany. They are not to be interrupted. However, measures are to be taken in co-operation with the *Ordnungspolizei* for looting and other special excesses to be prevented. . . . The arrest of about 20–30,000 Jews in the Reich is to be prepared. Propertied Jews above all are to be chosen. More detailed instructions will be issued in the course of the present night.[42]

It was unthinkable that Müller, a career policeman who had been in the force since 1919, would have sent this telex without having been told to by his superiors, either Himmler or Heydrich or both.[43]

Müller's telex was the only document sent by a leading police official that stated the number of Jews to be arrested, a number that tallied with the figure noted in Goebbels' diary on 10 November as having been ordered by Hitler himself ("The Führer has ordered that 20–30,000 Jews are to be immediately arrested").[44] The "more detailed instructions" mentioned in the telex were sent out to German police units about one and a half hours later, at 1:20 A.M. on 10 November 1938, this time directly by Himmler and Heydrich. This second telex instructed the police and Security Service all over Germany not to get in the way of the destruction of Jewish property or obstruct violent acts committed against German Jews. "Demonstrations against the Jews," it warned, "are to be expected in the course of this night—9th to 10th November 1938—in the entire Reich . . . The demonstrations which occur are not to be hindered by the police." Only a few restrictions were placed on the action:

a) Only such measures may be taken as do not involve any endangering of German life or property (e.g. synagogue fires only if there is no danger of the fire spreading to the surrounding buildings).

b) The shops and dwellings of Jews may only be destroyed, not looted. The police are instructed to supervise the implementation of this order and to arrest looters.

c) Care is to be taken that non-Jewish shops in shopping streets are unconditionally secured against damage.

d) Foreign nationals may not be assaulted, even if they are Jews.[45]

Thus the police were explicitly ordered not to intervene in the destruction except in these four very particular circumstances.

Crucially, I also discovered persuasive evidence to suggest that Himmler had been in contact with Hitler before these telexes were sent off to the German police. A consultation late on 9 November 1938 was mentioned by two SS officers, Karl Wolff and Luitpold Schallermeier, after the war.[46] A report by the British Consul in Munich on 11 November 1938 also said that Himmler had been in contact with Hitler that evening.[47] There was thus a strong likelihood that the police telexes reflected Hitler's own intentions.

So how did Irving deal with this evidence? In *Goebbels,* he ignored the information indicating a meeting between Hitler and Himmler, despite the fact that he was familiar with the sources suggesting it.[48] He failed to mention the telex sent by Müller in his narrative, hiding it in a footnote.[49] And he misrepresented the content of the telex sent out by Himmler and Heydrich at 1:20 A.M. According to Irving, it was not until one in the morning that the two top SS men finally discovered what was going on. When Heydrich learned that the Munich synagogue, next door to the Hotel *Vier Jahreszeiten,* was ablaze, Irving wrote, he "hurried up to Himmler's room then telexed instructions to all police authorities to restore law and order, protect Jews and Jewish property, and halt any ongoing incidents."[50] The only historical truth in this account was the assertion that Heydrich sent a telex to the German police authorities. Everything else was a blatant manipulation of the historical record. Even a cursory glance at the telex showed that it ordered the opposite of what Irving claimed it did. What Heydrich was telling the police was *not* to prevent the destruction of Jewish property or get in the way of violent acts against German Jews.

Irving went on to suggest that when Hitler discovered what was going on, after one in the morning, he was very angry and tried to stop it. Irving referred at one point to Hitler's "fury" at the news of the pogrom.[51] He based this claim in the first place on postwar testimonies by members of Hitler's entourage. But these people were close associates of the Nazi leader and often remained sympathetic to his memory. It seemed obvious to me that their testimony had to be treated with great caution, and indeed I devoted considerable attention to assessing its value in general, although in the end this did not prove a very useful exercise for the purposes of the trial, which demanded a concentration on issues of a more precise and limited nature. Irving reported that Julius Schaub, "the most intimate of his aides," reported that Hitler had been furious and sent "Schaub and his colleagues out into the streets to stop the looting (thus Schaub's post-war version)."[52] I discovered plenty of evidence in the archives indicating that Julius Schaub was indeed one of Hitler's most loyal followers, having joined the Nazi Party in the early 1920s, taken part in the failed putsch of 1923, for which he had served a term in prison, and been decorated with various prestigious Nazi awards. He had been Hitler's personal adjutant since 1925 and was a *Gruppenführer* in the SS by the time of the pogrom. After the war he did his best to exonerate Hitler for the crimes of Nazism, claiming he had cursed the war and "was always for peace."[53] He was not a very trustworthy witness, therefore.

Schaub's postwar claim that Hitler was outraged at the actions against the Jews and tried to "rescue what could still be rescued"[54] seemed to me to be a self-serving lie, for if Hitler had known of them and given his approval, then Schaub, as his closest personal aide, must have been in the same situation, and the anti-Jewish actions of 9–10 November 1938 were the subject of criminal proceedings in Germany after the war. Moreover, according to Goebbels' diary, Schaub, far from trying to stop the violence, was in the thick of it: "The *Shock-troop Hitler* gets going immediately to clear things out in Munich," Goebbels reported: "That then happens straight away. A synagogue is battered into a lump. . . . The Shock-troop carries out frightful work. . . . We go with Schaub to the Artists' Club, to await further reports. . . . Schaub is completely worked up. His old shock-troop past is waking up."[55] This contemporary document totally exploded Schaub's later claims.

Irving also misrepresented the testimony of other members of Hitler's entourage, claiming, for example, that "according to Luftwaffe adjutant Nicolaus von Below, Hitler phoned Goebbels. 'What's going on?' he snapped, and 'Find out!' "[56] However, this claim was not backed up by Below's own published postwar memoirs, where he reported that Hitler phoned Goebbels privately from his own living-room, so that he could not be heard, and indeed Below made no claim to have heard what Hitler said.[57] Below repeated this assertion when interviewed by Irving in 1968.[58] Irving also cited the testimony of another adjutant, Fritz Wiedemann, in support of his claim that "Goebbels, now in no doubt where Hitler's real favour lay, also spent the night on the telephone trying to extinguish the conflagration that his mischievous tongue had ignited."[59] He later backed up this claim with the assertion that Wiedemann "saw Goebbels spending much of that night of November 9–10 'telephoning . . . to halt the most violent excesses.' "[60]

Irving had previously dismissed Wiedemann as an untrustworthy witness, so this change of heart was surprising.[61] Whether or not he was untrustworthy, however, what he said was not what Irving claimed it was anyway: "There is absolutely no doubt," Wiedemann reported, "that this action slipped out of the hands of those who instigated it. It is reliably reported that Göbbels (*sic*) as well repeatedly telephoned from Munich during the night to stop the worst outrages."[62] So Wiedemann did not actually see Goebbels make any phone calls, he merely repeated one of the many rumors circulating in Germany after the pogrom. In any case, Goebbels was not preoccupied with halting the violence, as Irving surely knew. The Supreme Party Tribunal report of 13 February 1939 stated that Goebbels was phoned at about two in the morning on 10 November 1938 and told of the first death of a Jew in the pogrom. It continued:

> According to the statement of the deputy *Gauleiter* of Munich-Upper Bavaria, Party Comrade Dr Goebbels answered to the effect that the man reporting it should not get upset because of one dead Jew; thousands of Jews had better believe it in the coming days. At this moment in time, most of the killings could have been prevented by a supplementary order. If this did not happen, the conclusion has to be drawn from this fact, as from the comment in itself, that the end result was either intended, or at least taken into account as possible and desirable. Then the individual perpetrator had put . . . The correctly recognized, if unclearly expressed will of the leadership into effect.[63]

Thus Goebbels was explicitly intervening to *stop* attempts to protect Jews and threatening further violence "in the coming days" with his menacing language.

His attitude was underlined in his diary entry for the night of the pogrom, where he noted the excesses with obvious approval:

> In Berlin 5, then 15 synagogues burn down. Now the people's anger is raging. Nothing more can be done against it for the night. And I don't want to do anything either. Should be given free rein. . . . As I drive to the hotel, windows shatter. Bravo! Bravo! The synagogues burn in all big cities. German property is not endangered.[64]

Yet, according to Irving, Goebbels had been spending the night desperately telephoning all over Germany to get this kind of thing to stop! In fact, Goebbels' only concern is likely to have been to prevent looting and forestall damage to German property, which must have been what he was referring to when he wrote in the same diary entry for an earlier point in the evening: "I now issue a precise circular in which is set out what may be done and what not."[65] As the rest of the diary entry and the evidence of the Supreme Party Tribunal both demonstrated, he encouraged attacks on Jewish persons and property and greeted news of their occurrence not with alarm but with jubilation.

Irving also made use of a third telex sent out to the local Nazi Party bosses at 2:56 A.M. on 10 November 1938 by Rudolf Hess, Hitler's deputy. What did this telex say? In 1983, Irving claimed that it read as follows: "On express orders issued at the very highest level, there are to be no kind of acts of arson or outrages against Jewish property or the like on any account and under any circumstances whatsoever." This meant, Irving added, italicizing the point, that *Adolf Hitler himself has ordered that all this outrage has got to stop forthwith.*"[66] But when I looked at the actual text of the telegram, it was immediately clear that the telex merely stated that "on the express command of the highest instance, fire-raising in Jewish shops or the like must in no case and under no circumstances take place."[67] The German original for shops in the telex was *Geschäften.* Irving must have deliberately mistranslated *Geschäften* as *property* in order to give the impression that the order also covered houses, apartments, and synagogues, instead of shops and similar commercial premises. The telex in fact was entirely consistent with the earlier orders sent out to the police by Müller and by Heydrich and Himmler, imposing only limited restrictions on the scope of the action. The telex referred only to arson, not to any other kind of "outrage." Other kinds of destruction, such as trashing the shops' contents, shattering their windows, breaking up their furnishings and fixtures, setting fire to synagogues, beating up and killing individual Jews, were exempted and could continue.

Irving also used the diaries of the diplomat Ulrich von Hassell, later a prominent member of the resistance movement which culminated in the attempt to kill Hitler on 20 July 1944, to back up his assertion that "Hess confirmed that in his view Goebbels alone was to blame" for the pogrom.[68] The diaries were readily available in published form. On consulting them, I discovered that what Hassell wrote in the entry to which Irving referred was as follows:

> On 23.12 Hess spent two hours at the Bruckmanns'. They said he had been more depressed than ever before. He had left them in no doubt that he completely disapproved of the action against the Jews; he had also reported his views in an energetic manner to the 'Führer' and begged him to drop the matter, but unfortunately completely in vain. Hess pointed to Goebbels as the actual originator.[69]

Thus Hassell never reported Hess as saying Goebbels *alone* was to blame, simply that he was the man who initiated the action. Irving omitted all mention of the crucial sentence which reported Hess as saying his attempt to get Hitler to stop the action had been futile.

Irving did not quote the following passage in von Hassell's diary, relating to a conversation he had on 17 December 1938 with the Prussian finance minister, Johannes Popitz, about the destruction and violence of 9–10 November. "Popitz said to Göring, those responsible must be punished. Answer: 'My dear Popitz, do you want to punish the Führer?' "[70] According to this source, therefore, Göring, who was far closer to Hitler than the old-conservative Popitz, considered that Hitler himself was responsible for the pogrom.

So the available evidence pointed to Hitler's having backed it from the outset. I found strong indications that he actually approved of it before he left the Old Town Hall in Munich. In any case, the evidence made it clear that Hitler did not order that "all this outrage has to stop." Irving knew this evidence. Yet he deliberately chose to suppress or distort it in his efforts to exculpate Hitler from responsibility. This was not a mere case of carelessness or sloppy research on Irving's part. He surely decided to suppress information of which he was aware, deliberately misconstrue other information, and manipulate the material in order to serve his own purpose of absolving Hitler from blame for the anti-Jewish excesses of the night in question.

IV

In his diary account of the events of 10 November 1938, Goebbels wrote: "New reports rain down the whole morning. I consider with the Führer what measures should be taken now. Let the beatings continue or stop them? That is now the question."[71] How did Irving treat this entry? On page 277 of *Goebbels*, he wrote: "As more ugly bulletins rained down on him the next morning, November 10, 1938, Goebbels went to see Hitler to discuss 'what to do next'—there is surely an involuntary hint of apprehension in the phrase." The claim that Goebbels was apprehensive had no basis in the diary, but was Irving's own invention. In fact, Goebbels' diary entries were jubilant about the whole affair and about his own part in it.

When Hitler and Goebbels talked on the morning of 10 November as reported in this diary entry, therefore, no decision had yet been taken. But following this conversation, Goebbels drafted an order to bring the pogrom to a halt. He reported on it in his diary on 11 November: "Yesterday, Müller reports on the events in Berlin. There, all proceeded fantastically. One fire after another. It is good that way. I prepare an order to put an end to the actions. It is now just enough."[72] His diary entry went on to describe how he then took his draft order for approval by Hitler over lunch at the Osteria restaurant.

> I report to the Führer in the Osteria. He agrees with everything. His views are totally radical and aggressive. The action itself has taken place without any problems. 17 dead. But no German property damaged. The Führer approves my decree concerning the ending of the actions, with small amendments. I announce it via the press and radio. The Führer wants to take very sharp measures against the Jews. They must themselves put their businesses in order again. The insurance companies will not pay them a thing. Then the Führer wants a gradual expropriation of Jewish businesses.[73]

This entry clearly suggested to me, as it surely would have done to any historian approaching it with an open mind, first, that Hitler approved the pogrom, and second, that it was Hitler who devised some of the economic measures ordered against the Jews at a subsequent meeting chaired by Göring on 12 November 1938.

How did Irving deal with this material? In 1992, when Irving first read the recently discovered Goebbels diary entries for the period 9–10 November 1938 in Moscow, he was convinced that they showed that Hitler approved of the pogrom. I found his account of this in a videotape of a television interview he gave to the Canadian Broadcasting Corporation shortly after his Moscow visit, one of the large collection of such tapes the defense had obtained under the legal terms of Discovery from Irving's own personal collection. The events of 1938 had not been covered in any of the sections of Goebbels' diary which had previously been available. Irving made the most of them:

> According to his diary [Goebbels], and I can't emphasise those words enough, according to his diaries, Hitler was closely implicated with those outrages. And that's a matter of some dismay to me because it means I have to revise my own opinion. But a historian should always be willing to revise his opinion.[74]

In another videotape in the collection, containing a recording Irving made a year later for his audience in Australia, where he had recently been banned from appearing in person, he was sounding a slightly more skeptical note. Goebbels' diary, Irving said,

> describes how Hitler thoroughly endorses what he, Goebbels, has done, namely starting that outrage that night. This was a deep shock for me and I immediately announced it to the world's newspapers that I had discovered this material, although it appeared to go against what I had written in my own book *Hitler's War*. But even there you have to add a rider and say, 'Wait a minute this is Dr. Goebbels writing this.' Dr. Goebbels who took all the blame for what was done. So did he have perhaps a motive for writing in his private diaries subsequently that Hitler endorsed what he had done? You can't entirely close that file.[75]

By 1996 this slightly skeptical note by Irving had been transformed in the biography he published of the man he called the "Mastermind of the Third Reich" into a total conviction that Goebbels was lying. Irving's change of mind was not influenced by any further discoveries of new documentary material. Unable to manipulate the diary's clear statement that Hitler took an extreme antisemitic line, Irving tried to explain it away. He suggested that Goebbels was lying when he said that Hitler approved of his action. Irving now claimed that Goebbels had been acting against Hitler's wishes, but tried to give the opposite impression in his diary by saying that he had actually been carrying them out.

Irving's reason for claiming that the diary entry dealing with the meeting between Goebbels and Hitler on 10 November 1938 was partially untrue and perhaps slanted was the fact that it "stands alone, and in direct contradiction to the evidence of Hitler's entire immediate entourage."[76] But far from standing alone, it tied in well with the contemporary documents that I had examined. And the testimony of members of Hitler's entourage was either manipulated by Irving to say something it did not in fact say, or was suspect on any one of a number of grounds. It seemed to me in the light of the available evidence that Goebbels' report of Hitler's radical views at the meeting in the Osteria restaurant was accurate and truthful. I looked at various contemporary documents supporting this reconstruction of events. They showed that the order by Goebbels to stop the pogrom went out in the afternoon of 10 November 1938.[77] Irving accepted that this order went out on 10 November 1938, but claimed that it was broadcast at 10:00 A.M., in order to suggest that it merely put the seal on the previous night's supposed attempts to end the pogrom. Once again, Irving presented no contemporary documentary evidence to support such a claim.[78]

In order to emphasize his point that almost all of the Nazi leaders, except Goebbels, opposed the pogrom, Irving claimed that after things had quietened down, Hess "ordered the Gestapo and the party's courts to delve into the origins of the night's violence and turn the culprits over to the public prosecutors."[79] But when I looked at it, the document he cited in support of this claim said something quite different:

> The aim of the investigation by the Party Courts is to establish which cases can and must be held responsible by the action itself and which cases arose out of personal and base motives. In the latter cases a referral to the state prosecution service will be unavoidable, indeed it will be just.[80]

Thus the state judicial investigations were never meant to examine all the incidents that had taken place during the pogrom. Already on 10 November 1938, the Ministry of Justice had instructed its officials that "material damage to synagogues, cemetery halls and graveyards through fire, blowing up etc." as well as "damage to Jewish shops" should not be prosecuted. This covered many of the criminal offenses committed during the pogrom and left only cases of looting, killing, grievous bodily

harm, and the destruction of Jewish homes out of selfish motives.[81] The
criminal courts still left the initial investigation of these cases to the
Gestapo and the party courts.

By no means all culprits investigated by the party courts, as Irving
claimed, were later to be turned over to the criminal justice system.
Offenders were only to be treated in this way if they were judged by the
party courts to have acted out of base motives. In all other cases, the participants in the violence of 9–10 November 1938 were to be spared criminal prosecution. What Hess's directive did, therefore, was the exact
opposite to what Irving claimed it did. It ensured that only a small number of offenders ever reached the criminal courts. Had Hess and the leading Nazis wanted the criminal courts to deal with the numerous crimes
committed during the pogrom, then they would have left the investigations to the public prosecutors, rather than the Gestapo and the party
courts. However, this was precisely what leading Nazis wanted to avoid.[82]

On 13 February 1939, Göring was informed of the outcome of the
investigations in sixteen cases which the Supreme Party Court had undertaken. In only two of the sixteen cases, both involving the rape of Jewish
women, had the Party Court transferred the perpetrators to ordinary
criminal courts (and in these two cases the party judges were not motivated by concern for the victims, but simply by the fact that Nazi Party
members had committed 'racial defilement' or in other words compromised what the party regarded as their own racial purity). In all the other
fourteen cases, the Supreme Party Court asked Hitler to quash proceedings. These cases included the brutal murder of twenty-one Jews,
who had been shot dead, stabbed to death, or drowned by Nazi Party
members. The worst punishment meted out to these murderers was an
official warning and barring from any Nazi Party office for a period of
three years. The great majority of offenders received even milder pun-
ishments, or none at all.[83]

V

In all of his books, writings, and speeches, Irving's references were almost
exclusively to original sources. He made a point of almost never citing the
work of other historians. It was all the more surprising, therefore, that in

his account of the pogrom of 9–10 November 1938 in *Goebbels*, he referred no fewer than six times in seven pages to an author by the name of Ingrid Weckert. Irving's references to Weckert were extremely vague. I could not find out anything about her from his footnotes. Nor could I locate her work in any of the mainstream academic journals or bibliographies. Eventually I found her in cyberspace. Irving's own professionally constructed and well presented Focal Point website, which the defense team monitored regularly, was only one of a range of such sites put onto the Internet by self-styled 'Revisionists.' This was where, in the historian David Cesarani's memorable phrase, the "cyberwarriors of Holocaust denial" now peddled their wares. In addition, the legal process of Discovery once more came to my aid, as the material by Weckert that served as the basis for some of Irving's statements about the events of 9–10 November 1938 turned up in his personal collection of documents.

As I looked through Ingrid Weckert's work, it became clear that its cumulative effect was to play down or deny the crimes of the Third Reich. In an article published in 1994, for instance, she declared that "the claim that Germans killed thousands of people in 'gas vans' is to be categorized as rumour."[84] In an article published in 1985, Weckert openly acknowledged her sympathy for the Nazis, confessing that "the youth of Adolf Hitler's Germany was the finest of all Europe and perhaps of the entire world. The same ethical standards," she continued, "applied to the SS and SA. . . . It was their faithfulness and gallantry which saved Germany from chaos and Communism." Irving had evidently read this article, since the copy made available in the Discovery process from his personal library contained pencil lines in the margin that were unlikely to have been made by anyone except Irving himself.[85]

In 1997, Weckert suggested in another article that conditions in the Dachau concentration camp were better when it was run by the SS than when it became a U.S. internment camp after the end of the Second World War. The article in which she put forward this claim was first published in the extreme right-wing magazine *Sleipnir*. To make it more difficult to track her down, she had adopted a pseudonym in this particular instance.[86] Moreover, according to information posted on a 'Revisionist' website, Weckert had also been sentenced in 1998 by the local court in Berlin-Tiergarten to a fine of over 3,000 German marks for her article in *Sleipnir*.[87]

Weckert was best known, however, for her manipulation of the historical record of the pogrom of 9–10 November 1938. She published a series of articles on the subject in the late 1970s, at least one of which was read at the time by Irving.[88] Her book *Feuerzeichen: Die 'Reichskristallnacht,'* was first published in 1981. When I looked at it, I found it full of crude and offensive antisemitic remarks and praise for Hitler's Third Reich. It absolved all the leading Nazis of any blame and suggested that it was master-minded by German 'traitors' and 'World Jewry' in the hope that such violence would reflect badly on the (blameless) Nazi regime and cause it to fall. The real victims of the pogrom were the Germans, not the Jews. Not surprisingly, the German authorities had blacklisted the book. It was illegal to sell or lend it to any person under the age of eighteen. The German authorities not only described the book as likely to corrupt young minds by arousing antisemitic feelings in them, but also declared that it showed no evidence even of a minimal attempt at truthfulness and objectivity.[89] Irving's source Ingrid Weckert thus turned out to be an antisemitic propagandist who had been sentenced for her antisemitic and pro-Nazi outpourings. No wonder that Irving concealed the true identity of his source from his readers and withheld full references to her work from his footnotes. Nevertheless, he knowingly made use of her work in his biography of Goebbels, including the claim that Goebbels broadcast an order calling a halt to the pogrom at 10:00 A.M. on 10 November 1938.

Irving also gave credence to claims that the assassination of vom Rath was a Jewish conspiracy and alleged that there had been little violence against Jewish persons. On page 272 of *Goebbels,* Irving suggested that there was "some frail evidence that LICA, the Paris-based International League Against Antisemitism," had a hand in the assassination. But he provided no evidence for this insinuation at all. In the 1991 edition of *Hitler's War,* Irving wrote:

> Revisionist historians now argue that the Nazis had fallen into a Zionist trap. The Haganah officials with whom Adolf Eichmann negotiated on his trip to Palestine in November 1937 had hinted that it would serve their interests if things were made hot for Germany's Jews, to accelerate Jewish emigration to Palestine. It deserves comment that Grynszpan, although a destitute youth, was able to reside in a hotel in 1938 and purchase a handgun for 250 francs, and that

his defence counsel Moro Giafferi was the best that the money of
the International League against Anti-Semitism (LICA) could buy:
LICA's Paris office was around the corner from Grynszpan's hotel.[90]

Irving again seemed to have taken some of the details from Ingrid Weckert, this time however without acknowledging his debt to her in any way
for once again the Discovery process had yielded a copy of her article from
Irving's private collection with the tell-tale pencil marks in the margin.[91]

Grynszpan's activities in France had been intensively researched by
the German historian Helmut Heiber in the 1950s. The young Pole had
actually been living until the day before his assassination attempt with his
uncle Abraham Berenbaum. He left after a quarrel, renting a room in the
Hôtel Suez on the Boulevard de Strasbourg for 22 francs 50 centimes a
night. With 320 francs in his pocket, he bought a gun and cartridges from
the weapons dealer Carpe for a total cost of 245 francs on the morning
of 7 November 1938. His defense lawyer was paid by a non-Jewish committee in the United States set up by the journalist Dorothy Thompson
in November 1938 specifically to help the young Pole. A subsequent
investigation by the Gestapo failed to come up with any links at all
between Grynszpan and Jewish organizations. When Grynszpan finally
fell into German hands after the Nazi invasion of France in 1940, the official appointed by the Propaganda Ministry to represent the interests of
the German Reich in the Grynszpan affair in France, Professor Friedrich
Grimm, admitted on 10 July 1942 that "one cannot prove any direct relationship between the murderer and Jewish organizations."[92] What did
Irving know that the Nazis themselves had failed to discover? Neither his
text nor his footnotes gave me any clue.

Irving's entire portrayal of the events of 9–10 November seemed to
me designed to diminish the suffering of the Jews. In his book on Göring,
published in 1989, and his biography of Goebbels, published in 1996, he
cited a figure of thirty-five or thirty-six dead, apparently basing it on an
early, incomplete report by Heydrich, and omitted to mention the figure
of ninety-one provided by the fuller investigation of the Supreme Party
Tribunal.[93] When I examined Irving's earlier work, it was clear that he
knew that the lower figures were wrong. His overall presentation of the
events reached a low point of tastelessness in the relevant chapter head-

ing of the Göring biography, which he entitled "Sunshine Girl and Crystal Night," trivializing the murderous destruction of the pogrom by linking it in this way to a section on Göring's daughter Edda.

In his Goebbels biography, Irving's manipulation of the figures of destruction was even more openly designed to minimize the suffering of the Jews in Germany. Here Irving devoted one short paragraph to the statistics of the pogrom:

> By dawn on November 10, 191 of the country's fourteen hundred synagogues had been destroyed, about 7,500 of the one hundred thousand Jewish shops had had their windows smashed. Thirty-six of the country's half-million Jews had been murdered, and hundreds more badly beaten.[94]

What Irving failed to tell his readers is that, once more, he had taken information from the notorious Ingrid Weckert, including the figure of one hundred thousand Jewish shops.[95] Not one of these claims was accurate.

The only source that Irving provided for his claims was a preliminary report submitted by Heydrich to Göring, available in print as a document presented to the Nuremberg War Crimes Trial. This mentioned not 191 synagogues destroyed, but 276 (191 burned down, and a further 76 completely smashed).[96] It was clear even at the time that the real figure was much higher. The organization of the Social Democrats in exile, the SOPADE, which had informants all over Germany, estimated in November 1938 that 520 synagogues had been completely or partially destroyed.[97] More detailed investigations of the damage carried out after the war arrived at higher figures still.[98] Heydrich did not report that these shops had merely had their windows smashed, as Irving claimed: Heydrich wrote baldly that they had been destroyed.[99] It was also misleading to claim, as Irving did, that only about one Jewish shop in every thirteen was attacked. As Avraham Barkai, an expert on the economic life of Jews under the Nazis, had discovered, the Nazi thugs had in fact targeted the vast majority of Jewish shops in Germany, since there were only some nine thousand Jewish shops left in the country as a whole by this time.[100]

It was clear after I had examined Irving's use of historical sources in his depiction of the anti-Jewish outrages of 9–10 November 1938 that he falsely attributed conclusions to reliable sources, bending them to fit his arguments. He relied on material that turned out directly to contradict his arguments when it was checked. He quoted from sources in a manner that distorted their authors' meaning and purposes. He misrepresented data and skewed documents. He used insignificant and sometimes implausible pieces of evidence to dismiss more substantial evidence that did not support his thesis. He ignored or deliberately suppressed material when it ran counter to his arguments. When he was unable to do this, he expressed implausible doubts about its reliability.

Irving did all this, it seemed to me, in order to minimize and trivialize the violence and destruction visited by the Nazis upon the Jewish community in Germany, and above all to dissociate Hitler completely from these events. Irving's conclusions were completely untenable. I thought his scholarship was sloppy and unreliable and did not meet even the most basic requirements of honest and competent historical research. If this was the case with his treatment of Hitler and Nazi antisemitism before 1939, how did he deal with the conception and execution of what the Nazis called the 'Final Solution of the Jewish Question in Europe' after the war had begun?

CHAPTER THREE

Hitler and the "Final Solution"

I

After the Nazi invasion of Poland in 1939, Jews in the occupied areas were forced into ghettos, where they were deliberately kept in overcrowded and insanitary conditions and isolated from the outside. The Nazi authorities restricted supplies of food and other vital resources. By the spring of 1941 the death rate in the Warsaw ghetto was running at nearly 4,000 a month. Conditions worsened still further after the German invasion of the Soviet Union in June 1941. The advancing German army was followed by four heavily armed task forces (*Einsatzgruppen*) organized by the Security Service of the SS. These task forces started shooting Jews found in the occupied territory. By 15 October 1941, Task Force A alone, working in the Baltic area, was reporting that it had executed 118,430 Jews. These actions continued through 1942 and well into 1943 and accounted for well over a million deaths.[1]

As these events unfolded, the Nazi leadership imposed fresh restrictions on the 164,000 Jews who were still living in Germany. From 15 September 1941 they were forced to wear a yellow star on their clothes.[2] On 18 September, Heinrich Himmler informed Arthur Greiser, *Gauleiter* of the occupied Polish area of the Warthegau, that the "Führer wishes that the Old Reich and the Protectorate (of Bohemia and Moravia) be emptied and freed of Jews from west to east as quickly as possible."[3] On 23 October 1941 Jews were banned from emigrating voluntarily. The SS and Gestapo now began deporting German Jews to the Eastern ghettos. Some of them were shot on arrival, but the Nazi leaders seem to have become alarmed at the effect on those Jews yet to be deported, and indeed on public opinion more generally, of reports filtering back to Germany about the killing actions that did take place. The arrival of thousands of German, Austrian, and Bohemian Jews in the ghettos did, however, cause the Nazi leadership to accelerate the killing of native Jews in the occupied East in order to make room for them, and it was at this point that the SS began to set up special camps designed for rapid mass extermination by poison gas, initially in mobile gassing vans.[4]

The Nazi leadership paid particular attention to deporting the Jews from Berlin. As Joseph Goebbels, who besides being Propaganda Minister had also been the party Gauleiter of Berlin since 1925, noted in his diary on 20 August 1941, "Berlin must become a city free of Jews. It is infuriating and a scandal that 76,000 Jews can still loiter around in the capital of the German Reich, mostly as parasites."[5] According to Irving, however, "Hitler was neither consulted nor informed" about the deportations of Jews from Berlin. As proof for this assertion he referred to remarks made by Hitler on 25 October 1941. According to Irving, Hitler claimed that the Jews had started the war and said:

> "Let nobody tell me," Hitler added, "that despite that we can't park them in the marshier parts of Russia!" "By the way," he added, "it's not a bad thing that public rumour attributes to us a plan to exterminate the Jews." He pointed out however that he had no intention of starting anything at present. "There's no point in adding to one's difficulties at a time like this!"[6]

The German original of this monologue was published in 1980. I looked it up and translated it. The whole passage read as follows:

> In the Reichstag, I prophesied to Jewry, the Jew will disappear from Europe if war is not avoided. This race of criminals has the two million dead of the [First World] war on its conscience, and now hundreds of thousands again. Nobody can tell me: But we can't send them into the morass! For who bothers about our people? It's good if the terror that we are exterminating Jewry goes before us. . . . I'm forced to pile up an enormous amount of things myself; but that doesn't mean that what I take cognisance of without reacting to it immediately, just disappears. It goes into an account; one day the

book is taken out. I had to remain inactive for a long time against the Jews too. There's no sense in artificially making extra difficulties for oneself; the more cleverly one operates, the better. When I read speeches from a person like Galen, I say to myself: pricking them with pins has no purpose; it's better to keep silent; unless one doubts the future of the movement! If I believe that the movement will exist in a few centuries, then I can wait. I wouldn't have dealt with Marxism either, if I hadn't had the power behind me.[7]

It was obvious from this that the translation presented by Irving contained numerous errors. In the German original there was no reference to Russia, and the action described was not the innocuous-sounding *park them,* which implied some kind of reasonably long-term stay, but *send them.* What might well have been meant by his statement was illustrated by an order given by Himmler to the SS in the area of the Pripet marshes on 30 July 1941 three months prior to this monologue: "All Jews must be shot. Drive Jew-women into the marshes." Reporting on their attempt to carry this order out, the mounted division of the second SS cavalry regiment noted on 12 August in terms that left no doubt as to the purpose of this action: "Driving women and children into marshes did not have the success that it was meant to, since the marshes were not deep enough for them to sink in. In most cases one encountered firm ground (probably sand) below a depth of 1 metre, so that sinking-in was not possible."[8] It seemed reasonable to me to suppose that Hitler was aware of these events by mid- to late October. Sending the Jews into the marshes in this manner was something very different from merely "parking them in the marshier parts of Russia."

But I found even more serious errors in Irving's version. Thus it had Hitler saying: "By the way . . . it's not a bad thing that public rumour attributes to us a plan to exterminate the Jews." What Hitler was really reported as saying was: "It's good if the terror that we are exterminating Jewry goes before us." Irving's book watered this down in several respects. The translation of *Schrecken* as "public rumour" was inadequate, as it failed to convey the element of terror and anxiety indelibly associated with the word *Schrecken.*[9] "Public rumour attributes to us" implied that it was, as so often with rumors, untrue. Hitler said nothing about *attribution,* but presented it as a fact. The word plan, which was wholly absent from the German original, appeared in Irving's book and made it seem that the rumored extermination of the Jews was not actually taking place but was still in the planning stage. In fact, of course, Hitler's actual recorded statement was unambiguous in its recognition of the fact that Jews were being exterminated behind the Eastern Front as the German army advanced into the Soviet Union following the invasion of June 1941, and crystal clear in its approval of the effect this had in terrorizing the inhabitants of the areas that were still to be conquered.

According to Irving, Hitler "pointed out however that he had no intention of starting anything at present." Irving here drew on his own account of the table talk in his book *Hitler's War* (1991), where he claimed that Hitler said that "with the Jews too I have found myself remaining inactive."[10] However, the German original made it clear that Hitler saw himself *no longer* as being inactive toward the Jews: "I had to remain inactive for a long time against the Jews too." This meant that the time of inactivity was over. Hitler was talking in the present tense about the Jews, not in the future tense.

Irving further reported Hitler as saying: "There's no point in adding to one's difficulties at a time like this!" But the German original said something subtly different: "There's no sense in artificially making extra difficulties for oneself; the more cleverly one operates, the better." Thus, Hitler was making the general point that when attacking one's enemies, one had to wait for the right moment to strike. While he thought that the time had come to deal with the Jews, he wanted to postpone the conflict with the Catholic Church, personified by Cardinal von Galen, who on 3 August 1941 had publicly attacked the Nazis' 'euthanasia' program (the killing of mentally and physically disabled adults and children). The translation presented by Irving completely obscured this important point.

As Irving himself pointed out when confronted with these criticisms, he had not translated the passage in question himself. In fact, he merely followed what he called the official translation in English, first published in 1953 by Weidenfeld. Indeed, as far as the 1977 edition of *Hitler's War* was concerned, Irving had some justification for doing so. Until 1980, the German original was not officially accessible to historians, who had to rely on the English translation of 1953 instead.[11] Yet, by the time he published

Goebbels, in 1996, Irving had been familiar with the German original for almost twenty years. Irving claimed proudly that he "was the only historian in the world to whom the original German texts were made available by their physical owner, namely in October 1977."[12] He admitted in 1983 that the German original "is completely different from the published English translation."[13] Obviously the passages that he had used from the 1953 translation now had to be checked against the German original and amended if necessary. So for example, Irving dropped the phrase "terror is a salutary thing," falsely attributed to Hitler in the Weidenfeld translation, from his revised 1991 edition of *Hitler's War* because it was not in the German original.[14]

But while Irving cut out this phrase, which made Hitler appear in a bad light, he deliberately continued to use the other parts of the flawed (and in no sense 'official') Weidenfeld translation, if the original German text implicated Hitler in a way that the Weidenfeld translation did not. Thus in his book on Goebbels, he continued to claim that Hitler said that he was planning nothing against the Jews at present (Weidenfeld translation), while the German original had Hitler stating that "I had to remain inactive for a long time against the Jews too." In other words, Irving used both the German original, and the flawed translation, selecting from each of them whatever served his purpose of showing Hitler in a favorable light and dropping, if he could, anything that did not. Whether or not the Weidenfeld translation was accurate in any given case was of no interest to him; all that he was interested in was whether or not it supported his preconceived notion of Hitler's innocence. His version of the Hitler table talk in this instance thus amounted to a conscious and deliberate manipulation of the source-material.

In describing the deportation of German Jews from Berlin to the East, Irving also laid great stress on the influence which, he argued, was exerted by an antisemitic article by Goebbels, published on 16 November 1941 in *Das Reich*, his propaganda paper. Irving summarized the article as follows:

"The Jews wanted this war," he argued, "and now they have it." They were getting their just desserts. An eye for an eye. All Jews alike, whether languishing in an eastern ghetto or whining for war from

New York, were conspiring against Germany. The Yellow Star, he argued, was akin to a 'hygienic prophylactic', because the most dangerous were those otherwise not recognizable as Jews. To those who might bleat that the Jews were humans too he pointed out that the same could be said of muggers, rapists, and pimps. "Suddenly one has the impression that all of Berlin's Jews are either darling little babies who wouldn't hurt a fly, or fragile old ladies." "Were we to lose this war," he continued, "these oh-so-harmless Jewish worthies would suddenly turn into rapacious wolves. . . . That's what happened in Bessarabia and the Baltic states after the Bolsheviks marched in, and neither the people nor the governments there had had the slightest sympathy for them. For us, in our fight against the Jews, there is no going back."[15]

Irving claimed that "the article displayed a far more uncompromising face than Hitler's toward the Jews. When the Führer came to Berlin for Luftwaffe general Ernst Udet's funeral," he continued, referring to an entry in Goebbels' diary, "he again instructed Goebbels to pursue a policy against the Jews 'that does not cause us endless difficulties,' and told him to go easy on mixed marriages in future."[16]

It seemed a good idea to test Irving's account of these events by looking up the Goebbels diary entry to which he referred. The full entry in the published edition of the Goebbels diaries read as follows:

The Führer also completely agrees with my views with reference to the Jewish question. He wants an energetic policy against the Jews, which, however, does not cause us unnecessary difficulties. Evacuation of the Jews is to be undertaken city by city. So it is still uncertain when it is Berlin's turn; but when it is, the evacuation is then to be completed as quickly as possible. With reference to Jewish mixed marriages, the Führer recommended to me a somewhat more reserved procedure, above all in artistic circles, because he is of the opinion that these marriages will in any case gradually die out, and one should not allow any gray hair to grow on one's head over it.[17]

On checking this against Irving's account of these events in his biography of Goebbels, I quickly realized that Irving had manipulated this diary entry by omitting all reference to the crucial first sentence and the first half of the second sentence ("He wants an energetic policy against the Jews") from his text because it showed once again that Hitler thought about the 'Jewish Question' in the same way as Goebbels did. Irving only printed the first sentence hidden in the endnotes, directly followed by his comment that Hitler was "clearly" not in agreement with Goebbels.[18] The average reader could hardly be expected to plow through all the endnotes in the book, and anyone who did would, it seemed, be put at ease by Irving's gloss on the sentence, although to anyone familiar with the whole diary entry it would seem to lack any foundation in the document itself.

In his written submission to the court, Irving argued that Goebbels inserted the line concerning Hitler's approval as an alibi "for his own wrongdoing."[19] But what was the 'wrongdoing' in this case? Irving did not say. If Goebbels was so keen falsely to present Hitler as just as radical an antisemite as he was, why then did he note down that Hitler wanted him to go easier on mixed marriages? Here, as in his account of the so-called *Reichkristallnacht*, I could not find any indication of guilt in Goebbels' diary. As far as he was concerned, there was no 'wrongdoing' at all, nor was there any evidence that Hitler disapproved of his actions either. This seemed to me to be a clear attempt to make the sentence mean the opposite of what it actually meant.

As well as manipulating this diary entry by transposing a key part of it to an endnote, Irving also mistranslated it. According to Goebbels' diary, Hitler explained that he wanted to avoid causing "us unnecessary difficulties" in pursuing an "energetic policy against the Jews." What he meant by "unnecessary difficulties" was probably both the removal of Jews working in industries that were important for the war effort, and the printing of hostile reports about the expulsions in the foreign press.[20] However, Irving mistranslated "unnecessary difficulties" as "endless difficulties," thus removing the specific context and broadening the significance of what Hitler was saying beyond what the diary entry actually implied until it came to suggest a policy that would continue into the indefinite future.

Yet I found plenty of evidence that Hitler was voicing views concerning the Jews similar to those expressed by Goebbels at this time. On the evening of 10 July 1941, Hitler declared at his table: "I feel I am like

Robert Koch in politics. He discovered the bacillus and thereby ushered medical science onto new paths. I discovered the Jew as the bacillus and the fermenting agent of all social decomposition."[21] Many similar statements could be found expressing Hitler's extreme animosity toward the Jews at this time.[22] Thus after a meeting with Hitler, Goebbels noted in his diary on 19 August 1941:

> We speak about the Jewish problem. The Führer is convinced that his former prophecy in the Reichstag, that if Jewry succeeded once more in provoking a world war, it would end with the annihilation of the Jews, is being confirmed. It is being confirmed in these weeks and months with a certainty that seems almost uncanny.[23]

On 5 November 1941, Hitler was recorded as voicing similar sentiments in his 'table talk':

> I have always said that Jews are the stupidest devils there are. They haven't a single real musician, thinker, no art, nothing, nothing at all. They are liars, forgers, deceivers. Any one of them only ever achieved anything as a result of the stupidity of his surroundings. If he wasn't washed by the Aryan, the Jew wouldn't be able to see out of his eyes for dirt. We can live without the Jews, they can't live without us.[24]

All of this, and much more, gave the lie to Irving's claim that Goebbels' article in *Das Reich* "displayed a far more uncompromising face than Hitler's towards the Jews."

II

Irving's attempt to show that Hitler was not responsible for the mass killings of German Jews deported to the East made use of entries in the phone log kept by the SS leader and German Police Chief Heinrich Himmler. Reference to the entry for 30 November 1941 appeared repeatedly in Irving's work, and formed a key link in his chain of documents supposedly exculpating Hitler from involvement in the extermination of the Jews. In *Hitler's War* (1977), Irving wrote that Himmler "was summoned to the Wolf's Lair for a secret conference with Hitler, at which the fate of Berlin's Jews was clearly raised. At 1:30 P.M. Himmler was obliged to telephone from Hitler's bunker to Heydrich the explicit order that Jews were *not to be liquidated.*"[25] The phone log was made conveniently available while I was working on the report, in a printed scholarly edition, along with Himmler's appointments diary, another of the documents discovered in the former KGB Special Archive in Moscow after the fall of communism.[26] Irving had consulted the manuscript original of the phone log some years previously, although it was not until the late 1990s that he had access to the appointments diary. What did the phone log entry for 30 November 1941 actually say?

The phone log showed that Himmler had a phone conversation with Heydrich in Prague on 30 November 1941 at 1:30 P.M., summarized in the phone log as follows:

Verhaftung Dr Jekelius	Arrest of Dr Jekelius
Angebl. Sohn Molotow.	Supposed son of Molotov.
Judentransport aus Berlin.	Jew-transport from Berlin.
keine Liquidierung.[27]	no liquidation.

In the introduction to *Hitler's War,* Irving stated that this was "incontrovertible evidence" that "Hitler ordered on November 30, 1941, that there was to be 'no liquidation' of the Jews (without much difficulty, I found in Himmler's private files his own handwritten note on this)."[28] Later in the text, Irving several times referred to Hitler's "November 1941 order forbidding the liquidation of the Jews."

Yet, from the entry in Himmler's phone log it was perfectly clear to me, as it would be to anybody, that the subject of the conversation on 30 November 1941 between Himmler and Heydrich concerned *one* transport of Jews *from Berlin.* It was easy enough to check out whether there was such a transport, since the SS in the East had kept records and their activities had also been the subject of legal proceedings after the war. From these sources I discovered that a trainload of Jews had been transported from Berlin on 27 November 1941 and arrived in Riga on the night of 29–30 November just before a massacre of the local Jews by the SS police chief in the region, Friedrich Jeckeln, who took the Berlin Jews off the train on 30 November and had them machine-gunned into pits with the rest.[29]

Thus the phone log did not contain any *general* order from anyone to stop the killing of Jews. The telephone conversation between Himmler and Heydrich clearly referred to a *single* trainload of Jews, which could only have been the one from Berlin to Riga. Moreover, there was absolutely no evidence in the phone log that Himmler had been summoned to Hitler's bunker or had any conversation or meeting at all with Hitler before talking to Heydrich on the phone. The phone log did not record who had phoned whom, so it was at least possible that Heydrich had phoned Himmler and not the other way around, reporting on the situation in the Baltic and asking for instructions. It was doubtful whether Hitler and Himmler met that day before Himmler made the phone call to Heydrich telling him not to kill the Jews on the train from Berlin to Riga. The 'order' from Hitler was a figment of Irving's imagination.

This manipulation of the phone log had already been pointed out by Broszat and Trevor-Roper in their reviews of the 1977 edition of Irving's book.[30] As Trevor-Roper, Broszat, and the Hitler specialist Eberhard Jaeckel also pointed out, if Hitler had intervened personally to stop the killing of a single trainload of Berlin Jews on their arrival in Riga, then this strongly suggested that he was making an exception here, and that he therefore knew that there was a general policy of killing them on arrival.[31]

Irving subsequently claimed that only after the publication of the 1977 edition of *Hitler's War* had "colleagues provided him with the documentation which usefully narrowed down the reference in the Himmler-Heydrich phone note of November 30, 1941, to one particular trainload of Jews being shipped from Berlin to Riga at that time."[32] What was this fresh documentation to which Irving referred? The evidence that the phone call referred to a single transport of Jews from Berlin was unmistakably present in the document itself. Still, in *Goebbels: Mastermind of the 'Third Reich,'* published in 1996, as well as in the 1991 edition of *Hitler's War,* Irving did appear to have stepped back from some of his earlier claims.[33] All he argued in *Goebbels* was that the Berlin Jews who arrived in Riga on 30 November 1941 were killed "even as Hitler . . . was instructing Himmler that these Berlin Jews were not to be liquidated."[34]

Fresh evidence made available after the fall of the Soviet Union and the opening up of the former KGB archive in Moscow, with its hoard of captured German documents, led to further changes in Irving's position on the Himmler phone log. On his Focal Point website, Irving claimed that on 17 May 1998 he had received a document detailing Himmler's appointments for the 30 November 1941 from the Moscow archive. He reproduced this document on his website, with a translation. As emerged from this document, Himmler met Hitler at 2:30 P.M., that is, *after* he had made the phone call to Heydrich concerning the transport of Jews from Berlin, not before. It also showed that Himmler only arrived at Hitler's headquarters half an hour before his phone conversation with Heydrich, and recorded that he spent this half-hour 'working.' The likelihood of his having seen Hitler in this short period to receive a major policy order from him was thus vanishingly small. The summary on the Focal Point website (on which, oddly, Irving frequently referred to himself in the third person, as if it were being written by some neutral commentator) claimed: "This suggests that Mr Irving's original theory that Himmler discussed the matter with Hitler *before* phoning Heydrich is wrong." Irving, of course, had never presented this as a *theory,* but as "*incontrovertible evidence*" that Hitler ordered "that there was to be 'no liquidation' of the Jews."[35]

So Irving had now retreated from his claim that Hitler had ordered a stop to all liquidations of Jews on 30 November 1941. He had been forced to admit that the Heydrich–Himmler phone call only referred to one trainload of Jews from Berlin. He had also been obliged to give up his claim that Hitler had ordered Himmler to make the phone call. Absolutely nothing remained of his original assertions, which he had set out with such certainty in *Hitler's War* (1977) and repeated in modified form on a number of subsequent occasions, that the order referred to all Jews everywhere, and that it came from Hitler. So conclusive was the new documentary evidence that even Irving had to admit that a key link in his 'chain of documents' supposedly proving Hitler's opposition to the extermination of the Jews, was completely without substance.

Yet, extraordinarily enough, while Irving admitted that information received on 17 May 1998 suggested that he had been wrong to claim that Hitler had ordered Himmler to call Heydrich on 30 November 1941, he still continued to support his earlier claims in some of his subsequent publications. Thus on 31 August 1998, he posted another document on his website in which he argued that on 30 November 1941, Hitler had "demonstrably . . . ordered" that the Berlin Jews on the transport to Riga were not to be killed. This document could still be accessed on Irving's website on 11 April 1999. Evidently his 'theory' was not 'wrong' after all.[36]

III

Another key document that Irving repeatedly referred to in his 'chain of documents' proving Hitler's innocence in the matter of the Nazi extermination of the Jews was what he described in the preface to the 1991 edition of *Hitler's War* as

> an extraordinary note dictated by Staatssekretär Schlegelberger in the Reich Ministry of Justice in the Spring of 1942: "Reich Minister Lammers," this states, referring to Hitler's top civil servant, "informed me that the Führer has repeatedly pronounced that he wants the solution of the Jewish Question put off until after the war is over." Whatever way one looks at this document, it is incompatible with the notion that Hitler had ordered an urgent liquidation programme.[37]

According to Irving, "no other historians have quoted this document, possibly finding its content hard to reconcile with their obsessively held views" about Hitler's responsibility for the extermination of the Jews.[38] On various occasions, Irving had described this document as "the most cardinal piece of proof in this entire story of what Hitler knew about what was going on," "the most compelling document" showing that "Hitler didn't know about it" (the extermination of the Jews), a document that "refutes this lie" (that Hitler ordered the extermination of the Jews), and a document that "must acquit" Hitler because it proved that the "Nazis' determination to liquidate all of the Jews" was not supported by documentary evidence.[39]

What did this document actually say? I found the typewritten original in a folder of Reich Ministry of Justice files held at the German Federal Archives in Berlin (R 22/52). The full text of the typewritten document was as follows:

Reich Minister Lammers informed me that the Führer had repeatedly explained to him that he wanted the solution of the Jewish
Question put back until after the war. Accordingly the present discussions possess a merely theoretical value in the opinion of Reich
Minister Lammers. But he will be in all cases concerned that fundamental decisions are not reached by a surprise intervention from
another agency without his knowledge.[40]

It was not written on headed notepaper. It had no date, no signature, no
security classification, none of the abbreviations usually used by the leading officials in the Ministry of Justice when signing memoranda, and not
even an internal reference number (*Aktenzeichen*). The only direct clue
to the background of the document was the name of the state secretary
in the Ministry of Justice, Freisler, which appeared in the bottom left-
hand corner. The notion that it was authored by State Secretary Schlegelberger was a supposition, although not necessarily a wrong one.

The file (R 22/52) was not, it seems, an original file kept by ministe-
rial officials in the Third Reich but seemed to have been compiled from
Ministry of Justice papers by the Allies after the war.[41] If the document
dated from the spring of 1942, then it was most probably linked to discussions at the time regarding the fate of 'half-Jews' and Jews in 'mixed
marriages' which formed the context of three of the other four documents grouped with the memorandum in the file. This interpretation had
been advanced by several historians of Nazi Germany,[42] by one of the
leading prosecution attorneys at the Nuremberg trials,[43] and indeed even
by David Irving himself.[44]

The question of 'half-Jews' and Jews in 'mixed marriages' had been
discussed at length at the Wannsee Conference in January 1942, at which
there had been general agreement on the transportation and murder of
'full Jews' in the German sphere of influence—present and future—in
Europe. But the question of 'half-Jews' and Jews in 'mixed marriages' had
been left unresolved because of differences of opinion among the various different agencies involved. Were they to be deported? Or should
they be sterilized and left where they were? Should they be divided into
different categories and treated accordingly? Should 'mixed marriages'
be forcibly dissolved? Opinions were divided. These matters of detail
were thus debated at the meeting of fifteen lower-ranking state and party

officials on 6 March 1942 under the very general heading '*Endlösung der Judenfrage,*' 'Final Solution of the Jewish Question.' This was left-over business from the Wannsee Conference. So it was not surprising that it continued to be carried on under this general heading, as did subsequent correspondence on the matter.[45]

Three of the documents in the file containing the 'Schlegelberger memorandum' dealt with the aftermath of this meeting. The acting Minister of Justice, State Secretary Franz Schlegelberger, wrote to Hans Heinrich Lammers, the head of the Reich Chancellery, on 12 March 1942, complaining that the meeting of 6 March 1942 had prepared the ground for decisions "which I must hold to be in large part completely impossible." Schlegelberger asked Lammers for a meeting to discuss the issue.[46] This letter was followed by another, sent some three weeks later to seven of the state and party offices represented at the 6 March 1942 meeting, and also headed 'Final Solution of the Jewish Question.' It reiterated Schlegelberger's concerns about the treatment of 'half-Jews' and 'mixed marriages.' On 18 March 1942, Lammers, writing from Hitler's headquarters, under the heading: 'Re: Complete Solution of the Jewish Question,' agreed to meet Schlegelberger. A date for the meeting would be fixed upon Lammers' return to Berlin, which he expected to be at the end of March 1942.[47]

It seemed likely that Irving's document (the 'Schlegelberger memorandum'), if indeed it did date from the spring of 1942, was Schlegelberger's record of this meeting with Lammers, which according to the historian Eberhard Jäckel took place on 10 April 1942.[48] What then was the cause of the uncertainty shown by Hitler in this particular area of policy? Unlike those Germans classified as 'full Jews,' the 'half-Jews' and Jews in 'mixed marriages' were not yet totally cut off from the rest of the German population, as they still often had one parent classified as German, or were married to a German partner. That these 'Aryan' Germans would not necessarily allow deportations to go ahead without resistance was powerfully confirmed in February 1943, when a large crowd of 'Aryan' German women successfully staged a public demonstration against the Gestapo in the Rosenstrasse in Berlin to force the release of their arrested Jewish husbands and even the return of a handful who had already been sent to Auschwitz.[49] For most of the war, Hitler was worried about repercussions such as these.

In the light of all this, Irving was misleading his readers and listeners when he argued that the document was "incompatible with the notion that Hitler had ordered an urgent liquidation programme" and showed that Hitler "ordered 'No Final Solution.' "[50] The "present discussions" to which the document referred were probably the discussions taking place in the spring of 1942 about divorce proceedings for Jews in 'mixed marriages' and measures against 'half-Jews,' discussions which took place under the general heading 'Final Solution of the Jewish Question' (*Endlösung der Judenfrage*). In this context, the likelihood was that Lammers' reference to views Hitler had expressed in the past that the solution of the 'Jewish question' should be postponed until after the war was over, referred only to the fate of 'half-Jews' and Jews in 'mixed marriages.' The fate of 'full Jews,' by contrast, had already been decided upon in principle. Yet, until the position of the borderline categories was finally clarified, the 'Jewish Question' as many Nazis understood it could not be regarded as completely solved. Lammers' reference to a possible surprise intervention from another agency was probably meant to reassure Schlegelberger that more radical officials in other party or state positions who favored a more drastic solution would not be allowed to resolve the issue without Schlegelberger's considerations being taken into account.

This interpretation of the document seemed to me to have the best fit with the surrounding historical context and with the other documents in the same file. Irving's version, however, raised serious problems for his own views on a wider scale. It occurred to me that if the term *final solution* was really understood to mean here the total physical extermination of the Jews in Europe, as Irving implied in his writings, then the document would mean that Hitler did know about the policy of exterminating Europe's Jews, even if he did want it postponed until after the war. Surely Irving would not have wanted this implication to be drawn from the document in question; the inference would have run counter to everything he had previously argued about Hitler. On the other hand, if it meant the deportation of the Jews to the East, then how could Hitler have repeatedly said he wanted it to be postponed, when he had ordered it the previous autumn and knew that it was in full swing? How indeed could Irving justify his reading of the Himmler phone log of 30 November 1941 as expressing Hitler's command that deported Jews were not to be shot, a command which in Irving's view showed that Hitler recognized that deportations were going on and yet also made it clear that he did nothing at all to stop them? Irving's 'chain of documents,' when I looked at each one in context, seemed to be a chain of contradictions.[51]

In any case, the policy of the Ministry of Justice toward the Jews from spring 1942 on was absolutely incompatible with the Ministry officials having received any general order from Hitler that commanded no killing or deportation of Jews. In his own doctoral dissertation on Hitler's prisons, my research assistant Nik Wachsmann had come across documents in the German Federal Archives indicating that on 16 April 1942, only six days after Schlegelberger's presumed meeting with Lammers, the Ministry of Justice issued a directive to all chief state prosecutors in Germany stating that the Ministry supported the 'evacuation' to the East of the Jewish inmates of all German penal institutions. The same principle was applied to Jewish prisoners awaiting trial on remand, "unless," the Ministry added in a revealing phrase, "it is expected that they will be sentenced to death," showing that judicial officials probably understood that *evacuation* was a synonym for *execution*.[52] This process was completed when the last remaining Jews in state penal institutions were handed over to the police (together with other selected 'asocial' state prisoners) after a meeting between Himmler and the new minister of justice, Otto-Georg Thierack, on 18 September 1942, "for annhihilation through labour." More than one thousand Jewish prisoners were transported straight to Auschwitz following this agreement.[53] Thus the Ministry of Justice was actively involved in the deportation and extermination of Jews in the months following the consultation with Lammers. So whatever Schlegelberger had come away with from his meeting with Lammers, it was clearly not the impression that it was Hitler's wish that Jews generally were not to be evacuated or killed.

Ten years previously, after first demolishing Irving's interpretation of the document, Eberhard Jäckel had written that Irving knew full well how limited its significance was. "But," Jäckel added, "he only ever sees and collects what fits his story, and even now he will not let himself be dissuaded from understanding what he wants to by the phrase 'postponement of the solution of the Jewish question.'" Jäckel predicted that Irving would soon repeat it in his books once more. That he would still be repeating it so many years after it had been disproved, would come as no surprise to him.[54] This supposedly key document in Irving's arsenal of

alleged documentary proof of Hitler's lack of culpability for the extermination of the Jews had long been regarded by professional historians as
nothing of the kind. He could only present it as such by ignoring the logical contradictions in his reading of the document, by disregarding its
immediate context, and by suppressing all the uncertainties with which
it was associated.

IV

By the time the discussions were being held in March and April 1942
about the future of 'half-Jews,' those people classified by the Nazis as full
Jews were already being exterminated in large numbers, not just by mass
shootings, but also by gassing, first in mobile vans, then in specially constructed facilities at camps, such as Belzec, behind the Eastern Front. In
the first edition of *Hitler's War* (1977), Irving claimed in several passages
that Hitler was kept in the dark by other Nazi officials such as Goebbels
and Himmler about the extermination of Jews in the East. This was part
of his general argument that Hitler knew nothing of the 'Final Solution.'
In one such passage, Irving wrote:

> The ghastly secrets of Auschwitz and Treblinka were well kept.
> Goebbels wrote a frank summary of them in his diary on March 27,
> 1942, but evidently held his tongue when he met Hitler two days
> later, for he quotes only Hitler's remark: "The Jews must get out of
> Europe. If need be, we must resort to the most brutal methods."[55]

By this stage in my investigations, I had come to regard all of Irving's references to the Goebbels diaries with a good deal of suspicion. So once
more, I looked up the full diary entry in the published edition of
Goebbels' voluminous journals. What did it say?

The full—and very lengthy—diary entry gave a very different
impression from that conveyed by Irving:

> The Jews are now being pushed out of the General Government,
> beginning near Lublin, to the East. A pretty barbaric procedure is
> being applied here, and it is not to be described in any more detail,
> and not much is left of the Jews themselves. In general one may

conclude that 60% of them must be liquidated, while only 40% can be put to work. The former Gauleiter of Vienna [Globocnik], who is carrying out this action, is doing it pretty prudently and with a procedure that doesn't work too conspicuously. The Jews are being punished barbarically, to be sure, but they have fully deserved it. The prophecy that the Führer issued to them on the way, for the eventuality that they started a new world war, is beginning to realise itself in the most terrible manner. One must not allow any sentimentalities to rule in these matters. If we did not defend ourselves against them, the Jews would annihilate us. It is a struggle for life and death between the Aryan race and the Jewish bacillus. No other government and no other regime could muster the strength for a general solution of the question. Here too, the Führer is the persistent pioneer and spokesman of a radical solution, which is demanded by the way things are and thus appears to be unavoidable. Thank God, during the war we now have a whole series of possibilities which were barred to us in peacetime. We must exploit them. The ghettos which are becoming available in the General Government are now being filled with the Jews who are being pushed out of the Reich, and after a certain time the process is then to renew itself here. Jewry has nothing to laugh about.[56]

Irving did not tell his readers that Goebbels described Hitler as having pushed for this "radical solution." He simply omitted the entire passage relating to Hitler, as he did in the 1991 edition of *Hitler's War*, because this statement by Goebbels discredited his claim that Hitler knew nothing about the extermination camps in the East.[57] If Hitler was ignorant, how could he be "the persistent pioneer and spokesman of a radical solution"? Thus, Irving manipulated the diary entry to argue the exact opposite of what it actually showed.

Irving claimed that Goebbels did not inform Hitler of the murderous activities taking place in Auschwitz and Treblinka when he met him on 29 March 1942.[58] But it was clear from Goebbels' diary entry for 30 March 1942, which recorded the events of the previous day, that the Propaganda Minister did not meet Hitler on the 29 March 1942.[59] Hitler's remark ("The Jews must get out of Europe. If need be, we must resort to the most brutal methods") was made on 19 March 1942, as recorded in Goebbels' diary on 20 March 1942, and could not therefore be used, as Irving used it, as evidence that Goebbels "held his tongue when he met Hitler" after writing his "frank summary" of the "ghastly secrets" of the extermination camps on 27 March. Nor did Irving publish the complete passage from Goebbels' diary entry of 20 March. Goebbels recorded: "We speak in conclusion about the Jewish question. Here the Führer remains, now as before, unrelenting. The Jews must get out of Europe, if necessary, with the application of the most brutal means."[60] In both editions of *Hitler's War*, Irving omitted Goebbels' characterization of Hitler's stance as unrelenting.

I found several other documents indicating Hitler's knowledge and approval, to put it no more strongly, of the 'Final Solution.' For example, on 28 July 1942, Himmler wrote to the head of the SS Head Office, Gottlob Berger, and explained that "the occupied Eastern territories will be Jew-free. The Führer has laid the implementation of this very difficult order on my shoulders."[62] At this time, between the end of July 1942 until the end of September 1942, some of the worst excesses of mass murder of the entire 'Final Solution' occurred in the Polish General Government. Apart from mass gassings, German police forces also exterminated entire villages by shooting their Jewish inhabitants.[63] Historians later estimated that around 1.75 million women, men, and children were murdered in Belzec, Treblinka, and Sobibor by the time the camps were dismantled the following year.[64]

On 22 September 1942, at the height of this unprecedented mass murder operation, Himmler had a lengthy meeting with Hitler. Here we found another problem with Irving's account of Hitler's role in these events. Judging from Himmler's handwritten agenda notes, one subject may have been the extermination of the Jews. Under the heading "Race and Settlement," Himmler noted:

1. Emigration of Jews
   how to be further proceeded?

   2. Settlement Lublin—   Circumstances
   Lorrainers   Gen[eral] Gouv.[ernement]
   Germans from Bosnia   Globus
   Bessarabia[65]

The fact that Himmler discussed the emigration of the Jews, as well as Globus, his nickname for Globocnik, who was responsible for this program of mass extermination in the General Government, immediately raised in my mind the suspicion that the mass annihilation of the Jews was one of the topics of conversation between Hitler and Himmler on that day.

But such suspicions seem to have been far from Irving's thoughts. In his written submission to the court, Irving conceded that he had neglected the Himmler note in question:

> It is admitted that the plaintiff did not draw attention to this minute, but it is denied that this is relevant. . . . The Defendants have failed to inform us of the minute's 'obvious significance', which escapes the Plaintiff. . . . Himmler's jotted agenda for his meetings with Hitler are crowded with names, pet or otherwise, and in the absence of collateral evidence it is imprudent in the extreme to spin fanciful theories around them.[66]

Yet it was not a fanciful theory to suggest that the note indicated that Hitler was updated by Himmler on the mass murder of Jews in the East, or that the two men decided on the next steps in the 'Final Solution.' The documents left me in no doubt that at this time important decisions by the Nazi leaders were being made.[67] Globocnik's involvement in all this was as the man responsible for clearing out the Jews from Lublin to the death camps in order to make way for ethnic German settlers brought there from other parts of Europe, part of the vast plan of resettlement, deportation, and murder with which the Nazis were seeking to redraw the ethnic map of Europe.

Oddly enough, I discovered that Irving was in fact wrong in thinking he had not used the note by Himmler in his own work. In the 1991 edition of *Hitler's War*, Irving used the minute to support his claim that Himmler did not enlighten Hitler about the true fate of the Jews in the East:

> Himmler meanwhile continued to pull the wool over Hitler's eyes. On September 17 (*recte*: September 22) he calmly jotted in his notes for that day's Führer conference: "1. Jewish emigration—how is to

be handled in future? 2. Settlement of Lublin," and noted next to
these points: "Conditions in Generalgouvernement," and "Globus"
(Globocnik's nickname).[68]

Irving's claim lacked all factual foundation. First, there was no indication that Himmler took down the agenda for the meeting "calmly" or
kept Hitler in the dark about the mass annihilation of the Jews. Second,
the fact that the mass murder of the Jews was not mentioned openly in
Himmler's notes, which Irving seemed to have taken as proof for Himmler's having misled Hitler, was no surprise. The Nazis generally used camouflage terms when noting details of the extermination of the Jews at this
time. There was no question of trying to pull the wool over Hitler's eyes
with regard to the mass killings. If anyone had spun fanciful theories
around this document and pulled the wool over people's eyes, it was Irving himself.

V

As the war progressed, the Nazis began to round up and transport Jews
from all over Europe to the death camps. Even where they did not
directly control areas with large numbers of Jewish inhabitants, they
started to exert pressure for mass murder. The sovereign nation with the
largest number of Jews untouched by the Nazis at the end of 1942 was
Hungary. During the Second World War, Hungary was ruled by a strongly
authoritarian, right-wing regime, which had come to power in a bloody
counter-revolution at the end of the First World War. Led by Admiral
Horthy, whose title derived from the defunct Habsburg Empire and who
functioned as regent for the absent Habsburg emperor, the Hungarian
regime allied itself to Nazi Germany from early on, principally in order
to recover territory from small neighboring countries which it considered
belonged to Hungary by the historic right of the Habsburg tradition.
In 1938–39 Hungary joined Germany in the dismemberment of
Czechoslovakia. In return for German backing in obtaining territory from
Romania in August 1940 and Yugoslavia in April 1941, the Hungarian
government sent troops to participate in the German invasion of Russia

in June 1941. Having achieved its principal goals in annexing territory from its small neighboring states, Hungary now tried to pull out of the war on the Eastern Front, and withdrew substantial numbers of troops. Following the defeat of the German armies at Stalingrad, Hitler began to put pressure on Admiral Horthy to reverse this policy, and summoned him to a meeting on 16 and 17 April 1943, at which the German foreign minister, Ribbentrop, was also present. Hitler and Ribbentrop also used this opportunity to discuss with Horthy the question of Hungary's Jews, of whom there were perhaps three-quarters of a million at that time. These people were already subjected to massive legal discrimination by the strongly antisemitic Horthy regime. However, the Hungarian government made clear that it was extremely jealous of its sovereign rights over native Hungarian Jews and insisted to the Germans that any 'solution' of the Hungarian dimension of the 'Jewish question' would have to take the specific circumstances in Hungary into account.[69]

The meeting between Hitler and Horthy on 16 and 17 April 1943 was in part designed to escalate the pressure that the German government had already put on Horthy to 'solve' the 'Jewish question' in Hungary once and for all and to persuade Horthy to remove the obstacles that he had so far put in the way of the forcible deportation of all of Hungary's Jews to territory controlled by the Nazi regime. The minutes of the meeting were taken by Dr. Paul Otto Schmidt, who confirmed them and added his own recollections at the Nuremberg trials.[70] The minutes for the second day's meeting, on 17 April 1943, recorded a statement by Ribbentrop, in Hitler's presence, to a point made by Horthy:

> On Horthy's retort, what should he do with the Jews then, after he had pretty well taken all means of living from them—he surely couldn't beat them to death—the Reich Foreign Minister replied that the Jews must either be annihilated or taken to concentration camps. There was no other way.[71]

This blunt statement by Ribbentrop contributed to the conclusion of the judges at the Nuremberg trials in October 1946, that the foreign minister was guilty of war crimes and crimes against humanity.[72]

Hitler almost immediately confirmed Ribbentrop's explicitly murderous statement at some length:

Where the Jews were left to themselves, as for example in Poland, gruesome poverty and degeneracy had ruled. They were just pure parasites. One had fundamentally cleared up this state of affairs in Poland. If the Jews there didn't want to work, they were shot. If they couldn't work, they had to perish. They had to be treated like tuberculosis bacilli, from which a healthy body could be infected. That was not cruel, if one remembered that even innocent natural creatures like hares and deer had to be killed so that no harm was caused. Why should one spare the beasts who wanted to bring us Bolshevism more? Nations who did not rid themselves of Jews perished.[73]

Despite this remarkably open language, Horthy was clearly not convinced about the need to murder large numbers of Jews, much to Hitler's annoyance.[74]

How did Irving deal with this incriminating document? I had by this time become familiar with his tactics when confronted with material such as this, and in this instance too, he did not disappoint. In the 1977 edition of *Hitler's War*, Irving started off by hiding away in a footnote Ribbentrop's statement that all Jews had to be either "annihilated or taken to concentration camps." He resorted to the same tactic in his 1991 edition of *Hitler's War*.[75] Having disposed of this awkward remark to a place where many readers would not trouble to consult it, Irving then placed Hitler's following references to Poland, bacilli, and so on in an entirely different context. Irving's summary of Hitler's statement read:

Events in Poland were pointed to as providing an ugly precedent: there were reports of Jews roaming the country, committing acts of murder and sabotage. . . . In Warsaw, the fifty thousand Jews surviving in the ghetto were on the point of staging an armed uprising—with weapons and ammunition evidently sold to them by Hitler's fleeing allies as they passed westward through the city. Himmler ordered the ghetto destroyed and its ruins combed out for Jews. "This is just the kind of incident that shows how dangerous these Jews are."

Poland should have been an object lesson to Horthy, Hitler argued. He related how Jews who refused to work there were shot; those who could not work just wasted away. Jews must be treated like tuberculosis bacilli, he said, using his favourite analogy. Was that so cruel when one considered that even innocent creatures like hares and deer had to be put down to prevent their doing damage? Why preserve a bestial species whose ambition was to inflict bolshevism on us all? Horthy apologetically noted that he had done all he decently could against the Jews: "But they can hardly be murdered or otherwise eliminated," he protested. Hitler reassured him: "There is no need for that." But just as in Slovakia, they ought to be isolated in remote camps where they could no longer infect the healthy body of the public; or they could be put to work in mines, for example.[76]

Yet whoever said "This is just the kind of incident that shows how dangerous these Jews are," Adolf Hitler certainly did not say it to Admiral Horthy at their meeting on 16–17 April 1943. Hitler did not mention the Warsaw ghetto uprising at all, which was not surprising, since it did not even begin until two days later. Nor did the uprising involve fifty thousand armed Jews, as Irving implied, but at most a few thousand of them. Nor was there any evidence that they had been supplied with arms by Hitler's fleeing allies.[77] Irving also watered down the expression used by Hitler to describe the fate of those Polish Jews who could not work—*verkommen*—by translating it as "wasted away," as if they had no assistance toward this fate from Nazi authorities who deliberately starved them of food.

Most seriously of all, however, the exchange reported at the end of Irving's account, beginning "Horthy apologetically noted," did not occur on 17 April, as Irving clearly portrayed by placing it immediately after his summary of Hitler's speech, but on the previous day, and in another context, during the first of the two men's meetings. On 16 April, Horthy stated: "He had done everything which one could decently undertake against the Jews, but one could surely not murder them or kill them in some other way. The Führer replied that this was also not necessary. Hungary could accommodate the Jews in concentration camps just like Slovakia did."[78] At this point in the meeting, Hitler and Ribbentrop were not being as open as they became on the 17th. It was because he was not satisfied with Hitler's response, and was aware that he had still not satisfied the Nazi leaders with his, that Horthy repeated his question on the 17th ("he surely couldn't beat them to death"), eliciting this time far more explicit statements of what they expected him to do, both from Ribbentrop and from Hitler, namely that they were to be put in camps if they could work, and killed if they could not. Finally, it is worth noting that the majority of the Slovakian Jews were by no means only put into concentration camps, as Hitler claimed on 16 April 1943. In fact, they were killed. According to SS statistics, 57,545 Slovakian Jews had been transported to Nazi-occupied Polish territory between 26 March 1942 and 31 March 1943 (only about 25,000 Jews were still left behind in Slovakia). The transports went to the extermination camps at Auschwitz, Sobibor, and Majdanek.[79]

I could not avoid the conclusion that Irving, to use some of the phraseology employed by Lipstadt in her general criticism of his and the Holocaust deniers' work, bent this reliable source to suit his argument, misprepresented the historical data, and skewed the documents on which he relied, by placing quotations in a false context, removing part of the record to a footnote, and mixing up two different conversations in the text so that it looked as if Hitler was telling Horthy that the Jews should not be killed, only interned in camps.

The significance of the meeting between Hitler and Horthy on 16–17 April 1943 was made clear by what happened subsequently. In May 1943 the Hungarian Prime Minister Kállay rejected the idea of 'resettlement' of Hungary's Jews until he received a satisfactory answer to the question of where the resettlement was to take place.[80] But the Nazi government did not abandon its designs for the extermination of the Hungarian Jews. In March 1944, Horthy was again summoned to meet Hitler. According to Horthy, at the meeting on 18 March 1944 Hitler complained that "Hungary did nothing in the matter of the Jewish problem, and was not prepared to settle accounts with the large Jewish population in Hungary."[81] Meanwhile, German troops marched into Hungary and took the country over, and a puppet government was installed in March 1944. On 19 March 1944, the Eichmann *Sonderkommando* arrived in Budapest to organize the deportation of the Hungarian Jews. By July 1944, over 430,000 Jews had been deported to Auschwitz. All of this demonstrated clearly the paramount importance the extermination of Hungary's Jews had for Hitler.

Irving was clearly at pains to obscure this in his account of the German leader's meeting with Admiral Horthy on 16–17 April 1943. He conveyed the impression in his book *Hitler's War* that Hitler was actually opposed to the extermination of the Hungarian Jews, demanding merely their confinement in internment camps, a measure for which, Irving insinuated, events in Poland (including the Warsaw ghetto uprising, which had not actually taken place at the time of the meeting between Hitler and Horthy) provided the spur. On reading the actual minutes of the meeting, I had no doubt that Irving's account of what Hitler was telling Horthy should be done with the Hungarian Jews could not be reconciled with what the minutes actually reported.

VI

Hungary was not the only foreign country whose Jewish population the Nazis attempted to remove in the latter part of the war. Italy was another. Initially Germany's allies, the Italians had pulled out in July 1943, following a string of military reverses. The Italian dictator Mussolini was overthrown. By the autumn of 1943, Italy was under occupation by the German army, and Mussolini had been installed as the head of a puppet regime in the north. These new circumstances brought a serious threat to Italy's Jews. Once again, however, Irving did his best to dissociate Hitler from the attempted round-up. As he explained in the 1991 edition of *Hitler's War*:

> Himmler evidently also considered the eight thousand Jews in Rome a potential threat to public order; Ribbentrop brought Hitler an urgent telegram from his consul in Rome reporting that the SS had ordered that "the eight thousand Jews resident in Rome are to be rounded up and brought to Upper Italy, where they are to be liquidated." Again Hitler took a more "moderate" line. On the ninth Ribbentrop informed Rome that the Führer had directed that the Jews were to be transported to Mauthausen concentration camp in Austria instead, where they were to be held "as hostages."[82]

This meant, as Irving explained in his written submission to the court, that they were to be "kept alive." Irving had been using this document for over two decades, for the same example appeared, with variations, in the 1977 edition of his book *Hitler's War*.[83]

How convincing was Irving's reading of this document? In order to unravel its meaning, I had to get clear in my mind who was who in Nazi-occupied Italy—not an easy task in view of the complex and overlapping sources of authority in that war-torn country in 1943. Basically, however, three different agencies of the Third Reich had a role to play, and all three were involved in the exchange of messages on which Irving relied: the SS, which had overall responsibility for the 'Final Solution,' the Foreign Office, since Italy was a foreign country, and the army, which had control of day-to-day events on the ground.[84] Here the key figure was Field Marshal Albert Kesselring, who had overall control in southern Italy, including Rome. Local control of Rome was exercised by military Commandant General Rainer Stahel, but he did not command all the forces in the city, since some of the police were under the German police attaché in Rome, *SS Obersturmbannführer* Herbert Kappler.[85]

On 12 September 1943, Kappler received a telephone call from Hitler's field headquarters in East Prussia informing him that Himmler wanted him to proceed with the round-up and deportation of the Roman Jews.[86] This telephone call was followed by a secret cable confirming this order.[87] On 24 September Himmler's office in Berlin sent a second secret cable calling for the 'Final Solution' to the Jewish problem in Rome. All Jews were to be arrested and sent to the Reich "for liquidation." This action was to be prepared in secret and carried out by surprise.[88] On 25 September Himmler's Reich Security Head Office sent a circular to all its branches at home and abroad, announcing that "in agreement with the Foreign Office" all Jews of listed nationalities could now be included in the deportation measures. Italy headed the list.[89]

Although the cable from Himmler was marked *confidential* and *personal*, the military commandant of Rome, Stahel, read it and contacted the German consul in Rome, Eitel Moellhausen. By chance Moellhausen had become the chief representative of the Reich in German-occupied Rome when his superior, ambassador Dr. Rudolf Rahn, had been injured in a car accident the day before. Both Moellhausen and Stahel agreed that the action was a mistake. Regardless of their motivations, Moellhausen in turn agreed to take the matter up with Kappler, and proceeded to do so on 26 September. Moellhausen drew Kappler's attention to Tunisia, where in 1942 the Jews had been saved by drawing them into forced labor on fortification work. Both Rahn and the current military commander of southern Italy General Field Marshal Kesselring had been involved.[90] Moellhausen and Kappler then called on Kesselring, who told them that he would be unable to spare any soldiers for the action, and that if Berlin considered it necessary to do something about the Jews within his jurisdiction, he would approve using Jewish labor for fortification work around Rome.[91]

At the beginning of October *SS Hauptsturmführer* Theodor Dannecker of Section IV-B-4 of the RSHA arrived in Rome at the head of a mobile 'task staff.' Dannecker had already played a prominent part in the deportation of Jews from France and Belgium. He had with him an authorization from Gestapo Chief Heinrich Müller ordering the local police chief to furnish all necessary assistance.[92] It was in this context that Moellhausen sent a cable on 6 October, cited by Irving both in *Hitler's War* and in his submission to the court. It was marked *very very urgent* and addressed to the Reich foreign minister personally. This cable, Telegram 192, read in full:

> *Obersturmbannführer* Kappler has received orders to arrest the eight thousand Jews resident in Rome and bring them to Upper Italy, where they are to be liquidated. The City Commandant of Rome, General Stahel, informs me that he will permit this action only if it corresponds to the intention of the Herr Reich Foreign Minister. I am personally of the opinion that it would be better business to employ the Jews for fortification work, as in Tunis, and, together with Kappler, I will propose this to Field Marshal Kesselring. Please advise. Moellhausen.[93]

Consul Moellhausen followed this with a second dispatch on 7 October, again marked *very very urgent* and to *the Reich Minister personally*. It was numbered 201 and headed "following telegram of 6th, no. 192+." Irving completely omitted this document from his account, although the Foreign Ministry's reply, document number 98 which he did cite, clearly read "in response to no. 201 of 7.10." Telegram 201 read as follows:

> Field Marshal Kesselring has asked Obersturmbannführer Kappler to postpone the planned Jew-action for the time being. But if something has to be done, he would prefer to use the able-bodied Jews of Rome for fortification work here.[94]

On 9 October, Moellhausen received an answer from Dr. Franz von Sonnleithner of the Foreign Office to his telegram 201:

> The Reich Foreign Minister requests that consuls Rahn and Moell-hausen be informed that, on the basis of a Führer instruction, the 8,000 Jews resident in Rome should be taken to Mauthausen (Upper Danube) as hostages. The Reich Foreign Minister requests that Rahn and Moellhausen be told under no circumstances to interfere in this affair, but rather to leave it to the SS. Sonnleithner.[95]

But Irving then omitted another vital document from his account. A few hours later a second, unequivocal message was sent to Rome from the same source:

> The Herr Reich Minister of Foreign Affairs insists that you keep out of all questions concerning Jews. Such questions, in accordance with an agreement between the Foreign Ministry and the Reich Security Head Office, are within the exclusive competence of the SS, and any further interference in these questions could cause serious difficul-ties for the Ministry of Foreign Affairs.[96]

Nowhere did Irving even mention the existence of this document, let alone cite or refer to its contents.

Moellhausen's telegram of 6 October, not cited by Irving, made it clear that not merely was Stahel objecting to the *Aktion,* but that he was refusing to comply with it unless it was sanctioned by Ribbentrop him-self. Moreover, he had not only the stupidity to use the word *liquidate* in official correspondence with the foreign minister, but also the audacity, before a response could be given to his first telegram, to contact Field Marshal Kesselring and obtain his agreement that the Jews of Rome be engaged in fortification work. The senior figures in Rome, Moellhausen, Kesselring, and probably also Kappler, had effectively formed a triumvi-rate to block deportation. Any prospect of a 'clean' round-up was fading fast in this entanglement. Hitler's order cut decisively through the mess and made clear in no uncertain terms that the Jews of Rome were still to be deported and not to be kept in Italy on fortification work.

Appended to the order outlining the Führer's instructions in this matter was a clear order that Moellhausen and Rahn were "under no cir-cumstances" to interfere in the affair. They were instead to leave it entirely to the SS. It was clear to me that Irving manipulated this document by omitting all mention of this part of it both in the 1991 edition of *Hitler's War* and in his submission to the court. I had no doubt that he was suppressing this important information in order to underline the impression that Hitler was intervening purely and simply to stop the Jews being killed.

Ribbentrop must have discussed with Hitler all the major aspects of the situation, including Himmler's liquidation orders, the impending round-up by the SS, and the attempts to block it by the Consul and the army. Ribbentrop's injunction to leave the "Jew-action" to the SS must have been an integral part of the discussion, and Hitler must have approved it. Thus Irving was caught here in the same logical trap into which he fell in a number of his other attempts to present documentary evidence that Hitler did not know about, or disapproved of, the mass murder of the Jews. If Hitler was intervening to stop the Roman Jews from being killed, then he knew that the Roman Jews were to be liquidated, he knew it was on Himmler's orders, and he must have known it was part of a much wider pattern of mass murder of Jews by the SS, or in other words, he must have known it was part of an exterminatory 'Final Solution of the Jewish Question in Europe.'

As it was, on 16 October 1,259 people were seized and after two days and a sifting process, just over a thousand Jews were shipped off, not to Mauthausen, but to Auschwitz.[97] On arrival on 23 October, 149 men were admitted to the camp and given the numbers 158491–158639, and 47 women were admitted and given the numbers 66172–66218. Investigating the killings after the war, Robert Katz traced 14 male and one female survivor. The rest were gassed.[98] Irving completely failed to mention the fate of these Jews in the account he gave in *Hitler's War* in 1991 or in his written submission to the court.

Still, was it possible to reconcile "liquidation" in "upper Italy," "hostages" in Mauthausen, and deaths in Auschwitz? The standard authority on the extermination of the Italian Jews made it clear that the first large concentration camp on Italian soil (Fossili near Carpi) was not operational until December 1943.[99] "Upper Italy" was probably a convenient euphemism for "the East."[100] The verbal camouflage surrounding the 'Final Solution' was always hard to penetrate. That Moellhausen used the word *liquidate* was reason enough to surmise that Hitler's order used *Mauthausen* and *hostage* to reassert the prescribed phraseology.[101] As for Mauthausen, if Hitler did indeed mean what he said when he ordered the Roman Jews to be sent there, he was surely aware that it was perhaps the deadliest of all concentration camps. In January 1941 the head of the Reich Security Service *SS-Obergruppenführer* Reinhard Heydrich divided the concentration camps into three grades to determine conditions of detention and work in each.[102] Grade III was intended to deal with the worst category of prisoner, and was reserved solely for Mauthausen. The mortality rate, especially for Jews, was terrible. Deportation to Mauthausen was effectively a death sentence, often by forced labor in the quarries or in camp construction.[103]

Thus Hitler's intervention was not one that 'mitigated' the lot of the Jews of Rome. On the contrary, it counteracted a concerted local attempt to save them and condemned them to extermination. Hitler's order was not a revision of Himmler's, but a forceful reaffirmation of it. Hitler surely knew that for the Jews to be deported from Italy 'as hostages' was their death warrant, whether it was to Mauthausen or whether this was simply a euphemistic deception on his part. I could not avoid the conclusion that in this instance, too, Irving had manipulated and falsified the documentation. He suppressed material that he knew ran against his case, in order to support an untenable conclusion which was in fact the exact opposite of what the documents indicated.

VII

After this lengthy examination of Irving's 'chain of documents,' I had to conclude that Irving consistently and repeatedly manipulated the historical evidence in order to give the impression that it supported his view that Hitler did not know about the extermination of the Jews, or, if he did, opposed it. Irving's method of working with documents had been noted by previous investigators, who had trodden the same path through the obscure undergrowth of his footnote references. Thus, for example, Irving's use in *Hitler's War* of Foreign Minister Joachim von Ribbentrop's Nuremberg prison notes to support the thesis that Hitler knew nothing of the 'Final Solution' had already been exposed as a falsification in the 1970s.[104] In a footnote on page 851 of the 1977 edition of *Hitler's War*, Irving had reported:

> Writing a confidential study on Hitler in his Nuremberg prison cell, Ribbentrop also exonerated him wholly. "How things came to the destruction of the Jews, I just don't know. As to whether Himmler began it, or Hitler put up with it, I don't know. But that he ordered it I refuse to believe, because such an act would be wholly incompatible with the picture I always had of him."

The journalists Gitta Sereny and Lewis Chester had tracked down this reference for a critical assessment of Irving's book in 1977. The original document in the Bavarian State Archives contained an additional sentence, not included by Irving: "On the other hand, judging from his (i.e., Hitler's) Last Will, one must suppose that he at least knew about it, if, in his fanaticism against the Jews, he didn't also order it." When confronted with the omission, Irving had said that the sentence concerned was "irrelevant" to the logic of his argument and that he did not "want to confuse the reader."[105]

Following the appearance of the article by Chester and Sereny, Irving had written to the editor of *The Sunday Times* on 14 September 1977 claiming: "The passage from Ribbentrop's statement which I omitted is totally irrelevant to my claim that *up to October 1943* there is no evidence for the claim that Hitler knew what was going on."[106] But this irrelevant observation did nothing to justify Irving's manipulation of the record, which revealed, once again, how he had plucked out the part of a single statement which suited his purposes and suppressed the other part which did not. At no other point in this letter or in his subsequent correspondence did Irving try to defend his editing of the Ribbentrop note.[107] Despite such devastating criticism by Chester and Sereny, the quotation remained intact and was still without the missing sentence on page 809 of the 1991 edition of *Hitler's War*.

Irving's argument that Hitler did not know or approve of actions against the Jews thus clearly rested on a substantial number of historical falsifications. Although some of them, looked at individually, might appear relatively insignificant, there were others that, in my view, were extremely serious. Above all, their cumulative effect was very striking. It became clear that, taken as a whole, they amounted to a systematic distortion of the historical record. To the unwary reader—and there have been many such—Irving's books gave the appearance of scholarly solidity. The footnotes and sometimes the text cited innumerable archival sources, documents, interviews, and other material that seemed at first glance to conform to the normal canons of historical scholarship. All this conspicuous display of research was bolstered by Irving's extravagant self-promotion as a discoverer of new historical material and his arrogant denigration of other researchers in the field. Again, to the unwary, this probably seemed convincing. It was only when I subjected all of this to detailed scrutiny, when I followed Irving's claims and statements about Hitler back to the original documents on which they purported to rest, that Irving's work in this respect was revealed as a house of cards, a vast apparatus of deception and deceit. Lipstadt was therefore right to describe Irving as a Hitler partisan who manipulated the historical record in an attempt to portray his hero in a favorable light.

Few historians or reviewers had had the persistence, knowledge, or time to expose Irving for the fraud that he was. Broszat, Trevor-Roper, Sydnor, and Sereny had already done so in 1977 in relation to Irving's *Hitler's War*, widely praised by reviewers who were less well informed than they were. Looking again at Irving's record more than two decades later confirmed their diagnoses of deception and added fresh evidence. Too many writers and reviewers seemed to have forgotten their work in the intervening period. Many seemed to have assumed that Irving had been an honest historian for most of his career and had only recently gone off the rails. Yet Broszat and the others had already showed in 1977 that Irving's falsifications of the historical record were not the result of some recent aberration in the career of an otherwise respectable historian. One of the most shattering things I had discovered was that Irving's deceptions were there from very early on in his career and had remained an integral part of his working methods across the decades.

CHAPTER FOUR

Irving and Holocaust Denial

I

At issue in the case brought by Irving against Lipstadt was not only her contention that he falsified history, but also her allegation that he was a Holocaust denier (*Denying the Holocaust*, p. 111). What exactly did this mean? The term *Holocaust*, derived from an ancient Greek version of the Old Testament, originally meant a burnt sacrificed offering dedicated exclusively to God. Many scholars had reservations about its application to the Nazi extermination of the Jews, who were not being sacrificed or offered to God, but were brutally murdered in the name of ethnic purity. Used in German, some argued, the word had a distancing and almost euphemistic effect. However, despite these reservations, the word had gained currency until it was difficult to avoid using it altogether.[1]

The meaning of the term *Holocaust* might have been metaphorical rather than literal; common usage made what it referred to abundantly clear. The standard work by the distinguished Canadian historian Michael Marrus, *The Holocaust in History* focused on, to use his own words, "the Holocaust, the systematic mass murder of European Jewry by the Nazis."[2] Similarly, Sir Martin Gilbert, in his documentary compilation *The Holocaust: The Jewish Tragedy*, concurred in referring to "the systematic attempt to destroy all European Jewry—an attempt now known as the Holocaust." Another author, Ronnie S. Landau, put forward a similar definition: 'The Holocaust involved the deliberate, systematic murder of approximately 6 million Jews in Nazi-dominated Europe between 1941 and 1945.' Numerous other writers employed the term in roughly the same sense.[3]

The use of the term *Holocaust* was ultimately a secondary issue. However it was labeled, there was wide agreement among historians that there was a systematic attempt undertaken by the Nazi regime in Germany between 1941 and 1945 to kill all the Jews of Europe, and that it succeeded to the extent of murdering between 5 and 6 million of them in a variety of ways, including mass gassings in camps specially constructed for the purpose. These events were known about from a variety of sources. There was testimony from Jewish survivors of the camps (principally, Auschwitz) and the ghettos. The Nazi authorities also left contemporary documentation providing details of the policy of extermination and its implementation. After the war, the International Military Tribunal at Nuremberg presented a mass of testimony and documentation in a series of trials both of leading Nazis and of lesser but still important figures. Other trials followed over the years, yielding more evidence. The physical remains of at least some of the camps, notably Auschwitz, were also available for inspection. Hundreds of scholars from many different countries had published detailed research based on all this material.[4]

Standing apart from this scholarly literature was an attempt by a small number of writers to deny that there was any systematic or organized extermination of Europe's Jews by the Nazis; to suggest that the number of Jews killed was far smaller than 5 or 6 million; and to claim that there were no gas chambers or other specially built extermination facilities. Who were these people? I knew something about them from my reading of Lipstadt's book, but reading them in the original was an altogether different experience from encountering them through the filter of Lipstadt's cool, academic prose. They inhabited an intellectual world that was far removed from the cautious rationality of academic historical scholarship. What moved them seemed to be a strange mixture of prejudice and bitter personal experience.

After the war, perhaps the earliest proponent of these views was the Frenchman Paul Rassinier (1908–67). Rassinier had apparently been beaten by a communist fellow-prisoner in the Buchenwald concentration camp for failing to recognize or pay his respects to the imprisoned German communist leader Ernst Thälmann (subsequently murdered by the SS in 1944). His fellow-prisoners seemed more dangerous than the SS guards to him. Rassinier eventually got a relatively easy job in the infirmary on his

transfer to camp Dora in the Harz mountains, where he was evidently
well treated by his boss, a senior SS officer. These experiences seem to
have prejudiced him in favor of the Nazis. He initially published a
defense of the SS against its critics and denied reports by survivors of
atrocities in the camps, then went on to dispute the existence of the gas
chambers and to assert that it was the Jews who had started the Second
World War.[5]

Another relatively early denier was Austin J. App, author of *The Six
Million Swindle: Blackmailing the German People for Hard Marks with
Fabricated Corpses*. App estimated the total number of Jewish casualties
of the Third Reich at around three hundred thousand, and declared the
'six million' to be "an impudent lie." Born in 1902, App was for a time
president of the Federation of American Citizens of German Descent,
and in 1942 he campaigned in the United States in support of Nazi war
aims. In the early years after the war, he defended the Nazi mass murder
of the Jews and similar atrocities as legitimate acts of war, minimized the
numbers of victims, and denied the existence of gas chambers. In his
book, he argued that the "fraudulent six million casualty" figure for Jewish deaths at the hands of the Nazis was used "vindictively as an external
club for pressuring indemnities out of West Germany and for wringing
financial contributions out of American Jews." He alleged that at least five
hundred thousand of the Jews supposedly gassed in the camps had gone
to Israel. The perpetuation of the 'swindle' was due to Jewish domination
of the media. The Americans and the British and above all the Soviet
Union colluded in the deception in order to distract attention from their
own war crimes.[6]

Perhaps the most influential proponent of such views was Arthur R.
Butz, an engineering professor at Chicago's Northwestern University,
whose book *The Hoax of the Twentieth Century*, published in 1976, constituted the first attempt to present Holocaust denial in a pseudo-academic form. Its eight chapters were adorned with 450 footnotes, 5 appen-
dices, and 32 plates and diagrams and it looked at first glance like an
academic treatise. The book argued, *inter alia*, that the Allied bombing
of Dresden produced more corpses than had ever been found from the
camps, that Zyklon-B gas was used strictly as an insecticide, that
Auschwitz was an industrial plant, that deaths there were mainly caused

by typhus, and that no gassings took place there. In Butz's view, when the Nazis talked or wrote about *Judentum* ('Jewry'), they meant the destruction of Jewish power, not of Jewish human beings, and when they used the word *annihilation* (*Vernichtung*) or *extirpation* (*Ausrottung*) in this context, they did not mean actual killing. He alleged that the failure of the Yad Vashem memorial to the Holocaust, in Jerusalem, to collect 6 million names of those who had died, proved that the number of dead was far fewer than 6 million. The Nuremberg trials were a frame-up in Butz's view, and the myth of the Holocaust was propagated after the war by the Jews for their own advantage.[7]

Perhaps the most active and vocal of the deniers in the 1980s and 1990s was the Frenchman Robert Faurisson, a former university teacher of French literature who had argued over many years that "the alleged massacres in the 'gas chambers' and the alleged 'genocide' were part of the same lie," which "is essentially Zionist in origin" and "has allowed a huge political and financial swindle of which the state of Israel is the principal beneficiary." Faurisson concentrated in particular on attempting to prove that the gas chambers at Auschwitz and in other camps never existed. He was tried in his native France for slander, violation of Article 382 of the Civil Code by wilfully distorting history, and incitement to racial hatred, which had been outlawed under a law of 1972, and was found guilty on all three counts.[8]

As well as these three figures, a role was also played in the denial phenomenon by Wilhelm Staeglich, an academically qualified German lawyer whose book *Der Auschwitz-Mythos: Legende oder Wirklichkeit* (The Auschwitz Myth: Legend or Reality), published in 1979 by the far-right Grabert-Verlag in Germany, followed Butz in presenting Holocaust denial in a pseudo-academic form. The book argued that there had been no mass extermination of Jews in Nazi extermination camps, and that guilty verdicts in postwar trials of the perpetrators were wrong. Staeglich used minor discrepancies in postwar documents and reports of the extermination to dismiss all such documents as forgeries and falsifications. As a result of this book Staeglich was dismissed from state employment and his doctoral title was withdrawn by his university.[9]

Figures such as these operated on the fringes of public life. Their books were mostly distributed by mail order and could seldom be found on the shelves of respectable bookshops or libraries. They seemed to belong in the world of sensational newspapers such as you could buy in American supermarkets, recounting the experiences of people who had been abducted by little green aliens or who had seen Elvis Presley still alive. There was indeed a distinct genre of historical writing about Nazi Germany that could be slotted into this category and seemed to find enough readers for publishers to be willing to sell it. The past few years, for example, had seen books published claiming that the bodies in the Berlin bunker in 1945 were not really those of Hitler and Eva Braun, and that the Heinrich Himmler, who committed suicide when he was arrested a few weeks later by the British, was not really Heinrich Himmler; that Hitler's aide Martin Bormann was spirited away from Berlin at the end of the war by the British agent Ian Fleming, later author of the James Bond spy novels, and given a new identity as a doctor in the English home counties in exchange for information about Nazi gold; that Hitler became an antisemite because he studied at the same school as the young Ludwig Wittgenstein, a Jewish boy who became the twentieth century's most influential philosopher, and hated him because of his superior intelligence; that Klaus von Stauffenberg, who tried to blow up Hitler in July 1944, was not acting as part of a recently founded German resistance movement but in the service of a centuries-old secret society whose tradition reached back to the time of Christ; and so on.

All of this work tried to present its arguments as the outcome of serious historical scholarship, resting on a combination of detailed documentary research and careful scholarly reasoning. Often it was extremely ingenious and required a considerable effort to unpick and to refute. Its authors, however fantastic the theories they were putting forward, in most cases really seemed to believe what they were saying. I had reviewed a few of these books over the years and often wondered why their authors had written them. They did not seem to have any particular political axe to grind. What they were offering was more a perverse kind of entertainment to the reader. They belonged to a paranoid style of historical writing: nothing was quite what it seemed, and terrible secrets had been suppressed by mainstream historical scholarship for decades or even centuries. Unlike genuine historians, however, these writers were never willing to accept criticism, and stuck to their theses, however convincing the documentary evidence that was thrown at them.

For the most part, engaging with work such as this seemed pointless. It might be irritating, but on the whole it seemed fairly harmless. The writings of people like Rassinier, Butz, Faurisson, and Staeglich were different, however. For a start, it was surely deeply offensive to the many thousands of Hitler's victims who had been through the camps and the persecution and were now confronted by people telling them that virtually nothing of what they had suffered had ever happened. Those who had lost relatives and loved ones in the Nazi extermination program were now being told that they had not lost them at all, or if they had, it was through disease or secret emigration to Palestine. Moreover, while events such as the death in 1945 of Hitler, Eva Braun, Himmler, and Bormann, or Stauffenberg's attempt on Hitler's life, were discrete happenings that were not difficult to verify, the denial of such a large and complex chunk of history as the systematic extermination of millions of Jews by the Nazis was on a vastly larger scale, and called in question a huge mass of historical evidence carefully gathered and interpreted by professional historians over the decades.

Moreover, much of the writings of the Holocaust deniers seemed neither morally nor politically harmless. On the contrary, a good deal of them seemed to be linked to racial hatred and antisemitic animosity in the most direct possible way. And, unlike the purveyors of historical fantasies about the survival of Bormann or the relationship between Hitler and Wittgenstein, the Holocaust deniers were not maverick individualists but fed off each other's work and organized journals, conferences, and institutes to exchange views and disseminate publications.

It was for these reasons that they had attracted a good deal of attention from serious scholars in recent years. Deborah Lipstadt's book, published in the United States in 1993, was the most thorough study of the deniers, but it was by no means the first. Others who sought to describe and explain the phenomenon included the British political scientist Roger Eatwell,[10] the distinguished French historian Pierre Vidal-Naquet, writing in 1980,[11] the Israeli scholar Yisrael Gutman, author of *Denying the Holocaust*,[12] the German political scientist Armin Pfahl-Traughber,[13] and Limor Yagil, a researcher working for the Project for the Study of Anti-Semitism at the Faculty of Humanities, Tel Aviv University.[14] An important early book on this phenomenon was Gill Seidel's *The Holocaust Denial: Antisemitism, Racism and the New Right*, published in 1986.[15]

Clearly there were some differences among these various authors'
depiction of Holocaust denial, and equally clearly, not all Holocaust
deniers subscribed to all the views which they mentioned, or held them
to the same degree. However, reducing them all to a lowest common
denominator, it seemed clear that Holocaust denial involved the minimum following beliefs:

(a) The number of Jews killed by the Nazis was far less than 6 million; it amounted to only a few hundred thousand, and was thus
similar to, or less than, the number of German civilians killed in
Allied bombing raids.

(b) Gas chambers were not used to kill large numbers of Jews at any
time.

(c) Neither Hitler nor the Nazi leadership in general had a program
of exterminating Europe's Jews; all they wished to do was to
deport them to Eastern Europe.

(d) "The Holocaust" was a myth invented by Allied propaganda during the war and sustained since then by Jews who wished to use
it to gain political and financial support for the state of Israel or
for themselves. The supposed evidence for the Nazis' wartime
mass murder of millions of Jews by gassing and other means was
fabricated after the war.[16]

Lipstadt had alleged in her book that Irving belonged to the weird
and irrational world of Holocaust denial. Whether or not he could reasonably be called a 'Holocaust denier' could be determined by examining his public statements to see if these four basic principles of Holocaust
denial were present. Did what he had said and written about the Nazi
extermination of the Jews conform to what Rassinier, Butz, Faurisson,
Staeglich, and others had said and written? And did he have any contacts
with such individuals or with organizations devoted to Holocaust denial?
I determined to find out.

In his written submission to the court, Irving wrote: "It is a particularly mischievous and damaging libel to call the Plaintiff 'a Holocaust
denier,' a lie worthy of the Nazi propaganda minister Dr Goebbels himself."[17] Irving asserted "that the whole of World War Two can be defined
as a Holocaust." He considered it "invidious to single out one single act

of mass murder of innocents and to label it 'The Holocaust,' as though there was none other." He went on:

> If however the Defendants seek to define the Holocaust as the mass murder of Jews by the Nazis and their cohorts during World War II, then the Plaintiff maintains that he has at no time denied it; on the contrary, he has rendered it more plausible by investigating documents, questioning witnesses, and uncovering fresh sources and making no secret of for example the alleged liquidation of 152,000 Jews at Chelmno on December 8, 1941, about which he wrote in *Hitler's War,* 1991 edition, at page 426. At page 7 of his book on aerial warfare against civilians *Von Guernica bis Vietnam* (From Guernica to Vietnam), the very first page of text, the Plaintiff emphasised: "The massacre of minorities by the National Socialists in Germany . . . probably cost more lives than all the air raids carried out to the present date."[18]

Similarly, Irving maintained that he had "at no time denied that the Nazis established concentration camps throughout their territories." He had "at no time denied that the murder of the Jews began in about June 1941 when the Germans invaded the Soviet Union, or that hundreds of thousands of Jews were shot to death." In this context he referred to pages 270–71 of the 1977 edition of *Hitler's War,* pages 380–81 of the revised 1991 edition of the same book, and unnumbered pages of his 1996 biography of Goebbels.[19]

When I looked at them more closely, however, it became clear that these points did not really relate to the Holocaust as defined by most historians. Irving wrote only of an *alleged* liquidation at Chelmno; he did not accept, therefore, that 152,000 Jews were actually killed there. He referred to concentration camps, but the existence of such camps was not at issue, for nobody denied that concentration camps were built to imprison those whom the Nazis regarded as their enemies, above all within the borders of the Reich, at Dachau, Buchenwald, Bergen-Belsen, Flossenbürg, and elsewhere. What was at issue was a different category of camp, namely those constructed in occupied Eastern Europe, such as Belzec, Sobibor, Treblinka, and Chelmno, and built specifically and exclusively to exterminate Jews, or, in the case of Auschwitz-Birkenau, with extermination as one of its principal aims: in other words, the extermination camps. Finally, the murder by shooting of hundreds of thousands of Jews was not the same as the extermination by shooting, gassing, starvation, and deliberate neglect of millions of Jews which formed an essential part of the Holocaust as conventionally understood.

Moreover, the book on aerial warfare to which Irving referred was published in 1982. On reading through his many books and speeches, I soon realized that Irving's views on these issues had not stood still over time. In his introduction to the first edition of *Hitler's War*, Irving referred to "the methodical liquidation of Russian Jews during the 'Barbarossa' invasion of 1941," and also to the fact that the Nazis "kept the extermination machinery going until the end of the war."[20] Leaving aside for the moment Irving's view of Hitler's role in all this, it was clear that in 1977 Irving accepted that the Nazis had systematically killed the Jews of Europe in very large numbers. In the index to the 1977 edition of *Hitler's War*, for example, there were seventeen entries under the heading "Jews, extermination of, documenting responsibility for and knowledge of," referring to thirty-one pages of text. Another entry in the index was for "Auschwitz, extermination camp at." These pages made no attempt to deny the fact of the extermination. When the Jews were deported to the East on Hitler's orders, Irving wrote on page 391, their fate was determined by lower-level officials. "Arriving at Auschwitz and Treblinka, four in every ten were pronounced fit for work; the rest were exterminated with a maximum of concealment." Similarly, on page 332 of the 1977 edition of *Hitler's War*, Irving referred to "the extermination program," which, he wrote, "had gained a momentum of its own."

All this had made it plain to most commentators that Irving was not a hard-core Holocaust denier in the 1970s or early 1980s.[21] By the end of the 1980s, however, all this had changed, and Irving had clearly moved from 'soft-core' to 'hard-core' Holocaust denial.[22] When I looked at the 1991 edition of *Hitler's War*, it became clear that the picture painted by Irving here was very different from what it had looked like in the first edition. The references made in 1977 to "the extermination of the Jews," "the methodical liquidation of Russian Jews," and "the extermination machinery" had all been deleted from the introduction by 1991. Indeed, the word *extermination* no longer appeared at all. Instead, Irving referred vaguely to "the Jewish tragedy," "the Nazi maltreatment of the Jews," or "the entire tragedy." The index entry was still there in 1991, as in 1977, for "Auschwitz, extermination camp at," as it was for "Treblinka, extermination camp at." But on the pages in question (463–47 in 1991, 390–93 in 1977) the account had undergone some significant alterations. In 1991, the 1977 references to the "murder machinery" and "the extermination center at Treblinka," had gone. In their place was new material describing Himmler's visit to Auschwitz on 18 July 1942 and citing the postwar interrogation of Albert Hoffmann, an SS man who accompanied Himmler on the visit, noting that "maltreatment did occur" but adding that he "totally disbelieves the accounts of atrocities as published in the press" after the war. Irving explicitly denied that there was any documentary sanction for the story that Himmler witnessed the 'liquidation' of a trainload of Jews on this occasion, and added: "By late 1945 the world's newspapers were full of unsubstantiated, lurid rumors about 'factories of death' complete with lethal 'gas chambers.'"

Perhaps most noteworthy of all was the difference between the two versions of Irving's account of Hitler's address to a group of generals about Hungary's Jews on 26 May 1944:

> 1977: In Auschwitz, the defunct paraphenalia of death—idle since 1943—began to clank again as the first trainloads from Hungary arrived.
>
> 1991: Four hundred thousand Jews were being rounded up in Hungary; the first trainloads arrived in Asuchwitz as slave labor for the now completed I. G. Farben plant.

In 1977, Irving made it clear that the Hungarian Jews were killed. In 1991, he made no mention of this fact but claimed instead that they were being used merely as workers in a chemical factory.

Thus Irving's views had altered substantially between the two editions. The turning-point seemed to have been the 1988 trial of Ernst Zündel, a German-Canadian antisemite, Holocaust denier, and self-confessed admirer of Hitler. Zündel's books included *The Hitler We Loved and Why*, published by a firm called White Power Publications, and *UFOs: Nazi Secret Weapons?*, which argued that unidentified flying objects, which used to be known as flying saucers, were still being deployed by survivors of the Nazi regime from bases underneath the Antarctic.[23] There could be no doubt as to which worlds of thought Ernst Zündel belonged to, then: unusually, perhaps, he combined in one person two of the most bizarre fantasies in modern America. Zündel's defense lawyers called a number of Holocaust deniers as expert witnesses in an attempt to demonstrate that the information Zündel had been spreading about the Holocaust was not false. Irving also appeared as an expert witness in this trial. Irving repeatedly admitted under questioning in the court that he had changed his mind since 1977 on the issues of the numbers of Jews killed and the use of the gas chambers. "My mind has now changed," he said, "because I understand that the whole of the Holocaust mythology is, after all, open to doubt."[24]

In examining the question of whether or not Irving was a Holocaust denier, I had therefore to concentrate on his publications and statements at and after the Zündel trial in 1988, not before. For Irving himself said quite openly in 1991 that he had removed all references to extermination camps and death factories from the second edition of the book.[25] I could thus disregard work published by Irving before 1988 since it was plainly irrelevant to the issue of whether Lipstadt was correct in 1994 to call him a Holocaust denier.

II

The first basic element of Holocaust denial was a minimization of the numbers of Jews killed. I looked through Irving's various books, articles, and speeches to see what his estimation of the numbers was. They revealed that until the late 1980s, Irving had paid little attention to this question. In 1986, for example, while confessing that he thought "the six million figure is probably marginally exaggerated," Irving described the minimal figure of one hundred thousand as being put forward by a "school of thought" that was "right out at the fringe," and added that "I have to admit that I haven't examined the Holocaust in any detail."[26]

In his evidence to the Zündel trial in Canada in 1988, however, which he had put in full on his own website for all to consult, Irving was asked to comment on the following statement (put to him by the defense lawyer): "If the 'Holocaust' is represented as the allegation of the exter-

mination of 6 million Jews during the Second World War as a direct result
of official German policy of extermination (*sic*), what would you say to
that thesis?" Irving replied:

> I am not familiar with any documentary evidence of any such figure
> as 6 million . . . it must have been of the order of 100,000 or more,
> but to my mind it was certainly less than the figure which is quoted
> nowadays of 6 million. Because on the evidence of comparison with
> other similar tragedies which happened in the Second World War,
> it is unlikely that the Jewish community would have suffered any
> worse than these communities.[27]

As he himself said in 1996, "cutting the Holocaust down to its true size
makes it comparable with the other crimes of World War II."[28]

This applied not just to gassing and extermination camps, but also to
the mass shootings carried out by the Security Service and Security Police
task forces, the *Einsatzgruppen*. In his evidence to the Zündel trial in
1988, Irving cast doubt, for example, on the reports filed by task force
leaders giving numbers of Jews shot by their forces. "I don't trust the statistics they contain," he said. "Soldiers who are out in the field doing a job
or murderers who are out in the field doing a job, they don't have time to
count." Each leader, he suggested, submitted reports whose aim was to
"show he's doing a jolly good job," and by inference, therefore, seriously
exaggerated or even invented the numbers killed. "Statistics like this are
meaningless," Irving said. "I'm suggesting," he continued, "it is possible
that at the time some overzealous SS officer decided to put in a fictitious
figure in order to do Heinrich Himmler a favour." This of course was pure
speculation, unsupported by any documentary evidence. This was characteristic of Irving's methods in disposing of inconvenient documents. If
a document did appear that Irving was unable to suggest was not genuine, or in some way unreliable, such as a memorandum from Himmler
to Hitler in which three hundred thousand Jews were referred to in 1942
as having been exterminated, Irving said he was "unhappy about it
because it is such an unusual, isolated document."[29] But of course, it was
only "isolated" because Irving had dismissed or ignored other documentary evidence that pointed in the same direction: there was no genuine
documentary warrant at all for this remark.

By the middle of the 1990s, Irving was deploying a range of arguments to buttress his minimal estimates for the numbers of Jews killed by the Nazis. In *Nuremberg: The Last Battle,* he claimed that the Auschwitz death books gave 46,000 names of people who had perished in the camp, mainly from disease.[30] Citing British decrypts of German code messages from Auschwitz to Berlin, Irving suggested on a number of occasions that some 25,000 Jews possibly died in Auschwitz by killing, the rest from disease, the cause given in most of the reports.[31] On occasion, he went so far as to suggest that *all* the Jews who died in Auschwitz died from disease: "Probably 100,000 Jews died in Auschwitz," he said in 1993, "but not from gas chambers, they died from epidemics."[32]

Irving actually claimed that the official history of British Intelligence during the Second World War, by the late Professor Sir Harry Hinsley,

> states . . . that upon analysis of the daily returns of the Auschwitz concentration camp, it becomes completely plain that nearly all of the deaths, nearly all of the deaths, were due to disease. The others were by execution, by hanging, and by firing squad. There is no reference, and I'm quoting this page, there is no reference whatever to any gassings. So why hasn't this extraordinary revelation been headlined in the newspapers around the world? It's not just some cranky, self-appointed, British, neo-fascist, neo-Nazi pseudo-historian. And you journalists who are present can take those words down. It's not just some pseudo-historian from Britain saying this. This is the British official historian, Professor Hinsley, who had unlimited access to the archives of the SIS, the Secret Intelligence Service, and to the archives of the British code-breaking agency, who says that in Auschwitz nearly all the deaths were due to disease. There is no reference whatsoever to gassings. (Applause).[33]

In fact, when I looked up the passage, Hinsley did not claim that nearly all the deaths were due to disease; all he wrote was that the British decrypts of encoded radio messages sent from Auschwitz did not mention gassings, which was hardly surprising, given the Nazis' policy of not mentioning the gas chambers explicitly in any of their communications with one another.

Moreover, although Irving claimed that the radio reports from Auschwitz to the central administration of the camps in Berlin were decrypted by British intelligence at Bletchley Park "from 1942 to the end of 1943,"[34] in fact the decrypts ended on 1 September 1942, when the authorities stopped reporting deaths by radio, and reported them only in writing. The returns to which Hinsley referred covered early to mid-1942, which was the only period during which the total number of prisoners in the camp corresponded to the total number of inmates mentioned in the decrypts. It was only subsequently that numbers increased (to 135,000 in March 1943) and mass gassing began on a really large scale with the completion of Crematorium II in March 1943.[35] Crucially, too, the decrypts were decipherments of radio reports of the additions and subtractions to the *regular, registered* camp population: these reports omitted all *unregistered* Jews (as well as gypsies) selected for gassing immediately on arrival. Thus they proved nothing, except that there were numerous deaths from executions and disease among the long-term camp inmates.[36] Finally, as Hinsley himself pointed out in reply to a letter from Irving on 17 June 1991, he had not in any case seen the original intercepts himself: "I saw only a summary of them, compiled afterwards, and they were probably not translated and circulated at the time."[37] The originals certainly contained information not purveyed in the summaries, and it was anybody's guess as to what it might have been. The decrypts therefore completely failed to substantiate Irving's allegation that there were no deaths by gassing in Auschwitz.

This was far from being the only attempt Irving made to twist the evidence in order to minimize the numbers of Jews deliberately murdered by the Nazis. "Despite the most strenuous efforts," he also claimed, "the Yad Vashem Museum, Jerusalem, has compiled a list of no more than three million possible Holocaust victims. The same names appear in this list many times over."[38] This did not mean, of course, that the same names referred to the same people; nor did the fact that the number of names compiled totaled less than 6 million mean that 6 million were not killed. The figure of 6 million, Irving said, originated in a guesstimate based on a comparison of European Jewish population figures in 1929 and 1946. It had no basis, he declared, in documented historical fact.[39] Yet the discrepancy in population was a documented historical fact.

When it came to suggesting ways in which the missing Jews might in fact have survived the war, Irving suddenly and conveniently forgot his demand for documented historical fact. Nobody, he alleged, had "explained what became of the one million cadavers" which it was claimed "were produced by killing operations at Auschwitz," nor for that matter what happened to the alleged corpses produced by supposed gassings in other camps.[40] There was no trace in Allied aerial photographs of mass graves at Auschwitz, so where had the bodies gone? he asked.[41] Irving himself supplied more than one answer. He claimed that the Jews who disappeared did not die but were secretly transported to Palestine by the Haganah, the Zionist underground, and given new identities. He suggested some of the missing Jews were killed in the February 1945 bombing raid on Dresden: "Many other raids were like that. Nobody knows how many Jews died in them. Nobody knows how many Jews died on the road of hunger or cold, after the evacuation of concentration camps in late 1944 and early 1945. Nobody knows how many Jews survived in displaced persons' camps. None of the Holocaust historians have researched this."[42]

Such wild and unfounded speculations commonly occurred in Irving's speeches. They derived in part from the Holocaust denier Paul Rassinier's unsubstantiated assertion that four-fifths of the 5 to 6 million Jews most historians agreed had been killed in fact "were very much alive at the end of the war," repeated by Arthur Butz in his Holocaust denial tract *The Hoax of the Twentieth Century.*[43] Irving did concede in his 1992 speech that there were some unauthorized mass shootings of Jews behind the Eastern Front. On this point, he was explicitly supported by Robert Faurisson, who, speaking on this occasion from among his listeners, confirmed: "We assume that there were massacres and hostages and reprisals and so on. . . . There is no war without massacres, especially on the Russian front where you had Jews, and partisans, women, and children all mixed together." Irving agreed: "It's important to say this because we are called Holocaust deniers, and the television screens show you the mass graves and all the rest of it, which we don't deny."[44] Irving repeated this point once more, in 1995, conceding that "there is no doubt in my mind that on the Eastern front large numbers of Jews were massacred, by criminals with guns—SS men, Ukrainians, Lithuanians, whatever—to get rid of them."[45] Atrocities always occurred during wars.[46]

Did this amount to 'Holocaust denial'? I thought it did. Irving admitted in 1992 without qualification that "Eichmann's memoirs are an important element of the refutation of the Holocaust story."[47] If engaging in a refutation of the Holocaust story was not Holocaust denial, then what was? "For me as a historian," Irving said in 1992, "the Holocaust is a mere footnote to history. I write about world history; I write about Real History, and I am not going to talk at any great length about something which is of far more obsessive interest to other historians, revisionists, or whatever."[48] Speaking in Toronto on 1 November 1992, Irving declared:

> The legend was that Adolf Hitler ordered the killing of six million Jews in gas chambers in Auschwitz. This is roughly how history has had its way for the last forty or fifty years. . . . Well, I am not a Holocaust denier, and that word really offends me, but I am a Holocaust analyst, I think we are entitled to analyse the basic elements of the statement: Adolf Hitler ordered the killing of six million Jews in gas chambers at Auschwitz, and to ask, is any part of this statement open to doubt?[49]

Once again Irving, as in another speech made during his Canadian lecture tour in 1992, was using the term *analysis* as a euphemism for *denial*; the difference between analysis and denial here was nonexistent: "I don't like this word 'deny,' " he said in 1993 with reference to the figure of 6 million Jewish victims of Nazism: "the word 'deny' is only one step away from lying, really. I challenge it, I contest it."[50] There was nothing about the word *denial* that implied telling a lie, however, any more than there was anything about the words *challenge, contestation,* or *analysis* that implied telling the truth.

At the beginning of his videotape *The Search for Truth in History,* Irving said once more: "The Holocaust with a capital 'H' is what's gone down in history in this one sentence form, so to speak: 'Adolf Hitler ordered the killing of six million Jews in Auschwitz.' "[51] But nobody had ever argued that 6 million Jews were killed by gassing in Auschwitz. Irving's claim that this was what the term *Holocaust* meant was a figment of his own imagination. The standard works on the Holocaust made it clear both that a substantial proportion of those killed were shot or starved to death or deliberately weakened and made susceptible to fatal disease as a matter of policy, that gassings took place at other centers besides Auschwitz, including notably Belzec, Chelmno, Sobibor, and Treblinka, and that the number killed in Auschwitz was around 1.1 million.[52]

Only on one recorded occasion, during an interview with the Australian journalist Ron Casey on 27 July 1995 (after the publication of Deborah Lipstadt's book) did Irving depart at all significantly from his minimization of the numbers killed:

> CASEY: What is your estimate of the number of Jews who died at the hands of Hitler's regime in the war years? What number—and I don't like using this word—what number would you concede were killed in concentration camps?
>
> IRVING: I think, like any scientist, I'd have to give you a range of figures and I'd have to say a minimum of one million, which is a monstrous crime, and a maximum of about four million, depending on what you mean by killed. If putting people into a concentration camp where they die of barbarity and typhus and epidemics is killing, then I would say the four million figure, because, undoubtedly, huge numbers did die in the camps in the conditions that were very evident at the end of the war.[53]

Even in giving, exceptionally, a figure of between one and 4 million however, it was noticeable that Irving strongly qualified his remarks by claiming that "barbarity and typhus and epidemics" were the main causes of death. Irving had a long record of blaming the high mortality rate in the camps—insofar as he conceded it at all—on epidemics rather than on deliberate, systematic killing. Thus, for example, in 1986 he told an audience, again in Australia, that the piles of dead filmed in Buchenwald and Bergen-Belsen at the end of the war had been the result of epidemics that "had only broken out in the last two or three weeks of the war." And who, in Irving's view, was responsible for these epidemics?

> We have to admit probably that we, the British and the Americans, were partially responsible, at least partially responsible for their misfortune. Because we vowed deliberate bombing of the transportation networks, deliberate bombardation, bombarding the German communications, by deliberate destruction of the German pharmaceutical industry, medicine factories. We had deliberately created the conditions of chaos inside Germany. We had deliberately cre-

ated the epidemics, and the outbreaks of typhus and other diseases, which led to those appalling scenes that were found at their most dramatic in the enclosed areas, the concentration camps, where of course epidemics can ravage and run wild.[54]

In fact, of course, conditions for epidemics were deliberately created by the Nazis, who ran the camps in a way that deprived the inmates of hygiene and medical attention as a matter of policy.[55] Yet Irving had a repeated tendency to blame virtually all the deaths of the Second World War on the Allies in general, the British in particular, and above all on Winston Churchill. Thus he told an audience in South Africa in 1986:

> We went in and we bombed the Belgians, and the Poles, and the French, and the Dutch. We did appalling damage. We killed millions of people in Europe in the most bestial way, in defiance of all conventions. In a way which eventually damned with infamy on the name of the British, and it all goes back on Winston Churchill's name.

Indeed, he said on another occasion, probably in the same year: "We'd killed 20 million people."[56] Winston Churchill, in Irving's view, "bears at least a partial share of the blame for the tragedy that befell the Jews in Europe, because Churchill fought the war five years longer than was necessary and provided the smokescreen behind which the tragedy could occur."[57]

Closely linked to these views was the denial of the existence of gas chambers at Auschwitz and elsewhere. Irving declared in his written submission to the court: "It is denied that the Plaintiff has denied the Holocaust; it is denied that the Plaintiff has denied that gas chambers were used by the Nazis as the principal means of carrying out that extermination; they may have used them on occasion on an experimental scale, which fact he does not deny."[58] This sentence was remarkably self-contradictory. Was he saying that he accepted that the gas chambers were the principal means of killing, or that their use was only possible ("may have used") and if it did occur, was he merely saying that it was only experimental in scale?

It was also contradicted by another line of defense he took against the accusation of being a Holocaust denier, namely, to deny that there was any authentic wartime archival evidence for the existence of gassing facilities at Auschwitz-Birkenau, Chelmno, Belzec, Sobibor, and Treblinka—a cautious statement stopping short of an outright denial but clearly designed to imply that those gassing facilities therefore did not exist.[59] If Irving was implying here that he would not accept any evidence about the Second World War unless it was written at the time, then how did he justify his own extensive use of the postwar testimony of members of Hitler's entourage given in interviews with them conducted by himself? Here again, he was applying double standards in his approach to different types of evidence. The fact was that historians had to take all kinds of evidence into account, and apply the same standards of criticism to all of them. Irving was wrong to imply that there was no authentic wartime evidence of gassing facilities in the camps he mentioned. But even if he had been right, this would not have meant that there was no authentic evidence of any kind for their existence.

Nevertheless, Irving clearly meant to imply that there was not. In his testimony to the Zündel trial in 1988, he explicitly rejected the use of the term *extermination camps* apart from Chelmno, which "was operating on a very small scale," and by shooting, not gassing.[60] In 1992, he put forward the same kind of argument in describing the memoirs of Adolf Eichmann. Irving said:

> He also describes—and I have to say this being an honest historian—going to another location a few weeks later and being driven around in a bus; then being told by the bus driver to look through a peephole into the back of the bus where he saw a number of prisoners being gassed by the exhaust fumes. So I accept that this kind of experiment was made on a very limited scale, but that it was rapidly abandoned as being a totally inefficient way of killing people. But, I don't accept that the gas chambers existed, and this is well known. I've seen no evidence at all that gas chambers existed.[61]

This minor concession was characteristic of his technique in admitting small-scale, limited instances of what he devoted much of his attention to denying on the large scale, as a kind of alibi that enabled him to deny that he was really doing the latter at all. He alleged that "equal tonnages of Zyklon-B pesticide granules were delivered to Auschwitz and Oranienburg camps, at which latter camp nobody had ever suggested that gas chambers existed, and to camps in Norway." Recently discovered documents in former Soviet archives showed that Auschwitz prisoners, he said, were released to the outside world on completion of their sentence. This was "incompatible with the character of a top-secret mass extermination centre." This again applied only to registered prisoners, and only to a minuscule number of them.[62]

Irving also denied "that diesel engines could be used for killing operations. These engines," he said, "exhaust non-lethal carbon dioxide ($CO2$), and only minute quantities of toxic carbon monoxide (CO). These howlers," he says, "typify the flawed historical research into 'the Holocaust' even now, fifty years after the tragedy."[63] In his videotaped speech *The Search for Truth in History,* made in 1993, Irving also asked: "How can you gas millions of people with hydrogen cyanide gas and leave not the slightest significant trace of chemical residue in the walls of the gas chambers?" This was a reference to the so-called Leuchter Report, a document commissioned by the French Holocaust denier Robert Faurisson for use in Zündel's defense in the 1988 trial. In this report, the American Fred Leuchter (pronounced 'Looshter'), designer of gas chambers and lethal injection devices used in the administration of the death penalty in some states in the United States, declared that his examination of the cyanide residues in the inner walls of the gas chambers in Auschwitz proved that they had not been used for gassing at all. Irving accepted the report's findings and published them in Britain. Indeed a reading of the report had proved decisive in bringing Irving round to full-scale Holocaust denial in 1988.[64] Irving went on to claim that Dr. Franciszek Piper of the Auschwitz State Museum had had the tests secretly replicated and when the State Forensic Laboratory in Cracow had confirmed Leuchter's findings the museum suppressed the fact and filed the report away.[65]

It was not difficult to check up on Irving's arguments. They turned out to be specious and derivative, and corresponded closely to a number of the same points put forward by well-known Holocaust deniers such as Robert Faurisson.[66] I was able to establish that the Polish authorities did not suppress findings of their own investigations of the former gas chambers, and these findings did not confirm Leuchter's claims. And of course

the literature made it abundantly clear that prisoners sent to Auschwitz
for extermination were not enrolled on the camp's list of inmates, but
were sent straight away to the gas chamber; so naturally there was no
record of their release.[67] As for the unfortunate Jews who were crammed
into gas vans, eyewitness reports described them as being slowly asphyx-
iated by carbon monoxide, which is one reason why it was eventually
replaced by the somewhat faster-acting Zyklon-B, to spare the distress
caused, not to the victims, but to the perpetrators who waited outside for
them to die and had to listen to their screams and bangings on the sides
of the van.

The Leuchter Report had long since been exposed as an incompe-
tent and thoroughly unscientific document compiled by an unqualified
person; it was completely discredited, along with its author, at the second
Zündel trial in 1988. Leuchter had removed samples from the inner walls
of Crematorium II at Auschwitz-Birkenau and had them analyzed, with
the result that the concentration of cyanide residues was found to be
slight, compared with the concentrations found in the delousing facilities, thus showing, he had triumphantly declared, that the crematorium
was not used for gassing people. But he had taken great chunks out of the
wall instead of scrapings off the surface, thus greatly diluting whatever
residues were to be found there. Even more crass, he had ignored the
fact that the concentration of cyanide gas needed to kill humans was far
lower than that needed to kill lice in clothing, and so failed to understand
that, far from disproving the existence of the gas chamber, his findings
actually tended to confirm it. Yet Irving, in his continued championing of
the report, had completely ignored—or suppressed—these fatal objections to its credibility.[68]

In his book on the Nuremberg trials, published in 1996, Irving also
noted (p. 131) that evidence was presented at Nuremberg that there
were lethal gas chambers at Dachau. "The German government has cer-
tified that no lethal gas chamber was ever operated at Dachau." But of
course the Nuremberg evidence and the German government statement
said two different things. Not even Irving claimed that the evidence presented at Nuremberg said that the gas chamber at Dachau ever actually
came into use.[69] Irving's technique here was to present (sometimes real,
sometimes invented) minor mistakes and propaganda legends at Nurem-

berg while ignoring the overwhelming mass of evidence on major matters of fact, using the former to discredit the latter. "There were no gas
chambers in Auschwitz," he said on 5 March 1990. In his view, only
"30,000 people at the most were murdered in Auschwitz . . . that's about
as many as we Englishmen killed in a single night in Hamburg."[70] In 1995
he repeated this view: "We revisionists," he declared, "say that gas chambers didn't exist, and that the 'factories of death' didn't exist."[71] "I'm a gas
chamber denier," he told a television interviewer in 1998. "I'm a denier
that they killed hundreds of thousands of people in gas chambers, yes."[72]

Irving repeatedly denied that there were *any* functioning gas chambers and that *any* Jews or other victims of Nazism were killed in them,
with the sole exception of a small number who he conceded were gassed
during experiments. I found plenty of instances of such comprehensive
denial in his speeches. In 1989, for instance, he confessed himself "quite
happy to nail my colours to the mast on that, and say that to the best of
my knowledge, there is not one shower bath in any of the concentration
or slave labour camps that turns out to have been some kind of gas chamber."[73] On 5 March 1990 he declared roundly to an audience in Germany
once more that there were no gas chambers at all in Auschwitz during
the war:

> There were no gas chambers in Auschwitz, there were only dum-
> mies which were built by the Poles in the postwar years, just as the
> Americans built the dummies in Dachau . . . these things in
> Auschwitz, and probably also in Majdanek, Treblinka, and in other
> so-called extermination camps in the East are all just dummies.

Repeating this claim later in the same speech, Irving added that "I and,
increasingly, other historians, . . . are saying, the Holocaust, the gas chamber establishments in Auschwitz did not exist."[74] On 8 November 1990
he repeated the same claim to an audience in Toronto: "The gas chambers that are shown to the tourists in Auschwitz are fakes."[75] These statements were clear and unambiguous. Irving's statement to the court of his
position on this issue—"it is denied that the Plaintiff has denied that gas
chambers were used by the Nazis as the principal means of carrying out
that extermination"—was a falsehood.[76]

A third element in Holocaust denial was a refusal to accept that the extermination of the Jews was systematic, organized, or centrally directed. Where did Irving stand on this issue? Even before he changed his mind on the numbers killed and the use of gassing as a murder technique, Irving was denying that the Nazi extermination of the Jews had been carried out in a systematic manner, because he had always denied that it had been ordered by Hitler. Thus, for example, in 1986, two years before his change of mind on these other issues, Irving told reporters in Brisbane, Australia, that

> the Jews were the victims of a large number of rather run-of-the-mill criminal elements which exist in Central Europe. Not just Germans, but Austrians, Latvians, Lithuanians, Estonians, feeding on the endemic antisemitism of the era and encouraged by the brutalization which war brought about anyway. These people had seen the bombing raids begin. They'd lost probably women, wives and children in the bombing raids. And they wanted to take revenge on someone. So when Hitler ordered the expulsion, as he did—there's no doubt that Hitler ordered the expulsion measures—these people took it out on the person that they could.[77]

Irving did not explain how Allied bombing raids on Germany had turned Latvians, Lithuanians, and Estonians against the Jews. The extermination of Jews in Eastern Europe during the war, he repeated in 1988, in places like Minsk and Kiev and Riga, was "conducted for the most ordinary and repugnant motives of greed and thievery" by "individual gangsters and criminals," for whom the German state and people could not be held responsible.[78] In fact, of course, even those responsible on the ground for directing and carrying out the actual killing operations were not 'nameless' and most of them were not 'criminals' in the sense of having previous convictions; they were responsible officials acting on behalf of the Nazi state and Nazi agencies such as the SS and the police.

As so often when he dealt with these questions, Irving abandoned the pretence of original research and resorted to speculation and innuendo. Testifying at the 1988 Zündel trial, for example, Irving said he was

> puzzled at the apparent lack of logic: that the Nazis are supposed to have had a government policy for the deliberate, ruthless, systematic extermination of the Jews in Auschwitz and other places of mur-

der and yet tens if not hundreds of thousands of Jews passed through
these camps and are, I am glad to say, alive and well amongst us now
to testify to their survival. So either the Nazis had no such programme or they were an exceedingly sloppy race, which isn't the
image we have of them today. It's another of the logical questions
which is being asked in this history which the historians hitherto
have not asked.

"I don't think there was any overall Reich policy to kill the Jews," he
repeated later on the same occasion.[79] Of course, his argument here was
fallacious. Auschwitz was both a labor camp and an extermination camp,
so it is not surprising that many Jews interned there survived the experience. On the other hand, Treblinka, Chelmno, Belzec, and Sobibor,
which was presumably what Irving meant by "other places of murder,"
were designed purely for extermination; Irving presented no evidence to
show that any Jews at all survived from these camps, which is not surprising, for hardly any did.

Irving disputed the view, commonly held among historians, that the
Wannsee Conference, a meeting of senior officials held on 20 January
1942, drew up statistics of Jews in many European countries who were
to be taken to Eastern Europe for extermination, either in the near future
or, later, when, as evidently expected, these countries fell into German
hands. Irving told the 1988 Zündel trial:

> Several of the participants in the Wannsee Conference subse-
> quently testified in later criminal proceedings that . . . none of them
> had an idea that at that conference there had been a discussion of
> liquidation of Jews. . . There is no explicit reference to extermina-
> tion of the Jews of Europe in the Wannsee Conference, not in any
> of the other documents in that file.

This was a classic instance of the Holocaust denial technique described
by Vidal-Naquet, of taking the euphemistic language of Nazism at face
value, but casting doubt on any source that avoided euphemisms and
spoke directly and in unvarnished terms about murder and extermination. In fact, like others familiar with the Wannsee Conference minutes,
I was aware of the fact that Eichmann testified in 1961 that the talk at the

Conference had all been of killing and liquidation, disguised in the minutes (written by Eichmann himself but checked over and amended by
Heydrich) by euphemisms.[80]

However, Eichmann, said Irving, without any evidence for his claim
and forgetting how he had relied on the Nazi bureaucrat's 1961 testimony
on other occasions, "got confused about what he really recalled and what
he had in the meantime been told." "I don't now believe," Irving said in
1988, "there was anything you could describe as 'extermination machinery' other than the very disorganized *ad hoc* efforts of the criminals and
murderers among the SS who were carrying out the liquidations that we
described earlier."[81] This was a familiar part of the litany of Holocaust
denial. One of the earliest Holocaust deniers, Paul Rassinier, had also
described "the systematic mass extermination of the Jews in the gas
chambers" as an "infamous accusation" invented by the Jews.[82] Another
Holocaust denier, Austin J. App, had similarly asserted that there was no
"single document, order, blue-print" demonstrating the Nazis' intention
of murdering the Jews, and went on to argue, as Irving later did, that the
Nazis were so efficient that the fact that some Jews undoubtedly survived
proves that they never had any intention of murdering them all: had they
wanted to, "they would have done so."[83] Speculation such as this struck
me as wild, indeed almost desperate in its attempt to distract attention
from the hard evidence of various kinds that pointed to the extermination program having been large-scale, systematic, and comprehensive in
intent.

III

Reading through the work of Holocaust deniers like Arthur Butz, it was
clear that they wanted their readers to believe that the evidence for the
Holocaust was fabricated. In a number of speeches and writings, Irving
claimed that the 'Holocaust legend' was invented by the Political Warfare Executive of the British Government. "British intelligence," he said
in Toronto on 13 August 1988, "deliberately masterminded the gas chamber lie." "Who invented the myth of the gas chambers?" he asked rhetorically in Moers on 9 March 1990. His answer? "We did it. The English.
We invented the lie about the gas chambers, just as we invented the lie

about the Belgian children with their hands hacked off in the First World
War."[84] Repeated over the BBC, this myth, Irving claimed, was soon
common currency among the Germans:

> There's hardly a German who hasn't been listening clandestinely to
> the BBC who hasn't heard about the gas chambers. And they begin
> mentioning it in rumours to each other. From one washerwoman to
> the next, the rumour goes around Germany, until finally they've
> actually seen about it and their son's working in a unit and he's heard
> about it, too. And that's how the legend gains credibility from the
> German side too.[85]

So where did Irving believe that the gas-chamber 'story' originated?
In extracts from the forthcoming second volume of his Churchill biography Irving wrote that it was supplied to the British in 1942 by Gerhard
Riegner, director of the Geneva Office of the World Jewish Congress
from 1939 until 1945.[86] The Foreign Office disbelieved Riegner; the
whole story might have been invented. So when the British used the story
as propaganda, they knew it to be untrue. This was already some distance
from Irving's claim that they had invented it themselves.

What was the real documentary evidence for this account? I checked
it out in the British Public Record Office, in Kew, just to the west of London. The documents were well known and a number of other historians
such as Sir Martin Gilbert, author of *Auschwitz and the Allies,* published
as long ago as 1981, had cited them before. They revealed that on 8
August 1942, Riegner informed the Foreign Office that he had been told
by a well-connected German that the Nazis were intending to exterminate 3 to 4 million Jews.[87] The methods under consideration included
Prussic acid (hydrogen cyanide).[88] Foreign Office mandarins were reluctant to make use of "this story" in British propaganda against Germany
"without further confirmation."[89] In a minute of 27 August Roger Allen
of the Foreign Office wrote:

> This [Polish] aide-mémoire [on which the declaration was based] is
> in line with a good deal of information which we have received from
> time to time. There can, I think, be little doubt that the general
> picture painted is pretty true to life. On the other hand it is of course
> extremely difficult, if not impossible, for us to check up on the

specific instances or matters of detail. For this reason I feel a little
unhappy about the statement to be issued on the authority of His
Majesty's Government, that Poles "are now being systematically put
to death in gas chambers."

Allen considered that reports of gassings "may or may not be true, but in
any event I submit we are putting out a statement on evidence which is
far from conclusive, and which we have no means of assessing."[90] Another
Foreign Office mandarin, Victor Cavendish-Bentinck, added:

> In my opinion it is incorrect to describe Polish information regard-
> ing German atrocities as "trustworthy." The Poles, and to a far
> greater extent the Jews, tend to exaggerate German atrocities in
> order to stoke us up. They seem to have succeeded.
>
> Mr. Allen and myself have both followed German atrocities
> quite closely. I do not believe that there is any evidence which would
> be accepted in a Law Court that <u>Polish</u> children have been killed on
> the spot by Germans when their parents were being deported to
> work in Germany, nor that <u>Polish</u> children have been sold to Ger-
> man settlers. As regards putting Poles to death in gas chambers, I
> do not believe there is any evidence that this has been done. There
> may have been stories to this effect, and we have played them up in
> P.[olitical] W. [arfare] E. [xecutive] rumours without believing that
> they had any foundation. At any rate there is far less evidence than
> exists for the mass murder of Polish officers by the Russians at
> Katyn. On the other hand we do know that the Germans are out to
> destroy the Jews of any age unless they are fit for manual labour.
>
> I think that we weaken our case against the Germans by publicly
> giving credence to atrocity stories for which we have no evidence.
> These mass executions in gas chambers remind me of the story of
> employment of human corpses during the last war for the manufac-
> ture of fat, which was a grotesque lie and led to true stories of Ger-
> man enormities being brushed aside as being mere propaganda.[91]

The Foreign Office's doubts were telegraphed to Washington the
same day:

> On further reflection we are not convinced that evidence regarding
> the use of gas chambers is substantial enough to justify inclusion in

> a public declaration of concluding phrase of paragraph 2 of draft and
> would prefer if United States agree, that sentence in question
> should end at "concentration camps."[92]

As requested, the original declaration issued on 30 August stood, save
that it duly read that some children were "despatched with the women
and old men to concentration camps."[93]

There was no evidence here or anywhere else, indeed, that the
British Political Warfare Executive had invented the story of the gas
chambers: they had on the contrary received a report from people with
contacts in Central Europe about them. Nor was there any evidence that
the Foreign Office considered reports of gassings to be a lie; they were
simply unsure about them. Moreover, their real doubts related to claims
that *Poles* were being gassed. Even Cavendish-Bentinck agreed that the
Germans were "out to destroy the Jews of any age unless they are fit for
manual labour."

But Irving's speeches went much further than this in their allegations.
Irving also asserted that following on this supposed propaganda lie, further evidence for the Holocaust was fabricated after the end of the Second World War.[94] This included the eyewitness testimony of the thousands of former camp inmates and survivors of the Nazi extermination
program. In his videotaped lecture *The Search for Truth in History*, Irving, said his supporter Nigel Jackson, spoke of the alleged eyewitnesses
to the Auschwitz extermination machine "with sympathy," suggesting
they had fallen prey to distortions of memory and to pressure on the part
of their listeners to have the legend justified. He said that eyewitness testimony had to be submitted to psychiatric or psychological examination.[95]
In an interview with the right-wing magazine *CODE* in 1990, Irving,
answering a question about how he would judge the credibility of Holocaust survivors, responded in similar fashion: "I say that the psychiatrists
should concern themselves with this matter some time. There are many
cases of mass hysteria."[96] "I'm afraid I have to say I wouldn't consider
what a survivor of Treblinka could tell me in 1988 to be credible evidence," he told the court at the second Zündel trial; one could not rely
on "the very human and fallible human memories after a tragic wartime
experience forty years after the event."[97] (Irving would have been lucky

to have found such a survivor. Only *fifty-four* people are known to have survived of the million or so who entered the camp in 1942 and 1943; most of them escaped during an uprising of Jewish prisoners on 2 August 1943).[98]

Alleged extermination camp survivors would in Irving's view go to considerable lengths to prove their stories, "even the ones who've got tattoo marks on their arms," he told an audience at Latvian Hall, Toronto, on 8 November 1990:

> Because the experts can look at a tattoo and say, "Oh yes, 181,219, that means you entered Auschwitz in March 1943." So if you want to go and have a tattoo put on your arm, as a lot of them do, I'm afraid to say, and claim subsequently that you were in Auschwitz, you've got to make sure (a) that it fits in with the month you said you went to Auschwitz, and (b) that it's not a number which anyone has used before. (Laughter from the audience).[99]

"The eyewitnesses in Auschwitz . . . who claim to have seen the gas chambers," he said in another lecture in 1991, "are liars." They were "an interesting case for the psychiatrist. People over a period of years begin kidding themselves that they have seen something." This was because they had been through a traumatic experience (Irving did not say what this was), and "being in the centre of a traumatic experience is liable to induce strange thoughts in eyewitnesses."[100]

On another occasion he was even less "sympathetic." People claimed to be eyewitnesses of the gas chambers and extermination camps, he told a Canadian audience in 1990, "particularly when there's money involved and they can get a good compensation cash payment out of it":

> And the only way to overcome this appalling pseudo-religious atmosphere that surrounds the whole of this immense tragedy called World War II is to treat these little legends with the ridicule and bad taste that they deserve. Ridicule isn't enough, you've got to be tasteless about it. You've got to say things like: "More women died on the back seat of Senator Edward Kennedy's car at Chappaquiddick than died in the gas chamber at Auschwitz." (Laughter in audience). You think that's tasteless? What about this: (Laughter in audience) I'm forming an association especially dedicated to all these liars, the ones who try to kid people that they were in these con-

centration camps. It's called "The Auschwitz Survivors, Survivors of the Holocaust, and Other Liars"—"A.S.S.H.O.L.E.S." (Laughter in audience). Can't get more tasteless than that. But you've got to be tasteless because these people deserve all our contempt, and in fact they deserve the contempt of the real Jewish community and the people, whatever their class and colour, who did suffer.[101]

This was more than tasteless; and the laughter in the audience showed clearly what kind of people Irving was speaking to.

In 1995, Irving repeated the allegation: confronted with an alleged Holocaust survivor, he said, he would ask her " 'How much money have you made from that piece of ink on your arm, which may indeed be real tattooed ink?' And I'll say 'Yes. Half-a-million dollars, three-quarters of a million dollars for you alone?'" "There are now hundreds, thousands, hundreds of thousands of survivors. There are now millions of survivors. And I'm glad. But of course every survivor is living proof that there was no Nazi extermination programme."[102] In 1995 he repeated his claim that there were millions of survivors—"they defy all laws of natural decease and all laws of biology. The number of survivors is growing."[103]

Irving never used eyewitness testimony from victims of Nazism in any of his voluminous writings; he hardly ever discussed it or even mentioned its existence. When confronted with actual survivors, he picked on technical aspects of their testimony that he tried to use to discredit their memories. A discussion with a survivor in a program broadcast on Australian television in 1997, for example, included the following exchange:

IRVING: You said you saw the smoke coming from the crematoria.

SURVIVOR: Absolutely.

IRVING: Is that correct?

SURVIVOR: Correct.

IRVING: But crematoria don't smoke, Mrs. Altman. Go and visit your local crematorium in Sydney.[104]

The thought that the crematoria of Auschwitz might have been designed differently, and with less regard to the susceptibilities of onlookers and neighbors, than the crematoria in Sydney, did not, apparently, enter his mind.

Why, then, did Irving think that such evidence had been concocted? Who could possibly have gone to all the immense trouble necessary to fabricate such a vast quantity of documentary material? Describing various versions of Holocaust denial in 1986, Gill Seidel remarked in her pioneering survey of the subject:

> They all purport to show that Jews are liars and tricksters holding the world to ransom and continuing to extract war reparations. This is a continuation and an extension of the anti-Jewish prejudices and practices. The implication is that after all this time Jews are still liars, parasites, extraordinar[il]y powerful, and fundamentally dishonest—and that maybe Hitler was right.[105]

As I read Irving's writings and transcripts of his speeches dating from the 1990s, it became clear that after his conversion in 1988 he moved rapidly into line with these views. Fundamentally, he seemed to believe—against all the evidence of the massive amount of scholarly research carried out by non-Jewish historians in many countries—that the history of the Nazi extermination of the Jews had been written by Jewish historians. Thus he could refer, as he did in 1993, to "we independent historians, shall we say, the non-Jewish historians, the ones with an entirely open mind," as if all non-Jewish historians agreed with him.[106] Such agreement existed only in Irving's fantasy.

The political thrust behind such strange views became apparent when I read the following passage in Irving's preface to the English edition of the Leuchter Report, published by his Focal Point publishing house:

> Nobody likes to be swindled, still less where considerable sums of money are involved (Since 1949 the State of Israel has received over 90 billion Deutschmarks in voluntary reparations from West Germany, essentially in atonement for the "gas chambers of Auschwitz"). And this myth will not die easily: Too many hundreds of millions of honest, intelligent people have been duped by the well-financed and brilliantly successful post-war publicity campaign which followed on from the original ingenious plan of the British Psychological (sic) Warfare Executive (PWE) in 1942 to spread to

the world the propaganda story that the Germans were using "gas chambers" to kill millions of Jews and other "undesirables."

"The 'big lie,'" he declared in 1991, referring to the Holocaust, "allows Jewish fraudsters to escape unpunished and Israel to torture Arabs and ignore UN resolutions." And who were these Jewish fraudsters? "The big lie is designed to justify both in arrears and in advance the bigger crimes in the financial world elsewhere that are being committed by the survivors of the Holocaust."[107] The idea that survivors were engaged in large-scale financial fraud was new to me. I could not find any evidence in Irving's writings and speeches to support this sweeping claim.

On 7 July 1992 *The Guardian* printed an interview with Irving in which, consistently with views he expressed elsewhere, Irving predicted that

> one year from now the Holocaust will have been discredited. That prediction is lethal because of the vested interests involved in the Holocaust industry. As I said to the Jewish Chronicle, if a year from now the gas chamber legend collapses, what will that mean for Israel? Israel is drawing millions of dollars each year from the German taxpayer, provided by the German government as reparation for the gas chambers. It is also drawing millions from American taxpayers, who put up with it because of the way the Israelis or the Jews suffered. No one's going to like it when they find out that for 50 years they have been believing a legend based on baloney.[108]

Irving's confidence was misplaced. Moreover, many of his points were already familiar to me from a reading of the older Holocaust denial literature. The allegation that the Jews had used the Holocaust story to win reparations from the Germans could also be found in the texts of Paul Rassinier.[109] Austin J. App similarly argued that the Jews had "used the six million swindle to blackmail West Germany into 'atoning' with the twenty billion dollars of indemnities to Israel."[110] In fact, the true figure was $735 million; and the money was paid for resettlement of survivors, not as compensation for the dead; had the state of Israel actually wanted to maximize the amount of reparations, then, as Deborah Lipstadt pointed out, the state of Israel would have tried to argue that—as Irving himself tried to argue—millions of Jews were not killed by the Nazis, but fled to Israel instead.[111]

Irving of course denied being 'anti-Jewish' or 'anti-Israel,' just as he denied being a Holocaust denier. Speaking in Canada in November 1992, he told his audience: "I am not an antisemite."[112] But he realized that his ideas opened him up to the obvious accusation that he was:

INTERVIEWER: When one reads your speeches, one has the impression that Churchill was paid by the Jews, that the Jews dragged Britain into the war, that many of the Communist regimes have been dominated by Jews subsequently, and that a great deal of control over the world is exercised by Jews.

IRVING: Right, these are four separate facts, to each of which I would be willing to put my signature. They are four separate and unrelated facts. When you string them together like that, you might be entitled then to say: "Question five, David Irving, are you therefore an antisemite?" This may well have been—

INTERVIEWER: No, this wasn't my question.

IRVING: But the answer is this, these are in fact four separate facts which happen to be true, in my considered opinion as a historian. And I think we can find the historical evidence for it.[113]

From the end of the 1980s, Irving began referring to Jews as "our traditional enemies."[114] Who these precisely were, he made clear in a speech given in 1992: "our old traditional enemies . . . (are) the great international merchant banks (who) are controlled by people who are no friends of yours and mine," people who were "annoyed" by sixty-foot posters advertising the *Sunday Times* serialization of the Goebbels diaries "in all the Jewish ghettos of Great Britain."

Later in the speech he attacked the "odd and ugly and perverse and greasy and slimy community of 'anti-Fascists' that run the very real risk of making the word fascist respectable by their own appearance!"[115] His particular venom seemed to be reserved for the Board of Deputies of British Jews, to whom he referred in 1991 as "cockroaches."[116] "I never used to believe in the existence of an international Jewish conspiracy," he said. "I'm not even sure now if there's an international Jewish conspiracy. All I know is that people are conspiring internationally against me, and they do mostly turn out to be . . . (drowned out by laughter and applause)."[117] In April 1998 he spoke of American Jews

> "moving into the same positions of predominance and influence (media, banking, business, entertainment, and the more lucrative professions like law, medical and dentistry) that they held in Weimar Germany, which gave rise to the hatreds and the resulting pogroms; and that this being so, twenty or thirty more years might see in the USA the same dire consequences as happened in Nazi Germany."[118]

This was the classic language of antisemitism that I had encountered in reading texts from German antisemites from the late nineteenth century on: "ghettos," "greasy and slimy," "lucrative professions," "cockroaches," "international Jewish conspiracy." The use of the term *ghettos*, for example, suggested in standard racist manner that there were districts in Great Britain where Jews were in a majority and, by implication, not integrated into the wider society in which they lived. In fact, such ghettos existed nowhere in the United Kingdom. Irving's language expressed the classic ideology of antisemitism too, with its attempt to whip up jealousies and hatreds of Jews by portraying them—without a shred of evidence— as exerting predominance over key professions and institutions (although why this should have been a cause for pogroms, or indeed objections from anybody, Irving did not say). This alleged 'predominance,' in the view of Holocaust deniers, was behind the continuing widespread public acceptance of what they called the 'Holocaust myth.'[119]

Indeed, some of Irving's own speeches contained a veiled threat of violence against Jews in the future as a result of his own 'exposure' of the Holocaust 'myth':

> And gradually the word is getting around in Germany (Irving said in 1991). Two years there from now too the German historians will accept that we're right. They will accept that for fifty years they have believed a lie. And then there will come about a result not only in Germany, but around the world, which I deeply regret and abhor. There will be an immense tidal wave of antisemitism. It's an inevitable result. And when people point an accusing finger at me and say, "David Irving, you are creating antisemitism," I have to say, "It is not the man who speaks the truth who creates the antisemitism, it's the man who invented the lie of the legend in the first place." (Applause).[120]

Irving's crocodile tears were not to be taken too seriously. For in 1996, recounting the view of the publisher who eventually refused to publish the American edition of his book on Goebbels, Irving said:

> Maybe . . . the chairman of St. Martin's Press was right when he said: "This book suggests they (the Jews) had it coming to them." But if he's right, let me say in advance in my self-defence, it isn't David Irving who says that, it's David Irving reporting Dr. Goebbels who says that. Maybe I didn't make it plain enough, or maybe I didn't put enough distance between myself and Dr. Goebbels, or maybe I didn't put in all the counter-arguments I should have done to be politically correct.[121]

Fundamentally, however, as Irving conceded, he was in basic agreement with Goebbels in his belief that "they had it coming to them." For, Irving told an audience in Tampa, Florida, on 6 October 1995, referring to the Jews:

> What these people don't understand . . . is that they are generating antisemitism by their behaviour, and they can't understand it. They wonder where the antisemitism comes from and it comes from themselves, from their behaviour. . . . I said to this man from Colindale, this leader of the Jewish community in Freeport, Louisiana, I said . . . "You are disliked, you people. You have been disliked for three thousand years. You have been disliked so much that you have been hounded from country to country, from pogrom to purge, from purge back to pogrom, and yet you never asked yourselves why you're disliked. That's the difference between you and me. It never occurs to you to look into the mirror and say, why am I disliked? What is it that the rest of humanity doesn't like about the Jewish people, to such an extent that they repeatedly put us through the grinder?" And he went beserk. He said: "Are you trying to say that we are responsible for Auschwitz? Ourselves?" And I said, "Well the short answer is yes. The short answer I have to say is yes. . . . If you had behaved differently over the intervening three thousand years, the Germans would have gone about their business and not have found it necessary to go around doing whatever they did to you.[122]

Thus whatever atrocities Irving admitted had been suffered by the Jews over the centuries had been mainly their own fault.

After all, he said in 1991, "they (meaning the Jews) dragged us into two world wars and now, for equally mysterious reasons, they're trying to drag us into the Balkans."[123] Here too, in the 1990s, the machinations of a Jewish conspiracy seemed to be at work. Irving was confronted with his various statements along these lines in 1996:

> INTERVIEWER: At times in your speech to these groups you speak at, you ask if the Jews have ever looked at themselves to find a reason for the pogroms and the persecutions and the extermination. In other words, you're asking, "did they bring it on themselves?"
>
> IRVING: Yes.
>
> INTERVIEWER: Thereby excusing the Germans, the Nazis.
>
> IRVING: Let us ask that simple question: why does it always happen to the Jews? . . .
>
> INTERVIEWER: But isn't that an ugly, racist sentiment?
>
> IRVING: It is an ugly, of course it's an ugly, racist sentiment. Of course it is. You're absolutely right. But you can't just say, therefore let's not discuss it, therefore let's not open that can of worms in case we find something inside there that we don't like looking at.

After all this, it was not surprising that he considered that "the Madagascar solution would probably have been the most peaceful for the present world," because the Jews "would have had no neighbours, nobody who they could feel intimidated by, and of course, nobody whom they in turn could intimidate." In fact, as recent research had made clear, Irving was glossing over the fact that the Nazi regime, in drawing up its never realized plans to deport the Jews there in the early part of the war, would have made no provision to supply them with food and clothing and the basic necessities of life, and that the climate and economy of the island were entirely unsuited to sustaining millions of mostly highly urbanized European settlers.[124]

Irving thus shared the common position of Holocaust deniers that evidence for the Holocaust has been fabricated. He augmented these arguments with a wider range of assertions about the Jews' alleged influence in the postwar world, and their supposed responsibility for provoking attacks on themselves, assertions which in style and content could fairly be called antisemitic.

IV

Was Lipstadt right to charge Irving with maintaining connections to Holocaust deniers? The most important organization propagating Holocaust denial had for many years been the so-called Institute for Historical Review, based in California. I collected information about the Institute from a variety of sources, most notably its publications held, along with other right-wing literature, in London's Wiener Library, a German-Jewish emigré institution devoted to the study of Nazism and fascism. Other details, not disputed by Irving, were presented in Deborah Lipstadt's own thorough investigation of the Institute in the book that was at the center of the trial. All of this made clear that the Institute's main business was propagating in a pseudo-academic form the idea that there were no gas chambers, there was no systematic extermination of the Jews by the Nazis, there were no 6 million dead.

In her book, Lipstadt cited a resolution passed at the Institute's first convention, held in Los Angeles in 1979, declaring that "the facts surrounding the allegations that gas chambers existed in occupied Europe during World War II are demonstrably false," and stating its belief that "the whole theory of 'the holocaust' has been created by and promulgated by political Zionism for the attainment of political and economic ends, specifically the continued and perpetual support of the military aggression of Israel by the people of Germany and the US." The resolution urged the U.S. Congress to investigate, among other things, "deceitful wartime propaganda masquerading as fact . . . and the truth of the alleged extermination of 6 million Jews in Europe during World War II."[125]

The Institute for Historical Review purported from the outset to be a respectable academic body. In 1980, it began publishing a quarterly magazine, *The Journal of Historical Review*. Leafing through its pages in the Wiener Library, I noticed its classic academic format: plain covers, no color pictures, and lengthy articles with an elaborate apparatus of footnotes and bibliographies. The Editorial Advisory Committee of the journal included many prominent Holocaust deniers, most notably Arthur R. Butz, Robert Faurisson, and Wilhelm Staeglich. Articles in the *Journal of Historical Review* had titles such as "The Diesel Gas Chambers: Myth Within a Myth,"[126] "The Myth of the Extermination of the Jews,"[127] "How Many Jews Died in the German Concentration Camps?" (the author's answer was between 300,000 and 600,000), and so on.[128] The overall thrust of the journal's efforts was to present a wide variety of arguments in support of the thesis that, to quote one article among many, "the Holocaust story is absurd."[129] Thus for example it dedicated a special issue to an attempt to vindicate the Leuchter Report,[130] carried an article with the title "Neither Trace Nor Proof: The Seven Auschwitz 'Gassing' Sites,"[131] and devoted several issues and numerous articles to attempting to demonstrate that nobody was ever gassed at Auschwitz.[132] Another article in the journal underlined Holocaust deniers' tendency to inflate the influence of Jews in the postwar world by claiming that "Judaism, through the 'Holocaust' cult, has become the informal state religion of the West."[133] The centrality of Holocaust denial to the Institute for Historical Review and its journal could not be doubted.

Irving claimed in his written submission to the court that the Institute was a respectable and nonextremist institution whose board members held established academic qualifications; they were not antisemites or racists or ultra-right-wing. However, their academic qualifications were not in history but in other fields. Butz was an engineer, Faurisson a specialist in French literature, Staeglich qualified as a lawyer, and so on. None of them was an established professional historian, academic or otherwise. Moreover, the journal and its parent institute had a political rather than an academic background. They were founded and owned by the Noontide Press, whose proprietor, the Legion for the Survival of Freedom Inc., was owned in turn by Willis Allison Carto, a leading proponent of Holocaust denial. Carto's main publication was the extreme right-wing journal *Spotlight*, described by Irving in 1982 as an excellent publication. Irving was already familiar with Carto and his "efficient and dedicated staff" by the early 1980s and was well aware of what he publicly referred to as "the ties that exist between the Liberty Lobby and the Institute of Historical Review."[134] The booking for the Institute's opening convention

in September 1979 was made by Noontide Press, under the name of
Lewis Brandon, a pseudonym for David McCalden, formerly a leading
light in a racist breakaway from the extreme right-wing political organization the British National Front, founded in 1975.[135] McCalden, who
also wrote under the name David Berg, was director of the Institute for
Historical Review from 1978 until 1981 and a self-confessed 'racialist.'[136]
Throughout the 1980s and early 1990s, the Institute organized regular
conferences and actively propagated its academic image, while it remained in effect a subordinate part of Willis Carto's much larger and bet-
ter-funded Liberty Lobby nexus.

Its dependence on Carto for much of its effectiveness was dramatically revealed in 1993, when a multimillion-dollar bequest became the
subject of vicious infighting between Carto and the Institute's staff.
Eleven lawsuits took up a massive amount of time, energy, and money,
and agreements that the cover organization of the Institute, the Legion
for the Survival of Freedom, would get 45 percent of the legacy, or, later,
that Carto would hand over to it $1.2 million, did not seem to have been
honored. The Legion and the Institute did manage to wrest control of its
board from Carto, and in January 1993 the journal dropped its pseudo-
academic format. After that, it was published as a bi-monthly illustrated
glossy magazine. Its contents and its basic thrust, however, did not
change.[137] Carto's response revealed once more the paranoia that per-
meated such circles on the extreme right. He not only fired back in his
magazine *Spotlight* the accusation that the Institute had been taken over
by the Jewish Anti-Defamation League—a charge to which, not surprisingly, some of those who supported the existing line of the Institute and
its journal strongly objected—but evidently also withdrew his financial
backing, for in 1995 the Institute and the journal were forced to admit
that they were in financial difficulties because of what the journal editors
Mark Weber and Greg Raven called "the massive theft of IHR money by
former associates."[138]

In February 1994 the Institute's staff secured and circulated endorsements of their line from six leading supporters: Robert Faurisson, Ernst
Zündel, Bradley R. Smith, James J. Martin, Arthur J. Butz, and David Irving. Irving's endorsement praised the journal as "sincere, balanced,
objective, and devoid of polemics" and its editors and staff as "staunch

and unflinching soldiers in what our brave comrade Robert Faurisson has called 'this great adventure,' " meaning of course the 'adventure' of Holocaust denial.[139] However, the Institute never really recovered, since it now lacked the financial backing and know-how that Carto and his organization had provided. Its conferences, its journal, and its book-publishing and bookselling operation declined sharply from its heyday in the 1980s.[140] The journal also failed to regain the image of academic respectability it had so vigorously propagated earlier.

Like many individual Holocaust deniers, the Institute as a body denied that it was involved in Holocaust denial. It called this a smear that was "completely at variance with the facts" because 'revisionst scholars' such as Faurisson, Butz, "and bestselling British historian David Irving acknowledge that hundreds of thousands of Jews were killed and otherwise perished during the Second World War as direct and indirect result of the harsh anti-Jewish policies of Germany and its allies." But the concession that a relatively small number of Jews were killed was routinely used by Holocaust deniers to distract attention from the far more important fact of their refusal to admit that the figure ran into millions, and that a large proportion of these victims were systematically murdered by gassing as well as by shooting.

Irving denied that he was affiliated to the Institute in any formal capacity, and this was, strictly speaking, true. He was a member neither of its board nor of the editorial advisory board of its journal. However, his informal connections with the Institute and the journal were extremely close and were maintained over a considerable period of time. He was a frequent visitor to the regular conferences organized by the Institute for Historical Review. He spoke at the ninth, tenth, eleventh, and twelfth conferences in succession. It was hardly surprising that in 1993 the editor of the journal described him as "a good friend of the Institute."[141] There were articles about Irving in the fourth and sixth issues of volume 13 of the journal. Irving printed an advance copy of his introduction to the 1991 edition of *Hitler's War* in the journal, alongside a reassessment of Rommel and a scurrilous attack on Sir Winston Churchill ("almost a pervert—a man who liked to expose himself to people"). The first issue of volume 13 included one article by Irving and two others about him. The next issue had another article by Irving, and he also printed two more articles in the first issue of volume 15. Before he established his website on the Internet, it would not be going too far to describe the journal as the principal forum in which Irving disseminated work shorter than book-length but longer than a newspaper letter or article. This was certainly the case at the time when Lipstadt completed her book in 1993.[142]

Irving gladly continued to lend his support to the efforts of the *Journal of Historical Review* to win more subscribers. A leaflet advertising the journal carried a photograph of Irving and quoted him as follows: *"The Journal of Historical Review* has an astounding record of fearlessly shattering the icons of those vested interests who hate and fear truth. That is why I strongly endorse it . . . and suggest that every intelligent man and woman in America, Britain, and the dominions subscribe."[143] The Institute repaid this service. In the January–February issue of volume 13, a full-page spread was headed: "David Irving: Institute for Historical Review: Your Source for David Irving's Masterworks." After listing and describing five of his books and picturing the cover of each, the advertisement enjoined readers to "Order these fine books from the Institute for Historical Review," and gave the address.[144] Irving had close relations with leading figures at the Institute and included correspondence with them in his Discovery.[145]

In his reply to the defense, Irving maintained that lecturing at the conferences of the Institute for Historical Review did not associate him with Holocaust denial. He claimed that other lecturers had included not just Holocaust deniers but writers not concerned with this field at all, such as the Canadian journalist James Bacque, whom Irving described in 1991 as "a very good friend of mine."[146] James Bacque gained brief notoriety in the late 1980s and early 1990s not for Holocaust denial, in which he had never been involved, but for his book, *Other Losses: An Investigation into the Mass Deaths of German Prisoners of War at the Hands of the French and Americans After World War II*, published in 1979. This publication alleged that the Americans under General Eisenhower deliberately starved to death over a million German prisoners at the end of the Second World War—a thesis which might have made its author an obvious person to invite to a conference of Holocaust deniers, given their need to establish that Allied war crimes were as bad as, or worse than, German war crimes. In fact, the book's claims, which gained some credence on its publication through the appearance of careful archival research, were quickly challenged.[147] Another book by James Bacque claimed that the American occupation authorities deliberately starved to death as many as 9 million German civilians after the end of the Second World War.[148] Whatever Bacque's credibility as a historian, however, the fact was that he never spoke at an Institute conference or contributed to the Institute's journal or associated himself with Holocaust deniers or antisemites in any way. Bacque actually wrote to me after the trial, indignantly saying that he wanted nothing to do with antisemites of this or any other kind. I checked out the lists of conference speakers in the *Journal of Historical Review* and his name did not feature in any of them. The claim that he spoke at one or more of the Institute's conferences was pure invention on Irving's part.

Irving also pointed out that he had had disputes with well-known 'revisionists' like Robert Faurisson, and so by implication was not one of them. It was undoubtedly the case that Irving had his disagreements with Faurisson in particular. This was certainly true when he spoke to the Institute's conference in 1983, before his conversion to hard-core Holocaust denial.[149] By the early 1990s, Irving's and Faurisson's positions had converged, they were agreeing on the essentials, and they were only disputing minor points of disagreement within the Holocaust denial theses.[150] Irving praised Faurisson in 1991 as "a very distinguished intellectual in my mind, a very brave man indeed."[151] Irving made use of an article by Faurisson in the *Journal of Historical Review* in his book on Nuremberg.[152] In 1995 Irving referred to himself as part of this wider movement, "people like myself and the brave band of scientists, and writers, and journalists, and historians who have gradually fallen in. I won't say they've fallen in behind me because I'm not going to try and place myself at the head of this revisionist movement. They've fallen in shoulder-to-shoulder with us and are marching at our side in this extraordinarily interesting adventure."[153] By the middle of the 1990s Irving was talking to members of the Institute for Historical Review in terms of "we revisionists."[154] In all of their work, those associated with the Institute sought to avoid being labeled Holocaust deniers by describing themselves as 'revisionists,' and Irving's appropriation of this label to himself, and his association of his work with theirs, clearly indicated that he regarded himself as one of their number.

Despite all this, not everyone who studied Irving's writings and

speeches in the 1990s reached the conclusion that he had become a consistent and undeviating Holocaust denier. The American journalist Ron
Rosenbaum, interviewing Irving for his book *Explaining Hitler*, published in 1998, concluded that "Irving's stance in relation to Holocaust
denial has seemed to waver confusingly back and forth in the time since
I encountered him." On occasion, wrote Rosenbaum, Irving, for example in his Goebbels biography, "seems to argue that the Holocaust, or at
least mass killings of Jews, *did* happen . . . that there was *some* deliberate killing of Jews, perhaps a hundred thousand or so, but mainly wild-
cat, unauthorized actions in the blood heat of the fighting on the eastern
front."[155] Moreover, in the course of his conversation with Rosenbaum,
Irving admitted of some Holocaust deniers "that there are certain organizations that propagate these theories which are cracked anti-Semites,"
and that he only spoke at their meetings because "I've been denied a platform worldwide. . . . I know these people have done me a lot of damage,
a lot of harm," he confessed, without actually saying who he meant by this
or what kind of damage or harm he was referring to.[156] This was enough
for Norman Stone, sometime professor of modern history at Oxford University and author of a brief popular biography of Hitler, in reviewing
Rosenbaum's book, to conclude that "Irving . . . puts some blue water
between himself and the nutty 'revisionists' who claimed the Holocaust
never happened . . . even Irving is not blind to the facts."

However, Stone could only reach this rather startling conclusion by
overlooking Rosenbaum's statement in the same chapter that "to an ever-
increasing extent, Irving has become a fiery rabble-rousing Führer of the
Holocaust-denial movement." In addition, Rosenbaum made it quite clear
that Irving denied that people were deliberately killed at Auschwitz and
other camps by gassing, and cited his Action Report newsletters "which"
(Rosenbaum commented sarcastically) "seem to cater to his 'temporary'
cracked anti-Semite allies and Holocaust deniers."[157] No "clear blue
water" there, then. And why in any case should Irving have described the
members of the Institute of Historical Review—for to whom else could
he have been referring?—in such unflattering words when, as we have
seen, he had endorsed its work in such ringing terms in 1994? Moreover,
Irving's claim that mass killings of Jews did happen on a moderate scale
hardly put "clear blue water" between himself and the Holocaust deniers

either. His admission that a hundred thousand Jews were killed in largely unco-ordinated acts of war on the Eastern Front did not constitute an admission of the reality of the Holocaust in any meaningful or generally accepted sense of the term.

Some other distinguished experts on Nazi Germany had told me firmly that they did not believe Irving was a Holocaust denier. But when I looked closely at Irving's speeches and writings since the late 1980s, I could not escape the conclusion that he had become a Holocaust denier in 1988. He clearly held all four central beliefs of the deniers as defined at the beginning of this chapter. He argued that the number of Jews deliberately killed by the Nazis was far less than 6 million; it amounted to only a few hundred thousand, and was thus similar to, or less than, the number of German civilians killed in Allied bombing raids, which he portrayed as crimes of a similar or greater order. He argued that gas chambers were not used to kill large numbers of Jews at any time. If Jews did die in large numbers, it was as a result of epidemics for which the Allied bombing raids were in large measure responsible. If there was any wavering by Irving on these points, it was after the publication of Lipstadt's book; even here, however, insofar as it could be observed at all, it appeared to be more a matter of presentation than of content.

Irving continued to assert, as he had already done prior to 1988, that the Nazi state had no concerted policy of exterminating Europe's Jews; all the Nazi leadership, Hitler at its head, wished to do was to deport them to Eastern Europe. He alleged that the Holocaust was a myth invented by Allied propaganda during the war and sustained since then by Jews who wished to use it to gain political and financial support for the state of Israel or even for themselves. The supposed evidence for the Nazis' wartime mass murder of millions of Jews by gassing and other means, he claimed, was fabricated after the war. He referred repeatedly to the 'Holocaust myth' and the 'Holocaust legend' and described himself as engaged in a "refutation of the Holocaust story."

Irving was far from being a lone figure or an original, isolated researcher in this field. He had close contacts with virtually all the major Holocaust deniers, including Faurisson and Butz and the Institute for Historical Review. He was prosecuted for Holocaust denial in Germany and found guilty under German law. There was no doubt that he was a

Holocaust denier. Indeed he himself came close at times to agreeing with the application of this description to himself. "Until 1988," he told an audience in Calgary in 1991, "I believed that there had been something like a Holocaust." But since then, he continued, it had been clear to him that "that story was just a legend." It was not so much the label he rejected as its negative connotations—"Holocaust denier—as though there's something wrong in refusing to accept . . . the whole story."[158]

CHAPTER FIVE

The Bombing of Dresden

I

Reading through Irving's writings and speeches on Hitler, the Jews, and the Holocaust, I had no doubt that they were full of fabrications and distortions of the documents on which they claimed to be based. Some historians, however, had taken the view that these manipulations only affected a tiny part of Irving's work. The rest was solid. It was only when it came to Hitler's involvement in the extermination of the Jews that Irving abandoned his normally sound historical methods. So what of the other topics on which he had written? Irving had made his reputation with a book about the Allied bombing of Dresden in the German province of Saxony. How did it stand up to scrutiny?

The subject was certainly a controversial one. The city of Dresden was subjected to two fierce attacks by British bombers on the night of 13–14 February 1945, followed the next day by two further attacks by American bombers. The city was ill prepared for the attack. Flak batteries had been removed to the Eastern Front, and Dresden citizens had the illusion that their city would escape the fate of other German towns. German defense fighters remained grounded and the first attacking wave had unusually good weather, so that marking the target was achieved without hindrance. Dresden was an important center for administration, communications, and transport. After Berlin and Leipzig it was the largest city behind the Eastern Front, a military installation with garrisons and troops. Its industries were fully integrated into the structure of armaments manufacture.[1] Yet these war industries, although cited as a justification for the raid, were not directly targeted. Instead, the British attacked the maze of timbered buildings which made up the historic heart of Dresden and which were easy to ignite. In proportion to the Allies' declared aim of crippling Dresden as a transportation point, the attack was an act of overkill. Industrial production, although damaged, was not crippled. Even the main railway line remained severed for only four days.

The resulting firestorm blazed in the center of a city clogged with refugees fleeing the approaching Russian army. Fifteen square kilometers of Dresden were destroyed. The death-toll, whatever its final figure, was substantial. This, and the destruction of the historic heart of one of Germany's finest cultural treasures, became the focal point of impassioned postwar debate about the respective crimes of the Allies and the Axis. It proved hard to disentangle the strategic merits or limitations of Allied bombing from the ethical implications. Opinions were divided between those who saw the British bombing campaign as in some way effective and therefore justifiable,[2] and those who condemned it not merely as ineffective but as calculated 'terror.'[3]

The conclusion reached by most historians was that Dresden was bombed in an effort to kill German morale, and damage beyond repair the German people's will to resist the invading Allied armies on the Eastern and Western Fronts. The Soviet advance westward was to be aided by disrupting the German rail network and clogging the transport arteries with refugees.[4] An effort may well have been made to impress and intimidate the Soviet Union with Anglo-American air power.[5] None of this, however, succeeded in arguing away the impassioned moral debate surrounding the events of 13–14 February 1945.

Among the many authors to write on the bombing raids, Irving perhaps attracted the most attention and had the largest popular readership. *The Destruction of Dresden* was probably the most widely read of Irving's books. It went through numerous editions and translations.[6] In Germany the book was preceded by a more general account of the bombing offensive against various German cities, serialized in 1961 in the *Neue Illustrierte*, a glossy magazine, and published in book form as *Und Deutschlands Städte starben nicht* [And Germany's Cities did not Die], in Zurich, 1962 and 1963. I sent out one of my researchers to buy up or locate in libraries all the available English and German editions of the book. The resulting comparisons proved extremely illuminating.

How many people did Irving think had been killed in the raids, and on what evidence did he base his estimates? The first source he used was information supplied to him by Hans Voigt, who had been a local official in Dresden at the time of the raids. Four days after the attack, a missing persons search bureau was set up in the Saxon Ministry of the Interior. Voigt, at the time an assistant school master, was put in charge of establishing a dead persons department for the bureau to collect the records and personal effects of those people already dead, and of those still buried in the ruins. Irving said that it was this department which was "responsible for the identification of the victims and for arriving at some final estimate of the death-roll."[7]

Voigt's office had four different filing systems for different data. The first were garment cards, onto which samples of garments taken from unidentified bodies were pasted, together with date, location, and so on. Voigt told Irving that up to the time of the capitulation "we had almost twelve thousand of these cards completed." The second list was of miscellaneous personal belongings of the unidentified. The third was an alphabetical list of bodies identified by personal papers. The fourth was a list of wedding rings recovered from bodies. With these four indices the dead persons department was "able to clear up the identity of some 40,000 of the dead." Thus Irving arrived at an "absolute minimum" death toll of 40,000.[8] This in turn tallied with the figure of 39,773 given by Georg Feydt, the first person to write a reasonably considered account of the attack, in 1953.[9]

However, Irving did not accept 40,000 as the actual figure because Voigt had told Irving that he himself "estimated that the final number would have been 135,000."[10] In 1963 Irving was reported to have explained: "The Germans simply struck off the first digit to make the figure more acceptable to the Russians, who contended that Bomber Command was not a powerful weapon."[11] In other words, he apparently thought that the Russians wanted to reassure the citizens of the Eastern bloc that Western bombing was not very dangerous. There was no evidence for this supposition. Voigt wrote to Irving as early as September 1962, blaming the amendment on "Dresden officials" (especially the then mayor Walter Weidauer), who "reduced the figure out of fear of the 'Big Four,' so as not to speak ill of them."[12] This did not seem to me to be a particularly strong motive. The Russians were not involved in the bombing of Dresden. At the height of the Cold War, they would have had every incentive for inflating the figure, so as to put the Western Allies in a bad light. Yet Irving repeated the claim in 1995.[13]

There was no corroborative evidence of any kind about the missing digit. Moreover Voigt was apparently not a popular man with the communist authorities in Dresden. Weidauer decried him as a "virulent fascist" who had been rightfully thrown out of East Germany. This was typical of the language the Communists used for people who proved a nuisance to them. Still, Voigt, then living in West Germany, may have had a political motive in accusing the Soviet and East German authorities of falsifying the statistics. Weidauer added that the death register was still extant in the Dresden Town Hall with a highest card number of 31,102 for an unidentified body. In addition there were the so-called street books. The numbers in the street books, which were compiled according to the streets and houses where the dead were found, exactly matched those on the registration cards.[14] Irving could only sustain the figure of 135,000, therefore, by relying on a postwar speculation which he must have known was shaky and was discounted by most other writers on the raid, with good reason. This did not say much for his claim that he based his work on careful research into contemporary documentation. Not long after the first publication of his book, however, Irving discovered a source that seemed not only more plausible, but also gave an even higher estimate than that Voigt had supplied by suggesting the addition of a '1' to the figure in the documents.

Between the English editions of 1963 and 1966 and the German editions of 1965 and 1967, Irving acquired a copy of a document entitled Order of the Day no. 47 [*Der Höhere SS und Polizeiführer, Dresden: Tagesbefehl Nr. 47, Luftangriff auf Dresden,* henceforth TB 47]. TB 47 was dated 22 March 1945 and attributed to a Colonel Grosse. It introduced itself as "a brief extract from the concluding statement of the Police President of Dresden," evidently an earlier document. Irving's copy of the report, besides detailing other physical damage, put the final death-toll at 202,040 and expressed the expectation that the figure would rise to 250,000 by the time all the victims had been recovered. Irving gave the document full prominence in the English edition of 1966 and the German edition of 1967, and reproduced it in both as an appendix. This, then, was the source of his frequently repeated upper estimate of 250,000.

Irving was not in fact the first person to have seen or written about TB 47. Max Seydewitz had photographically reproduced a copy of it and had dismissed it as a forgery as early as 1955. Irving had accepted this.[15] He had in fact cited Seydewitz in 1963 himself, branding the document an ingenious piece of propaganda and as thoroughly spurious.[16] He was familiar with the reasons for Seydewitz's dismissal of the document, therefore, and found them convincing. But now he changed his mind, reporting that he had previously not seen the report himself. Seydewitz had only quoted a few sentences, but on seeing the 'whole' Irving could no longer agree that it was a forgery.[17]

What was Irving's justification for withdrawing his earlier skepticism? He was coy in print about naming his source, referring to him as a "Dresden private citizen" and a "doctor" who had been one of many medical officials and local officers to have received the document through official channels in March 1945.[18] But Irving had been obliged to make available to the defense solicitors all the private correspondence and notes relating to his research, under the rules of Discovery. These documents proved extremely revealing about Irving's research methods. It was not difficult for me to check up on his sources and to establish for a start that the indirect source was indeed a Dresden citizen, Dr. Max Funfack.[19]

In fact, the documents showed that Irving obtained TB 47 from a Dresden photographer, Walter Hahn, who was a friend of Funfack's. Funfack had "confidently" shown Hahn the document and "without Funfack's knowledge, Hahn transcribed the entire document, and made a typewritten copy of it."[20] Irving in turn had visited Hahn on 18 November 1964 and had chanced upon the document on Hahn's desk, whereupon he asked him to copy it. Hahn's wife had begun to type a transcript,

while in the sitting room I, Hahn and [Walter] Lange [Director of the Dresden City Archive] began to discuss the implications of the "200,000" figure. Lange had not realised that it gave this figure, and I at once realised why Hahn had seemed reluctant to show it to me (in fact he had had that probably since 1950 or so, yet he had not shown it to me on any of my previous visits in 1962 and 1963). As soon as Lange began to expostulate on this document being a patent forgery, Hahn became very worried, and when his wife brought in the typed copy, plus four carbon copies, and I took one of the copies, he urgently asked me to give it back to him—but realising that they

> could not very well fight me for it if I was the guest of the Lord Mayor
> I folded it up and put it into my wallet and assured them that I too
> thought it highly unlikely that the figure mentioned was genuine.[21]

Irving's proposal to visit Funfack that day was rejected by Lange and
Hahn, and Irving apparently contented himself with an intention to write
to Funfack on his return to England.[22]

Irving's subsequent correspondence showed that he was extremely
pleased with his find. No sooner had he returned to England than he
wrote to Donald McLachlan of *The Sunday Times* informing him of its
existence: "Having now examined the document minutely myself, I am
satisfied of its authenticity. It remains to be established whether the
'200,000' figure contained is equally genuine."[23] On 28 November he
wrote to his German publisher, Dr. Dieter Struss, that the figure was a
"sensational" piece of information, and suggesting they publish it as an
appendix if a new edition of his book were to appear in German. Now
that he had seen a copy "with my own eyes" he no longer had any doubts
as to the "authenticity of the document."[24] In a letter to the provost of
Coventry Cathedral concerning Irving's suggestion for staging an exhibition of Walter Hahn's photographs of the raid on Dresden, he wrote that
TB 47 should be reproduced "in large type" to "drive home the impact
of the exhibition" because "its nonchalance and the casualties it mentions
have a shattering effect."[25]

The death toll "constantly grows," Irving told *Stern* magazine. "Is that
not very impressive?"[26] Likewise he wrote to his Italian publisher reas-
suring her that if anything the 135,000 figure was too low and asked if she
could insert TB 47 into the next Italian edition.[27] Yet what Irving had
obtained in Dresden was not an authentic original at all. It was merely a
carbon copy of a typed-up transcript of another typed-up transcript of a
handwritten transcript of an extract from an unknown document, unauthenticated by any distinguishing marks such as a signature or an official
stamp of any description. Had it not contained information congenial to
his purposes, Irving would doubtless have had little hesitation in dis-
missing it as inauthentic. But the figures it contained led him to suspend
his much-vaunted critical approach to archival sources altogether.

Nevertheless, of course, Irving needed to back up his conversion to
belief in the document's authenticity by whatever means he could, and

to convince others too that TB 47 was the genuine article. In December 1964 Irving and his German publisher, Sigbert Mohn, set about marketing TB 47 as authentic to the English and West German public. A reader's letter from Irving's publisher, Dr. Dieter Struss, to a West German newspaper on 10 December read:

> Mr. Irving has found a new document a copy of which I enclose to you. The document has been examined and has been established as authentic. The figures originate with the then deputy Chief Medical Officer, Dr. Max Funfack. Therefore the dead of Dresden need in future no longer be guessed. They are precisely counted and they were 202,040 in all. The truth is therefore much worse than one had previously imagined.[28]

On 19 January 1965, after six weeks of frantic marketing, Irving finally received a letter from Max Funfack. The East German doctor wondered in a puzzled tone:

> Why I should now, after twenty years, be put in the spotlight with the mention of my name in the West German papers and be named as a witness to the number of dead is a complete mystery to me. Exactly like every one else affected I have only ever heard the numbers thirdhand: from city commandants with whom I was friends, from the civilian air-raid protection etc. But the numbers always differed greatly. I myself was only once present at a cremation on the Altmarkt, but otherwise completely uninvolved. Likewise I was never Dresden's Chief Medical Officer or even deputy Chief Medical Officer; rather I always worked as a specialist urologist in a hospital. How one comes to such suppositions, is incomprehensible to me. I did not have the slightest to do with rendering any such services. The photos of the cremations on the Altmarkt as well as the "Order of the Day 47" were also given to me by acquaintances. Therefore I can give no firm information about the figure of the dead but only repeat what was reported to me.[29]

Irving's reply to Funfack's letter on 28 February 1965 made it clear that Irving had made no attempt to establish the provenance of Hahn's copy, no attempt to check Funfack's for stamps or signatures if it were an original, and no attempt to confirm Funfack's alleged hand in TB 47 before going to press.

Yet both Irving and his German publisher wrote further letters defending TB 47 in the West German press, Irving in full knowledge that Funfack explicitly denied being the author of TB 47. On 12 February 1965, Dr. Dieter Struss wrote to *Die Welt*, "besides Mr. Irving found the doctor who had calculated the figures and reached the conclusion that the figure of 202,040 dead was not propaganda, but is authentic." Struss then announced his intention of giving TB 47 full prominence in a new edition of the book.[30] In an accompanying letter Irving defended his rejection of Seydewitz's conclusion that TB 47 was a fake and declared: "One learns from this that one should not accept everything one reads in books as facts. Two thirds of an historian's efforts lie not in getting hold of exact facts, but in verifying the authenticity and reliability of his sources and documents [*sic*]." Irving piously rounded off his defense of TB 47 with the words "God knows, I as an Englishman have the least grounds to exaggerate the effects of the air raid on Dresden."[31] Once again, it should be recalled that what Irving had was not an original source at all, but a typed-up transcript at several removes from the original, which he had not seen himself. He had in fact done nothing in the way of verifying the authenticity of the document through tracing its provenance.

In a draft article written in February for the *Sunday Telegraph* propagating the new source, Irving continued to insinuate that Funfack had an official connection with TB 47:

> The document's pedigree is certainly impressive. It came out subsequently that my host [Walter Hahn] had obtained a copy of it some years before from one Doctor Max Funfack, who still lives in and practices in Dresden. <u>Funfack, during the war a senior medical officer (Oberstabsarzt) in the German army, was in 1945 Deputy Chief Medical Officer, Dresden District; as such he was responsible for supervising the disposal and cremation of all the city's air-raid victims during the three months following the attack.</u>
>
> According to Funfack, the report had reached him during the war through the normal official channels.[32]

As late as May 1965 Irving triumphantly sent a copy of TB 47 to the RAF historian Dr. Noble Frankland, informing him that he had obtained it "from the doctor (still in Dresden) who during the war was Deputy

Chief Medical Officer of the city."[33] Funfack had explicitly denied holding any such position and Irving had not obtained the document from him. Evidently nothing was going to stand in the way of Irving's eagerness to capitalize on his new-found belief in TB 47.[34]

Yet a number of factors should have alerted him to the suspicious nature of his find. In early March 1945 an unsparing report on the attack on Dresden had appeared in the Nazi weekly *Das Reich*.[35] This contained what was later described as "a fictitious top-secret estimate that the casualties had probably reached 250,000."[36] This was the original of the version of TB 47 which Irving took from Hahn, an extract made from a longer official report. The figures cited in it made an appearance in Nazi foreign broadcasts in the final weeks of the war. Goebbels leaked it to representatives in Berlin of the press in neutral countries.[37]

As Goebbels' Propaganda Ministry evidently hoped, the figures hit a real vein of revulsion in the neutral press during the final phase of the war, especially in Swiss and Swedish newspapers. They duly dwelt on the extent of the destruction and the apparently immense death toll, and questioned the military sense of the action. Previous to TB 47 the neutral press had merely guessed at how many might have been killed. The *Dagens Nyheter* of 16 February 1945 had reported "several tens of thousands" dead. On 17 February 1945 the *Svenska Morgenbladet* noted that "currently 100,000 dead are talked of."[38] Following the deliberate leaking of TB 47 by Goebbels' Propaganda Ministry, the *Svenska Dagbladet* wrote on 25 February 1945:

> No one knows with certainty how many people lost their lives because thousands of corpses remain buried under the rubble and will long stay there. But according to information compiled a few days after the destruction the figure is closer to 200,000 than 100,000.[39]

The propaganda effect was therefore twofold: to shock the world and to shock the German people. The Allies were portrayed as monsters in a believable way while at the same time the German population was goaded on to futile efforts at final resistance. This also explained how an inflated number so resolutely remained in the minds of the Dresden population and of former Nazi officials for long after the war.

So the original of Irving's transcript of TB 47 achieved its circulation above all through the efforts of Goebbels' Propaganda Ministry. This should have been enough in itself to alert anybody to the fact that it could not be trusted. A number of facts should have warned the commonsense reader, as they did Max Seydewitz, of the likelihood that the document was a clumsy forgery. The document started off: "In order to be able to counter wild rumours, there follows a brief statement from the concluding statement of the Police President of Dresden" and closed: "As the rumours far exceed the reality, open use can be made of the actual figures. The casualties and the damage are grave enough."[40] This was the key sentence. Rumors of 200,000 dead did indeed appear to have circulated at the time. But what kind of figure could have been mentioned in a rumor that the death-toll would "far exceed" the supposed reality of a quarter of a million? For this there was no evidence at all.

Even if the attack on Dresden could be considered the worst of the war, the number of deaths would still have remained in some proportion to the extent of the physical destruction. In raids that had cost Hamburg 3.3 percent of its population, 48 percent of dwellings became uninhabitable; in Kobe the destruction of over 50 percent of its dwellings went with the death of one percent of its population. Even allowing for the unique circumstances of Dresden, a figure of 250,000 dead would have meant that 20 to 30 percent of the population was killed, a figure so grossly out of proportion to other comparable attacks as to have raised the eyebrows of anyone familiar with the statistics of bombing raids, as Irving was, even if the population had been inflated by an influx of refugees fleeing the advance of the Red Army.[41] And how was it imaginable that 200,000 bodies could have been recovered from out of the ruins in less than a month? It would have required a veritable army of people to undertake such work, and hundreds of sorely needed vehicles to transport the bodies. The effort actually undertaken to recover bodies was considerable, but there was no evidence that it reached the levels required to remove this number. Irving claimed that disposing of large numbers of bodies at Auschwitz would have been impossible. Such skepticism vanished entirely, however, when it came to his estimation of the number of corpses to be disposed of in Dresden.

TB 47 gave a figure of 68,650 dead bodies incinerated on the Dresden market square, the *Altmarkt*. This referred to the decision by the

Dresden authorities two weeks after the attack to burn some of the corpses dug from the rubble to avoid the spread of typhus. Common sense should have given Irving pause for thought before swallowing this. After all, it was he who had brought the gruesome photos of the cremations on the *Altmarkt* to light in the first place.[42] He himself had given prominence to the cremations and talked of scores of police helping in the last-ditch attempt to identify the bodies.[43] The *Altmarkt*, which everyone agreed was the only place where bodies were burned, was 100m by 125m square, a marketplace half taken up by a huge water tank clearly visible in photos. It would have taken weeks and an army of men and materials to burn such a vast number of corpses in an area of this size. As Irving pointed out, gallons of gasoline were needed for each pyre at a time when it was sorely needed by the military.[44] None of Irving's sources or anybody else's even hinted at an undertaking of these dimensions. Bewilderingly for the attentive reader, Irving reproduced TB 47, including its figure of 68,650 cremated, in his book, but elsewhere in the same book he put the figure of those burned on the *Altmarkt* at only 9,000.[45]

Finally, and quite basically, I wondered how he explained the incongruity of the 250,000 figure with Voigt's 135,000, on which he also placed considerable weight. At no point in the revised account of 1966 did Irving attempt to reconcile the figures. One or the other of them must have been wrong. Nevertheless, Irving brushed aside these problems in his eagerness to publicize TB 47. When he learned from his original publisher, William Kimber, in May 1965, that Corgi planned to publish the paperback edition of *The Destruction of Dresden*, Irving requested that "one sensational document" be inserted as an appendix.[46] Irving also sent Corgi twenty-one pages of amendments that he wanted inserted into the original Kimber text, many of them concerning TB 47.[47]

II

Irving's correspondence and notes also contained a good deal of information about his attempts to provide plausible support for his championing of TB 47. He claimed to have been able to talk to a number of "wartime police associates" of the report's author, Colonel Grosse, who "have spoken out for its *general* authenticity."[48] However, he never identified any of them in his published work. He wrote to the *Bundesarchiv*, the German Federal Archive, in December 1964 asking them to comment on TB 47 and to help him establish its authenticity.[49] They replied that they could not comment on the authenticity of the document, but supplied Irving with the address of Frau Grosse and five former members of the Dresden police.[50] Thus Irving was able to establish that there had indeed been a Colonel Grosse, but was no closer to vouching for the document's authenticity.

In March 1965 the German illustrated magazine *Stern* conducted investigations into TB 47 (presumably at Irving's suggestion). On 15 March Irving received the results of their researches. Of the five people named in the letter from the Federal Archive, two would seem to have died and one was marked as "away."[51] A reporter had managed to interview Major Ludwig Nölke, one of those people suggested to Irving by the Federal Archive. Nölke was unable to comment on the authenticity of TB 47. He had not seen it at the time as it lay outside his area of competence. However, Nölke was willing to comment on the figures in TB 47 based on his position as the then police commander of Central Dresden: "Based on his experience and memory the figures about buildings in the Order of the Day could be correct, but not the figure of the dead. Nölke considers the figure of 35,000, which was given by the Lord Mayor Weidauer after the war and that the Soviet officials also adopted, as correct."[52] A reporter likewise interviewed Wolfgang Thierig, who had been responsible for air-raid precautions in Dresden.[53] Thierig considered the document authentic, including the number of dead.[54] Irving had no way of knowing it, but Wolfgang Thierig's signature was to turn up a year later on a document which recorded that, as of 10 March 1945 (i.e., twelve days before the issue of TB 47), the police had been able to establish 18,375 persons as 'killed.' In view of this document, it was clear to me that Thierig was lying.

As far as I could see, Irving had contacted only one former official himself. In June 1965 Irving approached Werner Bühlmann, a former army officer in Dresden, again at a later suggestion of Herr Teske of the Federal Archive, asking him if he would care to comment on TB 47.[55] Bühlmann wrote back that he was unable to comment on TB 47 as he had been hospitalized in Bad Elsten from 20 February 1945 until the end of the war.[56] Taken together, these three statements by Nölke, Thierig,

and Bühlmann did not amount to an endorsement of the 'general authenticity' of the document by any stretch of the imagination. But Irving also
interviewed Frau Eva Grosse, the widow of Colonel Grosse. He reproduced his notes of the interview with her on 10 July 1965, as Appendix 5
to the German edition of his Dresden book.[57] Since *Stern* magazine had
contacted her in February on Irving's behalf, Frau Grosse had collected
and sorted all the papers of her husband, and at the time of Irving's visit
was occupied with her son in sifting these papers for reference points to
TB 47's authenticity. His papers consisted of (a) his military identification, driving license, etc.; (b) military assessments of his superior officers
from 1930 to 1943; and (c) Frau Grosse's correspondence with the Allied
authorities to secure her husband's release. This was not very much.
There was certainly no copy of TB 47 in the collection. The only papers
Frau Grosse possessed that could provide any comparison on which to
confirm the authenticity of TB 47 were letters her husband had written
to her during his imprisonment after the war.[58]

Without even the slightest hesitation, Irving solemnly declared in
point 10 of his interview: "There are clear similarities between the style
and expression of the Order of the Day and some of Grosse's letters from
the period May to July 1945."[59] The copy of TB 47 in Irving's possession
was of course a typewritten transcript, so the similarity alleged by Irving
referred to the content of the letters and the report, not to the handwriting. But he provided no evidence whatsoever to show what these
supposed similarities were, beyond the fact that both were presumably
written in German. I thought it unlikely that Frau Grosse's emotional
nourishment during the painful period of uncertainty and separation
from her husband would have consisted of letters written in the style and
expression of a bureaucratic police document such as TB 47. Nevertheless Irving obviously concluded that he had been able to confirm the
authenticity of a report putting the Dresden death-toll at three times that
of the atomic bomb attack on the Japanese city of Hiroshima. Irving's
notes recorded that the interview had lasted from 9.30 P.M. until 10.30
P.M. Allowing for a minimal amount of small talk and perhaps ten minutes' perusal of the documents that Frau Grosse handed him to glean the
background information contained in points 1–9, it looked to me as if this
achievement had been the result of no more than half an hour's work.

Irving also claimed that Frau Grosse confirmed to him that her husband had mentioned the final figure of 250,000 to her. Point 8 read that Frau Grosse "remembers very well how her husband confided in her the daily number of victims found in the weeks after the attack—it grew daily from a figure of 10,000. She remembered his *prediction* that the final figure *would be* a quarter of a million."[60] In the 1966 English edition of his book, Irving wrote that Frau Grosse "confirmed to the author that her husband spoke of the death-toll *as having been* a quarter of a million."[61] In reporting the details of the interview in 1995, Irving again failed to include the word *prediction*.[62] In Irving's hands, the future tense became the past, and a prediction became a report.

I did not think the material Irving had garnered from Frau Grosse was worth very much. What else did Irving have to go on? Funfack had offered to show Irving his copy of TB 47 if Irving obtained permission from the East German authorities. He also suggested a number of people Irving might find it useful to contact:

> Therefore I can give no firm information about the figure of the dead but only repeat what was reported to me. The city commander Herr General Mehnert spoke on about 22 February 1945 of 140,000, Herr Professor Fetscher of the civilian air defence of 180,000. Nevertheless I have never seen written documentation to this effect. I set great store by these facts to tell the truth. The International Red Cross delegation headed by a Swiss man should actually know best. All the figures were put at their disposal when they as commissioners enquired about prisoners of war. Unfortunately I do not know their names, but was briefly with them at a meeting.[63]

Irving duly wrote to the Red Cross asking if they could confirm that a Red Cross official had been shown the official casualty figures at the time, and if so, whether they could they send him the report it might be contained in.[64] The Red Cross replied: "It is correct to say that one of our delegates, Mr. Walter Kleiner, was in the Dresden area during the period you mention, for the purpose of carrying out his duties of visiting camps. We have in fact in our possession the reports he made at the time on prisoner-of-war camps. We have, however, no information concerning the victims of the Dresden air raids."[65] In a second reply to a second letter, presumably inquiring into the exact contents of Kleiner's report, the Red Cross replied, "There were no PoW camps in Dresden itself, consequently Mr. Kleiner's reports did not even allude to the air raids on the town."[66]

In his published account of this correspondence, Irving wrote that Mr. Walter Kleiner, the Swiss leader of an International Red Cross delegation, toured Allied PoW camps in the Dresden area on 22 February 1945 and "was in the presence of witnesses informed by the Dresden city commandant, General Karl Mehnert, that the current death-roll was 140,000."[67] Funfack did not mention Mehnert and the Swiss Red Cross official in the same context; rather he had named himself as the person who had heard Mehnert's figure.[68] I could find no evidence, not even of an indirect nature, that a figure of 140,000 was supplied to the Red Cross. However, this small elision gave the story a ring of authenticity to the unsuspecting reader by associating the figure with the Red Cross, when in fact no such association existed.

In the 1995 edition of his book, Irving wrote: "It is also known that on February 22 a representative of the International Red Cross had visited Dresden to inquire after the fate of the prisoners of war; his report to Geneva may well have contained other information than about the number of prisoners amongst the casualties."[69] But the Red Cross had expressly told Irving that Kleiner's report "did not even allude to the air raids on the town" and Irving's own letter to Kleiner—returned to him marked *not known*—stated that 'they [the Red Cross] have informed me that you made no reference to the air raid in your reports, as of course there was no reason why you should."[70] So I could only conclude that Irving's suggestion about his report was his own invention.

Not much remained of Irving's attempts to provide some plausibility to the figures mentioned in TB 47. All that was left to him in 1995 was a last passing jibe at Funfack:

> Grosse's figures were allegedly provided by Dr med. Max Funfack, described as the deputy surgeon-general of Dresden. Funfack, still living in the Soviet zone, protested at having his name dragged into the newspaper columns of West Germany as a witness for the death-roll figures. He claimed to have learned such figures at third hand only, and never to have been surgeon-general. . . . He will have had good reason in the Soviet zone to express himself thusly. He did not however take the opportunity to repudiate the figures.[71]

This was pure sophistry. Funfack had quite clearly stated he was in no position to comment on the figures. I had no reason to doubt that he was telling the truth, and Irving had no evidence that it was that Funfack was under pressure from the East German authorities that he denied having provided the figure of 250,000. On the contrary, Funfack was surprisingly frank in expressing his personal doubts about the official East German figure of 35,000, even after he had fallen foul of the authorities thanks to the unsolicited exposure Irving had given him in the media.[72]

Irving had no chance to interview Mehnert, who had died in the late 1950s or early 1960s.[73] But he did correspond with Theo Miller, a member of the Dresden Clearing Staff in 1945. In his first letter of February 1965 Miller described his work to Irving (in English) in the following terms:

> At the wall of my bunker [the Staff Quarter in the bunkers under the Brühl'sche Terrasse] I had pinned up a big map of the town. Every evening the commanders of rescue units had to report on the figures of corpses found and on the shelters which had been cleared of deads [*sic*]. The streets and shelters which had been cleared of corpses I marked with red colour in my map. Furthermore, I had to keep book on the figures of deads. In the middle of March, 1945, our task was almost completed. The town was free of corpses. I then received the order to return to my division in Latvia.
>
> Soon after the attack we heard in the radio Joseph Goebbels reporting on the attack on Dresden. He spoke of 300,000 deads. In your book you mention the figure of 135,000 victims. My records at the Clearing Staff showed 30,000 corpses. If you assume the amount of deads completely burnt etc. would reach 20%, the total figure of victims will not exceed 36,000. Still this figure—two full divisions— is terrible enough.[74]

In a second letter of 25 February 1965 Miller added more detail. He first outlined how, in an attempt to prevent double book-keeping, army logistics had confiscated all brandy and cigarette stocks in Dresden and offered SS salvage teams fifteen cigarettes and a half-bottle of brandy if they reported their figures to the army team.

He then went on to describe a conversation with General Mehnert, telling Irving:

One day General Mehnert visited our Staff. I had seen the general the last time in summer 1939 when he had inspected our battalion. In March 1945 he looked like a very old, broken man. He asked me for the figures of deads [*sic*] and I showed him my book-keeping, and the map showing the freed areas. He shook his head and said: "These figures are much too low, I do not believe them, it must be much more, I have seen them." Well, he was an old man and completely desperated [*sic*] like we all, but generally nobody, no police man, no civilian believed my figures. Maybe only the Lord in Heaven knows whether my figures were right or wrong. However, I had figures to count based on the reports of all salvage units and my counterparts only estimated figures. Their figures, so I believe, were an expression of the dantesque pictures of horror they saw everywhere on their ways through the town.

My counting system was very simple. I used a thick book like that of a book-keeper. In this book I wrote down exactly the names of the reporting unit, the name of the reporting officer, the figure of corpses found and the areas of the town, where they had been collected, and the place they had been buried. When I left the Staff on about March 20 with the order to return to my tank-division in Latvia, I handed this book over to another officer. My last figure of deads [*sic*] was about 30,000—this figure I remember well, because after my return to my division I was asked by many of my comrades, who were born in Dresden and did not know anything about their relatives.[75]

Miller added, "P.S. By the way, the figures of deads [*sic*] were reported every day to a Central Air Defence Staff. This authority was in Berlin."[76]

In a postscript typed a day later Miller wrote to Irving with further details:

P.S. I have again to come back to the high figures of victims which I deny as far as they overgo 50,000. It is a fact that all corpses found have either been buried or burnt on the Altmarkt. Now we come to mathematical problems: Do you believe it possible to burn in about three weeks 110,000 corpses on a fire-grate of railway rails with a dimension of about 70 x 10 meters? In fact we started collecting corpses not before February 17 when the town stopped to burn and enough transport media had been brought together from other cities. The burning of corpses started about February 21 (one week after the air raid) and <u>only</u> on the hermetically closed Altmarkt because we feared the reaction of the population. The burning was finished to the best of my knowledge about March 15. When you can find out how long corpses are burning you will believe that a maximum amount of 10,000—rather 7,000—has been burnt. For the transportation of the deads [*sic*] we had only horse-drawn carts and some rickety trucks which run with producer gas due to the lack of diesel oil or gasoline. This poor transport capacity could not transport the gigantic figures of deads [*sic*] overgoing 100,000 which are mostly reported. You must check again this problem as one of logistics. But can anybody really imagine what also 40,000 corpses mean? If you put them down in a line foot by head it is a street of 42 British miles! The inner district of Dresden has only a dimension of 2 times 4 miles! So the streets of Dresden looked to the frightened population like overfloated with corpses, and as a normal human reaction the survivors reported gigantic figures out of their phantasy.[77]

Here was a lucid, sober, and detailed account by a witness who had obviously taken some time and care to recollect his activities following the bombings. Theo Miller's unequivocal conclusion, imparted to Irving early in 1965, was that all estimates exceeding fifty thousand were inherently implausible.

According to his evidence, Miller, like Voigt, had occupied a key position in the attempts to record the death toll. It seemed to me that he was therefore ideally suited to give an estimate, albeit, like Voigt, from memory, of the numbers killed. Miller's figures corresponded roughly to those given by the East Germans, by the engineer Feydt, and to Voigt's reported minimum. I thought the information he provided on Mehnert's state of mind was convincing and needed to be put against Funfack's rather different account. He gave a perfectly plausible explanation of why some eyewitnesses had exaggerated the figures. Moreover he had raised some telling points about the sheer logistics of any death toll put at higher than 50,000. Yet Miller, his testimony, and his criticisms remained unmentioned in Irving's published work. It was all obviously too embarrassing for Irving's championing of a high death toll. TB 47 was too important in this context for Irving to allow it to be questioned.

As if Irving's new evidence were not already threadbare enough, the single most important document to date in helping historians decipher the true Dresden death toll was discovered just as he set about publishing his own 'sensational' source. Following a lecture in Bad Schandau in East Germany in 1965, a Frau Jurk showed Walter Weidauer a document belonging to her father-in-law. It was the Final Report issued by the Dresden police on 15 March 1945.[78] Max Jurk had formerly been with the Dresden police. He had been a colleague of Wolfgang Thierig, the police colonel responsible for the report. The Final Report bore Jurk's dictation initials and was signed by Thierig.[79] This was the very document from which TB 47 claimed to be an extract.[80] It contained exact details of all the material damage the city had sustained. The key passage read: "Until early 10.3.1945 established: 18,375 fallen, 2,212 badly wounded, 13,718 slightly wounded, 350,000 homeless and long-term re-quartered."[81] Unlike the copy of TB 47 obtained by Irving, the Final Report bore both an identifiable signature and was stamped *secret*. It ended with the commentary: "The above report was submitted after agreement on the documents with the district committee of the NSDAP." Weidauer was the first to publish the document in 1966 in a second edition of his book *Inferno Dresden*.

The Dresden City archivist Dr. Walter Lange kindly informed Irving of the existence of this crucial document on 5 April 1966. Irving replied: "As you know I continue to believe in the authenticity of *Tagesbefehl 47* signed by *Oberst* Grosse" based on its stylistic similarity with other documents signed by Grosse.[82] Lange then sent Irving a copy of the new document on 27 May 1966, informing him that he would be interested in hearing his opinion on it.[83] This was the final piece of evidence any self-respecting historian would have required to halt the printing of TB 47 as authentic. Simultaneously, on 13 May, the West German archivist Dr. Boberach drew Irving's attention to the discovery of a document in the Federal Archive in West Germany that confirmed the authenticity of the Final Report.[84] Among the "Situation Reports on Air Raids on Reich Territory" dated between 23 February and 10 April 1945, Situation Report No. 1404 of the Berlin Chief of Police, dated 22 March 1945, had appeared, a document dated the very same day as TB 47. In it the same data were recorded as in the Final Report, including the then current death toll of 18,375, a predicted death toll of 25,000, and a figure of 35,000 missing. As Boberach informed Irving: "These figures are in complete contradiction to the Order of the Day [i.e., TB 47] of the BdO [*Befehlshaber der Ordnungspolizei*] Dresden, likewise dated 22.3. The number of dropped bombs and destroyed buildings mentioned deviate only slightly or not at all from the figures in the Order of the Day."[85] Boberach refrained from pushing the implications of this find further, but it was obvious to me, as it should have been obvious to Irving, that (1) the Final Report was authentic beyond doubt and (2) someone had tampered with the death toll in Irving's version of TB 47.

A further passage in the Final Report drew attention to a possible source of statistical confusion in Voigt's earlier statements to Irving of a minimum figure of 40,000.

> The exact establishment of the number killed will first be possible when the police bureau of missing persons and the registration office establish which people have left Dresden. At the moment some 35,000 missing persons entries have been submitted to the bureau of missing persons and the city authorities.[86]

Apparently Voigt's office had also included information on those registered as missing, although many of them had probably fled Dresden following the attack. The last document to strengthen this substantial chain of evidence was published by Bergander on 13 February 1975. The final wartime document to quote a figure for those who had died in Dresden was Situation Report No. 1414 of the Berlin Chief of Police, dated 3 April 1945. It read: "BdO [*Befehlshaber der Ordnungspolizei*] Dresden. Up to 31.3.45 the number of killed recovered numbers 22,096 persons."[87]

With the appearance of the Final Report and these various supporting documents, it had been conclusively proven that no weight could be given to TB 47 and that it was more likely than ever that it was a forgery. Irving was forced to make a humiliating climb-down. On 16 May 1966 he informed Dr. Boberach that he fully realized the implications of the document of which Boberach had apprised him, and announced his intention to give the facts "fullest prominence" in both England and Germany to counter the "false impression" given by TB 47. Unfortunately, he would have to delay any announcement by about a month on "diplomatic grounds" as the new edition of his book had appeared only fourteen days earlier.[88] A letter, first drafted and discussed on 29 and 30 June, duly appeared in *The Times* on 7 July 1966.[89] Irving brought readers' attention to the new documents, concluding that he had "no interest in promoting or perpetuating false legends."[90] Likewise he wrote to the *Sunday Telegraph* asking them if they would help him "to correct what might otherwise become a dangerous legend."[91] This was too little, too late. Irving had had no grounds for printing TB 47 in the first place. As L. A. Jackets, chief historian to the Air Ministry, commented in a memorandum shortly after Irving's letter to *The Times* had appeared: "It is practically impossible to kill a myth of this kind once it has become widespread and perhaps reprinted in other books all over the world."[92]

Although I could find no evidence that Irving undertook a similar effort in Germany, his correspondence files showed that he wrote to Kimber and to his Italian publishers in August outlining the alterations that needed to be made in light of the Final Report.[93] Likewise Corgi wrote to Irving in September, presumably in reply to a similar request, to say that, as no new edition of his book on Dresden was planned in the foreseeable future, the changes could not be made. In reply to Corgi, Irving wrote that he hoped that Corgi did not think he was pushing them for a new edition, but "otherwise I would lay myself open to charges of having done nothing to bring this to the attention of my various publishers' attention."[94]

Irving's recantation was not as whole-hearted as it might at first glance have seemed. On the very day his letter appeared in *The Times*, Irving recorded his conversation with a journalist from the *Sunday Telegraph* as follows: "I told him that I had lost faith in statistics now, but was still a little suspicious of the new Dresden figure as the man who wrote the report was responsible for civil defence in the city."[95] Likewise in answer to a reader's letter he wrote: "You probably detected the note of reservation I introduced into my letter to *The Times*, because it is unlikely that the Germans could have counted accurately the large numbers of victims in such a short time, and in a catastrophe like that who was there left to register relatives as 'missing' anyway?"[96] This begged an obvious question. If in July 1966 Irving now doubted the police's ability to count 18,375 dead by 10 March, why had he never previously doubted their

ability to count 202,040 dead by 20 March? In reply to another reader
who expressed the opinion that the real figure was nevertheless still much
higher, Irving wrote: "I share your disbelief regarding the authenticity of
the number of losses given by the Dresden police officer."[97] Irving then
turned down a request from his Italian publishers to print his letter to
The Times. "They [the alterations] are not too sweeping because despite
what I wrote to the Times I do not think too much importance can be
attached to the figures given in the new German documents. On the
other hand, they cannot be ignored."[98]

The new German edition of Irving's book appeared in October 1967.
Looking through it, I could see that TB 47 was still given the same prominence as it had been in the Corgi edition of 1966. Irving had not revised
his "most probable" figure of 135,000.[99] Worse still, the requested
changes were not instituted in the Corgi edition of 1971, despite Irving's
prior communication to this publisher of his book about the evidence of
the Final Report. TB 47 was still printed in the 1971 Corgi edition as an
appendix, five years after Irving had described the figure it gave as a 'legend.' All Irving did was to reduce his estimate in the text back to 100,000,
which still ignored entirely the much lower figure given in the Final
Report.

The final stone in the mosaic of real and authentic sources for the
number killed in the bombing raids on Dresden fell into place in 1977,
when TB 47, which had long been strongly suspected as a forgery, was
conclusively proven to be so. A copy of the original document was discovered by Götz Bergander. He had found a reservist, Werner Ehrlich,
who reliably reported that not only had he held the original TB 47 in his
hands, but, as a then member of the Dresden police force, he had also
made one typed and one handwritten copy of it as part of his official
duties. The copy was still in Ehrlich's possession. It started "In order to
be able to counter wild rumours. . . ," and proceeded to list all the details
listed in the version of TB 47 used by Irving—with one crucial difference.
In Ehrlich's copy the actual death figure was put at 20,204, the expected
dead at 25,000, and the number of bodies cremated at 6,865. What had
clearly happened was that someone, probably in Goebbels' Propaganda
Ministry, had crudely doctored the document by simply adding a zero to
the end of each number it contained. What Irving had claimed as authentic documentary evidence was a blatant forgery.[100] In neither England

nor Germany had Irving made much of an effort to revise his book in the light of the mounting documentation. He had ignored new evidence that not merely contradicted, but invalidated, his findings. It was not until 1977 in Germany that Irving finally described TB 47 as a Nazi fake, as Seydewitz had argued all along and he himself had originally accepted. Yet he still reprinted it as an appendix, and published the Final Report alongside it.[101]

It was not until 1995 that Irving was at last willing to come clean with his English-language readers and make Seydewitz's explanation his own again, namely that TB 47 was in fact a product of the Propaganda Ministry's "machinations."[102] Without expanding on the information given by Weidauer, Irving wrote imperiously to the Dresden City Museum:

> We have recently re-published my work about the massive Allied attack on Dresden, which will be well known to you. . . . In this volume . . . I have revised the number of losses, and independently from the research named by you, I come also to the conclusion that the so-called *Tagesbefehl 47* is a forgery of the Ministry of Propaganda.[103]

How or on what grounds Irving's conclusions were arrived at "independently" he did not make clear. In fact, of course, this was pure bluster, and there was nothing independent about his change of mind at all. The truth seemed to be in fact that he finally felt unable to persist with his allegiance to TB 47 in the light of the overwhelming weight of evidence, dating back twenty years, indicating that it was a forgery.

III

Despite having been finally forced to disown TB 47, Irving continued subsequently to keep the legend of a higher death toll alive. In 1985 Irving wrote to a Munich newspaper, the *Süddeutsche Zeitung*, claiming that the police chief responsible for the Final Report had the "most reason to minimise the losses," because he was the person charged with air-raid protection. Irving was implying therefore that the figure of 18,375 given in the Final Report was a politically motivated underestimate.[104] Yet Irving was quite happy in other places to accept the authenticity of police statistics on air-raid losses. As he himself commented with regard to the October 1943 attack on Kassel, the Germans "kept records of all air raid losses with meticulous care—even those on livestock."[105] He wrote this in the 1995 edition of the Dresden book about the September 1944 raid on Darmstadt: "Once again the police chief's post-raid report provides the best documentary description of the attack."[106] Irving, indeed, quoted the Final Report no less than eighteen times in 1995. Why therefore should it be unreliable? Moreover TB 47 itself had also been signed by the police chief for Dresden. Yet for a long time Irving had accepted the figure of 202,040 to 250,000 given in the forged version of the document as entirely plausible. Here was yet another example of the double standards that Irving applied in the evaluation of evidence that suited his case, and evidence that did not.

Although the existence of the Final Report, he wrote in 1995, "must inevitably cast doubt" on higher estimates, the report was by nature interim, concluded a mere three weeks after the attack.[107] I could not help wondering why, if Irving once again doubted the police's ability to count the dead by 10 March, he had never previously doubted their ability to count 202,040 dead by 20 March. Yet, Irving went on, the city had been overcrowded, it had had no shelters and no defenses worth talking of, and there was no expectation of raids on such a large scale: "The key element is probably, over and above the identified death-toll, the vast number of missing people which even the Dresden Police Chief put at thirty-five thousand."[108] The night Dresden was hit it was, according to Irving, "swollen to twice its peace-time population by the [massive] influx of refugees from the East, Allied and Russian prisoners of war, and thousands of forced labourers."[109] Dresden had had a "permanent" population of 650,000 and "hundreds of thousands of refugees." In the 1995 edition these had become "one or two million refugees."[110] It seemed obvious to me in the light of the increase which they underwent between the 1966 and 1995 editions of his book that these figures were entirely arbitrary. At no point did Irving give a source for any of them. They were figments of his own imagination.

Establishing just how many refugees there were in the city at the time of the raids was obviously not a simple task. Dresden was undoubtedly hit in the early part of 1945 by a wave of refugees fleeing westward from the advancing Red Army. The literature on the raids by Bergander and others made it clear that schools and pubs, cinemas on the Prager Strasse, and even the palace in the *Grosse Garten* were given over to accommodating refugees. None of the refugees was meant to stay longer than three days, and all available manpower was committed to keeping the trains and carts flowing through Dresden. Undoubtedly some became stationary in Dresden, but one or two million? How were so many refugees accommodated? According to Irving, they were not. "These endless, well organised refugee 'treks,' each with its own designated 'Führer,' had been directed one after another to the designated reception areas—like the *Grosse Garten*."[111] In other words, they slept under the open skies.

In the Corgi edition of 1966, Irving claimed that the Dresden City authorities had issued a total of 1,250,000 ration cards to the city's population by the time of the raids.[112] Here would be official documentary proof of the number of people in Dresden at the time of the attack. The source given by Irving simply read: "Ration statistics were provided by Mr. Howard Gee who was given them during a visit to Dresden in June 1963."[113] Who Mr. Gee was remained entirely unclear. Without knowing who he was, or where he got his information from, this apparent 'fact' remained nothing more than hearsay. Irving saw fit to allow the 'fact' to disappear from the 1995 edition.[114] Why? Because in the meantime the truth about the 1,250,000 ration cards he claimed had been issued to the Dresden population had now become clear to him. Far from being genuine, many if not most of them had been produced by the Allies in order to confuse the population and hamper the local Nazi administration. In 1995, and in the 1985 German edition of his Dresden book, Irving admitted he had made a mistake on this point in 1966, and conceded that to add to the long-term dislocation the RAF dropped "millions of fake ration cards." He quoted the Final Report of March 1945, which recorded that such cards had been dropped "in large masses."[115] Yet this openly admitted mistake did not prevent Irving from continuing to claim that Dresden had been packed with immense numbers of refugees in early February 1945, swelling the city's population to two or three times its normal size.

As early as 1953, the Dresden civil defense engineer Georg Feydt had struggled to defeat the myth of the city saturated with refugees. He wrote: "I cannot imagine a more peaceful and calm picture than Dresden on the afternoon of 13 February 1945."[116] Götz Bergander likewise confirmed from his own memory that at no point did Dresden become crammed with refugees. He himself had been called on to help place refugees in accommodation, and apart from those stragglers around the station and the influxes that came with each train, he remembered most being somehow quartered.[117] Scarcely any, in other words, had been sleeping in the open. Bergander then proceeded to calculate the number of refugees in Dresden on 13–14 February 1945 on the basis of what source material he could find: 9,000 had been temporarily lodged in the stations (through which the majority came), 6,000 had been trekking with carts spread out over the whole of Dresden, and 85,000 had been staying in emergency accommodation. Somewhat boldly, Bergander doubled the number to include all those who might have somehow found their own lodgings that night. This made a round total of 200,000. Bergander admitted that this was also a guess, but at least a sensible one arrived at through due process. It was more likely to have been a maximum than a minimum. To have accommodated any more refugees would have required one of two measures: either forced billeting in private homes on a massive scale, or huge temporary camps. Neither of these two measures was in fact undertaken.[118]

The Dresden historian Friedrich Reichert went one step further. He quoted witnesses who attested that no refugees were billeted in Dresden houses and that no billeting took place in the parks or squares. He then pointed out that the Dresden population was not at its prewar level because of the numbers of men away on active service. Not 630,000, but 567,000 were resident in the city at the time. To that he added 100,000 refugees.[119] This was already a very considerable number in view of the city's overall population; but nowhere near the one or 2 million suggested by Irving in 1995. And it meant that the number of people in Dresden on the night of the raids was not much greater than the number given in the official figure of the city's population anyway.

How many of these refugees were likely to have been killed? The total figure of just over 18,000 dead given by the Final Report of course included refugees as well as local citizens. Irving implied that many thousands of those killed had officially only been listed as missing and so had been excluded from the official death toll.[120] The Final Report put the missing figure known to the register of missing persons and the city administration at 35,000, but 10,000 of those missing were later found to be alive.[121] Given the chaotic situation of the final weeks of Hitler's Germany, with millions of refugees streaming through Europe, many more might have escaped official attention. Irving quoted a refugee from Dresden as saying: "None of the neighbouring towns could send help [after the attack] because all the approaches to Dresden were crowded with refugee columns, peasant carts, pushcarts and army vehicles."[122] Thus even on Irving's own evidence, the missing must have included many thousands who had left the city immediately after the raids were over. Even if a considerable number of those registered as missing had in fact been killed in the raids, it was still clear to me that they would have added no more than a few thousand to the overall death toll, not the numbers needed by Irving to make up the shortfall between the Final Report figure of 18,000 and his own estimate of 100,000 or even 250,000.

Conclusive evidence was supplied by burial figures. According to Irving, "history relates that the last mortal remains of 28,746 of the air raids' victims found their last resting place on the Heidefriedhof cemetery."[123] The figure of 28,746 in the Heidefriedhof came from the cemetery's head gardener Zeppenfeld, who was quoted by Seydewitz as having given this total from the head-count of those buried and the ashes of 9,000 bodies burned on the *Altmarkt*.[124] In fact, a rather smaller total of 6,865 corpses were burned on the *Altmarkt* (the forged TB 47 had turned this into an implausible 68,650 by adding a zero). Weidauer quoted the director of the Johannisfriedhof cemetery as reporting that 3,660 victims of the attack had also been buried there.[125] In 1993, new official material was found from the Dresden burial offices confirming the exact number of those buried.[126] Quite contrary to Irving's image of chaotic and botched mass burials,[127] this material made it clear that the counting of the dead was conscientiously carried out, with the figures being reported regularly to the city administration. Exactly 17,295 bodies had been buried in the Heidefriedhof cemetery, including the ashes of the 6,865 people burned on the *Altmarkt*. In addition to 3,462 burials in the Johannisfriedhof cemetery, 514 were buried in the Neue Annenfriedhof cemetery. This gave a total of 21,271 registered burials.[128] Head gardener Zeppenfeld's figure of 28,746 thus overestimated the true number by more than 7,000, unsurprising perhaps, given the fact that, despite its apparent precision, it lacked any written authentication and was arrived at only in a rough and ready way. The official figures were far more likely to be closer to the truth.

Another possible point of statistical confusion, according to Irving, lay in the fact that many people had searched for missing relatives to "spare them the indignity of mass burial in a common grave" or even resorted to digging up their next-of-kin already buried in mass graves.[129] There were indeed witnesses quoted elsewhere as rescuing bodies from the rubble themselves. But it seemed highly unlikely to me that people had broken open sealed mass graves in the hope of finding their relatives among the number buried there. Moreover, this in no way precluded the victims from appearing on one of the official lists. On the contrary, people who had by then identified their relatives would have been bound to have reported their death to the authorities. Or did Irving think that thousands had been secretly buried in unconsecrated grounds and their deaths for some strange reason kept secret from the authorities? Reichert added that the burials in the smaller graveyards were scrupulously recorded and did not exceed 2,000.[130] The total number of burials, therefore, approximated to the total figure of deaths in the raid already known from other sources such as the Final Report, namely, 21,000 compared to 18,000.

Irving's last refuge was to claim that too much of Dresden remained unexcavated to say how many bodies might still be buried there.[131] Some corpses, of course, were buried beneath the rubble and were not discovered until later. Weidauer, who as sometime mayor of the city was in a position to know, pointed out that between 8 May 1945 and 1966, exactly 1,858 bodies had been dug from the ruins of Dresden. Only in four instances had it been impossible to establish the number of victims in one place. The total for the four could not have been higher than a hundred.[132] He likewise made it clear that by all accounts the majority of victims had died through suffocation and that only in a small number of cases were bodies so mutilated or burned that the exact number could not be ascertained. Reichert quoted a slightly smaller figure for between October 1945 and late 1957 of 1,557 bodies.[133] Yet, although he must have been aware of Weidauer's figures, Irving still wrote in 1995 of an immediate postwar Dresden "where *thousands* of victims were still being recovered *each week* from the ruins."[134] He himself, however, had written in 1963 that "most of the bomb sites in Dresden's Inner City have been cleared anyway."[135] Reichert added in 1994 that not a single body had been found

since 1990, despite heavy building and despite archaeological excavations
on the *Altmarkt* and around the Taschenberg Palace.[136]

Thus all of Irving's attempts to justify a high figure rested on fantasy,
invention, speculation, the suppression of reliable evidence, the use of
unreliable sources, or, most shockingly, the repeated deployment of a
document that he knew to be a forgery. An honest historian would have
taken due consideration of the convergence of the major authentic
sources around estimates in the area of 25,000 dead. When Reichert
added the three sums together cited above he came to the inescapable
conclusion that the final number of deaths for the raids of 13–14 February and 17 April was 25,000, corresponding to the real TB 47's prediction
of the same number, and all of it based on documentary evidence, not the
kind of hearsay, third-hand reports, and unauthenticated copies of forged
documents, on which Irving relied.

Irving's book on Dresden was published right at the beginning of his
career. Reflecting on the distortions that it contained, I found it striking
that Irving had massaged up the death toll from the Allied bombing raids
in Dresden long before he began to argue that Hitler had been a friend
of the Jews, and more than two decades before he started to deny the existence of the gas chambers. Even as a young writer Irving seemed to have
used his manipulations of the evidence on the bombing of Dresden to
peddle what was then relatively 'soft' form of revisionism. Irving variously
claimed that his interest in Dresden was first awakened either by reading
an article in the German magazine *Stern* in March 1960 or by conversing
with fellow-workers while employed at a steel mill in Mülheim. In April
1961 he placed advertisements in British and American newspapers to
trace the surviving air personnel. William Kimber was one of the people
to answer his advertisement and subsequently became his publisher.[137]

That Kimber's relationship with Irving was an uneasy one was borne
out by the correspondence between the two that I was able to consult
thanks to the Discovery rules. Kimber wrote to Irving on 3 April 1963,
after his legal advisers had suggested he check the proofs for "certain
allegedly historical statements." Once they had started, wrote Kimber,

> it became abundantly clear that the first proofs were riddled with
> falsifications of the historical facts. The picture painted by these

falsifications led to the inescapable conclusion that your book could
be interpreted as the work of a propagandist for Nazism who had
not scrupled to distort many facts and omit numerous others in
order to vilify the British War Government and in particular Winston Churchill. . . . I have no doubt that it was a scoop for the Germans to find an Englishman prepared to concoct a mixture of
fact and fiction which would vindicate or extenuate Nazi actions
(because of course there is an extensive movement trying to achieve
this aim in Germany and elsewhere) and at the same time to deni-
grate English leaders.[138]

Irving stiffly denied this and argued that in Germany he had been
accused of being a lackey of British Air Command.[139]

According to Irving, Kimber then instituted a number of textual
changes against his wishes. He altered chapter headings, softened criticism
of Churchill and the head of RAF Bomber Command, Arthur Harris, and
erased the more "harrowing" details of the attack; all testimony to Kimber's
"sincerely held belief that, after all, perhaps the Germans had merely been
repaid, with interest in their own coin."[140] Although Irving told his readers
in 1995 that it was "several years before I noticed these little modifications,"
there was documentary evidence to the contrary. In the same letter of April
1963, Kimber had written to Irving informing him that after "intensive
work" by the office staff checking and changing the proofs, "we now believe
the book to be cleansed of its somewhat evil undercurrents." Later in April
Irving had berated Kimber for changing some of the historical sections in
the book.[141] So he had known about them right away.

Irving wrote to Kimber in 1963 declaring his view that the crime of
World War II had not been genocide but "innocentocide," the killing of
civilians, and that therefore the Eastern and Western powers were just
as guilty in his eyes as the Germans and the Japanese. For him Dresden
was a crime.[142] Nowhere in the earlier editions was there an *explicit* effort
to draw the parallel. Instead, Irving allowed others to draw this obvious
conclusion and then somewhat disingenuously congratulated them on
their independence of mind. Thus he wrote to Sydney Silverman MP,
who had reviewed the book in *Tribune*: "I am not someone who holds
political views similar to your own, but I really must congratulate you—
in spite of this—for having stuck your neck out so firmly and unmistak-

ably by drawing a parallel between the Nazis' atrocities and what happened in Dresden; this is something I myself did not claim in my book."[143]

Three decades later, Irving was making the parallel explicit. In a speech delivered in Toronto on 8 November 1992, he estimated the numbers who died in Auschwitz ("most of them from epidemics," he said) as 100,000. "Around one hundred thousand dead in that brutal slave labour camp." Around 25,000 of these had been killed by shooting or hanging, according to German radio reports from Auschwitz received and decrypted by the British, he added. He continued:

> Twenty-five thousand killed, if we take this grossly inflated figure to be on the safe side: That is a *crime*; there is no doubt. Killing twenty-five thousand in four years—1941, 1942, 1943, and 1944—that is a *crime*; there is no doubt. Let me show you a picture of twenty-five thousand people being killed in twenty-five *minutes*. Here it is, in my book, a vivid picture of twenty-five thousand people being killed in twenty-five minutes by the British (in February 1945) in Pforzheim, a little town where they make jewellery and watches in Baden, Germany. Twenty-five thousand people were being burned alive. . . . That is what it looks like when twenty-five thousand civilians are being burned alive in twenty-five minutes. One person in four, in twenty-five minutes. One person in four in that town. As I said when I was speaking in Kitchener yesterday, it is as though somebody came to Kitchener, a town of about a hundred thousand people, and killed one person in four in twenty-five minutes. That too is a crime. Twenty-five minutes! In Auschwitz it was a crime committed over four years. You don't get it spelled out to you like that. Except by us, their opponents. When you put things into *perspective* like that, of course, it diminishes their Holocaust—that word with a capital letter.[144]

Irving's almost incantatory repetition of the figures "twenty-five thousand" and "twenty-five minutes," mentioned in this passage respectively four times and five times, compared with his figure of twenty-five thousand for Auschwitz mentioned only twice, left no room for doubt about which crime he considered the greater.

In fact, quite apart from the fraudulent minimization of the

Auschwitz figures, Irving's equivalence did not stand up to examination because of his wild exaggeration of the number of deaths caused by the Pforzheim raid, which was estimated in a report of the Statistical Office of the City of Pforzheim in 1954 not as 25,000, as Irving claimed, but as 17,600.[145] And the bombing of Dresden, however indefensible it might have been in moral terms, was never legally condemned as a crime against international law. Irving's efforts to boost the numbers killed in the Dresden bombing raids seemed designed from the very beginning to establish a moral equivalence with the Nazi killing of the Jews.

By the 1990s this position had hardened, as Irving had come to propagate a far lower number of Jews killed than he had accepted two decades before. When it suited, him, he still repeated the 'innocenticide' refrain. In answer to the rhetorical question, put to him in 1995, if there was a parallel between Dresden and Auschwitz Irving replied: "To my mind both teach one lesson: that the real crime of war and peace alike is not Genocide—with its implicit requirement that posterity reserve its sympathy and condolences for a chosen race—but Innocenticide. It was not the Jewishness of the victims that made Auschwitz a crime; but their innocence."[146] There was of course no implication in the concept of genocide that posterity should reserve its sympathy and condolences for a 'chosen race'—this was purely Irving's invention, for the concept of genocide had been applied to many other victims of genocide besides the Jews.

While Irving always maintained a more balanced tone in his books, in his public speaking his opinions became increasingly strident. Despite his frequent rhetoric against the propagating of other myths in history, especially the 'myth' of the Holocaust, and despite his earlier pronouncements to the contrary, Irving seemed to me to be proud of his own role in keeping alive what he himself had described at one point as the legend of a Dresden death toll many times higher than the official estimates.[147] During a speech in South Africa in 1986 he told his audience:

> I realised that I was being told [about Dresden] of what we would now call a Holocaust I suppose, of which we English at that time, 1961, knew absolutely nothing at all. Of course now everybody talks about Dresden in the same breath as they talk about Auschwitz and

Hiroshima. That's my achievement ladies and gentlemen. I'm a little bit proud when I look at the newspapers every 13th or 14th of February, when the anniversary comes and they mention Dresden, because until my book was published on that subject the outside world had never heard of what happened in Dresden when 100,000 people were killed in one night by an RAF and American air force air raid on one undefended German town at the end of the war.[148]

It was more than coincidence that Irving, his mind perhaps constrained by a convenient symmetry, stubbornly maintained a false figure of 100,000 deaths in Dresden in the face of all evidence to the contrary, while at the same time he manipulated his figure of deaths at Auschwitz down to a similar number.

In a television documentary screened on 28 November 1991 Irving made the comparison explicit in the following interchange:

INTERVIEWER: So what's the point in quibbling about the exact number of Jews that were killed by Hitler?

IRVING: Exact numbers are important. Look at Auschwitz. About 100,000 people died in Auschwitz. Most of them died of epidemics, as we now know, from code breaking. So even if we're generous and say one quarter of them, 25,000, were killed by hanging or shooting. 25,000 is a crime, that's true. 25,000 innocent people executed by one means or another. But we killed that many people burning them alive in one night, not in three years, in a city like Pforzheim. We killed five times that number in Dresden in one night.

INTERVIEWER: So we're as bad as that?

IRVING: I've pleaded for equality in the writing of history. Not just truth but also equality.

INTERVIEWER: So lining up Jews in pits and machine gunning them was as bad as bombing Dresden?

IRVING: I see very little difference.[149]

What he really meant, it seemed to me, was that bombing Dresden was as bad as killing Jews.

Following his conversion to Holocaust denial toward the end of the 1980s, Irving's utterances connecting Dresden and Auschwitz became increasingly bizarre. Launching the Leuchter Report in 1989, he told journalists:

> Obviously if the gas chamber now turns out to have been phoney then we have to try and explain what happened to the figures. Now, one possible reason is the large number that turned up in the state of Palestine, what's now the state of Israel. The Jews that were in Israel didn't come from nowhere. Another part of them, when Auschwitz was liberated were set out on the roads to be shipped westward where they ended up in cities like Dresden. I don't have to tell you what happened in Dresden three weeks after Auschwitz was evacuated by the Germans. There were one million refugees in the streets of Dresden at the time that we burned Dresden to the ground, killing anything between 100,000 and 250,000 of them. Large numbers of people on the streets in Europe that winter also suffered normal deaths of exposure and starvation epidemic. I'm offering to you alternative solutions to where the people went.[150]

Irving repeated this explanation in a 1993 promotional video intended for viewing in Australia, where he had been refused an entry visa:

> Many concentration camps as the Russians approached were evac-uated and set out on the long cold march through the European win-ter of December 44, January 1945 to the West. The concentration camp inmates arrived in Berlin or in Leipzig or in Dresden just in time for the RAF bombers to set fire to those cities. In Dresden a million-and-a-half people camping out in the streets on the night of February 13, 1945. Nobody knows who they were. Refugees, con-centration camp prisoners, citizens of Dresden itself. After the bombers retired, 45 minutes later another wave came, and then at noon on February 14 the American air force joined in. Over 130,000 people died in that particular air raid. The same kind of raids took place on Leipzig, Berlin, Cottbus: refugee centres up and down the centre of Germany. Nobody knows how many Jews died in those air raids, nobody knows how many Jews died on the roads of hunger or starvation or just sheer cold.[151]

This attempt to bring together the raids and the marches was speculation, unsupported by any contemporary documentary evidence.

In fact, the 'death marches' took place in the closing months of the war as the Nazi authorities cleared concentration camps and ghettos in the East in the face of the victorious Red Army. Between 17 and 23 January 1945, some 60,000 prisoners of Auschwitz were evacuated, mainly on foot. Many of them died of cold, physical exhaustion, thirst, and hunger, or were beaten or shot to death on their way to other concentration camps within the Reich. There was no evidence that any of those prisoners forcibly evacuated from Auschwitz passed through Dresden, nor those marched out of other camps either. It was not credible that the deporting authorities would have quartered thousands of starving and emaciated Jews in the historic heart of Dresden. The suggestion that the Allies were somehow responsible for killing Auschwitz prisoners in Dresden in what were their last agonizing weeks of suffering was completely fantastic. It sprang full-grown from Irving's own fantasy and had absolutely no basis in any kind of documented fact.

In ways such as this, Irving played a pivotal role in keeping the myths of the Dresden attack persistent in the public mind. This involved deliberately falsifying statistics, misrepresenting testimony, attributing false conclusions to reliable sources, using evidence that he knew to be unreliable or forged, and bending reliable sources to fit his argument in order to arrive at conclusions that were historically untenable—precisely the kind of historical falsification itemized by Lipstadt in her book. Irving's estimation of the purposes and biases of those compiling historical sources varied not according to the sources themselves or their authors, but according to the extent to which he found them useful in his attempt to maximize the numbers killed.

It was clear to me that Irving's overriding purpose was to drive up the figure of those killed in the raids by any means until it became many times greater than the actual number, and began to achieve implicit and in the end explicit comparability with the mass murders carried out by the Nazis at Auschwitz and elsewhere. In the light of his consistent and deliberate falsification of the historical evidence to this end, and the amount of time and energy he spent on these manipulations, I thought it somewhat hypocritical of him to put the rhetorical question to the *Süddeutsche Zeitung,* a reputable Munich newspaper, in 1985: "Is the question of the number of deaths really of consequence?"[152] and to say to *The Times* that "It is odious to debate whether we killed 200,000 or 'only' 35,000 that night."[153] In 1991, after all, Irving was once again to insist that "exact numbers are important."

Few historians defended the Allied bombing raids on Dresden on 13–14 February 1945 without equivocation; certainly it had always seemed to me that they were extremely hard to justify, to put it no more strongly than that. The war was virtually won anyway, and it was extremely doubtful whether the raids saved more lives in terms of Allied and other troop losses than they cost in terms of civilian deaths. I could see no evidence that they weakened the German war effort in the final months of the conflict, or damaged the German will to fight to the end. Nor could I underestimate the terrible cost they wrought in terms of human life and suffering, or to ignore the wanton destruction of some of Europe's most beautiful and significant buildings, whose reconstruction was still not complete when I visited them in the late 1980s and saw some of the damage for myself.

But the way to reach a reasoned judgment on these events was not to falsify the evidence, which was already horrifying enough: all that did was to obscure the real issues. Irving's manipulations and exaggerations merely got in the way of a proper discussion of these events, rather than assisting it, since dealing with his falsifications took up time and effort that would have been better spent on researching other aspects of the bombings. Although his distortions of the truth had long since been exposed, Irving persisted for decades in presenting them to his readers as an accurate depiction of the historical record. Perhaps the best way of dealing with his version of the destruction of Dresden was found in 1985 by his German publishers, who appended to the title page of his book the description, "a novel."

CHAPTER SIX

In the Witness Box

I

Such were the results of my investigations into Irving's way with historical documents, a task that took all of 1998 and much of 1999 to carry out. This was only part of a wider effort put into the preparation of the case by the defense solicitors, the experts, and their researchers. While the experts and their researchers got the reports ready, the solicitors were compiling dossiers containing copies of all the documents listed in the two sides' Discovery and referred to in the experts' reports. That meant, for example, that everything I referred to in the footnotes to my own report had to be copied and placed in the courtroom for consultation during the trial if necessary. A whole team of paralegal assistants was deployed on this mammoth task. The resulting mass of paper was neatly stored in several hundred red-backed lever-arched files, quaintly referred to in legal terminology as 'bundles,' as if they were still made of parchment and tied up with red tape.

Affidavits were drawn up for the various interim actions before the Master of the Queen's Bench requiring Irving to disclose yet more documents from his vast private collection, and various assistants were engaged in reading through these, copying them, scouring Irving's diaries and letters for any evidence of racism, antisemitism, or contacts with far-right extremists, viewing many hours of videotapes of his speeches, and listening to one audiocassette after another of Irving talking to audiences of like-minded people in obscure meeting-halls in various parts of the world. Deborah Lipstadt flew over frequently to keep an eye on how things were going, and cheered everybody on from the sidelines, but obviously could play no part in the compilation of the expert reports.

By the summer of 1999, the experts' reports were complete, and in July and August they were handed in to the court and passed on to the Plaintiff. Taken together, the reports ran to over two thousand pages. Clearly, Irving had a lot of reading to do. By getting everything as far as possible out into the open beforehand, the rules governing pre-trial proceedings tried to ensure that there were no unnecessary delays in the trial itself. Still, when the public hearing actually began in Court 37 in the huge, rambling Victorian High Court building on London's Strand on 11 January 2000, it was scheduled to last for a full three months, and many suspected it might go on for a good deal longer. How would Irving deal with the defense's case? Was the High Court the right kind of place to settle the issues involved? Many had serious reservations, which increased among the reporters who crowded into the press gallery as the trial got under way. David Robson, one of the most perceptive observers of the trial, confessed himself all at sea. "The libel court is somewhere to fight battles," he wrote, "score points and collect damages. But for seekers of light, understanding and historical truth, it is very often not the place to look." David Cesarani argued that "evidence in history is not like evidence in court. . . . In a court of law, context and circumstance are the least important evidence; they may be deemed inadmissible, not real evidence. The court wants physical evidence, a fingerprint that no one can argue with, but in history context and circumstance matter a great deal."[1] A law court was "the worst possible place" to conduct "historical disputes about Auschwitz," agreed Geoffrey Wheatcroft.[2]

Neal Ascherson also had doubts. All too often, the issues, he thought, got drowned in a mass of confusing detail, and history was reduced to a kind of "toxic sludge." In a trial such as this, "fragments of history are snatched out of context, dried, treated and used as firelighters to scorch an adversary." The fact was that "for establishing what really happened in history, an English libel court is the worst place in the world." What went on had something to do with truth, to be sure; but it had far more to do with the personalities of those involved, their motives, and their ability to withstand the strain of cross-examination. The tale of the Holocaust was "neither entirely simple nor entirely known." Ascherson seemed to think it unlikely that the trial would add very much to the tale or do very much to fill in the gaps.[3]

Daniel Jonah Goldhagen, Harvard-based author of a controversial book arguing that virtually all Germans were "Hitler's willing executioners" because they were rabidly, murderously antisemitic and had been for many decades before the coming of the Third Reich, thought the trial absurd because the Holocaust was "an established historical fact." "The ruling of a court," he declared, "has no bearing on historical fact: the court is a place where legal issues are adjudicated according to the particular legal standards of a given country, not where historical issues are decided according to the different and well-established standards of historical scholarship."[4] Even one of the expert witnesses, Peter Longerich, found the experience of working with the court in matters of history somewhat alien, noting that the court demanded "a painfully exact presentation of evidence, beyond any reasonably provable doubt, going beyond the standards customary in the Humanities."[5]

The philosopher A. C. Grayling reminded readers of *The Guardian* that the Irving case showed the importance of arguments about whether historians were engaged in creating present narratives of a past that was irretrievably lost, or in constructing an accurate picture of what happened by the discovery of verifiable facts.[6] He cautiously refrained from coming down on either side, however. That was left to modish relativists like Anne Sebba, writing in the *Times Higher Education Supplement* shortly before the trial began. She asked rhetorically:

> What chance is there that legitimate issues about interpretations of the Holocaust will be adequately aired in a court of law? The grave danger of this costly case is that grave issues that are being aired in the current spate of war crimes trials could be reduced to sound bites and personalities. . . . A court—even one without a jury where a learned judge has studied the papers as here—may be the right place to decide on issues of defamation, but it is surely an inappropriate setting to rule on the interpretation of history.[7]

Similarly, Werner Birkenmaier, writing in the *Stuttgarter Zeitung*, asked pointedly whether a judge was really capable of meting out justice to history:

> Can he, may he establish as if by virtue of his office what is 'correct' in history, how it really was? In that case he could be able to achieve more than all the historians put together. Historical scholarship is the effort to approach what objectively happened, based on sources, documents and witnesses. The rest is interpretation and opinion, but also the sceptical knowledge of the fact that witnesses make false reports, and sources and documents can be overtaken or reinterpreted in the light of new research.

Birkenmaier thought that Irving exploited such uncertainties in order to cast doubt on the Holocaust. Like many other observers, he had serious doubts about the court's ability to settle anything, let alone reach a defensible verdict on what was historical research and what was falsification of the documentary record.[8]

In fact, however, in many respects the High Court turned out to be a good place to settle the historical and methodological points at issue in the Irving case. There were, for a start, none of the usual constraints of time and space that limit what can be said or written in other arenas of debate. In a radio or television program, each side has at best only ten or fifteen minutes to make its points, at worst little more than a couple of sound-bites; in court, however, we could pursue every point, no matter how minor, for hours on end (often to the frustration of the attending journalists), until we had exhausted the subject or the judge was satisfied that everything had been said that was necessary and asked us to move on. In an academic seminar or conference, the speaker is never allowed to go on for more than an hour, and discussion seldom extends even to that amount of time. In the High Court, proceedings went on for the best part of three months. Academic controversies in journals, newspapers, and magazines are limited by the space available, and books are subject to severe restrictions on their length which are imposed by the economics of publishing even in quite arcanely academic subject areas. There were no such limits on the space the experts had to write their reports in the Irving trial: we simply wrote as much as we needed to fulfill the commissions we had been given, which in Robert Jan Van Pelt's case was over six hundred pages and in mine over seven hundred.

The court proceedings turned almost entirely on Irving's interpretation of original historical documents. The red lever-arch 'bundles' that now lined the bookshelves on three out of the four walls of the courtroom were filled mainly with photocopies of Irving's works and the original, mostly German, mostly wartime documents that they used, or, as the defense claimed, misused to support their various controversial theses. We spent hours going over detailed matters of research such as the interpretation of particular sentences in the original sources, the translation of individual words, the reading of a series of letters in a handwritten manuscript. Journalists frequently found this extremely irritating.

Even Neal Ascherson, one of Britain's most intelligent and perceptive journalists, with a keen eye for history and a good knowledge of the recent European past, expressed some impatience with the proceedings, complaining,

> We spend hours on the timing of a scribbled Himmler phone-note about how a transport of Berlin Jews should be treated in Riga, on a bugged conversation between captured SS men in London about whether somebody said he had an order from Hitler to kill Latvian Jews, on the meanings of words such as *Vernichtung* (destruction) or *Judentum* (Jewry).[9]

The Irish reporter Rachel Donnelly did a reasonable job of reporting the issues, but even she showed some irritation with "circular arguments about the position of a full stop" in one particular document.[10] As Simon Rocker observed in *The Jewish Chronicle*, "The finer points of German grammar, the position of a full-stop in a document . . . it is easy to see why the two sides considered the case too much for a jury."[11]

This was, however, a trial about historical research at the most detailed and basic level, about the very creation of historical knowledge from the remains the past has left behind. Seldom does either a historical controversy or an academic debate touch on such fundamental issues of the historian's business, or treat them with such close attention over such a long period of time. "For many of us squeezed into the court," the reporter Cal McCrystal complained, "there are times when the sheer volume of information being exchanged seems almost a *barrier* to historical truth." The information overload was "stupefying," he thought. "Stacked in teak bookshelves around the walls are nearly 400 files of information. Teak tables groan beneath the weight of further boxes, books and laptops."[12] Like many journalists, he was simply unfamiliar with the enormous quantity of source material with which modern historians customarily work.

In historical debate it is often possible to evade your opponent's question or to get away with irrelevant answers. But not in court. This was the first time that Irving had been put to the question in a court of law on these issues, and the procedure was far more rigorous than it had been in the occasional debates in which he had taken part on television or in the press. The court's proceedings were surprisingly informal, and Mr. Justice Gray in general applied the rules in what seemed to me to be a fairly relaxed way. But the obligation on the witnesses, including Irving himself, to tell the truth, allowed merciless, relentless questioning, particularly by Richard Rampton, if the cross-examiner felt that the truth was being evaded, argued around, or denied. Every word spoken in court was taken down by stenographers, fed into the laptops that all the main protagonists had on the desk in front of them, and distributed in corrected, hard-copy form the same evening. There could be no dispute, therefore, about what anyone had said. Leading counsel frequently referred to the transcripts in the course of cross-examination. What was said on oath in the witness box was supposed to be true and therefore dealt with in a definitive manner. This rule, designed not least to save time that would otherwise be lost through repetition, led to an almost immediate intervention when a witness contradicted something he had said earlier, though in practice it did not prevent either repetition or contradiction from taking place. All of this was immensely helpful in moving the court toward a definite conclusion on the issues before it.

As it turned out, the rules of evidence in court were not so different from the rules of evidence observed by historians. In criminal cases a prosecution has to be proved beyond reasonable doubt. Here, in a civil trial, the issue hung on the balance of probabilities, much as it does in history. Irving requested that the standard of proof demanded of the defense be set high, since the allegations made against him were particularly serious, and the judge agreed. Yet in the end this did not seem to make a great deal of difference. Since the trial turned for the most part on how historians used historical evidence, the context and circumstances in which an original document had been written proved to be all-important. The same was true of the language in which the documents were couched. Whether or not the word *Vernichtung* meant physical annihilation could indeed often be judged only from the context—in 1939, for instance, it might mean something vaguer than it meant in 1943, as all the experts agreed, and Irving himself accepted as a general principle, even if he frequently disputed its application in practice. The standards of proof were in the end not much higher than those used by historical researchers in their own work.

Despite the lawyers' wigs and gowns and the judge's red sash, the proceedings were generally informal. The language used by the court was for the most part plain English. As Ralf Dahrendorf remarked ruefully: "In Continental Europe, the open drama might possibly have been sterilized by juridical terminology."[13] This was not so in the High Court, and while historical technicalities abounded, legal jargon was mercifully absent. The normal course of trials of this nature was followed, albeit with occasional interruptions and variations. The plaintiff and the defense presented their cases, and then the plaintiff was cross-examined. The defense called its witnesses, who were cross-examined in turn by the plaintiff. There were concluding pleas, and finally, after an interval, judgment was delivered.

Three features of the trial stood out as unusual. The first was the absence of a jury. Everyone agreed that the mass of documentation was too vast, the issues too intricate, for a jury to cope with. Even the judge found the minute examination of original source material "extremely difficult and taxing." Irving, perhaps flattered by this argument, agreed. Although Irving had agreed to all this in advance, there were moments when he came to question his own wisdom in having done so.[14] A jury might have proved susceptible to his bluster, his rhetoric, and his self-advertisement, or found itself as much at sea in the welter of historical argument and counterargument as the vast majority of the journalists did. The judge was immune to all of that. Or, jurors might have been numbed by the detail and concluded that the two parties were somehow on the same level and there was nothing to choose between them. Mr. Justice Gray's extraordinary mastery of detail proved decisive in this, as in other respects. Yet of course the presence of a jury would have altered the nature of the proceedings profoundly. No doubt the defense would have put its case more simply. The defense witnesses would have spent weeks in the witness box presenting their testimony orally under the guidance of defense counsel, instead of just handing in written reports. And even the soft-spoken defense counsel Richard Rampton QC might have raised his voice and inserted a little drama into its tones, instead of speaking, as he seemed to, mainly for the sake of the transcript, which he knew the judge would study every night after the proceedings were over for the day. My guess was that had there been a jury, however, the defense would still have been able to put its case across convincingly, albeit in a rather different way.

Second, the role of the expert witnesses loomed unusually large in this trial. What we researched and wrote was also exceptionally independent from the Instructing Solicitors, who simply lacked the necessary expertise in historiography, the deciphering of handwritten German documents, and the detailed knowledge of the Second World War and the Nazi extermination of the Jews. The expert reports provided the basis for Richard Rampton's lengthy cross-examination of the plaintiff; destroying the credibility of the witnesses and the points they made became the main object pursued by Irving when his turn came to cross-examine us. Almost every aspect of the assessment of Irving's work reached in the final judgment derived ultimately from the expert reports and the way Irving had dealt with them in court. Despite the fact that the defense case was conducted in masterly fashion by one of Britain's top defamation QCs, who seemed to know what was in the expert reports better than we did ourselves, the main role in drawing up the defense case was ultimately played by the historians.

The third unusual aspect of the trial was the fact that the plaintiff was representing himself. This lent the whole proceeding a directly personal quality often missing when most of the talking is done by lawyers. It was unclear whether Irving decided to represent himself because he could not afford the legal fees or whether he was so convinced that he knew more about the subjects under discussion than anyone else could ever do, that he simply did not trust a lawyer to put his case. He did not call any expert witnesses to testify on the substantive issues, only two historians to comment, favorably as he hoped, on his reputation among professional historians, and one Kevin Macdonald, a Californian "evolutionary psychologist," to defend him against the charge of antisemitism by supporting his view that Jews had always stuck together throughout history in pursuit of their own interests. Interviewed on BBC Radio 4, Irving admitted being "self-confident to the point of arrogance." His interviewer, the psychologist Oliver James, suggested that this derived from the fact that he was "actually very short of self-esteem," and suffered "from feelings of inferiority" which made him "far more anxious about who you are and far more in need of kicking everyone and trying to make a big fuss and being the centre of attention than you realise."[15] These feelings were to emerge in curious ways during the trial.

Finally, Irving could probably not trust a barrister to extract the maximum publicity from the case in the way he wanted. *The Economist* pointed out that Irving, "an astute self-publicist," was widely suspected by critics of "using his three-month stint in court to try to revive the flagging public interest in his work."[16] And on many occasions indeed, Irving seemed to be addressing more the press and the world outside than the judge and the court, indulging, for example, on one occasion in the sensational gambit of asking the judge to prevent him from extradition in the middle of the trial to Germany to face charges of Holocaust denial there, a ploy that duly reaped its reward in the Pavlovian response of the panting headline-writers in the next morning's daily newspapers.[17]

II

As the trial got under way, it quickly became apparent that Irving was going to find it difficult to set the agenda. The bias of the English law of defamation brings its own perils for the unwary plaintiff. By placing the entire burden of proof on the defense, it allows them to turn the tables and devote the action to destroying the reputation of their accuser. Indeed, once the defense has admitted, as Lipstadt's did without hesitation, that the words complained of mean what they say and are clearly defamatory, justifying them in detail and with chapter and verse is the only option left to them. A successful libel defense therefore has to concentrate, in effect, on massively defaming the person and character of the plaintiff, the only restriction being that the defamation undertaken in court has to be along the same lines as the defamation that gave rise to the case in the first place, and that it has, of course, to be true. The defense had to prove that Lipstadt's accusations of Holocaust denial and historical falsification were justified in Irving's case. Thus it was Irving, not Lipstadt, whose reputation was on the line. By the end of the third week of the trial, as Neal Ascherson observed, the defense had succeeded in turning the tables, "as if David Irving were the defendant and Deborah Lipstadt the plaintiff,"[18] an observation shared by other commentators too.[19] "In the relentless focus on Irving's beliefs," wrote Jenny Booth in *The Scotsman*, "it was easy to forget that it was actually Lipstadt's book which was on trial. Increasingly it seemed that was Irving himself."[20]

In the welter of argument and counterargument, many of the journalists who attended the trial found themselves more and more at sea, and it was perhaps not surprising that newspaper interest dropped off once the trial got into the meat of the allegations. Listening to it all, the writer Dan Jacobson found himself feeling "as if I were sitting in a kind of grim version of Wonderland . . . a region of illogicality and topsy-turvydom."[21] At times even the defense counsel Richard Rampton QC thought the same. When Irving spent some time trying to show that well-known British politicians and authors of the interwar period such as John Buchan had made antisemitic remarks, Rampton exclaimed:

> My Lord, this is a kind of insanity. I feel as though I was in one of Lewis Carroll's books. Mr. Irving brought this action in respect of words published by my clients. The only defence is that what is said is true, amongst them that Mr. Irving is an antisemite. What can it matter that there may have been some author from the distant past, the *39 Steps*, who also, on some occasion, might have made a remark as an antisemite?[22]

The sense of unreality felt by reporters was heightened by the fact that while all the participants in the proceedings—the judge, the defense counsel, the plaintiff, and the witnesses—were supplied with copies of the documents under discussion at any given moment, they themselves, obviously enough, were not, so that for them, much of the discussion took place in a kind of vacuum, in which they could do no more than guess as to the nature of the text whose contents or status were being disputed. For the majority of British pressmen attending the trial, matters were made still worse by the fact that a large portion of these texts were in German, a language that they were unable to understand. The same applied as well to many of the spectators who crowded the public benches every day.

All of this gave uninformed, or inattentive, observers the impression that Irving was doing quite well as the trial went on. Jonathan Freedland reported perceptively on the fog of uncertainty that Irving tried to spread over the evidence for the Holocaust. After Irving had dismissed the memories of survivors as the product of delusion or conspiracy, all that remained were the documents:

> This is where Irving is happiest, rolling around in swastika-embossed paper. He knows these documents so well, he knows their mannerisms. On this terrain, Irving can be frighteningly convincing. . . . The trouble with Irving is that he refuses to accept the basic rules of evidence. . . . It is history itself which is on trial here, the whole business of drawing conclusions from evidence. If Irving is able to dismiss the testimony of tens of thousands of witnesses, where does that leave history? If we can't know this, how can we know that Napoleon fought at Waterloo or that Henry VIII had six wives? How can we know anything? . . . If we start to doubt corroborated facts, how can we prevent oursleves being swallowed up in doubt, unable to trust anything we see? It might all be a conspiracy, a legend, a hoax. This is the bizarre, never-never world inhabited by David Irving. Now the court has to decide: is this our world too?[23]

Irving of course was not doubting whether one could find the truth; on the contrary, he was bending the rules of evidence to impose the validity of what he claimed was the truth. But it took a lot of knowledge and a lot of expertise to recognize this.

As James Dalrymple observed of Irving's performance in court:

> Like a magician producing rabbits from a hat, he produces questions that are disturbing, puzzling, confusing, even bewildering. Remorselessly, he plants tiny seeds of doubt in the minds of even intelligent and reasonable people. . . . On and on it goes. Find some tiny inconsistencies, discover some flaws in eye-witness accounts, present logistical anomalies as Zionist lies—and soon the minds of those who were not even born during the Holocaust are filled with the possibilities that it could all be a lie.[24]

Nevertheless, despite all this fog of linguistic incomprehension and documentary obscurity, Jonathan Freedland of *The Guardian* found the proceedings "a daily performance of extraordinary theatre."[25] Simon Rocker of the *Jewish Chronicle* thought them "more like trench warfare, slugged out with documents, the full significance of which might emerge only days later, a ray of light through a thicket of paperwork. The horrible details of human depravity became pieces in a game of legal chess."[26] The strangeness of it all was heightened by the tense atmosphere created partly by Irving's decision to represent himself, partly by the enormous public interest the case aroused. So many people wanted to get into the public gallery that the judge moved the trial to a larger court, Court 73, after the first couple of days, and even then there were perpetual queues outside the courtroom. Holocaust survivors, Jewish activists, academics, and right-wing extremists sat cheek-by-jowl on the public benches throughout the proceedings.

A history teacher from Royal Holloway College brought his students along to witness the spectacle. Holocaust historian Sir Martin Gilbert attended every day and took copious notes from his seat in the public gallery. Visiting American academics like Eric Johnson, author of *Nazi Terror*, dropped in for a day or two, coincidentally just as, unbeknown to him, Irving was handing extracts from his book around the courtroom. A large bearded and turbaned Sikh, connected with the anti-racist magazine *Searchlight*, sat within easy reach of Irving sympathizers identified by the magazine as activists in the far-right British National Party, who were sporting flat of St. George badges in their lapels. I noticed one young spectator wearing a death's head signet ring.

According to one observer, one of them had an American paper on his lap, the headline "News of Phoney Survivors" facing up at his neighbor, an Auschwitz survivor who had rolled up his sleeve to display the number the SS had tattooed on his left arm. Behind Irving sat a well-dressed, heavily made-up, forty-something blonde who was known to *Searchlight* as the London contact for the Holocaust-denying Adelaide Institute in Australia. Often accompanying him to lunch, she set the tone for the small claque of his admirers to whom he would occasionally address his remarks, eliciting predictable chuckles when he made what he indicated to them was a joke or a winning point. Mostly they sat close behind Irving, although on one occasion, one of Irving's supporters positioned himself behind me and my research assistants and almost fell out of his chair in the attempt to read the notes we would occasionally hand to each other on the yellow post-it stickers we used to pass forward to Richard Rampton with information on the rare occasions on which he missed something. Strangest of all was a man whom the *Searchlight* described as "the arch conspiracy theorist Alexander Baron, who put out on the press benches a note declaring: 'Irving is a paid agent of political Zionism. This trial is staged. Don't be deceived.'"[27]

Expectations on all sides were high. Irving's supporters clearly thought this would be his opportunity to wipe the floor with the liberal Establishment and resurrect his flagging career as a writer and political activist. On the other side, Neal Ascherson, noting the camp survivors in the courtroom, observed:

> Some of them hope this trial will be a sort of Last Judgment, the breaking of the Seventh Seal to reward the righteous and drown the wicked, and flood the Earth with truth too blinding to deny. . . . Idealists, like some of those vigilant old people on the public benches, dream that this trial will culminate in a mighty rite of transmission. It will lay out one last time the evidence about what was done in the Holocaust (to how many, by whom, in what manner and why). The young generations will lose the voice of the witnesses. But they will be armed instead with a judgment.

Whether the end result would actually deliver such a clear-cut result, he doubted.[28]

All of this not only created a tense atmosphere but also lent the proceedings a surreal aspect, as Philipp Blom observed in the *Berliner Zeitung*:

> Amidst the courtly ceremoniousness of an English court, with its wigs, its gowns and its deliberate politeness, the debate here was about mass murder, about bizarre arithmetical tasks, that sounded as if they came from a textbook from the gates of Hell: if you have two gassing lorries with a capacity of sixty individuals and you have 172 days to kill 97,000 Jews, how many journeys must each lorry make each day?[29]

James Dalrymple of the *Independent* was another observer who clearly felt uneasy at the discrepancy between the style in which the court proceedings were held and the matters with which they dealt. "I felt," he wrote, "like a man in some kind of Kafkaesque dream. What was going on here? Was this some kind of grotesque *Monty Python* episode? Everybody seemed to be in such good spirits. As if they were taking part in some kind of historical parlour game. Spot the gas chamber for 20 points."[30]

Every lunchtime, after a morning of cross-examining Irving on the dispatching of trainloads of starving Jews in cattle trucks and the committing of mass murder in the gas chambers of Auschwitz, the defense team walked across the road to Richard Rampton's chambers in the Middle Temple, sat down to a sandwich lunch, exchanged impressions of the morning's play, swapped legal and academic gossip, and planned tactics for the afternoon. Often, even in court, one had to pinch oneself to realize the enormity of the events we were discussing. Much of the time, however, merely to keep oneself from becoming uncontrollably angry, it was necessary to erect some kind of emotional curtain between the court proceedings and the death camps, to distance oneself from the horrors of Auschwitz and Treblinka. On one level the trial was indeed played out as a kind of intellectual and forensic game, and given the fact that in the end the decisive issues as far as the court was concerned were intellectual and legal rather than moral or political ones, it was necessary that this should be so.

On another level, however, the more the trial went on, the more moral significance the case seemed to take on in the face of Irving's seemingly limitless capacity for telling lies, distorting the truth, and insulting the memory of the dead. This too required its tactics of emotional self-preservation. Before going into the witness box to be cross-examined by Irving, I had two pieces of sound advice that constituted in fact the only kind of coaching I received from the defense. "Remember, Richard," said Anthony Julius, "you're on the stand for two and a half hours without a break, so don't take too many sips of water from the glass they give you; it would be embarrassing to have to ask the judge for a pause while you go to the loo." I followed this as closely as I could, although the dry atmosphere of the air-conditioned courtroom obliged me to have frequent recourse to the water-glass all the same, and on one or two occasions, it was touch and go.

The other piece of advice was from Robert Jan Van Pelt, who went into the box before me. "Don't look Irving in the eye," he said, "it'll just make you angry." On my first day of cross-examination I was foolish enough to forget this sage counsel, and it turned out to be just as Robert Jan had foretold: I became irritated by many of the things Irving was saying or implying, especially when he tried to tackle me on reports written by other expert witnesses whom the defense had chosen not to call—reports for which I was not responsible and did not have the expertise to discuss. This did not make a good impression on the court. Over the weekend, I had a rethink, and for the remaining five days of cross-examination I did not make eye-contact with Irving once. This was much better; as the disembodied questions, statements, innuendos, and insults volleyed in from my left, I was able to take them in an impersonal manner and answer them in relative calm, addressing my remarks either to the court in general, or to the judge. Later I noticed that Richard Rampton never looked Irving in the eye either. Confronting Irving in a personal manner would have made it more difficult to deal with the issues at hand in a dispassionate way. For all of us he became someone with whom the least contact was defiling.

III

Rampton's decision to cross-examine Irving on the basis of a chronological run-through of the events to which the evidence referred made strategic sense, for in doing so he built up a narrative of Nazi antisemitism that was designed to trap Irving in the logic of historical events. Irving may have been aware of this; and Dan Jacobson observed: "Risking the anger of the bench mattered a good deal less to him than trying to disrupt the story which was being unfolded, and which not even the curious format of the trial could prevent from being unfolded." Irving, he thought, was determined to prevent the emergence of a narrative of "consequence, of events having necessary connections, of one thing leading to another," and constantly attempted to break it all down into isolated discussions of detail.[31] But as Rampton's remorseless questioning went on, I could not see any such subtle tactics in Irving's responses. Irving seemed too concerned to duck and weave as Rampton probed and prodded, to think of anything apart from the topic of the moment.

After many days of being questioned by Rampton on the issues of falsification and manipulation of the sources, it was Irving's turn to put the defense experts into the witness box and attempt to refute what they had written in their reports. Some observers found much to admire in the way he went about his task. "Mr. Irving's performance was very impressive," wrote Sir John Keegan, defense editor of the *Daily Telegraph,* after observing him conducting a cross-examination. "He is a large, strong, handsome man, excellently dressed, with the appearance of a leading QC. He performs well as a QC also, asking, in a firm but courteous voice, precise questions which demonstrate his detailed knowledge of an enormous body of material."[32]

Not many people who were in court for more than the few hours that he was there found themselves sharing Sir John's favorable impressions. Irving struck me as being impressive neither as a witness nor as a cross-examiner. A lumbering hulk of a man, he did not look well dressed to me; his suit did not seem to fit him properly, and his graying hair for the first few weeks was untidy and clearly needed cutting. Knowledgeable Central European commentators were generally unimpressed by Irving's performance. Robert Treichler, writing for the Austrian magazine *Profil,* found Irving "was not an impressive thinker or rhetorician. In the trial, in which he is representing himself, he acts chaotically."[33] And Eva Menasse, writing in the *Frankfurter Allgemeine Zeitung,* found that "the biggest disappointment in this trial up to now has been the intelligence of David Irving, which was so famous before the case and which supposedly made him so dangerous." He knew his way around the documents well enough, but "It is painful to have to hear how Irving tries to bend every detail, even the tiniest, every translation, every word in his direction. In doing so he is not in any way convincing, not for a second."[34]

In his own published work, Irving often seemed obsessed with trivial detail, unable to see the wood for the trees. The same intellectual weakness now became apparent as he launched into his cross-examination. His technique was to go through my report page by page, indiscriminately picking up any errors that he thought he could identify, as if he were writing a lengthy book review rather than trying to argue a legal case. "It is," he said hopefully, "a barrage of tiny points, It is death by a thousand cuts."[35] Inevitably, given the pressure of time with which the report had been researched and compiled, and the large amount of ground it had to cover, he did succeed in finding a few minor errors. Some mistakes identified by Irving turned out not to be mistakes at all. But whether he was right or wrong, most of his points were completely irrelevant to the central issue of falsification. The judge became increasingly irritated with these irrelevancies, and grew ever more insistent in directing Irving's attention to the central issues in the report with which he had to grapple. On the third day of Irving's cross-examination of me, the judge finally lost his patience, describing one question of Irving's as "an absolutely futile point." The danger to Irving of his failure to understand what he had to do was immediately made clear by defending counsel:

> MR. JUSTICE GRAY: This cross-examination does not appear to me to be grasping the nettle of the criticisms against you. You keep finding tiny little points on which you hope, and sometimes succeed, in tripping up Professor Evans, but you are not grappling with what the criticisms are of your account. . . . You are taking tiny little points like whether a sentence has been left out of an account he gives as part of his testimony. That just does not really affect the issues that I have to decide at all.

> MR. RAMPTON: I would have to say this, my Lord. It is as well perhaps I say it now. Unless Mr. Irving challenges Professor Evans on this and other topics, upon the foundation of his criticisms of Mr. Irving's writings, which is not in every case but in most cases and in all important respects the way in which Mr. Irving has treated contemporary documents, then I am afraid I will take it that Mr. Irving has accepted the criticisms.

> MR. JUSTICE GRAY: We will come back to that. That would, in the ordinary case, be a completely unarguable proposition for Mr. Rampton.[36]

Later, the judge remarked that while he was not in fact going to accept that Irving had conceded a point if he had not challenged it, he was going to take the fact that he had not disputed it into account when making up his mind about the issue in question.[37] And indeed the final judgment repeatedly noted where Irving had not challenged criticisms made of him, as well as summarizing the arguments he put when he had.

A major problem in dealing with Irving as a cross-examiner lay in the fact that he would frequently build into his often lengthy and elaborate questions assumptions that themselves rested on his falsification of the evidence, and so had to be disputed before the question itself could be dealt with. This tactic, whether conscious or not, did not escape the attention of the judge. "No, Mr. Irving, that will not do, will it?" he exclaimed on one such occasion: "You cannot put a question which has as its premise a misstatement about the date when gas chambers began operating. . . . If you are going to ask that question, and it is a relevant question, you must premise it correctly."[38] Moreover, it was clearly inadvisable to trust Irving's own account of the documents that he presented to me during cross-examination without checking them myself, so time and again, when he tried to initiate a discussion about the meaning or content of some particular source or text, it became necessary to hold up the proceedings by demanding to see a copy of the document to which he was referring. In many instances he was so badly prepared that he had neglected to supply the court with a copy, so that the discussion was aborted. As the judge remarked to Irving, "it is not terribly satisfactory to have cross-examination by assertion, if you follow me. . . . Sometimes I think it is going to be necessary to give chapter and verse for what you are asserting."[39]

Irving clearly found this insistence immensely irritating. After he put yet another point to me without providing any documentary evidence for it, the following exchange took place:

PROF. EVANS: First of all, I would have to see the document to accept your account of what is in it or rather—

MR. IRVING: Do you always ask to see documents?

PROF. EVANS: Yes, of course I do, Mr. Irving, because I do not trust your account of what is in documents. Still less do I trust the account—

MR. IRVING: Do you know your own name without being shown a document?[40]

For all of Irving's sarcasm, the advisability of insisting on seeing documentary evidence for everything he said quickly became obvious. Quoting from my report on one of many such occasions, for example, Irving put the following question:

MR. IRVING: On page 160 at line 4 of paragraph 36: "Irving casts doubt on almost all testimony at the Nuremberg War (Crimes Trials)"—is that an exaggeration, that I doubt almost all the testimony produced at Nuremberg?

PROF. EVANS: That is not what I say.

MR. IRVING: Well, you say that I say it does not fit my arguments; I say it was obtained by torture and threats?

PROF. EVANS: No, no I do not, Mr. Irving. I say: "Irving casts doubt on almost all testimony at the Nuremberg War Crimes Trials or during the prior interrogations if it does not fit his arguments, alleging it was obtained by torture and threats." Those are my precise words.[41]

But it was not only necessary to remain alert to Irving's distortion of my report; he even managed repeatedly to distort what I said in the witness box seconds after I had said it. Thus, for example, after I had quoted the passage in Hitler's Testament, written in the Berlin bunker shortly before his suicide, in which he said that the Jews would have to atone for what he called their guilt at having caused the deaths of millions of Aryans by burning, bombing, and starvation, "even if by more humane means," Irving almost immediately referred to the suggestion "that the Holocaust was humane, which is what you are proposing?" "I am not proposing it," I protested, "it is Hitler who is proposing it."[42]

Irving's cross-examination technique bore little resemblance to the calm, forensic probing of an experienced QC like Richard Rampton. Every time I started to give an answer he did not like, he tried to cut it off. Frequently the judge, and occasionally defending counsel, stepped in to stop him. Often I continued anyway, so that at times all three of us, Irving, the judge, and myself, were speaking at the same time. At the end of one day's proceedings, I leaned over to the stenographer and asked her whose words she recorded in such circumstances. "Whoever shouts the

loudest," was her reply. In practice, however, the tape-recording of each
day's proceedings made sure nothing got lost even when exchanges
became extremely heated. Irving even interrupted when he was being
told he should not interrupt:

> MR. RAMPTON: I do believe that Mr. Irving is occasionally guilty of
> discourtesy. My Lord, I would not interrupt a witness like that in
> that aggressive—
>
> MR. IRVING: I have to interrupt, Mr. Rampton, because otherwise—
>
> MR. RAMPTON: I am speaking to his Lordship, Mr. Irving. Please
> remain quiet. I am making an objection to the way in which Mr. Irv-
> ing is attempting to harass the witness.
>
> MR. JUSTICE GRAY: The objection is entirely well founded.[43]

"Please, Mr. Irving," the judge repeated a few minutes after this
exchange. "There is no point in asking questions if you constantly interrupt the answers."[44] But Irving could not see this. He seemed entirely
unaware of the impression he was making on the court.[45]

Irving dragged out the proceedings unnecessarily by repeating questions if he did not get the answers he wanted. On many occasions the
judge had to intervene to tell him he had got the point and Irving could
now move on.[46] But most of the time, Irving was impervious to such
advice. Sometimes this meant I had to repeat the same answer several
times. This was exasperating. "I have to say, Mr. Irving," I told him on one
occasion, "one of the reasons why this is taking so long is that you are constantly asking the same questions again and again, and I have to give the
same answers again and again." Now it was Irving's turn to be irritated.
"I do not really wish to be lectured by the witness on how I conduct my
cross-examination," he barked. "Well," interjected the judge, "take the
lecture from me and please, please move on."[47]

The central step that the defense had to make was to provide convincing evidence that Irving had not only made mistakes in his work but
had actually deliberately done so in order to bolster his preconceived and
politically motivated view of the past. As Irving correctly remarked in his
opening speech, the defense had to show not just "that I misrepresented

what happened, but that I knew what happened and that I perversely and deliberately, for whatever purpose, portrayed it differently from how I knew it to have happened."[48] Or, to be more precise, that he had deliberately falsified the evidence for what happened so that it indicated something different from what he knew it indicated. Irving tried to suggest in cross-examination that he would not have placed the documents he had discovered in the public domain had he been falsifying them. But, of course, most of the documents he misinterpreted and misrepresented were already in the public domain, in state archives, and in the long run it would not be possible to withhold the rest from other researchers. Irving got the point about the documents:

> MR. IRVING: Do you say that I misinterpreted and distorted them deliberately? Is that your contention?
>
> PROF. EVANS: Yes, that is my contention. You know there is a difference between, as it were, negligence, which is random in its effects, i.e. if you are simply a sloppy or bad historian, the mistakes you make will be all over the place. They will not actually support any particular point of view. . . . On the other hand, if all the mistakes are in the same direction in the support of a particular thesis, then I do not think that is mere negligence. I think that is a deliberate manipulation and deception.[49]

This was crucial. The defense's case was, after all, as Richard Rampton said in his brief Opening Statement, that "Mr. Irving calls himself an historian. The truth is, however, that he is not an historian at all but a falsifier of history. To put it bluntly, he is a liar."[50] Irving's line was of course that it was he who was telling the truth, he who was the *bona fide* historian. The purveyors of what he had called the 'Holocaust myth' were the ideologically motivated liars. "Although Irving relishes his status as a contrarian and historic mischief-maker," wrote Gerald Posner perceptively in *The Observer*, "he desperately wants to be accepted as a serious historian."[51] Beginning his cross-examination of Christopher Browning, Irving suggested collegiality by remarking that "we are going to have a joint journey of discovery and exploration over the next day or two."[52] At the same time, he was never reluctant to heap insults upon the tribe of professional

academic historians. Here, as in so many other respects, the contradiction in his own position was obvious. Yet on the face of it the issue
was clear. Falsification or truth? Historian or liar? On 11 January 2000,
battle was joined in the High Court.

IV

How did Irving deal with the detailed evidence of manipulation of the
historical record leveled at him in my report? He had several different
approaches, depending on the subject. Not all of them were mutually
compatible. Under cross-examination himself, for example, he had
boasted that he had read the entire eight thousand pages of the microfilmed transcripts of Hitler's trial for the beer-hall putsch in 1924. However, defending himself against the finding in my report that he had
deliberately suppressed evidence in the transcript that the man whom he
presented as a neutral witness on Hitler's behalf was actually the head of
the Nazi Party's intelligence service, Irving now argued that he had not
read the pages in the transcript where this was revealed, even though the
witness's entire testimony took up only five pages.[53]

Similar contradictions were to be found in Irving's attempt to show
that Hitler did not know about the pogrom of the *Reichskristallnacht* and
put an immediate stop to it when he found out. Despite his statement
elsewhere in the trial that he had a "gut instinct against eyewitnesses" and
"always preferred to use concrete documents rather than statements of
people,"[54] Irving tried to persuade the court to prefer the postwar testimony of a number of Hitler's adjutants who were with him at the time to
the contemporary evidence of Goebbels' diary and his speech at the Old
Town Hall and other documents which made it clear that the 'demonstrations' had been authorized by Hitler.[55] The adjutants had insisted that
Hitler knew nothing about the events until the middle of the night and
raged at Goebbels when he found out. This was far from convincing for
a number of reasons:

> PROF. EVANS: It is extraordinary, is it not, Mr. Irving? All these old,
> all these police officers and SS men have been with Hitler during

the appalling violence against the Jews in 1938, many years afterwards when it has become clear that society and the world disap-
prove very strongly of these events, all tell each other: "Well, I did
not know anything about it. I had not heard about it."

(. . .)

MR. IRVING: Do you, therefore, accept, Professor, that I had three
sources of what you would describe as being of variable quality, all
converging on an episode in Hitler's private quarters on the Night
of Broken Glass in which Hitler, apparently, vented his anger upon
receiving news of what was happening in Munich, at least?

PROF. EVANS: Yes, and I think they are all lying.

MR. IRVING: You think that all three are separately lying?

PROF. EVANS: Well, Mr. Irving, it is not beyond the bounds of possibility. You have already suggested in the course of this trial that
many thousands of Holocaust survivors are all collectively lying, so
it is not beyond the bounds of possibility that three people are lying,
is it?[56]

But it was left to the judge to point out another reason why their evidence might not have been reliable. One of the testimonies was given in
an interview of Nicolaus von Below carried out by Irving himself long
after the war.

MR. IRVING: Is there any indication that I am asking leading questions?

MR. JUSTICE GRAY: The first one is a leading question, but let us
move on.

MR. IRVING: My Lord, my interview technique is part of the criticism against me, that I have distorted history.

MR. JUSTICE GRAY: Yes, but you asked whether there were any
leading questions and the first question is a leading question, Mr.
Irving. Let us get to his answer.

PROF. EVANS: "You were with Hitler at his home when the news of
the *Reichskristallnacht* arrived there in Munich and he was rather

surprised by that. Can you depict that? Who else was there?" You
suggest to the witness that he was surprised. What you should have
asked was: "You were with Hitler in his home on the eve of *Reichskristallnacht,* can you say what happened?"—something neutral like
that.[57]

Irving was unable to sustain his claim that such evidence had to
be preferred to contemporary documents such as the Goebbels diary.
Indeed, under cross-examination by Richard Rampton, Irving had been
forced to concede that Hitler himself had been behind the two telexes
sent out to German police units at 11:55 P.M. and 1:20 A.M. on the night
of 9–10 November 1938 and that both these telexes were ordering the
police not to interfere with the action against the Jews.[58]

He also had to drop the claim that Hitler had called Himmler into
his bunker on 30 November 1941 and "required" him to stop the Jews
being killed. The Jews in question, he agreed, were in fact only a single
trainload from Berlin. And although he had said as much early in the trial,
he now had to abandon his claim that Hitler had summoned Himmler.[59]
Irving was also forced to drop his initial suggestion that he had misread
the singular *Judentransport* as the plural *Judentransporte* in the manuscript of Himmler's phone log when confronted, first, with a photocopy
of the original page, which showed quite clearly that there was no *e* at the
end, and then, conclusively, with a letter he had written in 1974 in which
he had transcribed the word with perfect accuracy. "When you go into
the witness box to answer questions on oath," Rampton commented
acidly, "you simply pluck an explanation out of the air, do you not? . . .
Yesterday's answer was a false answer."[60] Irving had said that he had
admitted that the order only covered Jews from Berlin when he was later
made aware of the documentary context. But the context was there in the
document itself, in the words *aus Berlin, from Berlin.* The omission of
these words from Irving's original account of the document in 1977 was
clear evidence of misrepresentation. Irving described this as a "smokescreen." "On the contrary," remarked the judge, "it is the whole point of
the criticism."[61]

This was not the only falsification in Irving's account of these events.
He had gone on to claim that on 1 December 1941, "Himmler tele-

phoned SS General Oswald Pohl, overall chief of the concentration camp system, with the order: 'Jews are to stay where they are.'"[62] Himmler's phone log for 1 December 1941, published in a scholarly edition in 1999, did indeed confirm that he spoke to Pohl that day. However, what he said was not what Irving claimed at all. I had looked it up in the edition. Himmler summarized the conversation as follows:

'Besuch bei Schwarz.
Koksagys.
Verwaltungsführer der SS
    haben zu bleiben.
Lappenschuhe u. Finnenstiefel'[63]

The relevant part of this entry for the matter under discussion consisted of the third and fourth lines, which together made a single sentence: "Administrative leaders of the SS are to stay." Thus, what Himmler talked about with Pohl was not that *Jews* were to stay were they were (i.e., safe from 'liquidation'), but that the *administrative leaders of the SS* had to stay where they were. The term *Jews* was not mentioned by Himmler in his phone call at all. It was simply fabricated by Irving, a fabrication that he continued to repeat in other books, such as the 1991 edition of *Hitler's War*.[64] It was clear that this had been a grotesque misreading of the word *haben* as *Juden* in a sentence that obviously began on the previous line. *H* had become *J, a* had become *u, b* had become *d*.

Irving tried to suggest this had been an honest mistake because Himmler's handwriting was difficult to decipher. Facsimiles of the original document were handed around the courtroom. The handwriting was clear enough to anybody who had learned to read the old Sütterlin, the script normally used in Germany up to the end of the Second World War. If it really was difficult to read, what should a diligent historian do? Certainly, in view of the importance attached to the passage, a wild guess would be out of the question.

> PROF. EVANS: When you are reading handwriting, if you find something difficult to read or ambiguous, you then search for other, similar letters, the same letter, in other words, in the same hand, to try

and figure out what that particular hand's version of a B or a D or an
E or a U actually looks like. . . . From the text there are a number of
indications which somebody who was not biased and looking for
some evidence to the contrary, that is (to) say an objective historian,
that this is *"haben zu bleiben."* First of all, the fact that it is indented,
the second line *"haben zu bleiben"* does suggest that it runs on from
the first line. The new entries here begin right next to the middle of
the page. They are not indented. Secondly, this writer, as is common
in this handwriting, generally puts a kind of what you might call a
little inverted circumflex over a U. . . . You were misled by your overwhelming desire to exculpate the Nazi leadership into misreading
this as *"Juden"* instead of *"haben,"* whereas to any objective historian, taking even a minimal amount of care about reading this, it was
very easy to establish that this meant *"Verwaltungsführer der SS
haben zu bleiben."* To that extent, therefore, I think you deliberately
misused and abused this text.[65]

Irving, in other words, wanted it to be *Juden zu bleiben*—despite the
ungrammatical nature of the phrase—and so it was. When Richard
Rampton took him to task for reprinting this mistranscription in the 1991
edition of *Hitler's War,* Irving tried to persuade him that the book had
gone to press before he had known about the error. But he had known
about the mistake in 1988, Rampton countered; and he had had time to
excise all references to the Holocaust from the text after that date. So Irving was forced to admit: "I could have taken it out, yes."[66]

In fact, the Jews did not stay in Berlin, if that was where Irving
claimed they were to stay. They were sent to Riga, and on the arrival of
the transport in question, they were immediately shot along with the Jewish inhabitants of the Riga ghetto. How many died in this action? Irving
claimed that on 30 November 1941, one thousand Jews from Berlin and
"four thousand of Riga's unwanted Jews were . . . machine-gunned into
two or three pits." Irving's assertion here, made with absolute certainty,
relied on an early report of *Einsatzgruppe A.* However, in a later report
compiled by the Reich Security Head office, the number of Jews shot in
Riga on 30 November 1941 was given as 10,600. After further detailed
investigation, a Hamburg court sitting in 1973 put the number at
between 13,000 and 15,000.[67] The total massacred on this day and in a

second mass killing very shortly afterwards reached no fewer than 27,800.[68] Only in his footnotes did Irving acknowledge that *Einsatzgruppe A* had reported in early December 1941 that a total of 27,800 Jews had been executed in Riga in these two killing actions at the end of November and the beginning of December 1941. Irving immediately cast doubt on these figures, however, claiming that they were "possibly an exaggeration."[69]

Irving also made use of the testimony of Walter Bruns, whose conversations with fellow-officers about these events had been secretly recorded by their British captors immediately after the war. Bruns described how the victims had been gunned down into three ditches (24 meters long, about 3 meters wide). Irving claimed that each ditch "would have held one or two thousand victims." Yet Bruns made no reference at all to the crucial missing dimension of the *depth* of the ditches. This led to one of the most absurd exchanges of the whole trial.

> MR. IRVING: Would you accept that I am expert in digging pits, having worked in my early years as a student as a navvy for many years in order to finance my way through university?
>
> MR. JUSTICE GRAY: Mr. Irving, come on. You can dig a pit as deep as you have got the energy to dig it.
>
> MR. IRVING: My Lord, that is a very hazardous operation if you are standing at the bottom of the pit and you dig it without any kind of shoring. I would now draw your Lordship's attention to one such pit which is photographed in the little bundle I have you . . .
>
> PROF. EVANS: And you are saying, are you, Mr. Irving, that this is one of the pits in Riga? . . .
>
> MR. IRVING: This is, well, as you can tell by the British soldiers standing around with machine guns, this is probably Bergen-Belsen or Buchenwald, where the victims of Nazi atrocities are being buried by some of the perpetrators.
>
> (. . .)
>
> PROF. EVANS: . . . This has no relevance whatsoever to the matter we are dealing with.

MR. IRVING: It is relevant to the matter of how deep you can dig a pit in circumstances like this—

PROF. EVANS: You can dig a pit any depth you like, Mr. Irving.

MR. IRVING: Is that your expert evidence as a pit digger or can we apply some common sense?

PROF. EVANS: As it happens, I have been having my house reconstructed, Mr. Irving, recently—

MR. JUSTICE GRAY: That is as may be.

PROF. EVANS:—and people have been digging pits and I have watched them, so I do know something about digging pits.

Irving too may have known something about digging pits, but he neglected to mention that photographs of SS killing pits in Eastern Europe showed them with shallow, sloping sides, not sharp, vertical edges that would need shoring up. But he plowed on anyway.

MR. IRVING: So if it was 2 metres deep and if it had straight sides and if there was no back fill—

PROF. EVANS: That is three "ifs," Mr. Irving.

MR. IRVING: —would you stop interrupting—you would get 1,500 bodies into that pit, is that right?

PROF. EVANS: Yes.

MR. IRVING: So if it was another metre deep, you would get another 750 in, so you can do an order of magnitude calculation, can you?

PROF. EVANS: On the basis of those four "ifs," yes, you can do any calculation you like.

MR. IRVING: So you can do a ball-park calculation of two or three pits of that kind of size and magnitude would hold of the order of, say, three to 7,000 bodies?

PROF. EVANS: Yes, on the basis of those four hypotheticals, yes.

MR. IRVING: Did you bother to do such a check sum before you criticised me?

PROF. EVANS: I did not know how deep the pits were, Mr. Irving. My criticism is that there is no evidence of the depth of the pits. You do not provide any. You simply make all these if, if, if assumptions and then somehow treat them as facts.

MR. IRVING: Do you accept that when you are writing history and you cannot get all these documents on hand, occasionally you have to make common sense calculations and deductions?

PROF. EVANS: This is not common sense, Mr. Irving. This is a systematic attempt to undermine the figure given of 27,800 Jews, suggesting that this is too large. This is typical of your minimisation of the statistics of the numbers of Jews killed in any number of instances.

MR. JUSTICE GRAY: Right. On to the next point, Mr. Irving. I think we have exhausted that.[70]

In the midst of all this surrealism, it was sometimes difficult to remember that what we were actually talking about was a large number of completely innocent civilian men, women, and children, having been brutally snatched from their homes, being summarily machine-gunned into pits for no other reason than that they were Jewish.

Irving had actually read out the whole of Bruns' report in his Opening Statement, in an attempt to prove to the court that he did not suppress evidence of Nazi atrocities. But confronted in court with a passage in Bruns' report indicating that Hitler had personally ordered the shootings, he now tried to pour doubt on Bruns' testimony. "Perhaps," he said, "he is not entirely unaware that somebody may be listening." Bruns, he suggested, had sought to exculpate himself before his hidden British listeners by blaming Hitler. But Irving had evidently forgotten what he had said only a couple of days earlier in his Opening Statement. This was now quoted back at him by leading defense counsel Richard Rampton QC. On 11 January, Irving had said that the General "has no idea that in another room British experts are listening to and recording every word."[71] Forced to accept the veracity of Bruns' testimony, Irving tried to discount it in another way, alleging that it was unreliable "because other evidence shows that Hitler had not issued the order"—a false claim in itself, since there was no such other evidence, only an absence of evidence, in the form of a document signed by Hitler, that he had. "I have to remind you," Irving told Rampton at this point, "of one of the basic principles of English law, that a man is innocent until proven guilty." One had to pinch oneself to realize that Irving was referring here to Adolf Hitler. "Hitler," commented Rampton, "is not on trial, alas."[72]

Irving's line on an entry in the diary of Hans Frank, the Nazi legal expert who ran the Polish General Government during the war, was even more brazen. In December 1941, Frank had noted in his diary that he had addressed his staff on the subject of the General Government's Jews. "What is to happen to the Jews?" he asked. "Do you believe that they will be lodged in settlements in the *Ostland*?" Clearly not, he told his staff. "In Berlin we were told, 'Why all this trouble? We cannot use them in the *Ostland* or the *Reichskommissariat* either. Liquidate them yourselves!'" This speech was delivered just a few days after Hitler had addressed a general meeting of senior Nazi officials in Berlin on 12 December, reported by Goebbels in his diary, declaring that "the annihilation of Jewry must be the necessary consequence" of the World War that had begun with the entry of America into the conflict the day before.[73] So what Frank was told in Berlin, he was in all probability told by Hitler himself, since Hitler's speech to the Nazi Party officials the day after the declaration of war on America was the only plausible reason for Frank's presence in Berlin at this time.

Irving first tried to argue that Hitler had not been in Berlin at the same time as Frank, as indeed he had claimed in *Hitler's War*, but was quickly forced to withdraw this suggestion and admit that he was. However, he refused to admit that the account he gave in the book of what Frank had actually said was manipulated. In court, he repeated the claim made in *Hitler's War* that on 16 December 1941, Hans Frank "makes a pretty lurid statement about, 'What do the people in Berlin think we are doing? We say liquidate them yourselves.'"[74] In other words, he tried to make his readers believe it was Frank telling the leadership in Berlin to liquidate the Jews, not the other way around. How could he justify such a blatant reversal of the sentence's meaning? As so often when driven into a corner, Irving took refuge in claiming that "as we know from other sources, Hitler was intervening constantly to stop these things being done." But those "sources" were also manipulated by Irving to say the opposite of what they meant, so the whole argument became entirely circular, as one falsification became the justification for another.[75]

One of the most important of these sources from Irving's point of view was the so-called Schlegelberger memorandum.[76] Irving quoted his summary of the document's contents from page 464 of the 1991 edition of *Hitler's War*:

> MR. IRVING: "Hitler wearily told Hans Lammers that he wanted the solution of the Jewish problem postponed until after the war was over, a ruling that remarkably few historians now seem disposed to quote."
>
> PROF. EVANS: Yes. That is a complete misrepresentation of what we are calling the Schlegelberger memorandum.
>
> MR. IRVING: In what way is it a misrepresentation?
>
> MR. JUSTICE GRAY: Do not let us go through it all over again.
>
> PROF. EVANS: There is nothing weary about it. He did not tell Lammers. There was not a ruling . . . , otherwise why would the Ministry of Justice have gone ahead quite shortly afterwards and arranged for the Jews in state prisons to be taken out and sent off for extermination? It beggars belief that this is actually a ruling which then does not leave a paper trail, as you describe Hitler rulings doing throughout the bureaucracy, saying, oh, the Führer has ordered that the solution has to be put off, hold it everybody, let us stop. The whole thing goes on.

Irving's response to this was to claim that there was no evidence that the prisoners had been sent off to be killed. *Vernichtung* did not necessarily mean killing, he said, although at this time, most historians are agreed that it did. He then asked why they should be killed when Germany needed manpower? In fact, of course, by this time the Nazi regime regarded the destruction of the Jews as one of the principal aims of the war itself.[77] Even if this were not so, the document did not provide any support for Irving's firm statement that it proved that Hitler had tried to stop Jews from being deported.

Irving's method of dealing with documents whose import was not convenient to his preconceived views was to cast doubt on their authenticity. This took up a good deal of the court's time on occasion. But it was seldom convincing. Fairly early on in the trial, Richard Rampton confronted Irving with a document reporting that 97,000 Jews had been killed in the gas vans at Chelmno. Irving had written and said on many occasions that the Nazis had only undertaken gassing on an experimental scale. Rampton, knotting his gown behind his back and pulling the ends tight, as he always did when he had the witness cornered, forced Irving to agree that the 97,000 had been gassed. Irving's response was inadvertently revealing:

MR. RAMPTON: . . . 97,000 people in three trucks in the course of five weeks.

MR. IRVING: It is a very substantial achievement when you work it out with a pocket calculator—

MR. RAMPTON: Clever SS!

MR. IRVING: —at 20 people per time, and they drove 20 kilometres into the countryside. I have read all the reports on this.

(. . .)

MR. RAMPTON: . . . Would you describe it as very limited and experimental?

MR. IRVING: Not on this scale. This is systematic.

MR. RAMPTON: It is systematic, huge scale, using gas trucks to murder Jews?

MR. IRVING: Yes. No question at all.[78]

Irving's written statements that gassing had only been used experimentally and on a limited scale were, he was forced to admit, "just plain wrong."[79] He was aware that he had made an important concession. He came back to the document much later in the trial. Irving noted that the words at the top, *Einzigste Ausfertigung*, literally, "onliest copy," could not be found on any other document anywhere, that the way it began, with the word *Beispielsweise* (for example), was "an unusual turn of phrase to begin a letter with." What was he trying to say? When the judge challenged him to come clean on whether he actually thought the document was authentic or not, he was forced to retreat:

> MR. JUSTICE GRAY: You rely on that as an indication that this is not an authentic document?
>
> MR. IRVING: I am trying to plant a seed of suspicion in your Lordship's mind, that is all.
>
> MR. JUSTICE GRAY: You are not succeeding at the moment because I would have thought, if you are trying to create a document that is going to deceive anybody, you would not do what you say is something obviously inappropriate, which is to refer to an example in the first paragraph.
>
> MR. IRVING: It would be inappropriate for me to do anything else . . .
>
> MR. JUSTICE GRAY: So you accept this is an authentic document?
>
> MR. IRVING: For the purposes of this morning, yes.
>
> MR. RAMPTON: I do have to know sooner or later, and so does your Lordship, whether Mr. Irving accepts for the purposes of this trial that this is an authentic document. If it is a forgery, we need to know why he says it is a forgery.
>
> MR. JUSTICE GRAY: You do not say it is a forgery?
>
> MR. IRVING: No.
>
> MR. JUSTICE GRAY: Then we can forget about *Beispielsweise,* can we not?

As Christopher Browning pointed out, the linguistic oddities were easily explained by the fact that the document was written by an uneducated mechanic in the motor pool in Berlin, and that "for example" referred back to the subject of the letter—technical changes in the gas lorries.[80] Innuendo of this kind was Irving's stock-in-trade. But it did not wash with the court, which insisted time and again on a clear view one way or the other.

When he was completely unable to defend himself on rational grounds against the accusation that he had doctored a source, Irving pleaded literary license of one kind or another. "We are writing a work of literature," he said grandly, and a "precise, literal translation . . . would end up with a ghastly book of the kind that academics and scholars write."[81] If he had abridged quotations, it was not because he wanted to suppress something inconvenient to his argument, but because he did not want to make his books too long by filling them with "acres of sludge."[82] On occasion, he even claimed that his American editors had removed passages from the 1977 edition of *Hitler's War* when it came to be reissued in 1991 without consulting him, a story that seemed barely credible in view of the fact that he also admitted that he himself had been over the text to remove the passages which mentioned the mass gassing of the Jews.[83]

V

Irving got himself into a similar tangle when trying to deal with the allegation that he had close contacts with the Institute for Historical Review, the leading Holocaust denial organization in the United States. First, he tried to claim that his contacts were not close. My report showed that he had been a frequent visitor to the Institute's conferences. He had spoken five times there, once in 1983 then again four times in succession at the ninth, tenth, eleventh, and twelfth conferences. Seventeen years had elapsed between his first speech in 1983 and the present trial.

> MR. IRVING: Five times in 17 years is not a frequent visitor, by any reckoning, is it?
>
> PROF. EVANS: Four times in four years is a very frequent visitor, Mr. Irving.
>
> MR. IRVING: What makes you think that the ninth, tenth, eleventh and twelfth conferences were on an annual basis?
>
> (. . .)
>
> PROF. EVANS: Are you telling me they are not, then? Would you like to tell me the dates of those conferences?

MR. IRVING: They are either every two or three years.

PROF. EVANS: So in that case, 17 years, . . . five visits is actually rather frequent; it is the majority of them, is it not?

MR. IRVING: Do you agree that five times in 17 years does not qualify for the word "frequent visitor"?

MR. JUSTICE GRAY: I think the point he is making is that if they are every two or three years, you have been to every single one.[84]

Since I was obviously unaware of the fact, and had not mentioned it in my report, Irving did not mention that he had also been the keynote speaker at the IHR's conference in 1998, which would have made it six conferences, not five.[85] In any case, if the Institute was a respectable academic institution, as he had claimed in his written submission to the court before the trial, then why was Irving trying to dissociate himself from it in this way?

Was he a Holocaust denier? It was absurd, Irving said, to label as a Holocaust denier "somebody who challenges a figure." But he did not challenge my definition of Holocaust denial in any detail. Irving's claim that 4 million Jews had been killed by the Nazis made the newspapers as if it had been some kind of retraction. But Richard Rampton forced him to admit that this number included deaths from disease. As far as the numbers were concerned, all Irving would admit was that up to one million Jews had been shot by the Nazis behind the Eastern Front.[86] His view of the rest was revealed dramatically when a woman confronted him one day as he stepped out of the Law Courts on to the Strand, and told him her grandparents had died in Auschwitz, "Well," he replied, "You can be comforted in the knowledge that they most likely died of typhus, just like Anne Frank."[87]

Irving admitted freely: "I denied the gas chambers."[88] Did he believe the extermination was systematic, then? In his published writings and speeches, Irving had claimed that the shootings of Jews behind the Eastern Front were the result of rogue elements in the SS acting on their own initiative, rather like the American army lieutenant who massacred villagers at My Lai during the Vietnam War. But faced with evidence that the *Einsatzgruppen* reports detailing, among other things, the numbers of Jews killed, were asked for by Heydrich in Berlin, sent to him regularly, and ordered to be shown to Hitler, Irving was forced to admit that "that was wrong" and that "there was a co-ordination . . . a systematic direction going on between Berlin and the Eastern Front where the killings were taking place."[89] He agreed that Hitler knew and approved of what was happening as well.[90] Irving had to make other concessions when confronted with hard evidence by the defense counsel. He conceded, for example, that it was probable that hundreds of thousands of Jews were deliberately killed in the 'Operation Reinhard' camps.[91] He also agreed that the Leuchter Report was fundamentally flawed, and that gassing of humans did take place on a limited scale in Auschwitz as well as on a larger than experimental scale at Chelmno. Irving was caught in a trap here: if he continued to defy the evidence and deny that these things had happened, then Lipstadt's charge that he was a Holocaust denier was proved correct; if he retracted his earlier views when confronted with hard evidence, then he was conceding her charge that he had denied the Holocaust in the face of facts that he knew to be true. Perhaps because of this, Irving issued the court with a written retraction of some of his concessions. But since he had made the concessions on oath, this did not count for much in the end.[92]

Irving evidently found it much easier to dispose of eyewitness accounts of the mass murder. His treatment of the description of Auschwitz by a former inmate, Marie-Claude Vaillant-Couturier, was characteristic: unable to discredit the detail it contained, he took refuge in the notes made on her testimony by an American judge at the Nuremberg trial. At the end of the short paragraph recording her evidence that the SS had kept brothels at the camps, Judge Biddle had added the parenthetical note: "(This I doubt.)" When Irving came to reproduce this note, he removed the brackets and rewrote it as: "All this I doubt.)" In this way, he made it refer to the entirety of Vaillant-Couturier's testimony, which of course included evidence of the gas chambers. On one occasion Irving had even claimed that Judge Biddle had written: "I don't believe a word of what she is saying. I think she is a bloody liar." He had to admit that this latter claim was wrong, but insisted he had been right to add the word *all* "to make it more literate for an audience."[93] Of course, it also altered the meaning at the same time.

Irving had also tried to discredit the diary kept by Anne Frank, a young Jewish girl, in Holland, before her deportation by the Nazis to Auschwitz, and eventually to Bergen-Belsen, where she died. An exhaustive scientific investigation by the Netherlands State Institute for War Documentation carried out after the death of Anne Frank's father Otto in 1980 had demonstrated conclusively that the diary had been written by one person and that all the materials used were in use in the 1940s. It had also found a limited number of minor stylistic emendations made later on, in ballpoint pen. Apart from these, however, the diary was undeniably authentic.[94] Disregarding these findings entirely, Irving had followed other Holocaust deniers in describing the diary as a 'novel,' alleging that the handwriting was not hers, suggesting that whole pages were written with a ballpoint pen, and asserting that a thirteen-year-old girl would not have had the maturity to have written such a document. He had made these fantastic allegations in 1993, long after the Netherlands State Institute for War Documentation had completed and published its work. He was also unable to explain away the fact that he had told CNN television news on 16 January 2000 that he had previously said the Anne Frank diary was a forgery and now admitted that it was not.[95]

Falsifications such as these, alleged the defense, were made in the service of Irving's racist and antisemitic ideology. Had he been antisemitic? Irving tried to argue that whatever remarks he had made about Jews and their organizations had been justified. But he was on sticky ground:

MR. IRVING: . . . I have made a speech in 1992 and you take exception to my description of the Board of Deputies (of British Jews), and the words that I use. Is any criticism of an organization like that permissible, do you think?

PROF. EVANS: I do think it is rather over the top to describe the Board of Deputies of British Jews as cockroaches.

MR. IRVING: If you are familiar with the methods that they have used to destroy a professional historian's career and family, would that professional historian be entitled to use pretty colourful language to describe these people who are secretly trying to destroy him?

(. . .)

PROF. EVANS: I would have to first of all see evidence to persuade me that such a secret dastardly campaign had been carried out. I do not want to answer a hypothetical question of that nature. I do think that professional historians should be reasonably measured in their language. I do not think that is an appropriate word to use.

MR. IRVING: If the court is shown a document showing that at this precise time that body was contemplating putting pressure on that author's publisher to stop publishing his books and thereby destroy his career and livelihood, and they were doing it behind armour plated doors in their headquarters—

MR. JUSTICE GRAY: Show the witness the document and then we can see.

What Irving showed me was a copy of the minutes of the Holocaust Educational Trust's Education and Academic Committee, not the Board of Deputies of British Jews, meeting on 12 December 1991, at which, as the minutes reported, "concern was voiced over the publication of the second edition of *Hitler's War.* There was debate over how to approach Macmillan publishers over Goebbels's Diary, It was agreed (to) await news from Jeremy Coleman before deciding what course of action to take."

So in fact the meeting did not decide to put any pressure on Irving's publishers. And since Irving had used the expression *cockroaches* on 5 October 1991, more than two months before the meeting took place, it was hard to see how the document Irving presented to the court could even begin to justify his using an expression of that kind.[96] Defeated on this point, Irving retreated:

MR. IRVING: . . . Witness, will you accept that, on the balance of probabilities, there are other documents of that nature in that bundle?

MR. JUSTICE GRAY: If I may say so, Mr. Irving, we must do better than that.[97]

An alternative tactic was to dispute the significance placed on some instances of his antisemitism in the report. This too proved difficult. When he tried to argue that the list of "traditional enemies of the truth" he had placed on his website contained many non-Jewish organizations, Richard Rampton was able to show that "Mr. Irving has identified as being not Jewish I think four that, in fact, are Jewish. The only two that are not that we can tell are the Australian and German governments."[98]

By the time he got to Dresden, Irving was clearly running out of steam. Under cross-examination himself, he had become visibly angry about the bombing, waving photographs of the dead at the court and almost losing self-control when Richard Rampton responded by saying "So what?"; for the issue was not what happened in Dresden, but how Irving had portrayed it in his book.[99] Astonishingly, he claimed under cross-examination himself that he had "always recognized" that TB 47 was a fake. Given this admission, he was unable to account for the fact that he had presented the figures that it gave as genuine.[100] And he ended on a bizarre note, with an elaborate excuse for the delays on his side in corresponding with Dr. Funfack, an excuse that I was happy enough to accept, given the fact that it had no bearing on the case against him.

Irving returned to a number of these issues in his lengthy Closing Statement to the court. "A judgment in my favour," he said, "is no more than a judgment that disputed points which I have made about some aspects of the narrative are not so absurd, given the evidence, as to disqualify me from the ranks of historians."[101] As a result of his work, and indeed of the trial, he claimed, the Holocaust had been "researched more, not less."[102] He had made mistakes in his work, to be sure, but so did all historians, and if any other historian had been subjected to the kind of critical investigation to which he had, the results would have been more or less the same. He admitted occasional lapses of taste in his speeches, but in his written works he had not distorted, falsified, or manipulated history at all. Professional historians, "including some whom you have heard in court," had "cheered from the sidelines as I have been outlawed, arrested, harassed, and all but *vernichtet* as a professional historian; and they have put pressure on British publishers to destroy my works."[103]

Irving had not, of course, presented a shred of evidence to support this wild and paranoid claim, nor could he have done so, because it was not true. Even if it had been, however, it had no more bearing on the case than did his equally wild claims about a world conspiracy to suppress his views, to which he devoted a substantial part of his Closing Statement.[104] On the substantive issues before the court, Irving had nothing new to say. At one point the defense counsel complained about his "continuous misrepresentation of the evidence of my witness."[105] And when it came to rebutting the defense charge of consorting with neo-Nazis in Germany, Irving's habit of improvising from his prepared text led him into a fatal slip of the tongue, as he inadvertently addressed the judge as "Mein Führer."[106] Everyone in court knew that he was referring to the judge as "Mein Führer" from the tone of voice in which he said it. The court dissolved into laughter.[107] "No one could believe what just happened," wrote one spectator. "Had we imagined it? Could he have addressed the judge as 'Mein Führer'?" Irving himself denied having made the slip.[108] But amid the laughter in court, he could be seen mumbling an apology to the judge for having addressed him in this way. Perhaps the slip was a consequence of Irving's unconscious identification of the judge as a benign authority figure. Whatever the reason for it, with the laughter still ringing in its ears, the court adjourned on 15 March 2000 as the judge prepared the final version of his judgment on the case.

CHAPTER SEVEN

Judgment Day

I

Throughout the trial, Irving posted more or less daily reports on the case on his website. These seldom bore a close relation to what had gone on in court. Day after day he trumpeted victories over the defense, when in fact he had suffered one defeat after another.[1] The "general satisfaction in the public galleries" which he reported consisted of the murmurs of appreciation he occasionally received from the tiny claque of supporters sitting behind him.[2] The judge's frequent admonitions of Irving for his conduct as a cross-examiner were simply not registered in Irving's self-styled 'Radical's Diary,' although virtually every intervention on Irving's behalf found a hopeful mention. Was it self-delusion when Irving told his website readers that the judge had said during the final speeches that the issue of racism had no bearing whatever on the trial? As so often with Irving, it was difficult to tell how far he had been taken in by his own hype.

There were already some indications during the trial that he was less than wholly optimistic about the outcome. He repeatedly alluded to the money and resources that he saw ranged against him. He tried to build up a picture of the 'revisionist' David against the orthodox Goliath despite claiming that he had supporters and researchers all over the world and a 'Gang' of assistants helping him prepare for each day's events. And in his Closing Statement he complained bitterly about the attitude of the press, which, he declared, had devoted eight times more reports to his cross-examination by Richard Rampton than it had to his own cross-examination of the defense witnesses. Clearly, by the end of the trial, Irving considered that the press had turned against him. If, as some had suspected, he had intended the whole case as a media event designed to gain a favorable hearing for his own views once more, then by his own confession he had lamentably failed to achieve his objective.[3]

When the verdict finally came, it was in the form of a 350-page reasoned judgment handed down by Judge Charles Gray. "Libel trials," wrote Clare Dyer in *The Guardian* after the judge had delivered his verdict, "rarely end with the feeling that the full story has been told. Irving v Penguin Books is a rare exception." If the trial had been held before a jury, all that would have happened at the end would have been a finding that Penguin had or had not libelled Irving. The judge would not have had the opportunity to write his lengthy judgment at all.[4] Now here it was. Plaintiff and defendant had received written copies of the judgment shortly before the final day's proceedings, but Irving still seemed stunned as he sat in front of Judge Charles Gray and listened to him read out, in a rapid monotone, the key sixty or so pages of his 350-page document. On his way into the High Court, Irving had been pelted with eggs by hostile demonstrators and had discarded his egg-stained jacket as a result, giving him an unwontedly informal appearance. His face reddened as he heard the judge read out his lengthy statement of findings on the case.

The judge began by sugaring the pill for Irving by accepting that as a military historian he had much to commend in him. He possessed an "unparalleled" knowledge of World War II and a "remarkable" command of the documents. He was capable and intelligent and had discovered much new material. Judge Gray rejected as "too sweeping" my assessment that Irving was not a historian at all. But, he went on, the case was not about Irving as a military historian, but about his treatment of Hitler and the Jews. Here, he concluded, the criticisms of Irving advanced by the defense were "almost invariably well-founded." In nineteen separate instances, the defense had proved that Irving had misrepresented the evidence.[5]

The judgment had a good deal to say about what an objective historian should do. "Whilst I accept that an historian is entitled to speculate," wrote Judge Gray, "he must spell out clearly to the reader when he is speculating rather than reciting established facts." Irving had not done this. "An objective historian," continued the judge, "is obliged to be even-handed in his approach to historical evidence: he cannot pick and choose without adequate reason." Irving was not even-handed. Objective historians had to take account of the circumstances surrounding the production of a document, and Irving had not. "I accept," wrote the judge, "that historians are bound by the constraints of space to edit quotations. But there is an obligation on them not to give the reader a distorted impression by selective quotation." Irving had not fulfilled this obligation. In sum, "Irving treated the historical evidence in a manner which fell far short of the standard to be expected of a conscientious historian." He "misrepresented and distorted the evidence which was available to him." It was also "incontrovertible" that "Irving qualifies as a Holocaust denier." His denial of the gas chambers and of the systematic and centrally directed nature of the mass shootings of Jews was "contrary to the evidence."[6]

However, the judge went on, this was still not sufficient to justify the defense's case. The defense had to "establish that the misrepresentation by Irving of the historical record was deliberate in the sense that Irving was motivated by a desire borne of his own ideological beliefs to present Hitler in a favourable light." "Historians are human," the judge noted. "They make mistakes, misread and misconstrue documents and overlook material evidence." But in all the instances in which Irving had done these things, the effect was to cast Hitler in a favorable light. There were no instances in which his errors worked in the opposite direction. His mistakes were thus "unlikely to have been innocent." His explanations for such errors in his work as he did concede were "unconvincing." Moreover, the judge declared: "In the course of these proceedings Irving challenged the authenticity of certain documents, not because there was any substantial reason for doubting their genuineness but because they did not fit in with his thesis." "His attitude to these documents was in stark contrast to his treatment of other documents which were more obviously open to question." There was "a comparable lack of even-handedness when it comes to Irving's treatment of eye-witnesses."[7]

The judge considered that Irving's change of stance on a number of issues during the trial when he was confronted with the documents showed his earlier "willingness to make assertions about the Nazi era which, as he must appreciate, are irreconcilable with the available evidence." Moreover, the fact that Irving withdrew some of these concessions indicated to the judge his "determination to adhere to his preferred version of history, even if the evidence does not support it."[8]

The judge explained with great clarity and force why he considered that Irving had departed from the normal standards of objective historical research and writing. It was clear from what he had said and written that "Irving is anti-semitic. His words are directed against Jews, either individually or collectively, in the sense that they are by turns hostile, critical, offensive and derisory in their references to semitic people, their characteristics and appearances." He was also a racist, and he had associated with militant neo-Nazis and right-wing extremists.[9] Over the past one and a half decades, he had become more active politically:

> The content of his speeches and interviews often displays a distinctly pro-Nazi and anti-Jewish bias. He makes surprising and often unfounded assertions about the Nazi regime which tend to exonerate the Nazis for the appalling atrocities which they inflicted on the Jews. He is content to mix with neo-fascists and appears to share many of their racist and anti-semitic prejudices. The picture of Irving which emerges from the evidence of his extra-curricular activities reveals him to be a right-wing pro-Nazi polemicist. In my view the Defendants have established that Irving has a political agenda. It is one which, it is legitimate to infer, disposes him, where he deems it necessary, to manipulate the historical record in order to make it conform with his political beliefs.

The inevitable inference was that this manipulation was deliberate.[10] Thus the defense had proved its case. On the central issues, Lipstadt was justified. Irving's libel action was rejected.

Irving rose stiffly to tell the judge that he intended to appeal. He had failed to make himself clear on the nineteen cases of alleged falsification, he said.[11] Mr. Justice Gray had failed to understand him. But this was no basis for an appeal, which Irving seemed not to realize would be allowed only on a point of law. Mr. Justice Gray rejected the application. Irving would have to apply for leave to appeal from the Court of Appeal itself. But as Richard Rampton made clear, the chances of success were minimal here too. The judgment seemed to him to be technically impeccable and legally unassailable. And indeed Irving's application was rejected

some months later by the Court of Appeal. As the security staff hustled
Irving out unceremoniously through a back entrance, Lipstadt and her
solicitors, along with Penguin's managing director, emerged through the
front gates to greet the assembled paparazzi.

Later, at a press conference, Lipstadt broke her silence for the first
time, declaring herself fully vindicated. During the whole period of
preparation from 1995 on, and during the trial itself, she had said nothing in public about the case. This was not unconnected with her consistent refusal to engage in debate with Holocaust deniers (on the reasonable grounds that it would dignify their views by granting them equal
status with those of genuine historians—a geography professor, after all,
does not waste time debating with people who think the earth is flat). Irving seemed particularly affronted that she had not gone into the witness
box during the trial to be cross-examined by him. Contrary to what many
journalists appeared to think, however, the decision not to call her had
not been Lipstadt's. She had been perfectly willing to take the stand. But
the defense lawyers had seen that there was no need for her to do so. To
accuse her of a lack of courage in not testifying, as Irving did, was, I
thought, mere spite, and responsible journalists like Neal Ascherson, who
similarly accused her of being "afraid of what Irving could do to her"
should not have swallowed his bile.[12]

And of course not only was there no obligation on the defense barrister to call her, her testimony would also have had no bearing on the
case, which was about Irving's work, not hers. Having provided Irving
with all the evidence that underlay her account of his work in her book,
as a part of the obligatory process of Discovery, there was nothing that
Lipstadt could usefully add to what the expert witnesses would say.[13] Her
motives in writing what she did about Irving in her book were irrelevant,
although no doubt Irving wanted to quiz her about her connections with
what he portrayed as the worldwide Jewish conspiracy to silence him. But
this, as the judge repeatedly tried to explain to him, did not matter. What
mattered was simply the truth or otherwise of what was on the printed
page of *Denying the Holocaust*. Suitably enough, when Lipstadt finally
spoke, after the trial, it was simply to declare that she was happy that the
truth of what she had written had been borne out by the trial.

Back at his Mayfair flat, Irving was confronting the prospect of a bill

for more than £2 million in costs from the defense, should the court agree
that he should pay it, as indeed was very likely. How would he react?
Speaking to journalists after the event, Irving called the judgment "inde-
scribable" and "perverse." He hinted that it was predictable in view of
the fact that the judge was "an up-and-coming member of the establishment."[14] Somehow, then, Irving had been defeated by the closed ranks
of an all-powerful 'Establishment.' He had "over-estimated the judge's
ability to grasp the intricacies of the German documents."[15] Unrepentant
in his antisemitism, Irving borrowed a phrase from Shakespeare's portrayal of Shylock, the Jewish villain of *The Merchant of Venice*, in the face
of the defense's intention of recovering costs: "Undoubtedly they will
come for their pound of flesh, but will find I'm made of British beef. I've
always suspected they were into money and gold, with a capital G."[16] But
this was only money he had made them spend. And he was evidently forgetting the tendency of British beef to transmit 'mad cow disease."[17]

And who were 'they'? Throughout the trial and long afterwards, Irving continually claimed on his website that the defense was being
bankrolled by Jews, both wealthy individuals and organized groups,
across the world. In fact, of course, there was no secret about the fact that
the bulk of the funds came from Penguin Books Ltd., and Penguin's
insurers. "Despite Irving's assertions to the contrary," noted Mark Bateman, Penguin's solicitor, "it was Penguin that paid the fees of the experts,
leading counsel, junior counsel and my firm."[18] They had also paid the
fees of all the researchers. Mishcon de Reya, Anthony Julius's firm of
solicitors, had indeed worked for the first two years of the case, in 1996
and 1997, *pro bono*, for no fee at all. They had only started to charge fees
when the final preparations for and conduct of the case began to con-
sume major resources within the firm (at one time, nearly forty people
were working on the case, many of them full-time). It was solely for these
costs that Deborah Lipstadt was obliged to pay, and for which she
received financial backing from supporters such as Steven Spielberg,
amounting in total to no more than a fraction of the overall costs.

Did Irving have the funds to pay the defense's costs? "No smart
accountants have been hired to hide funds away," he told *The Times* on 12
April 2000.[19] Accountants or no accountants, he certainly claimed to be
receiving about £2000 a day from his supporters during the trial.[20] One, he

reported, had handed him $50,000 in cash in a brown paper bag at Amsterdam airport. Most of his supporters, he said, were from the United States, and four thousand or five thousand people had sent him money by the end of the trial, by which time he claimed to have half a million dollars in his 'fighting fund.'[21] Yet Irving's Mayfair flat was mortgaged five times over and he earned little from his own writings and speeches. Indeed, according to *The Guardian*, "Irving's only real earnings of late have been in the courts." These included an estimated £75,000 paid to him out of court by *The Sunday Times* in 1994 as compensation for the newspaper's dropping the Goebbels diaries serialization.[22] Six years had passed since then. Another source put his monthly income from the sale of his books at around $10,000.[23] All that Irving achieved by boasting about the scale of his financial backing was to prompt Penguin's lawyers into applying for, and obtaining, an interim court order requiring him to pay the first £150,000 of the defense costs, a sum which he did not pay by the deadline.

Irving nonetheless tried to rescue some self-respect from the debacle. His boast that he had achieved what he wanted because he had stood alone against a battery of thirty witnesses met with general skepticism; after all, only five expert witnesses had actually appeared for the defense, and he had not been able to dent any of the central points they had made in their reports.[24] Irving claimed he had made the witnesses sweat. But he had not made us abandon any of the criticisms we had leveled at him, or modify any of the points we had made about the evidence for the Nazi extermination of the Jews or Hitler's part in it. On the contrary, it had been Irving who had been forced to recant on issue after issue as the trial had proceeded.[25] "Their experts were speaking a load of baloney, but mine spoke from the heart," he added.[26] What experts? Only four witnesses had appeared in court on Irving's behalf. One, Peter Millar, was testifying only to matters of fact in connection with the Moscow archives, so whether or not he spoke from the heart was completely beside the point.

Irving could only describe two others as 'his' experts with difficulty, since they had been forced to appear in court against their will. Finally, the "evolutionary psychologist" Kevin Macdonald's testimony had been disregarded altogether in the judgment. The writer Dan Jacobson pointed out that Macdonald was the only witness who appeared in court for Irving without being forced to.[27] No doubt Macdonald was sincere in his belief that Jews had an evolutionary strategy of sticking together and competing with gentile society. But did sincerity guarantee truthfulness? This was clutching at straws.

Irving also made a point, both in cross-examining the witnesses and in posting their fees up on his website, of implying (or more than implying) that they had been hired to destroy his credibility and would not have dared jeopardize their income by criticizing Lipstadt. This raised a general point about historians doing paid work outside the academy, the subject of some debate over the previous months in the context of colleagues commissioned to write histories of German instutitions such as the Deutsche Bank or Volkswagen AG, which had been involved in the use of slave labor or profiteering from Nazi gold during the Third Reich. Had they pulled their punches because they did not want to offend their paymasters? The evidence seemed unconvincing in most instances. Indeed, the firms' fortunes on the American merger and takeover scene virtually depended on their historians taking an uncompromisingly tough stance on their past misdeeds, to show that there was no intention of a cover-up. While this controversy rumbled on through 1998 and 1999, the expert witnesses in the Irving case were busy preparing their reports. At the end of it, we all had to make a declaration that we had told the truth and had not been influenced by our Instructing Solicitors. And this was indeed the case. We were after all being paid by the hour, not by results. My own report made it clear that Lipstadt was wrong on one issue, and nobody on the defense side made any attempt to change the passage in question; I would have resisted it if they had. Had she been wrong on more, I would have said so.[28]

Irving's attempts to brand the defense experts as corrupt tools of a monied Jewish conspiracy went largely unchallenged in his post-trial radio and television interviews, which were so numerous that the Board of Deputies of British Jews lodged an official complaint with the BBC. Why was the Corporation offering a platform to a man branded by the High Court as a racist and antisemite? Jewish observers complained that Irving "was allowed, in many instances, to spout his views, unchecked, and without the counter-argument."[29] As John Waters noted in the *Irish Times*, there were serious problems with "the conceited belief in the media that all discussion leads to enlightenment."[30] The BBC rejected the complaints. "Far from giving him a platform," it said, "we challenged him on his opinions and asked the kinds of questions many viewers and listeners wanted to see put to him."[31] Awkward questions were indeed asked. The problem lay in the way that interviewers dealt with Irving's answers. Discussion in this case had to be based on a detailed knowledge of the documents, the reports, and the court case that the journalists and interviewers simply did not possess. Few of the journalists who interviewed Irving after the trial proved capable of challenging the fresh distortions of the truth that he peddled.

The judge, Irving told Krishnan Guru-Murthy on Channel 4's 7 o'clock news, had described him as Britain's preeminent military historian. He had not. All that he had said was that there was much to commend in Irving as a military historian.[32] Irving claimed that the judge had admitted to being horrified when he discovered that there was not a single document that proved that the gas chambers existed. Nowhere in the 350 pages of his judgment did he say such a thing. On the contrary, he said that "the cumulative effect of the documentary evidence for the genocidal operation of gas chambers at Auschwitz is considerable."[33] Irving claimed that the judge said he was right to criticize Jews for what they had done to him. What the judge actually wrote was that while he had some sympathy for Irving's argument that Jews were not immune from his criticism, "Irving has repeatedly crossed the divide between legitimate criticism and prejudiced vilification of the Jewish race and people." Irving and his family had, it was true, the judge went on, been subjected to extreme pressure from time to time because of his views, but it was just in such circumstances, in the heat of the moment, that racial prejudice manifested itself.[34] None of these points was picked up by the interviewer.

Interviewing Irving on BBC World TV's 'Hard Talk' program a few weeks later, Tim Sebastian, one of the Corporation's most experienced journalists, did not dispute Irving's claim that the defense had cost 10 million pounds in a "really dirty fight" against him. He had enjoyed seeing the defense witnesses "crumble," Irving bragged: "I ran rings round them." This applied particularly to me. My knowledge of German was "on occasion lamentable," he declared, and he boasted that the judge had said he did not agree with "a lot of the negative things" I had to say about Irving. He also claimed that the Leuchter Report's findings had subsequently been replicated by reputable scientists. But the judge, he complained, had said "I believe the eyewitnesses and not the roof," although the judge had referred to drawings and photographs of holes in the roof used for dropping in poison gass pellets as evidence that the crematorium was a gas chamber. Irving repeated his lie that the word *Judentransport* in the Himmler phone log of 30 November 1941 had been there "just by itself, without context," as if the words *aus Berlin* had not been there too. Sebastian did not point out that the defense costs were 2 million pounds, not 10, and that the judge had only disputed one of my statements about Irving—that he was not a historian—not "lots." Sebastian appeared not to have read the trial transcripts, and I had not seen him in court at any time. Where he did manage to challenge Irving was on the simpler and more obvious issue of racism, where he succeeded in provoking a string of racist statements from Irving that the latter clearly did not recognize as such.

The only interviewer who did manage to unsettle Irving was the persistent Jeremy Paxman, on BBC2 television's *Newsnight*. Paxman was alert enough to spot that Irving was quoting selectively from the judgment ("typical of your methods," said Paxman with his inimitable sneer). He proved sufficiently effective in demolishing Irving's claim not to be an antisemite and racist for Irving, letting the mask slip for a moment, to say to him suddenly: "You're not Jewish, are you?" In another unguarded moment, when Paxman asked him, "Will you stop denying the Holocaust on the basis of this judgment?," Irving baldly replied, "Good Lord, no." No other interviewer was so effective.

What was wrong about the media's reaction to the verdict was not that they interviewed Irving, but that they failed to prepare properly for doing so. This contrasted strongly with the hard work and dedication of the lawyers involved in the case. Small wonder, then, that Irving thought he could make capital out of his media appearances after the verdict. For Irving himself, the 'feeding frenzy' of the media after the verdict prompted a reaction like that of an attention-seeking child:

> I do ITN, Australian ABC live, Today, Radio 4, Radio 5 . . . BBC World TV . . . Breakfast TV . . . Newsnight . . . The phone rings all morning every thirty seconds . . . BBC Radio 3 . . . Italian radio . . .

> Los Angeles Radio . . . Radio Teheran phones for an interview. Radio
> Qatar want to interview me. . . . How very satisfying it has all been.[35]

Thus a week after the verdict, Irving was claiming "I *have* managed
to win," because "two days after the judgment, name recognition
becomes enormous, and gradually the plus or minus in front of the name
fades."[36] The cartoons that had him denying the trial had ever taken
place, or the verdict ever delivered, were not far from the truth.[37]

The historian Andrew Roberts agreed with Irving's assessment of the
defense's triumph as a Pyrrhic victory because the trial had brought his
views to the attention of a worldwide audience. "The free publicity that
this trial has generated for him and his views has been worth far more
than could ever have been bought for the amount of the costs," he wrote
after the trial. It was Irving, not Lipstadt, who was being interviewed on
virtually every television channel. The law had let him propagate "his
repulsive political message." It had been a public relations triumph, and
all at the expense of Penguin.[38] Nevertheless, Irving's boast that even if
he had lost the courtroom battle, he had won the media war, was vain.
Reports about him in the press were overwhelmingly critical. Stories on
the verdict outnumbered those printed during the trial by a factor of
three to one. At sea for much of the courtroom battle, journalists now had
some solid ground on which to base their assessments.

Analysis of 55 newspaper articles published from 12 to 17 April 2000
revealed that while fewer than 15 had described Irving as a gifted
researcher, 40 had emphasized his activities as a Holocaust denier, 37 had
stressed the fact that he was a racist, and 35 had declared that he had falsified history.[39] "As post-verdict television interviews showed," thought
one commentator, "he has no idea how loathsome and isolated he is."[40]
Irving's frantic attempts on the afternoon after the verdict to find a legal
pretext for preventing television stations from showing video footage of
some of the more repulsive moments from his speeches failed completely, and millions of viewers were treated to the spectacle of Irving
describing Holocaust survivors as "ASSHOLES." This cannot have done
him much good. Lord Weidenfeld, publisher and pundit on matters Central European, noted too how only a few hours after the verdict, television viewers could see

> how this man, crafty, evasive, sometimes crude and even primitive,
> then once more skilled and almost artful, struggled again and again
> to piece together the fragments of his reputation. Master of innu-
> endo and of ambiguous formulations that he is, he repeatedly tried
> to assemble truth, half-truths and fiction into conclusive arguments.

Weidenfeld gave the impression that few took him seriously any more.[41]

On 29 April 2000, two and a half weeks after the verdict, Channel 4 broadcast a lengthy documentary, lasting almost two hours, at prime time, successfully juxtaposing well-chosen dramatized extracts from the trial transcripts with historical analyses and archive footage of the events to which they referred. Well before that, however, Irving had more or less disappeared from the airwaves once more, as the media circus moved rapidly on to other things. Meanwhile, Penguin reprinted Lipstadt's *Denying the Holocaust* in a paperback edition and rushed out the judg- ment in an inexpensive book format. Piles of both volumes could soon be seen in all good bookshops, and more were to follow in the shape of revised versions of the experts' reports and two comprehensive accounts of the trial by journalists who had been present in court throughout. Irv- ing might have cruised the airwaves with virtual impunity in the first flush of defeat, but over the long haul, his prospects of continuing but neu- tralized media fame did not look good.

Irving's reputation was damaged even in his own chosen milieu of right-wing extremists and Holocaust deniers. He had clearly let them down badly, and in more ways than one. To begin with, he had lost. This did not go down well on the far right. The views of other Holocaust deniers on the verdict ranged from incomprehension to defiance. Many were incoherent and abusive. Some of those which Irving put up on his own website were rabidly antisemitic, some more measured in tone. One report claiming to be from an eyewitness of the court proceedings was mostly pure invention (it put Richard Rampton's age at seventy, had him surrounded by twenty assistants telling him "Stop Irving. Stop Irving now," and so on).[42] More significant, however, was the fact that Irving lost a good deal of credit among hard-line Holocaust deniers by the conces- sions he was forced to make in court.

British National Party leader Nick Griffin criticized Irving as too soft on the Holocaust issue.[43] Ernst Zündel reported numerous telephone calls from supporters "anxious and upset, even angry," about "some far-reaching and off-the-wall concession David Irving is said to have made." Somewhat patronizingly, Zündel recalled his own experience of court proceedings and lamented the fact that "It is a pity for the cause of Truth in History and for Historical Revisionism that David Irving does not have that experience of how to fight a political trial to draw upon or to fall back on." Zündel claimed that there was resentment among 'Revisionists' that Irving had not called them as expert witnesses, and incomprehension that he did not want to be known as one of them. One of them, the gas chamber denier Germar Rudolf, thought that "Justice Gray made it pretty clear that refusing to present me as a witness forced him to reject Irving's law suit." Irving, concluded Zündel, was being dragged into the world of the Holocaust.[44] Robert Faurisson thought he had always been there, despite having been "subject, intermittently, to promising bursts of revisionism." Since Irving had not properly studied the Holocaust, Faurisson thought he was on weak ground in court. It was easy to trip him up. In any case, concluded the Frenchman, "he cannot be considered a spokesman for historical revisionism."[45]

Irving was going to have a lot of bridge-building to do if he was to have any friends left at all after the trial ended. At the end of May he flew to California to address an audience of 140 people at a meeting organized by the Institute for Historical Review. The location was kept secret. Characteristically he gave yet another figure, plucked as usual out of thin air, for the money he thought the defense had spent on the action—this time it was $6 million, or about 4 million pounds. One local Jewish organization described him as a "freak in a sideshow." Others objected. Meanwhile Irving's announcement that he was organizing a so-called 'Real History Conference' in Cincinnati suggested that the search for funds was going to take priority over mending fences with the Institute for Historical Review.[46]

II

In her book, Lipstadt had called Irving a particularly dangerous spokesperson for Holocaust denial. He was, as *The Guardian* put it after the trial, "the deniers' best shot . . . the best of this bunch, the 'Face' for those purulent haters behind the websites and the seamy pamphlets."[47]

Irving, commented *The Scotsman* newspaper, was dangerous because "he does not present himself to the public as a ranting ideologue or political extremist. Rather he wears the mantle of a serious academic historian, a man whose views are based upon research and erudition, not bile and prejudice."[48] Now his pseudo-academic mantle was in tatters. The damage done to the cause of Holocaust denial was shattering.

Yet Irving still had a few friends left, and in some rather unlikely places. Some still wanted to defend his early work. The journalist Tom Bower, a vigorous critic of postwar attempts to cover up Nazi crimes, still thought that the 1977 edition of *Hitler's War* was a masterpiece that offered "new insights which apparently were also factually accurate." Yet "Irving was never a reasoned historian. His falsification of history and his obsession with 'denying' the Holocaust was motivated by an uncontrollable hero-worship of Hitler." Irving was, in sum, "a brilliant historian ruined by a fatal flaw."[49] The fact was, however, that *Hitler's War* was not a 'masterpiece,' but an unreliable piece of work including massive falsification of the evidence. Nevertheless, others defended his early work too. The Irish political writer Conor Cruise O'Brien, for example, inspired by the trial to read the 1977 edition of *Hitler's War,* found it "a serious piece of historiography; solidly researched, lucidly presented and without apparent bias." It was only since the end of the 1980s, he thought, that Irving had gone downhill and suffered "the equivalent of a nervous breakdown," which turned a man who "had the makings of an excellent historian" into a man without intellectual balance who was no longer a "sound historian." There was, concluded O'Brien, "something movingly tragic, it seems to me, about the case of David Irving."[50] O'Brien's reading of the book cannot have been very careful if he thought it was without apparent bias. His views illustrated how easy it was for an intelligent layman to be impressed by the appearance of solid research that Irving's works often gave. At least, however, O'Brien was writing before the trial, when there was some excuse for such indulgence.

Further to the right of O'Brien, the columnist 'Peter Simple,' writing in the *Daily Telegraph,* considered it a "strange sort of country" which could consign Irving to "outer darkness while conferring the Order of Merit on another historian, the Marxist Eric Hobsbawm, an only partly and unwillingly repentant apologist for the Soviet Union, a system of tyranny whose victims far outnumbered those of Nazi Germany."[51] Leaving aside the numbers of victims, and ignoring the fact that Hobsbawm was not awarded the Order of Merit, which is in the personal gift of the queen, but was appointed a Companion of Honour, which is a government recommendation, the point here was, once more, that Irving did not lose his lawsuit because of his opinions, but because he was found to have deliberately falsified the evidence, something Hobsbawm, who in his day has attracted the most bitter controversy, has never been accused of doing, even by his most savage critics.

But it was not just journalists who spoke up for Irving. At the start of the trial, Stuart Nicolson, writing in *The Scotsman,* quoted an (inevitably) unnamed historian as saying that

> while historians like to have sparring partners when it comes to matters of academic dispute, this was a conflict in which many millions of people died, so it is not just a debating club matter, there are very serious issues at stake. Irving's track record is that of somebody who has made misleading statements about the Holocaust and who has supported others making such statements, and I would be very surprised if any serious historian gave him the time of day.[52]

How wrong he was. According to Tony Judt, a British specialist on twentieth-century France now based in the United States, Irving still had his defenders in the historical profession even after the judgment had been delivered. Some, he reported, argued that Irving was a conscientious and extremely knowledgeable collector of historical facts who only misused them for political purposes. Take away the conclusions and you still have the facts. Who is 'objective' anyway? "We may find his conclusions repulsive, but is that sufficient reason to exclude him from the community of historians?" Judt did not say which historians thought this, or how many of them there were. But he did make it clear that he disagreed with them. In his view, Irving simply selected facts to support his opinions. In fact, of course, he did far more than this: he molded the 'facts' so that they appeared to support his opinions even when in reality they did not. History, wrote Judt, always had to be rewritten and reinterpreted, but this had to be done with an integrity that Irving obviously lacked.[53]

All the more surprising, then, that he was still defended by some professional historians after the verdict. Three in particular took a stand on his behalf. The first of Irving's defenders was John Erickson, author of the standard military history of the war on the Eastern Front, and retired professor at Edinburgh University. Erickson evidently thought the verdict wrong-headed. He declared, for example, that the charge he would level against Irving "is not that he had 'denied' the Holocaust, which seems as fatuous as it is juvenile, but that he has contributed to diminishing an experience which had profound significance and which, as yet, has not been fully explained." For Irving, thought Erickson, did not deny the Holocaust, rather, he engaged in "whittling down" the scope of the Holocaust. He "does not deny mass killing of the Jews," but "distances himself from any admission of mass industrial murder" and thereby committed "contrived trivialisation for its own sake, a contrived parody of the Holocaust experience."

Erickson was "deeply concerned about the fate of the Holocaust at the hands of historians," since some "historians claim an exclusivity for the Holocaust" which he thought wrong because in the end "it belongs to us all."[54] Who these mysterious historians were, he seemed unable to say. Or what he meant when he said that the Holocaust had "not been fully explained." If Erickson had actually read the judgment, he would have been in no doubt that Irving had claimed that there were no gas chambers, no systematic extermination of 5 to 6 million Jews, no involvement of Hitler, no evidence apart from the inventions of the British and the Jews. If this was not denial of the Holocaust as historians understood it, then what was? And why was it juvenile to label it Holocaust denial? Moreover, the judgment made it crystal-clear that Irving was not engaging in denial for its own sake, but to further his own racist and antisemitic views.

If it was depressing that a historian of Erickson's standing could leap into print without actually having considered the details of the trial and the judgment, then it was, if anything, even more depressing that two other distinguished historians of the older generation, Sir John Keegan and Professor Donald Cameron Watt, actually testified on Irving's behalf in court. Admittedly, when asked by Irving to appear for him, both had refused, and he had issued a subpoena to force them to attend. Nevertheless, his choice by no means proved to be misguided. Keegan, a former teacher at Sandhurst military academy and now defense editor of the *Daily Telegraph*, had recently been knighted for his services to military history. He told the court that if he were to recommend to a starter a book "which would explain the Second World War from Hitler's side," it would be *Hitler's War*.[55] But he also described Irving's view that Hitler did not know what was going on with the Jews until October 1943 as "perverse . . . it defies common sense . . . it would defy reason."[56]

Keegan's praise was an important element in persuading the judge that Irving had much to recommend him as a military historian. But more was to come, for immediately after the verdict, Keegan rushed into print to justify what he had said in the witness box, and add a few more points in Irving's favor as well. Keegan declared that "the community of 20th-century historians" had generally thought before the trial began that "Irving might well persuade the judge of the unfairness of Professor Lipstadt's accusations of his bad historical method." As usual, these historians, whoever they might be, remained conveniently anonymous. At least Sir John did not. Asked to give evidence for Irving voluntarily, he had, he said,

> declined. Earlier experiences had persuaded me that nothing but trouble comes of taking sides over Irving. Decide against him, and his associates accuse one of prejudice. On this occasion I was accused of cowardice. Decide for him, and the smears start. I have written complimentary reviews of Irving's work as a military historian to find myself posted on the internet as a Nazi sympathiser.

No reasonable person would accuse Sir John of harboring Nazi sympathies. Yet, despite all the evidence that had been presented in the trial, despite the expert reports, Keegan still had a number of positive things to say about Irving. The judgment, to be sure, did support his view that Irving had an "extraordinary ability to describe and analyse Hitler's conduct of military operations, which was his main occupation during the Second World War." But Keegan went a good deal further than this in his newspaper article after the trial.

Sir John proved either unwilling or unable to rethink his earlier opinion that Irving was basically a sound historian who only had perverse opinions on the single issue of whether or not Hitler knew about the extermination of the Jews. This "nonsense" was "a small but disturbing element in his work." Driven by a desire for academic respectability, Irving overloaded his work with a massive apparatus of scholarship, footnotes, bibliographies, source references, and the like. "His books positively clank and groan under the weight of apparatus. Very good it is too." In most of Irving's work, he "sticks to the facts and makes eloquent sense of them." Unfortunately, Sir John concluded, Irving's desire to shock undermined this and propelled him

> to write the unprintable and to speak the unutterable. Like many who seek to shock, he may not really believe what he says and probably feels astounded when taken seriously. He has, in short, many of the qualities of the most creative historians. He is certainly never dull. Prof. Lipstadt, by contrast, seems as dull as only the self-righteously politically correct can be, Few other historians had ever heard of her before this case. Most will not want to hear from her again. Mr Irving, if he will only learn from this case, still has much that is interesting to tell us.

Although he had received the reports written by the expert witnesses for the defense, and was clearly aware of the terms in which the court's judgment had been cast, Sir John still insisted that Irving's "detailed knowledge of an enormous body of material" was incontestible. Yet "unfortunately for him, the judge has now decided that all-consuming knowledge of a vast body of material does not excuse faults in interpreting it."[57] In fact, the judgment had nothing to do with the interpretation of a body of knowledge at all. What it dealt with, on the contrary, was the creation of a body of knowledge that was not really knowledge at all but invention, manipulation, and falsification of the sources.

And the doctoring of the historical record was not a small part of Irving's work, but ran right through it. It concerned not merely Hitler's knowledge of the 'Final Solution' but also the actual conduct of events such as the *Reichskristallnacht,* Nazi antisemitism in 1933, the gas chambers at Auschwitz and elsewhere, the evidence of camp survivors, the bombing of Dresden, and much more besides. Among Irving's books, not only *Hitler's War* but also his works on General Sikorski, on Convoy PQ17, on Churchill, and other subjects, had also been criticized for their manipulation of the historical evidence. As for his writing of military history, others had serious reservations about accepting his account of Hitler's direction of the war. Gordon A. Craig, for example, had pointed out that Irving "accepted the Führer's attribution of all military setbacks

to the incompetence or disloyalty of the General Staff and the com-
manding generals, without making any appraisal of Hitler's own defi-
ciencies as a commander."[58] Hugh Trevor-Roper, indeed, had commented that when Irving wrote about Hitler's view of his generals, "it is
not clear who is pronouncing judgment on these 'undesirables,' these
'querulous generals,' this 'polyglot mixture of nobility and plebs.'"[59] Irving's view seemed indistinguishable from Hitler's. Both Charles Sydnor
and John Lukács had identified numerous inaccuracies in Irving's
accounts of military campaigns.[60]

The judge was bound to give weight to Keegan's opinion in the witness box. It must surely have swayed him to conclude that Irving had
much to commend in him as a military historian. His treatment of Hitler,
the bombing of Dresden, and other issues, however, were dealt with very
differently. Mr. Justice Gray found that Irving had repeatedly distorted
the historical record, manipulated documents, and applied double standards in evaluating evidence. The reason why Irving did all this was neither incompetence nor perversity. The evidence was overwhelming that
Irving was not merely propelled by a juvenile desire to shock, although
an element of that did seem at times to be present in his personality. He
was a racist, antisemitic, and neo-fascist ideologue, and an admirer of
Hitler, and there was little doubt that he believed what he said and wrote.

Finally, Keegan could not resist trotting out that hackneyed term of
abuse reserved by conservatives for views they do not like: political correctness. He was echoed in this by Brendan Glacken, a columnist for the
Irish Times, who also thought that there was "something odious in court
about Irving's nemesis, Prof Deborah Lipstadt, which had to do with her
smugness, her dullness and her self-righteous political correctness."[61]
However, whatever else might be said of Lipstadt's book, which it did not
seem either of her two critics had read, it certainly was not dull. Nor could
she justifiably be described as smug—on the contrary, Lipstadt was understandably extremely worried both before and during the trial, as anybody
would be with a libel action and the prospect of massive damages and the
discrediting and withdrawal of her book hanging over her. Despite her
cheerfulness and resilience, she visibly aged under the strain during the
two years in which I saw her before and during the trial. Keegan's gratu-
itous insults were despicable. For what is politically correct about criti-

cizing those who deliberately falsify historical evidence? What is politically correct about wanting to preserve the memory of those who suffered and died in the face of insulting attempts to deny the reality of what they were subjected to? If Keegan thought Irving was capable of learning anything from the trial, after three decades and more of being exposed to similar, if not quite such wide-ranging criticisms of his work, he was deluding himself. It would be Lipstadt's work that survived, not Irving's.

Keegan was followed into the witness box, and subsequently into the pages of the daily press, by the doughty figure of Donald Cameron Watt, retired Stevenson Professor of International History at the London School of Economics. Watt had collaborated with Irving on an edition of documents earlier in his career, but he too had refused to give evidence voluntarily and had to be issued with a court order to attend. Watt declared that he was an expert on documents up to 1940 but not beyond, so that Irving's attempts to draw him on the documentary record of the war itself fell flat.[62] Watt also said he found Irving's version of Hitler's personality and knowledge of the Holocaust "a very difficult one to accept." On the other hand, he told him, "in other areas where your particular political convictions are not involved, I am most impressed by the scholarship."[63] But it was the areas where Irving's convictions *were* involved, of course, that were at issue in the trial; and these were not just a small part of his work but, given his admiration of Hitler, his antisemitism, and his racism, involved a very high proportion of it.

Watt echoed Keegan in proclaiming that the vast majority of professional historians considered Irving to be a historian of repute: "Only those who identify with the victims of the Holocaust disagreed. For them Irving's views are blasphemous and put him on the same level of sin as advocates of paedophilia."[64] This analogy had previously been made in Irving's Opening Speech.[65] Yet Watt was simply wrong when he made his claim that most historians considered Irving to be a historian of repute. Particularly in Germany, there was a widespread view that Irving had lost almost all the reputation he had ever had among serious historians, and that he had brought the action not least in order to try and salvage something from the wreckage.[66] Indeed Irving himself had admitted to Ron Rosenbaum that his reputation amongst professional historians was low. Watt's statement was evidently not based on any serious canvassing of historical opinion or reading of recent reviews. Moreover, recognizing Irving's falsifications had nothing to do with identifying with the victims of Nazi racism and genocide.

Watt also thought that the challenge Irving had broadcast to the historical profession on the issue of Hitler's knowledge of the extermination of the Jews had "directly resulted in an enormous outburst of research into the massacres of the Jews, into the Holocaust and so on."[67] But the research which had been undertaken into the extermination of the Jews since the late 1970s was in no way stimulated by Irving's work. True, Broszat had developed his functionalist view of the decision-making process—a much narrower subject—in the context of a review of the first edition of *Hitler's War*. But his functionalism was not stimulated by Irving's denial of Hitler's knowledge, which he dismissed as untenable and based on documentary manipulation: the review of Irving's book had always seemed in the light of Broszat's other work little more than a pretext for putting it in concrete terms.

Similarly, the wider research into the decision-making process and implementation of the extermination process reflected in the first place wider developments in West German intellectual and academic culture in the 1960s, the impact of the Eichmann and Auschwitz trials in 1961 and 1964 respectively, and many other factors. To historians who were seriously interested in these topics, Irving's work was not important as a stimulus because they knew as a result of Broszat's critique, along with those of Sereny, Sydnor, Trevor-Roper, and others, that it was not based on a proper examination of the historical evidence.

III

Watt raised a more fundamental issue when he said in the witness box:

> I hope that I am never subjected to the kind of examination that Mr Irving's books have been subjected to by the defence witnesses. I have a very strong feeling that there are other senior historical figures, including some to whom I owed a great deal of my own career, whose work would not stand up, or not all of whose work would stand up, to this kind of examination.[68]

Writing in the aftermath of the trial, he added that Penguin had employed "five historians with two research assistants, for some considerable time, to produce 750 pages of written testimony, querying and checking every document cited in Irving's books on Hitler. Show me one historian," he asked with a rhetorical flourish, "who has not broken into a cold sweat at the thought of undergoing similar treatment." "Professional historians," he concluded, wisely not naming any names, "have been left uneasy by the whole business. Many distinguished British historians in the past, from Edward Gibbon's caricatures of early Christianity to A. J. P. Taylor, are open to the accusation that they allowed their political agenda and views to influence their professional practice in the selection and interpretation of historical evidence."[69]

Watt's defense of Irving in this respect seemed to pass over the difference between historians whose political views *influenced* their selection and interpretation of evidence, and people like Irving whose selection and interpretation of the evidence was *dictated* by their political views. Moreover, Taylor, Gibbon, and others did not knowingly and deliberately doctor the evidence by adding words, changing dates, mistranslating and misconstruing words, or omitting whole chunks from quotations because they ran counter to their preconceived notion of how things ought to have been. Watt had copies of the expert reports before he went into the witness box and before he put pen to paper in Irving's defense. But the arguments and opinions he put forward in his newspaper article after the trial did not suggest that he had taken the findings of the reports to heart.

Yet Watt was not the only commentator who thought that any historian subjected to the kind of critical examination Irving had received would come out of it similarly tarnished. The judge's repeated references to what an objective historian would do with the evidence Irving so abused proved particularly difficult for some to accept. The conclusion that Irving was not a historian, wrote one *Guardian* reader on 13 April, "makes a nonsense of the historian's craft, a craft where theoretical relativism has had some success in challenging old-fashioned positivist assumptions."[70] In similar if less pretentious vein, Anne McElvoy, writing in *The Independent*, thought that the judge's claim that Irving was not an objective historian was "marshy ground on which to pitch an argument and a sign that legal minds do not always grasp the pitfalls of referring

matters to the deceptive higher court of objectivity." After all, she suggested, "A lot of very good historians imbued their work with bias." A. J. P.
Taylor was one such, shaping his hostile interpretation of German history
"to fit his own anti-German views."[71]

But this was a mistaken analogy. First, Taylor in this instance was
writing a general textbook (*The Course of German History*), designed
specifically to put forward a controversial interpretation based on the
research of others; he was not creating historical knowledge from the
archives, but putting forward theses for debate. Second, although his
book did indeed verge on the tendentious, Taylor did not either consciously or unconsciously doctor the sources or manipulate the documents, insofar as any actually surfaced in his book.

I do not think that if I and my research assistants had looked at, say,
one of Cameron Watt's books and followed back his depiction of key
events via his footnotes to the sources as a kind of control sample to set
alongside our analysis of Irving's work, that we would have found the
same results. True, there have been too many cases in the past of historians *selecting* and *suppressing* evidence to support a particular point of
view, and nowhere more than in Watt's own field of diplomatic history,
where German historians in particular were unrestrained in their use
from the 1920s to the 1960s of such tendentious methods in their crusade to prove that Germany was not to blame for the outbreak of the First
World War. But cases of historians persistently *manipulating* documents
are fortunately altogether much rarer.

During the trial, there was a brief discussion of the case of the American historian David Abraham, a Marxist whom some had accused of falsifying and inventing documents in his attempt to prove that German big
business was responsible for the rise and triumph of Nazism. It was certainly true that Abraham's book *The Collapse of the Weimar Republic*
contained numerous errors, and these tended generally to be to the disadvantage of big business. There was one letter in particular where he
had reversed the meaning by leaving out the word *not*. He had also confused his (somewhat tendentious) notes on documents with the documents themselves and presented the former as direct quotations from the
original archival sources.

Yet while Abraham's book had been subjected to minute scrutiny by hostile and knowledgeable critics, who went back to the original archival documents, the errors in it were of a different order and frequency than those to be found in Irving's work. Abraham had done the research as a doctoral student, and confessed that it had been hasty, sloppy, and undermined by his poor knowledge of German. Irving's research had been carried out over decades, he claimed it was meticulous, and his knowledge of German was undoubtedly very good. Abraham admitted many of his mistakes when confronted with the evidence; Irving, except on very rare occasions, did not, and then more than once retracted or ignored the admission subsequently. Irving's errors were more consistently, indeed universally in one direction, whereas Abraham's research was so sloppy that a number of his mistakes actually counted against his principal argument. And the actual documentary falsifications that critics detected in Abraham's work were few, whereas those observable in Irving's work were numerous.

Moreover, the 'Abraham affair' aroused widespread debate in the academic world precisely because it was so unusual. Accusations, still more, proven findings of documentary falsification are extremely rare among professional historians, despite the frequency of lively and sometimes impassioned debate among them. Biased and tendentious work does occur, but it seldom involves the kind of blatant and direct doctoring of the sources that could be found in Irving's work. In the end, too, Abraham was driven out of the historical profession, unable to find a job because of the flaws detected in his work. This fate is also thankfully extremely rare.[72]

What, then, did the judge mean by an objective, fair-minded historian? Do such paragons exist? Irving's attitude to source material that ran counter to his argument was neatly summed up by his discussion of a passage in Eichmann's memoirs that he evidently found somewhat inconvenient to his attempt to argue that Hitler neither ordered nor even knew about the extermination of the Jews. In the memoirs, Eichmann records how in July 1941 Heydrich said to him: "I've come from the Reichsführer SS. The Führer has given orders for the physical destruction of the Jews." Irving told an audience at the Institute for Historical Review: "You've only got to change one or two words and you get a completely different meaning." Eichmann, he claimed, was worried when he was writing his memoirs in case he was later arrested and put on trial. So he tried to place the responsibility on Hitler in order to provide evidence for the argument that he had only been obeying orders. "Eichmann," concluded Irving, "may well have adapted the sentence that Heydrich actually uttered to him."[73]

In other words, if the source doesn't fit, then argue it out of existence if you can't ignore it altogether. If you want to alter a few words in a document in order to make it support your argument, then either do so (which, as we have seen, is the case with some of Irving's translations) or argue that the author would have done so had he been telling the truth. "To historians," Irving had written at the beginning of *Hitler's War,* "is granted a talent that even the gods are denied—to alter what has already happened!" Irving had gone on to describe this as a "scornful adage." But in a way what he was doing fitted it perfectly.

Two general questions are of vital importance here. They are interlinked and to a large extent interdependent. The first is, what are the boundaries of legitimate disagreement among historians? The second is, how far do historians' interpretations depend on a selective reading of the evidence, and where does selectivity end and bias begin? The answers to both are fundamental to the business of being a historian. Historians bring a whole variety of ideas, theories, even preconceptions to the evidence to help them frame the questions they want to ask of it and guide their selection of what they want to consult. But once they get to work on the documents, they have a duty to read the evidence as fully and fairly as they can. If it contradicts some of the assumptions they have brought to it, they have to jettison those assumptions. The pursuit of history, as Thomas Haskell has argued, "requires of its practitioners that vital minimum of ascetic self-discipline that enables a person to do such things as abandon wishful thinking, assimilate bad news, (and) discard pleasing interpretations that cannot pass elementary tests of evidence and logic."[74]

Those historians who have abandoned, or in some cases never acquired, this faculty of self-criticism and the ability to recognize when the evidence confounds their hypotheses, have received short shrift at the hands of their colleagues. Selecting evidence to support a case is one of the worst sins a historian can commit. "Far from just looking for evidence that may support his thesis," the late J. H. Hexter, professor of

history at Yale University, remarked, the historian "needs to look for vul-
nerabilities in that thesis and to contrive means of testing them. Then,
depending on what he finds, he can support the thesis, strengthen its
weak points, or modify it to eliminate its weaknesses."[75]

It is useless for example, merely to select quotations from the Goebbels
diaries to back up your argument; some other historian is bound to read
them and refute your argument by selecting other quotations that tell
against it. What a professional historian does is to take the whole of the
source in question into account, and check it against other relevant sources,
to reach a reasoned conclusion that will withstand critical scrutiny by other
historians who look at the same material. It is precisely for this reason that
there is so much agreement among historians on so many aspects of the
Third Reich, at least as much agreement as there is disagreement. Argument between historians is limited by what the evidence allows them to say.
Perhaps the point may be best put in the form of a metaphor.

Suppose we think of historians like figurative painters sitting at various places around a mountain. They will paint it in different styles, using
different techniques and different materials, they will see it in a different
light or from a different distance according to where they are, and they
will view it from different angles. They may even disagree about some
aspects of its appearance, or some of its features. But they will all be paint-
ing the same mountain. If one of them paints a fried egg, or a railway
engine, we are entitled to say that she or he is wrong: whatever it is that
the artist has painted, it is not the mountain. The possibilities of legitimate
disagreement and variation are limited by the evidence in front of their
eyes. An objective historian is simply one who works within these limits.
They are limits that allow a wide latitude for differing interpretations of
the same document or source, but they are limits all the same.

Reputable and professional historians do not suppress parts of quotations from documents that go against their own case, but take them into
account and if necessary amend their own case accordingly. They do not
present as genuine documents those that they know to be forged just
because these forgeries happen to back up what they are saying. They do
not invent ingenious but implausible and utterly unsupported reasons for
distrusting genuine documents because these documents run counter to
their arguments; again, they amend their arguments if this is the case, or

abandon them altogether. They do not consciously attribute their own conclusions to books and other sources which, in fact, on closer inspection, actually say the opposite. They do not eagerly seek out the highest possible figures in a series of statistics, independently of their reliability or otherwise, simply because they want for whatever reason to maximize the figure in question, but rather, they assess all the available figures as impartially as possible in order to arrive at a number that will withstand the critical scrutiny of others. They do not knowingly mistranslate sources in foreign languages to make them more serviceable to themselves. They do not willfully invent words, phrases, quotations, incidents, and events for which there is no historical evidence to make their arguments more plausible to their readers.

At least, they do not do any of these things if they wish to retain any kind of reputable status as historians. Irving has done all of these things from the beginning of his career. Not one of his books, speeches, or articles, not one paragraph, not one sentence in any of them, can be taken on trust as an accurate representation of its historical subject. Some of them may be. But we cannot know until we have checked. It may seem an absurd semantic dispute to deny the appellation of *historian* to someone who has written two dozen books or more about historical subjects. But if we mean by *historian* someone who is concerned to discover the truth about the past, and to give as accurate a representation of it as possible, then Irving is not a historian. Those in the know, indeed, are accustomed to avoid the term altogether when referring to him and use some circumlocution such as *historical writer* instead.[76] Irving is essentially an ideologue who uses history for his own political purposes; he is not primarily concerned with discovering and interpreting what happened in the past, he is concerned merely to give a selective and tendentious account of it to further his own ideological ends in the present. The true historian's primary concern, however, is with the past. That is why, in my expert report, in a passage that the judge did not in the end accept, I concluded that Irving was not a historian.

Many writers who commented on the trial's outcome took this point. As John Lukács wrote after the trial: "It is lamentable that certain professional and, by and large, respected historians have relied on some of Irving's research and given him qualified praise. They have not bothered to examine his writing carefully enough."[77] Watt and Keegan came in for particular criticism. Neal Ascherson's verdict on them was damning. In a biting article, he asked why they had succumbed to "a tendency to see the trial outcome as a form of censorship, a clamp on the limits of historical enquiry." "Both men," he conceded,

> are scrupulous scholars; neither could possibly be suspected of fascist sympathies. Yet both see Irving as still somehow "one of us"— wrong but romantic. But Lipstadt is a respectable historian too, more honest in her use of documents than Irving, and the trial vindicated what she said about him. So why is she being slighted as somehow *not* quite one of us?

Ascherson, perhaps wisely, did not answer his own, rather disconcerting question. But he went on to note that Lipstadt's view that there could be no argument about whether or not the Holocaust happened had "proved an unpopular view." "Most British commentators," he said, were,"worried that the judgment could deter 'genuine' historical argument about the details of the Holocaust." Ascherson rightly dismissed this fear out of hand, noting that Lipstadt's books and indeed the judgment itself asserted that research into debatable points like the number of victims and the genesis of the extermination program did not amount to "denial."[78]

Yet he was right to note that such fears proved to be remarkably widespread after the trial. The novelist Howard Jacobson worried that the verdict would result in "the Holocaust set as incontestable as stone. How will we adequately understand what it was, how it came into being, what it goes on being in men's minds," he asked, "unless we are forever asking questions of it?" Jacobson feared that Irving's defeat meant the triumph of "like-mindedness" and "uniformity." "I'm left wondering how it helps to have the field of conflict silent, and heaven hushed beneath its blanket," he concluded, "when we know that God himself has always needed the devil to contend with."[79]

"When a judge must judge a debate among historians," wrote the *Boston Globe*, in similar, if less poetic vein, "something of scholarly free enquiry is lost."[80] The columnist 'Peter Simple,' writing in the *Daily Telegraph*, admired Irving for defying "one of the most powerful of contemporary taboos." "The issue," he thought, "is the right of historians to examine and interpret all those innumerable events that have come to be known collectively as 'The Holocaust' . . . without being tied to a fore-gone conclusion."[81] But of course, Irving was not examining and inter-preting these events, he was twisting the evidence to make it appear that they had not taken place. There was no debate among historians on the basic factuality of the gas chambers.

Magnus Linklater thought after judgment had been pronounced that the real price of David Irving's lies was that "now even the most honest Holocaust scholar risks being smeared." "From now on," he wrote,

> anyone venturing to explore the facts about the Holocaust, the most sensitive area of 20th-century history, risks being tarred with the brush of Irving revisionism. However impeccable their credentials, their findings will be measured against his, and damned if any evi-dence of cross-infection is found. That could mean that a vital chap-ter in our past becomes forbidden territory.

Linklater feared that "because of Irving, historians will veer away from any reassessment of the Nazi extermination programme." And he quoted a historian, hiding as so often in this case behind a veil of anonymity, as expressing the view that "If they don't have the right to speak, then we don't have the right to criticise." "It is a defeat for all of us," the anony-mous 'historian' went on, "when history has to be decided in a court of law."[82] Jürgen Krönig, the London correspondent of the respected Ger-man weekly *Die Zeit*, quoted another inevitably anonymous 'British his-torian' as saying that the trial was not just about "the history of politics, but also about the politics of history."

This was not true either. David Welch, a leading specialist on the his-tory of Nazi propaganda, was cited as warning that "a serious historical debate must not be restricted by rigid political correctness. Researchers who challenge and change our way of seeing things stand in an hon-ourable tradition of scholarship." Whether he thought that Irving stood in such as tradition, Welch did not say, although he should have known that Irving's work had nothing to do with genuine scholarship; but Krönig certainly implied it. "Many historians," he summed up, "seem to be dis-turbed by the concern that historical scholarship could suffer damage" if a particular school of interpretation of the Holocaust achieved a monop-oly backed, he implied, by a court decision.[83]

"The courtroom defeat of David Irving, the Nazi-sympathising historian," declared a columnist in the *Manchester Evening News,* "has been hailed in the press as a victory for free speech. I'm not so sure. It could be the reverse. . . . We must not go down the road of outlawing any opinion, even one as extreme as Holocaust denial, just because we find it offensive."[84] Letter-writers to *The Guardian* seemed to share the view that Irving's defeat was a blow against free speech. One declared that "people angered by Irving should counter-argue rather than dogmatically cripple him, which just enforces this stubborn English mentality of a true and narrative history from above that is protected by the courts."[85] If this writer seemed to think Irving had been the defendant rather than the plaintiff in this action, then another went even further. Was Irving, he asked, "not entitled to ask for proof? May he not ask why Jews are hated? Did Hitler do nothing right? There is an unfortunate similarity between press headlines and Nazi propaganda in the common intent to silence. . . . Making a living or a lifestyle out of attacking a selected prejudice," continued this writer, "leads directly to McCarthy-style scenes, which Irving can reasonably claim to have endured. . . . Scapegoating never solved anything."[86] But who had been trying to scapegoat whom here? Who had issued the libel writ in the first place?

Magnus Linklater was worried too. He rightly pointed out that "Irving has been systematically selecting and suppressing facts to further his views for the best part of 30 years," and he quoted the historian Hugh Trevor-Roper's description of him as not a historian but "a propagandist who uses efficiently collected and arranged material to support a propagandist line."[87] Yet Linklater feared that Irving's supporters would

> point out, rightly, that all historical facts are debatable—that every version of history we are given contains elements of prejudice and even distortion. They will claim that there is no such thing as pure research, and that writers have always advanced their own theories and found the facts to support them.[88]

But this fear was misplaced on at least two grounds. First, it was unlikely that Irving's supporters would countenance such a determinedly relativist line on the historian's work. For them, as for all Holocaust deniers, the existence of the gas chambers and the extermination program are not a matter for open debate: their belief that none of this happened is, on the surface at least, absolute. For them, Irving was simply telling the truth; and their obsessive insistence on condemning all who disagreed with them as Jewish-inspired mythmakers merely underlined this rejection of relativism. Second, of course, there is the larger point that what real historians do is precisely not to gather material that supports their arguments and ignore or suppress or distort everything else. Still less do they doctor the evidence—a point that Linklater, like many others, seemed to have missed.

It was not the case that the trial only showed Irving's work to have "technical mistakes," as Dieter Ebeling claimed in the *Berliner Morgenpost*.[89] Too many failed to realize this crucial point. "During David Irving's libel trial," remarked the *Irish Times* columnist Brendan Glacken dismissively, "we were given little more than lists of facts and non-facts, assertions and counter-assertions."[90] To my knowledge, however, Glacken never visited the court during the trial, nor did he report on it while it was in progress. David Robson, writing in the *Daily Express*, hit the nail on the head: Irving was "not, as he pretends to be, a controversial historian posing difficult questions that need to be addressed, but a propagandist and liar, masquerading as a historian who needs, once and for all, to be exposed."

This was not the only point on which Robson proved to be more perceptive than some of the journalists writing for the 'quality' newspapers. Martin Mears declared in the legal columns of *The Times*: "The fact is that people such as Irving do us a service. They force us to examine the foundations of our orthodoxies and if the foundations are sound, what have we to fear? They remind us, too, that yesterday's orthodoxies become today's villainies and vice versa."[91] This was once more confusing fact and opinion. Irving was doing nobody a service by peddling his lies. Historians are constantly reexamining, extending, and refining the evidential basis for the history of Hitler's Third Reich. To suggest that the foundations of our knowledge somehow lay unexamined until Irving came along was to show a lamentable ignorance of historical research into the subject. But David Robson had the right thing to say about this argument too. "There are those who say that history needs its David Irvings," he noted, "especially Holocaust history where there is a tendency to resist every account that questions the accepted version of events. This would be true if one believed his questions were genuine. They are not. They are dishonest questions based on dishonest reading of the evidence."[92]

In a similar vein, David Cesarani also rejected the view that that the trial was "about interpretations of history." "By unmasking the methods of the deniers," he wrote, "the trial has actually made space for legitimate research and debate about the history of the Nazi era."[93] Deborah Lipstadt agreed, as she reaffirmed after the trial, that "we are not dealing here with sacred canon and I defend the right of historians to re-examine and ask questions. But," she went on, "it must be based on the evidence, not on what they want it to say."[94] As Jost Nolte correctly observed in the *Berliner Morgenpost*: "With his judgment, Judge Charles Gray proved himself a proponent of a free, decidedly critical debate within the historical profession."[95]

The German journalist Thomas Kielinger considered that by demonstrating in great detail the distinction between genuine historical research and propaganda, the case underlined the right of serious historians of the Nazi period to ask difficult questions. Not just Irving and the Holocaust deniers, but all those who wanted to impose a single meaning or political line on the interpretation of the Holocaust had been defeated. The legitimacy of rational inquiry into the Nazi extermination of the Jews had been underlined, and the enthronement of the Holcoaust as an icon, and thus in the end a taboo, prevented.[96] Watt and Keegan, as defense solicitors Anthony Julius and James Libson noted, had "missed the point. History does not need liars, ideologues prepared to subjugate truth to propaganda. If such people do decide to launch attacks on their critics (remember Irving sued Professor Lipstadt) and are then found out, they cannot then complain about the result—nor should anyone on their behalf."[97]

Who was trying to silence Irving or suppress debate? Certainly no one on the defense side. During the trial the British government announced that it was not going to implement a law against Holocaust denial, as had been promised, because of the threat it posed to freedom of speech. The defense agreed. Deborah Lipstadt opposed the outlawing of Holocaust denial as had happened, for example, in German law, because it made martyrs out of deniers.[98]

After the verdict, a leader in *The Times* pointed out that: "A British court has produced a more sophisticated and effective cross-examination of Holocaust denial than a ban could ever provide."[99] It was the *Daily Telegraph* that reminded those who, like Cameron Watt, evidently needed reminding, that "The downfall of David Irving does not mean the triumph of censorship. Nobody forced him to sue Deborah Lipstadt and her publisher, Penguin, for libel."[100] A leader in the *Daily Express* the day after the verdict pointed out in similar terms that Irving had been

> hoist by his own petard. It was, remember, Mr. Irving who brought this case. Despite his claims that he was being silenced, there was no silencing. In Britain, free speech has long been a proud boast and it is a tribute to our tolerance that even views as lacking in merit or basis in fact as Mr. Irving's were widely disseminated. Mr. Irving was the man who tried to silence debate by suing Penguin and Deborah Lipstadt for exposing his shameful record.

This record was one of spreading "his venomous ideology of hate" under the veneer of a "disinterested and valiant seeker after the truth."[101] Indeed, Irving was more than hoist by his own petard, for as Deborah Lipstadt herself noted, "the judge went further than I did in his ruling."[102] In place of Lipstadt's handful of rather generalized comments on Irving, we now had over three hundred pages of detailed condemnation from a High Court judge, branding Irving as a racist and antisemite as well as a Holocaust denier and a falsifier of history, and backed up by a whole battery of damning examples from Irving's speeches and writings which none of his critics, least of all Lipstadt herself, had even been aware of before the trial.[103]

Was the trial, then, a vindication of the British libel laws? The result of the trial persuaded some people that the law did not need reforming. "The civil law," concluded the *Daily Telegraph*, "acquitted itself well; a state prosecution under a statutory offence of Holocaust denial would have sent out illiberal signals."[104] Anne McElvoy thought that "British libel law . . . has served the admirable and civilised purpose of stripping bare the layers of false mystery which have long sheltered behind the description of the historian as 'maverick.'"[105] The most cogent and impassioned defense of the libel laws came from the victorious solicitors for the defense, Anthony Julius and James Libson. The verdict, they wrote, was "a sparkling vindication of British libel laws." Everyone, they argued, had the right to defend his or her reputation, and there was no doubt that Irving's reputation was seriously damaged by Lipstadt's criticisms. Even in the United States, she would "not have relied on putting Irving to proof of malice, she would have said 'everything I've written is true.'"

This was hardly the point, however. For even if Irving had proved what she said untrue, an American court would still have required him to prove malice on her part because he was a public figure, and his chances of succeeding in this were dubious, to say the least. Faced with such a hurdle to overcome, he would probably not have brought the action at all—as indeed he did not, waiting to launch it until the publication of an English edition of Lipstadt's book took it within the purview of English rather than American defamation law. Julius and Libson were honest enough to admit that "a fantastic result softens one's attitude to the courts and the litigation process" and their attitude might have been very different had Lipstadt lost.[106] Mark Bateman, Penguin's solicitor, was not so easily swayed by the euphoria of victory. "At present," he pointed out, "a number of presumptions in the law of defamation favour the claimant. There is the presumption that a claimant has a good reputation and that the words published are false. This tips the balance in the claimant's favour." Bateman called for a Human Rights Act to tip the balance back toward free speech.[107]

Most opinion was critical of the fact that the British libel laws, with their notorious bias in favor of plaintiffs, had allowed the action to be brought at all. *The Independent* declared on 12 January 2000 that "Britain has become the libel capital of the world," and British courts "a playground for the rich and the obsessive." The Irving case was the latest in a string of futile but costly defamation actions brought by the likes of Neil Hamilton, Jeffrey Archer, and Jonathan Aitken.[108] Geoffrey Wheatcroft, writing in *The Guardian*, agreed: the libel action "should never have been brought" and showed merely "how harsh and obscurantist our libel laws are." The requirement for the truth of the allegations at issue to be proved was often so demanding that newspapers threatened with a defamation suit often caved in without a fight. "Whatever the outcome, it is outrageous that Deborah Lipstadt should have to give up years of her life to this case, and spend many weeks in court, with nothing to gain."

Moreover, Wheatcroft continued, it was obvious from the outset that Irving would never be able to pay the defense costs if he lost, leaving the innocent objects of his libel suit with a seven-figure bill to pay. "What is the legal concept of the vexatious litigant for," he asked, "if not to prevent such an abuse?" And he ended with a call for a drastic reform of the libel law which would require the plaintiff to prove actual damage or material loss and allow a defense of public interest.[109] "England's libel laws are still rotten," declared *The Guardian* after the trial was over. The defendants were unlikely to get much of their money back. "Our libel laws present a formidable weapon against free speech to those who use them malignly. . . . It is a scandal that Penguin's and *The Observer's* defence of their writers should have cost the best part of £3m. . . . Free speech can be very expensive."[110] That the verdict was, in the end, a victory for free speech was, however, clear enough.

IV

There were some inevitable attempts to exploit the result for a particular political position. An Israeli government official concluded: "The court showed that the Holocaust should be approached from a moral point of view, so that the correct lessons can be learnt for future generations."[111] It did nothing of the kind. It had nothing to do with any moral issues or lessons of any sort for future generations, if indeed there were any. Decades of intermittent local and regional war and genocide since 1945, from Bosnia to Rwanda and beyond, seemed to indicate that nothing at all had been learned by the world community from the Nazi attempt to exterminate the Jews. More insidious was the argument that the verdict put paid to the debate about the public presentation and political exploitation of the Holocaust that had started with the publication of Peter Novick's book *The Holocaust and Collective Memory* and continued with Norman Finkelstein's polemic *The Holocaust Industry*, both published in London in the course of the year 2000, while the trial was still in the public eye.

Novick and Finkelstein had attacked, with widely differing degrees of detail and accuracy, the exploitation of the Holocaust in public discourse, from memorial museums that edited out the sufferings of non-Jewish

victims of Nazism, to the propagation of Holocaust education, which took
the topic out of history, where it belonged, and transported it into realms
of mysticism and identity-definition. They were backed up by Jonathan
Freedland, who called for the defense's victory in the trial to be taken as
a moment for "a pause and even, frankly, a rest: for it's time we gave the
victims and survivors of the Holocaust some peace." The "current Holocaust boom," he thought, made them a "dead people," building their
identity on the past, and it was time to end the "kitschy, quasi-mystical"
commemoration of it because it was "unhealthy."[112]

Such views were anathema to David Cesarani, who linked the trial
with what he described as "the growing backlash against the so-called
'Holocaust industry which . . . is taking hold in mainstream media and
academic circles." Because of this, Irving's accusation that, in effect, the
'Holocaust industry' and its exponent Deborah Lipstadt were trying to
silence him would, Cesarani said, "resonate beyond the odd collection of
his supporters huddled in the Irving corner of the public gallery." He
pointed to the art critic Brian Sewell's complaint of the Jews that "enough
has been made of their Holocaust and they are too greedy for our memories." The privileging of the Holocaust in modern public memory,
according to others, did more than anything to call forth Holocaust
denial; the two fed off each other.[113]

But all of this was beside the point. Irving's arguments cut no ice with
those who were critical of the political and cultural exploitation of the
Holocaust because such exploitation, like Irving's own work, had little or
nothing to do with genuine historical scholarship and debate. To attempt
to tar people like Novick or even Finkelstein with the brush of Holocaust
denial really was an attempt to impose a particular line of interpretation
on the basis of the Irving verdict. Finkelstein, after all, made a sharp distinction between the real 'Nazi Holocaust' and real scholarship on the
subject on the one hand, and the 'Holocaust industry' or the attempts to
create and exploit a mysticized and partly fictionalized version of what
had actually happened on the other. Neither he nor Peter Novick, nor
indeed scholars who debated whether, if at all, the Nazi extermination of
the Jews could be called historically unique, had anything at all to do with
Holocaust denial as practiced by people like Irving.

One of the strangest aspects of becoming involved in the case for me

as a professional historian was the way in which it brought me into contact not only with the bizarre mental world of the Holocaust deniers but
also with their counterparts in the outer reaches of 'Holocaust studies.'
Here too there were some obvious cases of falsification, most famously a
recently published book called *Fragments* by Binjamin Wilkomirski,
which had won high praise for its author's unsparing portrayal of a child-
hood spent in the terrifying environment of the Nazi death camps during the war. Investigations carried out initially by the son of a camp survivor and then deepened and extended by others showed, however, that
'Wilkomirski' had never been in the camps, and was not even Jewish. He
had made the whole story up from a mass of survivor literature which he
had somehow internalized and digested until he had become convinced
that the experiences these books recounted were his own.

A television program about Wilkomirski showed him on a lecture
tour of the United States being greeted by a woman who said she recognized him from their mutual time in Auschwitz; though no one, least of
all Wilkomirski himself, questioned her at the time, she too turned out
to be a fraud, who some years before had been exposed after claiming
that she had lost several children in satanic ritual murders. What was wor-
rying was not so much the fraudulent nature of *Fragments* itself, as the
ease with which the book's authenticity had been accepted by many of
those involved in Holocaust studies, a field dominated not by historians
but by people involved in other fields, from literature and aesthetics to
religious studies and education.

And the political exploitation of the Holocaust—itself a term with
which the trial left me no happier than I had been before—was also in
some ways a counterpart to the political payoff of Holocaust denial,
although it was often more subtle and seldom so directly dangerous or
offensive. Visiting the Holocaust Memorial Museum in Washington,
D.C., for example, I was struck by its marginalization of any other victims
apart from the Jews, to the extent that it presented photographs of dead
bodies in camps such as Buchenwald or Dachau as dead Jewish bodies,
when in fact relatively few Jewish prisoners were held there. Little attention was paid to the non-Jewish German victims of Nazism, from the two
hundred thousand mentally and physically handicapped Germans whom
the Nazis killed in the so-called euthanasia campaign to the thousands of

Communists, Social Democrats, and others who also met their death in the camps. The German resistance received almost no mention at all apart from a brief panel on the student 'White Rose' movement during the war, so that the visitor almost inevitably emerged from the museum with a belief that all Germans were evil antisemites.

Such crude and sweeping views were being popularized in some 'Holocaust' literature as well, most notably in Daniel Goldhagen's best-selling book, which portrayed the Germans as *Hitler's Willing Execution-ers*. At the end of the trial, I could not help agreeing with Peter Novick that the political exploitation of the Holocaust involved a good deal of distortion of the historical record as well; though the thesis, advanced by other critics, that Holocaust denial and the Holocaust business fed off each other seemed to me to go too far; after all, denial had its own political agenda, which would exist whatever the circumstances.[114]

One of Novick's central arguments was that the collective memory of the Holocaust had become more important to the Jewish community, at least in England and the United States, in recent decades, as religious sources of identification declined and the existence of Israel as the Jewish homeland came under threat. "The passage of time," Natasha Walter observed in *The Independent* during the trial, "doesn't seem to be making the past fade out. No, the Holocaust seems to loom ever larger. For many non-observant Jews like myself," she added, "it has become the touchstone of our identity." Thus the Irving case was "proving a magnet for people who wonder how we can ever ensure that our history is not twisted and turned against us."

Survivors themselves were understandably offended by Irving's denials. "I found Irving's views extremely insulting," said Trude Levi, a former inmate of Auschwitz, after the trial.[115] "This man should have spent five minutes in Auschwitz," said another former inmate, Ernest Levy. "It is salt in our wounds when people deny what happened," he added. But Levy also said that the distortion of the truth was particularly hard to understand while there were so many survivors alive.[116] Did this mean that it would become more understandable when there were no more survivors left? Some were clearly worried by this prospect. Speaking at a Holocaust Seminar for school students, Nadine Stark, the organizer, declared: "At present in the Old Bailey (*sic*) revisionist David Irving is trying to persuade a jury (*sic*) that the Holocaust never actually happened. This is a dire warning to us all that unless we act, the next generation could look upon the Holocaust as nothing more than a myth."[117] Anne Frank's stepsister, another former inmate of Auschwitz, confessed herself baffled by the trial.[118] The *Jewish Chronicle* thought that the trial still showed that "merely to suggest the fact of the Holocaust—so painstakingly and painfully recounted by those who survived—is somehow open to debate is obscene."[119]

The *Daily Telegraph* leader written after the verdict by a staff member who obviously had not been following the proceedings very closely, confessed itself disturbed by the fact that during the trial. "Auschwitz survivors were cross-examined by a man who clearly considered their traumatic experiences to be concocted."[120] In fact, of course, no survivors were called to the witness box. As Deborah Lipstadt pointed out, this "would have exposed people who have suffered mightily to denigration of their experiences and terrible attacks which none of us wanted when it was not necessary."[121] It was not necessary because the trial was not about proving whether the Holocaust happened or not; it was about proving the truth or otherwise about Lipstadt's allegation that Irving was a Holocaust denier who falsified the historical record. But it was not only not necessary, it was also not in the interests of the defense. It was important throughout the trial to keep the focus on Irving himself all the time, to plug away at his distortions and manipulations of the documentary evidence, and to expose the racist and extremist opinions that had led him to engage in such a betrayal of the historian's calling.

Putting survivors into the witness box would have taken the focus off him and put it onto them. Even the slightest slip of memory, easy enough after more than half a century, would have been enough for him to have cast doubt on the reality of their experiences. Irving's stock-in-trade is taking a small error or inconsistency in evidence and blowing it up out of all proportion so that the most far-reaching conclusions can be drawn from it. Making camp survivors relive their experiences in court was, as the Eichmann trial vividly illustrated, bad enough; that trial, in 1961, depended to a large extent on the testimony of survivors, and many of them found it deeply upsetting, even traumatic, to provide it despite the fact that the questioning was as sympathetic as possible under the circumstances. How

much more upsetting would it have been to have the validity of that testimony questioned, in the most brutal and aggressive manner, by someone who refused to believe it?

Yet this still left the issue of whether the trial was a triumph for the
memory of the Holocaust. Deborah Lipstadt did not think that memory
had won. Irving and his friends, after all, had not been silenced. Interviewed after the trial, Lipstadt described what she saw as the growing
danger of Holocaust denial as being "like a slow invasion of termites." "As
long as there are survivors," she went on, "the danger is mitigated. They
can stand up and say 'I am not lying about the Holocaust: where are my
parents and brothers?' I don't see deniers as a clear and present danger,
I see them as a clear and future danger."[122] "Soon," she added, "there
won't be people to tell the story in the first person singular and it'll be
easier to deny."[123] This had been a persistent theme in Lipstadt's work
for some time. Already in the preface to the paperback edition of *Denying the Holocaust* in 1994 she had predicted that "the public, particularly
the uneducated public, will be increasingly susceptible to Holocaust
denial as survivors die."[124] Even after her courtroom triumph, she
seemed unwilling to abandon this prediction. For Jonathan Freedland,
the verdict mattered not just to the families of Nazism's victims, but to

> all of us. For what became clear as this case unfolded was that Holo-
> caust revisionism is an assault not only on Jews but on history itself—
> the very business of understanding the past. Irving argued that we
> could not trust eyewitness testimony (both survivors and Nazis had
> made it all up) and that any document that pointed at the system-
> atic destruction of European Jewry was bound to be a forgery. With
> that as his method, Irving sought to sweep away the foundations of
> history and even of justice: for if we cannot believe the evidence of
> tens of thousands of witnesses, how can we believe anything? If Irv-
> ing had won yesterday, the ground beneath our feet would have
> begun to feel shaky. The court would have declared that we, like
> David Irving, live in a topsy-turvy world where nothing can ever be
> known. That's why this verdict is not a victory for the defence; it is
> a victory for memory.[125]

But it was not memory that triumphed, and it was not merely the evidence of tens of thousands of witnesses that was vindicated. For the judg-

ment was above all, as Freedland knew, a victory for history, for historical truth and historical scholarship.

So the real reason for the trial's importance was the fact that, as the
Austrian journalist Robert Treichler pointed out correctly, "It was not
perpetrators and victims who spoke as witnesses, but historians who
repelled an attack which aimed to defame historical truth."[126] If Irving
had won, it would have been a resounding defeat for professional history
rather than for collective memory. Eva Menasse, whose reports on the
trial for the *Frankfurter Allgemeine Zeitung* were in a class of their own,
pointed out that it took a considerable effort by a number of professional
historians to identify the falsifications in his books. To the lay reader, the
individual manipulations were hardly noticeable.

> The potential readers of Irving's books are in no way trained histo-
> rians. He wrote and writes for people who interest themselves in the
> Second World War in their spare time. Irving's name and reputation
> must now be ruined for the first time by this public defeat. To be
> sure, no-one can have hoped or expected that Irving himself or his
> hard-core supporters would be educated or converted by a court
> verdict. But because we now know much better how perversity
> functions and where it gets its ideological nourishment from, this
> court case has most definitely made sense.[127]

Thomas Kielinger, an experienced observer of the British scene, concurred. The judgment resulted in "the complete annihilation of the scholarly reputation of David Irving as a contemporary historian who is to be
taken seriously."[128] Anne McElvoy, writing the day after the verdict was
delivered, agreed, concluding that "this court case has done us a power
of good. It is worth a hundred Holocaust Memorial days," she added,
"because it provided a live example of the real nature of Holocaust denial
and its inseparability from vile and active anti-Semitism."[129]

What would have happened had Irving won? Asked the Israeli historian Tom Segev. "Big deal," was his answer: nothing, in other words.[130] But
this was trivializing the case in a big way. Had Irving not brought the case,
the few paragraphs which Lipstadt had devoted to him in her far from
best-selling book (Penguin admitted it had sold little over two thousand
copies before the trial) would probably have languished in academic
obscurity and gone unnoticed even by the majority of serious historians of

Nazi Germany, who by and large have never troubled themselves with the obscene and ridiculous fantasy-world of the Holocaust deniers. Irving, by contrast, was a well-known figure some at least of whose books had sold in their hundreds of thousands. The publicity generated by the trial catapulted Lipstadt to international fame, alerted people to Irving as a Holocaust denier (which even professional historians had doubted he was), and utterly destroyed his reputation as a genuine historian.

As James Dalrymple remarked, "The Holocaust libel action, in all its absurdity" had "cast a great spotlight" on Auschwitz, reminded people of what happened there, and educated those who did not know about it.[131] The trial taught the difference between real history and politically motivated propaganda. For truth, *The Guardian* rightly said, cannot be assumed, but "has to be worked at. . . . Even a casual reader of the case reports could quickly see how painstaking genuine historical scholarship is; it builds detail upon detail, avoiding casual inference and thin deduction." It was truth established in this way over many years that had been vindicated.[132] The trial demonstrated triumphantly the ability of historical scholarship to reach reasoned conclusions about the Nazi extermination of the Jews on the basis of a careful examination of the written evidence. It vindicated our capacity to know what happened after the survivors are no longer around to tell the tale. It showed that we *can* know, beyond reasonable doubt, even if explaining and understanding will always be a matter for debate. That is why, as the *Daily Telegraph* rightly concluded: "The Irving case has done for the new century what the Nuremberg tribunals or the Eichmann trial did for earlier generations."[133]

NOTES

CHAPTER ONE

1. Saul Friedländer (ed.), *Probing the Limits of Representation: Nazism and the 'Final Solution'* (Cambridge, Mass., 1992).
2. Witness Statement of Deborah E. Lipstadt, paragraphs 1–80.
3. David Irving, "On Contemporary History and Historiography: Remarks delivered at the 1983 International Revisionist Conference," *JHR*, vol. 5, nos. 2–4 (Winter 1984), pp. 251–88, here p. 265.
4. Videotape 175: speech at the Elangani Hotel, Durban, South Africa, 5 March 1986.
5. Irving's Statement of Claim, p. 1; and his Reply to the Defence of the Second Defendant, p. 2.
6. "David Irving on Freedom of Speech," speech presented in Victoria, British Columbia, Canada. 28 October 1992. Transcript on Irving's Focal Point website.
7. Deborah Lipstadt, *Denying the Holocaust: The Growing Assault on Truth and Memory* (London, 1994), pp. 181, 111, 161.
8. "The Defeat of the Denier," *The Bookseller*, 21 April 2000, p. 12.
9. Irving, Statement of Claim, Summary.
10. Paul Addison, "The Burden of Proof," *New Statesman*, 1 July 1977, p. 46.
11. R. Hinton Thomas, "Whitewashing Hitler?" *The Birmingham Post*, 22 June 1978.
12. Martin Gilbert, "Unobtrusive Genocide," *The Guardian*, 16 June 1977.
13. Michael Howard, "Hitler and the Dogs of War," *The Sunday Times*, 18 June 1978.
14. Gordon A. Craig, "The Devil in the Details," *New York Review of Books*, 19 September 1996.
15. Sir Martin Lindsay, "Too Decent for Hitler," *The Sunday Telegraph*, 15 January 1978.
16. John Charmley, *Churchill: The End of Glory* (London, 1993), p. 675 n. 51.
17. Hugh Trevor-Roper, "Hitler: Does History offer a Defence?" *The Sunday Times*, 12 June 1977.

18.   Martin Broszat, "Hitler und die Genesis der 'Endlösung': Aus Anlass der Thesen von David Irving," VfZG, vol. 25 (1977), pp. 739–75, reprinted in Hermann Graml and Klaus-Dietmar Henke (eds.), *Nach Hitler: Der schwierige Umgang mit unserer Geschichte. Beiträge von Martin Broszat* (Munich, 1986), pp. 187–229. References below are to the 1986 reprint unless otherwise noted.

19.   Charles Sydnor Jr., "'The Selling of Adolf Hitler: David Irving's *Hitler's War*," *Central European History*, vol. 12, no. 2 (June 1979), pp. 169–99; for the author's acknowledgments of financial support and research assistance, see p. 169.

20.   Ibid., p. 176.

21.   Peter Hoffmann, "Hitler's Good Right Arm," *New York Times*, 28 May 1989.

22.   John Lukács, reviewing *The War Between the Generals* in *The New York Times*, 8 March 1981; idem, *The Hitler of History* (New York, 1998), pp. 27–8, 132–3, 229–30.

23.   Ibid., pp. 27–28, 132–3, 229–30.

24.   David Cannadine, *History in Our Time* (London, 1998), pp. 223–4.

25.   Ibid., pp. 225–7.

26.   David Irving and Kai Bird, "Reviewed vs Reviewer," *New Statesman*, 8 May 1981, pp. 23–6.

27.   Videotape 232: Canadian Association for Free Expression, Carlton Inn, Toronto, undated (1986), 29 mins. 10 secs.

28.   Ron Rosenbaum, *Explaining Hitler* (London, 1998), p. 226.

29.   Sarah Lyall, "At War Over the Holocaust," *International Herald Tribune*, 12 January 2000, p. 5.

30.   Jenny Booth, "Humiliation for Holocaust Sceptic," *The Scotsman*, 12 April 2000, p. 4.

31.   Andrew Roberts, "David Irving, Truth and the Holocaust," *The Sunday Telegraph* (Early Edition), 16 January 2000, p. 37.

32.   Wolfgang Benz, "Ehrgeiz und Eitelkeit," *Die Welt* (Berlin), 12 April 2000; also Klaus Grimberg, "Ein Signal," *Neue Osnabrücker Zeitung*, 12 April 2000.

33.   "David Irving on Freedom of Speech," 28 October 1992.

34.   Irving, *Hitler's War*, 1977 ed., p. xii.

35.   Ibid., p. 6; also in the preface to *Hitler's War*, 1991 ed.

36.   Irving, *Hitler's War*, 1977 ed., pp. 7–8; also in the preface to the 1991 edition.

37.   *Hitler's War*, 1977 ed., p. xxii.

38.   Gitta Sereny, "Building Up Defences Against the Hitlerwave," *New Statesman*, 7 July 1978.

39.   Irving, "On Contemporary History," p. 273.

40.   *Hitler's War,* 1977 ed., p. 10 (also in the preface to the 1991 edition).

41.   Reply to the Defence of the Second Defendant, p. 29.

42.   Neal Ascherson, "The Battle May Be Over—But the War Goes On," *The Observer,* 16 April 2000, p. 19.

43.   See, for example, Paul Madden, *Adolf Hitler and the Nazi Epoch: An Annotated Bibliography of English-Language Works on the Origins, Nature and Structure of the Nazi State* (Lanham, Md., 1998), which runs to over seven hundred pages just on the literature in English.

44.   Robert Harris, *Selling Hitler: The Story of the Hitler Diaries* (London, 1986), pp. 319–26; Audiocassette 75, side 1, 300–370 (speech at 1983 International Revisionist Conference, reprinted as "On Contemporary History," pp. 251–88).

45.   Irving, "On Contemporary History," pp. 255–56.

46.   Audiocassette 75, side 1, 300–370. The German historian Eberhard Jäckel had earlier accepted some other forgeries from the same collection as genuine; his discovery that they were not was what led to his doubts about the diaries (Harris, *Selling Hitler*).

47.   Harris, *Selling Hitler,* pp. 339, 344.

48.   Ibid., p. 359.

49.   "David Irving on Freedom of Speech," 28 October 1992.

50.   Videotape 206: New Zealand television interview with Irving on the "Holmes Show," 4 June 1993, at 7 mins. 15 secs.

51.   Reply to the Defence of the Second Defendant, p. 7.

52.   "Speech by David Irving to a packed hall in the Primrose Hotel, Toronto, 1 November 1992." Transcript on Irving's Focal Point website.

53.   Sebastian Borger, "Herrn Irvings Erzählungen," *Format: Das Magazin für Politik* (Vienna), 17 January 2000.

54.   Michael Horsnell, "False Witness," *The Times,* sec. 2, 12 April 2000, p. 3. For the Institute of Historical Review, see chapter 4.

55.   Anne Sebba, "Irrational debates," *The Times Higher Education Supplement,* 7 January 2000, p. 16.

56.   John Mason, "Writer's Action Raises Thorny Questions," *Financial Times* (Early Edition), 12 January 2000, p. 6.

57.   Martin Mears, "You're Free to Say Anything I Want," *The Times* (Legal), 15 February 2000, p. 12.

58.   Peter Millar, "Why I Spoke Up for David Irving," *Sunday Times* (News Review), 19 March 2000, p. 6.

59.   "Corrections and Clarifications," *The Guardian,* 15 April 2000, p. 19 (referring to a report on page 4, 12 April).

60.   Joseph Sobran, "Labels and Libels," *Sobran's: The Real News of the*

Month, posted on Irving's website http://www.fpp.co.uk, on 6 April 2000.

61. Donald Cameron Watt, "History Still Needs Its David Irvings," *London Evening Standard,* 11 April 2000, p. 13.

62. Fiachra Gibbons, "Author with No Publisher and Few Funds Landed with £2.5m Bill," *The Guardian,* (Early Edition) 12 April 2000, p. 5.

63. Neil Tweedie, "Irving Libel Trial," *Daily Telegraph* (Early Edition), 12 April 2000, pp. 4–5.

64. "The Defeat of the Denier," p. 12.

65. Michael Horsnell, "False Witness," *The Times,* sec. 2, 12 April 2000, p. 3.

66. Stuart Nicolson, "Beliefs Turned Historian into International Pariah," *The Scotsman,* 12 January 2000, p. 2.

67. Jonathan Freedland, "The History Men," *The Guardian,* 1 March 2000.

68. Jürgen Krönig, "Ehrgeiz und Lügen," *Die Zeit,* 5 April 2000.

69. Ulrike Herrmann, "Einer der übelsten Schmutzfinken der Zunft," *Die Tageszeitung,* 12 April 2000.

70. Paul Spicker, in *The Guardian,* 14 April 2000, p. 23.

71. Robert Treichler, "Herrn Irvings Attacke," *Profil* (Vienna), 17 January 2000.

72. Jost Nolte, "Der falsche Saubermann," *Berliner Morgenpost,* 19 January 2000; Wolfgang Benz, "Ehrgeiz und Eitelkeit," *Die Welt* (Berlin), 12 April 2000.

73. Jonathan Freedland, "Let's Close the Book," *The Guardian* (Early Edition), 12 April 2000, p. 21.

74. Correspondence on Irving's website http://www.fpp.co.uk.

75. Videotape 190: Irving at Bayerischer Hof, Milton, Ontario, 5 October 1991, at 1 hr. 48 mins. 40 secs. to 1 hr. 50 mins. 50 secs.

76. These were two historians who emphasized Hitler's role in leading and co-ordinating the policies of the Third Reich: see Hans-Adolf Jacobsen, *Nationalsozialistische Aussenpolitik* (Frankfurt am Main, 1968), and Andreas Hillgruber, *Hitlers Strategie, Politik und Kriegführung 1940–1941* (Frankfurt am Main, 1965).

77. Audiocassette 88: Irving press conference in Brisbane, Queensland, 20 March 1986, side 2, no. 107–26.

78. Alan Hamilton, "Academic Buccaneer vs Bookish Schoolmaster," *The Times,* 12 January 2000, p. 3.

79. Helen McCabe, "Irving Sues over Holocaust Claim," *Courier Mail* (Brisbane), 12 January 2000, p. 19.

80.   Sarah Lyall, "At War Over the Holocaust," *International Herald Tribune*, 12 January 2000, p. 5.

81.   Ralf Sottscheck, "Verhandelt wird der Holocaust," *Die Tageszeitung*, (Berlin), 16 March 2000.

82.   Jost Nolte, "Der falsche Saubermann," *Berliner Morgenpost*, 19 January 2000.

83.   Caroline Fetscher, "Der Leichenrechner," *Der Tagesspiegel* (Berlin), 12 February 2000; Reinhart Häcker, "Niederlage für einen Unbelehrbaren," *Kölner Stadt-Anzeiger*, 12 April 2000.

84.   Caroline Fetscher, "Irvings Wendeltreppe," *Potsdamer Neueste Nachrichten*, 4 March 2000.

85.   Werner Birkenmaier, "Historie und Holocaust," *Stuttgarter Zeitung*, 13 March 2000.

86.   Walter Reich, "Look Again: This London Trial Is Not About the Holocaust," *International Herald Tribune*, 20 January 2000, p. 8.

87.   Werner Birkenmaier, "Wahrheit vor Gericht," *Stuttgarter Zeitung*, 12 April 2000; Reinhart Häcker, "Niederlage."

88.   David Cesarani, "Irving Exposed as a Liar with No Interest in Pursuit of Truth," *The Irish Times*, 12 April 2000, p. 16.

89.   Clare Dyer, "Judging history," *The Guardian*, 1 April 2000 (G2), p. 10.

90.   Sarah Lyall, "Historian Called Pro-Hitler Loses Libel Suit," *International Herald Tribune*, 12 April 2000, p. 4.

91.   See in particular his Opening Statement at the trial.

92.   John Mason, "Irving Branded a Racist and Active Holocaust Denier," *Financial Times* (Early Edition), 12 April 2000, p. 3.

93.   Petra Steinberger, "Der Fälscher," *Süddeutsche Zeitung*, 12 April 2000; Andrew Buncombe, "Judge Dismantles Author's Distorted View of History," *The Independent* (Early Edition), 12 April 2000; Freedland, "Let's Close the Book."

94.   Neal Ascherson, "In dubio pro Hitler? *Süddeutsche Zeitung*, 29 January 200.

95.   Ian Burrell, "Irving Finds Himself on Trial in His Holocaust Libel Case," *The Independent*, 4 March 2000, p. 10.

CHAPTER TWO

1.   Irving, *Hitler's War*, 1977 ed., p. xvi.

2.   David Irving, "Nachwort," in Paul Rassinier, *Die Jahrhundert-Provokation: Wie Deutschland in den Zweiten Weltkrieg getrieben wurde* (Tübingen, 1989), pp. 345–50, here pp. 347–48.

3.   Richard Overy, *War and Economy in the 'Third Reich'* (Oxford,

1994); Klaus Hildebrand, *Vom Reich zum Weltreich: Hitler, NSDAP und koloniale Frage* 1919–1945 (Munich, 1960); Gerhard Hirschfield (ed.), *The Policies of Genocide* (London, 1986).

4.   Hugh Trevor-Roper, "Hitler: Does History Offer a Defence?" *The Sunday Times*, 12 June 1977.

5.   Gordon A. Craig, *The Germans* (London, 1982), pp. 72–75.

6.   Robert Harris, *Selling Hitler: The Story of the Hitler Diaries* (London, 1986), pp. 188–89.

7.   Sydnor, "The Selling," pp. 171–72.

8.   Lukács, *The Hitler of History*, p. 26.

9.   Broszat, "Hitler und die Genesis," pp. 190–94.

10.   Rosenbaum, *Explaining Hitler*, p. 232.

11.   Guido Knopp (ed., *Hitler heute: Gespräch über ein deutsches Trauma* (Aschaffenburg, 1979), pp. 70–71; also in *Hitler's War*, pp. 423–24.

12.   Videotape 189: speech presented in Calgary, 29 September 1991; videotape 226: unedited material from *This Week*, 28 November 1991, at 1 hr. 36 mins. 40 secs.

13.   Audiocassette 88: press conference, Brisbane, Queensland, Australia, 29 March 1986, side 2, 224–29.

14.   Gerhard Botz, *Wien vom "Anschluss" zum Krieg* (Vienna, 1978), pp. 147, 154, 182, 278; J. Noakes and G. Pridham (eds.), *Nazism: A Documentary History* (4 vols., Exeter, 1985–99), p. 595; H. Boberach (ed.), *Meldungen aus dem Reich* 1938–1944 (Herrsching, 1984), pp. 37–38; *Deutschland-Berichte der Sozialdemokratischen Partei Deutschlands (SOPADE)* (Frankfurt am Main, 1980), vol. 5, pp. 415–28.

15.   "Book a Calumny on Victims of Hitler," *Jewish Chronicle*, 17 June 1977.

16.   Reply to Defence of Second Defendant, p. 29.

17.   "Book a Calumny on Victims of Hitler," *Jewish Chronicle*, 17 June 1977.

18.   David Irving, "On Contemporary History and Historiography: Remarks Delivered at the 1983 International Revisionist Conference," *JHR*, vol. 5, nos. 2–4 (Winter 1984), pp. 251–88, here pp. 274–75. Also in Audiocassette 75: International Revisionist Conference, September 1983, 307.

19.   Irving, "On Contemporary History," pp. 274–83. (Italics in original)

20.   Reply to the Defence of the Second Defendant, p. 13.

21.   Ian Kershaw, *Hitler 1889–1936: Hubris* (London, 1998), pp. 195–219.

22.   Irving, *Göring: A Biography* (New York, 1989), p. 59.

23.   Irving, *Hitler's War,* 1991 ed., p. 18.

24.   Reply to the Defence of the Second Defendant, p. 14.

25.   Irving, *Göring,* p. 518, footnote reference for p. 55.

26.   L. Gruchmann and R. Weber (eds.), *Der Hitler-Prozess 1924: Wortlaut der Hauptverhandlung vor dem Volksgericht München I* (2 vols. Munich, 1997–98), Vol. 2, pp. 545–46.

27.   Ibid., vol. 2, pp. 540–42; G. Franz-Willing, *Putsch und Verbotszeit der Hitlerbewegung* (Preussich Olendorf, 1977), p. 173.

28.   Die Polizeidirektion München an Generalstaatskommissar Kahr, 4.12.1923; reprinted in E. Deuerlein (ed.), *Der Hitler Putsch:Bayerische Dokumente zum 8./9. November 1923* (Stuttgart, 1962), p. 465.

29.   Gruchmann and Weber (eds.), *Der Hitler-Prozess 1924,* vol. 2, p. 546.

30.   Irving, *Goebbels, Mastermind of the "Third Reich"* (London, 1996), pp. 46–47.

31.   Ibid., pp. 547–48, n. 29.

32.   Walther Kiaulehn, *Berlin: Schicksal einer Weltstadt* (Munich and Berlin, 1958); Paul Weiglin, *Unverwüstliches Berlin: Bilderbuch der Reichshauptstadt seit 1919* (Zurich, 1955).

33.   A. Heider, "Deutsches Nachrichtenbüro," in W. Benz, H. Graml, and H. Weiß (eds.), *Enzyklopädie des Nationalsozialismus* (Munich, 1997), p. 427.

34.   "Die Juden in der Kriminalität: Ausführungen des Generalleutnants Daluege," *Deutsches Nachrichtenbüro,* 20.7.1935; disclosed as part of Irving's third supplementary list of documents, 51 (A).

35.   Daluege's subsequent career led to his execution in 1947 for war crimes: F. Wilhelm, *Die Polizei im NS-Staat* (Paderborn, 1997), p. 198; C. Browning, *Ganz normale Männer* (Reinbek b. Hamburg, 1996), pp. 45–46.

36.   "Die Juden in der Kriminalität," *Deutsches Nachrichtenbüro,* 20.7.1935; disclosed as part of Irving's third supplementary list of documents, 51 (A).

37.   *Statistik über die Gefangenenanstalten der Justizverwaltung in Preußen für das Rechnungsjahr 1925* (Berlin, 1928).

38.   BA Berlin, Film 14768, K. Daluege, manuscript for article "Judenfrage als Grundsatz," *Der Angriff,* 3.8.1935.

39.   *Kriminalstatistik für das Jahr 1932, Bearbeitet im Reichsjustizministerium und im Statistischen Reichsamt* (Berlin, 1935), p. 112.

40.   Bericht des Obersten Parteigerichts an den Ministerpräsidenten Generalfeldmarschall Göring, 13.2.1939, *Der Prozess,* vol. 32, ND 3063-PS.

41. Irving, *Goebbels,* p. 275.
42. Müller an alle Stapostellen und Stapoleitstellen, 9 November 1938, in *Der Prozess,* vol. 25, pp. 337–38, ND 374-PS.
43. A. Seeger, "Vom bayerischen "Systembeamten' zum Chef der Gestapo," in G. Paul and K.-M. Mallmann (eds.), *Die Gestapo* (Darmstadt, 1995), pp. 255–68.
44. *Der Spiegel,* 29 (1993), p. 128.
45. Heydrich an alle Staatspolizeileit- und Staatspolizeistellen, an alle SD-Oberabschnitte und SD-Unterabschnitte, 10.11.1938, 1 Uhr 20, in *Der Prozess,* vol. 31, ND 3051-PS, pp. 515–18.
46. *Der Prozess,* vol. 42, pp. 510–12; ibid., vol. 21, p. 392; IfZ ZS 526: Vernehmung des Luitpold Schallermeier, 23.6.1947; IfZ ZS 317/II: Karl Wolff, 22.3.1948.
47. *Der Prozess,* vol. 21, p. 392; IfZ ZS 317/11: Karl Wolff, 22.3.1948.
48. Irving, *Goebbels,* pp. 274, 276, 281, 613 n. 43; *The War Path,* (London, 1978) pp. 164–65 and notes.
49. Irving, *Goebbels,* p. 613 n. 38.
50. Ibid., p. 276. The footnote referred mistakenly to Nuremberg Document 3052-PS instead of 3051-PS.
51. Ibid., p. 277.
52. Ibid.; similarly, *The War Path,* p. 165.
53. IfZ/ZS 137, Ministries Division, Research Section, no date; BA Berlin, Film 55270: Vernehmung von Julius Schaub, 7.12.1946; BA Berlin, BDC, personal file Julius Schaub; IfZ/ZS 137: Vernehmung von Julius Schaub durch Dr. Kempner, 12.3.1947.
54. IfZ/ED 100/203.
55. GTB I/6, pp. 180–81. The Shock-troop had been created in 1923 as a personal paramilitary bodyguard for Hitler (W. Benz et al. [eds.], *Enzyklopädie des Nationalsozialismus* [Munich, 1997], p. 718).
56. Irving, *Goebbels,* p. 277.
57. Nicolaus von Below, *Als Hitlers Adjutant* (Mainz, 1980), p. 136.
58. Third supplementary list of documents, 51 (a), interview of 18 May 1968.
59. Irving, *The War Path,* p. 165.
60. Irving, *Goebbels,* p. 277, ellipses in the original.
61. Irving, *Hitler's War,* 1991 ed., introduction.
62. Third supplementary list of documents, 51 (a), Wiedemann papers.
63. Bericht des Obersten Parteigerichts an den Ministerpräsidenten Generalfeldmarschall Göring vom 13.2.1938, in *Der Prozess,* vol. 32, ND 3063-PS. The words "had better believe it,' *müssten dran*

glauben, contained a clearer threat of violence in German than a literal translation could easily convey in English.

64.   GTB I/6, p. 181.
65.   Ibid.
66.   Irving, "On Contemporary History," pp. 275–76.
67.   BA Berlin, BDC file 240/I: Fernschreiben an alle Gauleitungen, 10.11.1938, 2.56 Uhr.
68.   Irving, *Goebbels,* p. 281.
69.   Ulrich von Hassell, *Vom anderen Deutschland: Aus den nachgelassenen Tagebüchern 1938–1944* (Zurich, 1947), p. 43.
70.   Hassell, *Vom anderen Deutschland,* p. 39.
71.   GTB I/6, p. 181.
72.   Ibid., p. 182.
73.   Ibid.
74.   Videotape 199: Irving interviewed by Kurt Franz on the serialization of the Goebbels diaries, CBC Newsworld, 10 July 1992.
75.   Videotape 200: Irving, "The Search for Truth in History—Banned!" 1993.
76.   Irving, *Goebbels,* p. 278.
77.   IfZ, G 01/71: SD-Unterabschnitt Wien an den SD-Führer des SS-Oberabschnittes Donau, 10.11.1938; IfZ, G 01/91: Der SD-Führer des SS-Oberabschnittes Donau an das Sicherheitshauptsamt, 21.11.1938; Rundruf des Deutschen Nachrichtenbüros in Berlin vom 10. November nachmittags, in W.-A. Kropat, *"Reichskristallnacht"* (Wiesbaden, 1997), p. 233.
78.   Irving, *Goebbels,* p. 277.
79.   Ibid., p. 281.
80.   Mitteilung der Obersten SA-Führung, cited in: BA Berlin, BDC file 240/II, Der Führer der Gruppe Kurpfalz, 19.12.1938.
81.   Reichsministerium der Justiz an Generalstaatsanwalt Hamburg, 19.11.1938, cited in L. Gruchmann, *Justiz im Dritten Reich: 1933–1940* (Munich, 1990), pp. 487–88.
82.   Der Oberste Parteirichter an Hermann Göring, 13.2.1939; in *Der Prozess,* vol. 32, ND 3063-PS.
83.   Ibid. One of the fourteen cases involved a sex offense against a Jewish woman. In this case, the perpetrators were taken into police custody and probably sent to a concentration camp.
84.   Ingrid Weckert, "Die Gaswagen," in E. Gauss (ed.), *Grundlagen zur Zeitgeschichte* (Tübingen, 1994), http://www.codoh.com/inter/intgrweckert.html.
85.   I. Weckert, " 'Crystal Night' 1938: The Great Anti-German Spectacle,"

JHR, vol. 6 (1985), pp. 183–206, disclosed in Irving's third supple-
mental Discovery list, with pencil lines in the margin.

86.   Ingrid Weckert (alias Hugo Rauschke), "Zweimal Dachau," *Sleipnir*,
        vol. 3, no. 2 (1997), pp. 14–27.

87.   http://www.who.org

88.   I. Weckert, "Die Reichskristallnacht—2. Folge," *Güttinger Briefe*,
        März-April 1979, and Irving to Weckert, 3 June 1979, both in third
        supplementary Discovery list.

89.   Bundesprüfstelle für jugendgefährdende Schriften, Entscheidung
        4651 (V), 16 June 1994, in *Bundesanzeiger* 120 (30 June 1994); see
        also Entscheidung 3823, 30 April 1988.

90.   Irving, *Hitler's War*, 1991 ed., p. 148, footnote.

91.   Weckert, " 'Crystal Night' 1938," in third supplementary Discovery
        list, marked with pencil in the margins, presumably by Irving.

92.   Helmut Heiber, "Der Fall Grünspan," *VfZG*, vol. 5 (1957), pp.
        134–72.

93.   Irving, *Göring*, p. 237; idem, *Goebbels*, p. 276.

94.   Irving, *Goebbels*, p. 276.

95.   I. Weckert, " 'Crystal Night,' " p. 190.

96.   Heydrich to Göring, 11.11.1938, in *Der Prozess*, vol. 32, ND 3058-PS.

97.   *Deutschland-Berichte der Sozialdemokratischen Partei Deutsch-
        lands (SOPADE)*, vol. 5 (1938), p. 1, 187.

98.   S. Rohde, "Die Zerstörung der Synagogen unter dem National-
        sozialismus," in A. Herzig and I. Lorenz (eds.), *Verdrängung und
        Vernichtung der Juden unter dem Nationalsozialismus* (Hamburg,
        1992), pp. 153–72, here p. 170.

99.   *Der Prozess*, vol. 38, ND 1816-PS, p. 508; Stenographische Nieder-
        schrift von einem Teil der Besprechung über die Judenfrage unter
        Vorsitz von Feldmarschall Göring im RLM am 12. November 1938.

100.   A. Barkai, "Schicksalsjahr 1938," in W. Pehle (ed.), *Der Juden-
        pogrom 1938* (Frankfurt am Main, 1988), pp. 94–117, here pp. 96
        and 113.

CHAPTER THREE

1.   U. Herbert (ed.), *Nationalsozialistische Vernichtungspolitik
        1939–1945: Neue Forschungen und Kontroversen* (Frankfurt am
        Main, 1998); H. Krausnick and H. H. Wilhelm, *Die Truppe des
        Weltanschauungskrieges* (Stuttgart, 1981).

2.   GTB II/1, 20 August 1941.

3.   Himmler to Greiser, 18 September 1941, in P. Longerich (ed.), *Die*

Ermordung der europäischen Juden (Munich, 1990), p. 157; H. Safrian, *Die Eichmann-Männer* (Vienna, 1993), pp. 124, 134.

4.   Christian Gerlach, *Krieg, Ernährung, Völkermord* (Hamburg, 1998); Christopher Browning, *The Path to Genocide* (Cambridge, 1992); idem, *Nazi Policy, Jewish Workers, German Killers* (Cambridge, 2000).

5.   GTB II/1, p. 19.

6.   Irving, *Goebbels*, p. 377.

7.   W. Jochmann (ed.), *Monologe im Führerhauptquartier 1941–44. Die Aufzeichnungen Heinrich Heims* (Hamburg, 1980), pp. 106–8.

8.   I. Sagel-Grande, H. H. Fuchs and C. F. Rüter (eds.), *Justiz und NS-Verbrechen-Sammlung deutscher Strafurteile wegen nationalsozialistischer Tötungsverbrechen 1945–66*, Vol. XX (Amsterdam, 1979), No. 570, p. 113; F. Baade et al. (eds.), "Unsere Ehre heisst die Treue": *Kriegstagebuch des Kommandostabes RFSS, Tätigkeitsberichte der 1. und 2. SS-Kave.- Brigade und von Sonderkommandos der SS* (Vienna, 1965), pp. 227–9.

9.   Irving even claimed that this word meant "a childish kind of spook," confusing it, deliberately I thought, with *Schreckgespenst*, which was not the word Hitler used (Reply to the Defence of the Second Defendant, p. 24; also TS 17/1, pp. 174–75).

10.   Irving, *Hitler's War*, 1991 ed., p. 427.

11.   H. Trevor-Roper (ed.), *Hitler's Table Talk*, trans. N. Cameron and R. H. Stevens (London, 1953), pp. 87–92.

12.   Reply to the Defence of the Second Defendant, p. 23; Discovery doc. 2040: François Genoud to Irving, 4 November 1977.

13.   Irving, "On Contemporary History," p. 281.

14.   Reply to the Defence of the Second Defendant, p. 23; see also Irving, *Hitler's War*, 1991 ed., p. 427.

15.   Irving, *Goebbels*, p. 379. Ellipses in the original.

16.   Ibid.

17.   GTB II/2 (Munich, 1996), pp. 340–41, diary entry for 22.11.1941.

18.   Irving, *Goebbels*, pp. 379 and 645, endnote 39.

19.   Reply to the Defence of the Second Defendant, p. 37.

20.   GTB II/2 (Munich, 1996), pp. 169, 309, diary entries for 24.10.1941, 18.11.1941.

21.   IfZ, Sammlung Irving; reprinted in P. Longerich (ed.), *Die Ermordung der europäischen Juden* (Munich and Zurich, 1989), p. 76. Robert Koch discovered *Vibrio cholerae*, the bacillus that caused cholera, in 1884.

22.   A. Hillgruber, "Die 'Endlösung' und das deutsche Ostimperium als

Kernstücke des rassenideologischen Programms des Nationalsozialismus," in *VfZG*, vol. 20 (1972), pp. 133–53, here p. 142.
23. GTB II/1, p. 269.
24. Jochmann (ed.), *Monologe*, pp. 99, 131.
25. Irving, *Hitler's War*, 1977 ed., p. 332. Italics in original.
26. Peter Witte et al. (eds.), *Der Dienstkalender Heinrich Himmlers 1941/42* (Hamburg, 1999).
27. Witte et al. (eds.), *Der Dienstkalender*, p. 278.
28. Irving, *Hitler's War*, 1977 ed., p. xiv.
29. W. Gruner, *Judenverfolgung in Berlin 1933–1945* (Berlin, 1996); Y. Arad et al. (eds.), *The Einsatzgruppen Reports* (New York, 1989), p. 280; Institut für Zeitgeschichte Gh 02 47/3, Urteil des Schwurgerichts Hamburg in der Strafsache gegen J. und andere (50), 9/72, vom 23.2.1973.
30. Broszat, "Hitler" *(VfZG)*, p. 760; Trevor-Roper, "Hitler," *The Sunday Times*, 12 June 1977.
31. Eberhard Jäckel, "Hitler und der Mord an den europäischen Juden: Widerlegung einer absurden These," in Peter Märtheseimer and Ivo Frenzel (eds.), *Im Kreuzfeuer: Der Fernsehfilm Holocaust. Eine Nation ist betroffen* (Frankfurt am Main, 1979), pp. 151–62, here pp. 153–54; Broszat, "Hitler," *(VfZG)*, p. 761.
32. Reply to the Defence of the Second Defendant, p. 16.
33. Irving, *Hitler's War*, 1991 ed., p. 427: "a trainload of Berlin's Jews."
34. Irving, *Goebbels*, p. 379.
35. Irving, *Hitler's War*, 1977 ed., p. xiv. My italics.
36. Irving persisted in trying to sustain this 'theory' during the trial itself. (TS 17/2, pp. 104-106)
37. Irving, *Hitler's War*, 1991 ed., p. 18; Keith Brace, "Secret Memo Clears Hitler—Irving," *The Birmingham Post*, 9 March 1978; and Daniel W. Michaels, "Nuremberg: Woe to the Vanquished," review of Irving's *Nuremberg, JHR*, vol. 17, no. 1 (1998), p. 46, citing the memorandum again.
38. Cited in Reply to the Defence of the Second Defendant, p. 14, and Irving, *Goebbels*, p. 388.
39. Irving, "On Contemporary History" (speech presented at the Institute of Historical Review, 1983); audiocassette 199: speech presented in Toronto, 13 August 1988; videotape 186: speech presented in Moers, 5 March 1990; videotape 220: speech presented in Tampa, Florida, 6 October 1995; all quoted in defendants' Closing Statements, 5 (i) g.
40. BA Berlin R3001/52.
41. Office of U.S. Chief of Counsel for Prosecution of Axis Criminality,

Staff Evidence Analysis, 22 June 1946; third supplementary Discovery list, 51 (b).

42.   E. Jäckel, "Noch einmal: Irving, Hitler und der Judenmord," in Märthesheimer and Frenzel (eds.), *Im Kreuzfeuer*, pp. 163–66; N. Stoltzfus, *Resistance of the Heart: Intermarriage and the Rosenstrasse Protest in Nazi Germany* (London, 1996), p. 171; P. Hoffmann, "Hitler's Good Right Arm," *New York Times*, 28 May 1989.

43.   Dr. R. Kempner to Elke Fröhlich, 10.6.1972; third supplementary Discovery list, 51 (b).

44.   Irving, *Hitler's War*, 1991 ed., p. 464; also TS 19/1, p. 183; TS 20/1, p. 20.

45.   BA Berlin, 99 US 58013: Besprechungsniederschrift der Besprechung über die Endlösung der Judenfrage, 6.3.1942, ND: NG-2586.

46.   BA Berlin R 22/52, Bl. 155: Schlegelberger to Lammers, 12.3.1942.

47.   Ibid., Bl. 156: Lammers to Schlegelberger, 18.3.1942; ibid., Bl. 157: Schlegelberger to Klopfer et al., 5.4.1942.

48.   E. Jäckel, "Noch einmal," p. 165.

49.   Stoltzfus, *Resistance of the Heart*; J. Noakes, "Nazi Policy Towards German-Jewish 'Mischlinge,' " *Leo Baeck Institute Yearbook*, vol. 34 (1989), pp. 291–354, here p. 354.

50.   Irving, *Hitler's War*, 1991 ed., p. 18; David Irving, press release, 6.3.1978, third supplementary Discovery list.

51.   TS 19/1, p. 177; Hoffmann, "Hitler's Good Right Arm."

52.   BA Berlin, R 22/1238, Bl. 286: Der Reichsminister der Justiz an den Oberreichsanwalt beim Volksgerichtshof, die OLG Präsidenten, die Generalstaatsanwälte, 16.4.1942.

53.   BA R 22/4062, Bl. 35a–37: Besprechung mit Reichsführer SS Himmler am 18.9.1942 in seinem Feldquartier; N. Wachsmann, " 'Annihilation through Labor': The Killing of State Prisoners in the Third Reich," *Journal of Modern History*, vol. 71 (1999), pp. 624–59, here pp. 637, 650.

54.   Eberhard Jäckel, "Der Zettel mit dem schlimmen Wort," *Frankfurter Allgemeine Zeitung*, 22 June 1978; also idem, "Noch einmal."

55.   Irving, *Hitler's War*, 1977 ed., p. 392.

56.   GTB II/3, p. 561.

57.   Irving, *Hitler's War*, 1991 ed., pp. 464–65.

58.   Irving, *Hitler's War*, 1977 ed., p. 392.

59.   GTB II/3, pp. 578–583.

60.   Ibid., p. 513.

61.   Irving, *Hitler's War*, 1991 ed., p. 464–65.

62.   Himmler to Berger, 28.7.1942; third supplementary Discovery list 51 (b).

63.   D. Pohl, "Die Ermordung der Juden im Generalgovernement," Herbert (ed.), *Nationalsozialistische Vernichtungspolitk*, pp. 98–121, here pp. 98–99.

64.   I. Arndt and W. Scheffler, "Organisierter Massenmord an Juden in Nationalsozialistischen Vernichtungslagern," *VfZ* vol. 24 (1976), pp. 105–35.

65.   BA Berlin, NS 19/1447, Bl. 78–89, here Bl. 85: Vortrag beim Führer, Wehrwolf, 22.9.1942.

66.   Reply to the Defence of the Second Defendant, p. 28.

67.   Longerich, *Politik der Vernichtung. Eine Gesamtdarstellung der nationalsozialistischen Judenverfolgung* (Munich, 1998), p. 510; Himmler note, 9.10.1942, in third supplementary Discovery list, 51 (b).

68.   Irving, *Hitler's War*, 1991 ed., p. 467.

69.   Note from Sztójay to the German Foreign Office, 2.12.1942; reprinted in R. Braham (ed.), *The Destruction of Hungarian Jewry*, vol. 1 (New York, 1963), doc. 86.

70.   *IMT*, vol. 10, pp. 231, 244.

71.   A. Hillgruber (ed.), *Staatsmänner und Diplomaten bei Hitler*, vol. 2 (Frankfurt am Main, 1970), p. 256.

72.   *IMT*, vol. 22, pp. 605–6.

73.   Hillgruber (ed.), *Staatsmänner*, vol. 2, pp. 256–57.

74.   GTB II/8, p. 236.

75.   Irving, *Hitler's War*, 1977 ed., p. 872; also 1991 ed., pp. 541–42.

76.   Irving, *Hitler's War*, 1977 ed., p. 509; idem, "Hitler and the Jews," *The Spectator*, 30 September 1978 (correspondence column).

77.   R. Ainsztein, *Jewish Resistance in Nazi-occupied Europe* (London, 1974), pp. 624–25; E. Jäckel, P. Longerich, and J. Schoeps (eds.), *Enzyklopädie des Holocaust*, vol. 3 (Munich, 1995), p. 1,555; R. Ainsztein, *The Warsaw Ghetto Revolt* (New York, 1979), pp. 97–99.

78.   Hillgruber (ed.), *Staatsmänner*, vol. 2, p. 245.

79.   R. Hilberg, *Die Vernichtung der europäischen Juden*, (Frankfurt am Main, 1990), Vol. 2, pp. 779–785.

80.   Jagow to Foreign Office, 2 June 1943, reprinted in Braham (ed.), *Destruction*, doc. 107.

81.   Cited in Braham, *Politics*, p. 391.

82.   Irving, *Hitler's War*, 1991 ed., p. 590.

83.   Irving, *Hitler's War*, 1977 ed., p. 575; Reply to the Defence of the Second Defendant, p. 15, paragraph 17 (h).

84.   Hans-Jürgen Döscher, *Das Auswärtige Amt im Dritten Reich. Diplomatie im Schatten der 'Endlösung'* (Munich, 1987), pp. 310–11; Christopher Browning, *The Final Solution and the Foreign*

Office (New York, 1978), pp. 174–75; Raul Hilberg, *The Destruction of the European Jews* (New York, 1961), pp. 350–55.

85. Führer Order of 10 September 1943 in *Akten zur deutschen Auswärtigen Politik, Serie E: 1941–45*, vol. 6, *1 May–30 September, 1943* (Göttingen, 1979), pp. 533–34.

86. Meir Michaelis, *Mussolini and the Jews: German-Italian Relations and the Jewish Question in Italy, 1922–1945* (Oxford, 1978), p. 352; Robert Katz, *Black Sabbath: A Journey through a Crime Against Humanity* (London, 1969), p. 48; M. Tagliacozzo, "La Comunità di Roma sotto l'incubo della svastica. La grande razzia del 16 ottobre 1943," *Gli ebrei in Italia durante il fascismo, iii* (Quaderni del Centro di Documentazione Ebraica Comunità) (Milan, 1963), p. 9.

87. Michaelis, *Mussolini*, p. 353; Katz, *Black Sabbath*, p. 49.

88. Katz, *Black Sabbath*, p. 54; Michaelis, *Mussolini*, p. 354.

89. NG–2652-H: von Thadden to missions abroad, 12 October 1943, enclosing the RSHA circular dated 23 September 1943; Hilberg, *Destruction*, p. 427.

90. NG–2271, order by General Nehring, forwarded to Rahn, 6 December 1942; NG–2099, Rahn to Foreign Office, 6 December 1942.

91. Michaelis, *Mussolini*, p. 355; Katz, *Black Sabbath*, pp. 60–62.

92. Michaelis, *Mussolini*, p. 362; Katz, *Black Sabbath*, pp. 117–18 and 125–29.

93. NG–5027, Moellhausen to Ribbentrop, 6 October 1943. (Michaelis, *Mussolini*, p. 364-6)

94. Moellhausen to Ribbentrop, 7 October 1943, (PRO) GFM 33/147/123599. (Michaelis, *Mussolini*, p. 363)

95. Irving, doc. 97, NG–5027, Sonnleithner to Ribbentrop's Office, 9 October, 1943; similarly, NG–5027, von Thadden to Moellhausen, 9 October 1943. (Michaelis, *Mussolini*, p. 363-6)

96. NG–5027 as cited by Michaelis, *Mussolini*, p. 364.

97. IfZ NO–2427 (17–18 October, 1943), as cited in Michaelis, *Mussolini*, p. 367; Susan Zuccotti, *The Italians and the Holocaust: Persecution, Rescue and Survival* (London, 1987), p. 117, n. 43. Danuta Czech, *Auschwitz Chronicle 1939–1945* (London, 1990), p. 512; L. Picciotto Fargion, "Italien," in Wolfgang Benz (ed.), *Dimensionen des Völkermords, Die Zahl der jüdischen Opfer des Nationalsozialismus* (Munich, 1991), pp. 199–228, here p. 220.

98. Katz, *Black Sabbath*, pp. 275–79, 293–94, 341–45.

99. Fargion, "Italien," p. 204.

100. NG–5026, *Inland II* (signed Wagner) via Hencke to Ribbentrop, 4 December 1943; NG–5026, Hilger via Steengrach and Hencke to *Inland II*, 9 December 1943.

101. E. Kogon et al. (eds.), *Nationalsozialistische Massentötungen durch Giftgas* (Frnakfurt am Main, 1986), p. 23.
102. Helmut Krausnick et al., *Anatomy of the SS State* (London, 1973), p. 227.
103. Hans Marsálek, *Die Geschichte des Konzentrationslagers Mauthausen: Dokumentation* (Vienna, 1980), pp. 39–41.
104. Paragraph 30 in the Defence of the Second Defendant.
105. Discovery document: newspaper clipping from *The Sunday Times*, 10 July 1977, Gitta Sereny and Lewis Chester, "Mr. Irving's Hitler—the $1,000 Question."
106. Discovery document, letter from Irving to Harold Evans, *The Sunday Times*, 14 September 1977.
107. Discovery document in Irving's Discovery to the court consisted of the voluminous correspondence generated by Irving in response to this devastating attack on his integrity as a historian, including a complaint by him to the Press Council.

CHAPTER FOUR

1. Walter Laqueur, *The Terrible Secret: Suppression of the Truth about Hitler's "Final Solution"* (London, 1980), p. 7; Geoff Eley, "Holocaust History," *London Review of Books*, 3–17 March, 1982, pp. 6–9; Richard J. Evans, *In Hitler's Shadow: West German Historians and the Attempt to Escape from the Nazi Past* (New York, 1989), p. 142; preface by Eberhard Jäckel to Eberhard Jäckel, Peter Longerich, and Julius H. Schoeps (eds.), *Enzyklopädie des Holocaust: Die Verfolgung und Ermordung der Europäischen Juden*, 3 vols. (Berlin, 1993), vol. 1, p. xviii.
2. Michael R. Marrus, *The Holocaust in History* (London, 1989), p. 1.
3. Martin Gilbert, *The Holocaust: The Jewish Tragedy* (London, 1986), p. 18; Ronnie S. Landau, *The Nazi Holocaust* (London, 1982), p. 3.
4. Vera Laska, *Nazism, Resistance and Holocaust in World War II: A Bibliography* (Metuchen, N.J., 1985), p. xvii.
5. Lipstadt, *Denying the Holocaust*, chapter 2.
6. Austin J. App, *A Straight Look at the 'Third Reich': Hitler and National Socialism, How Right? How Wrong?* (Tacoma Park, Md., 1974), pp. 5, 18–20; and idem, *The Six Million Swindle: Blackmailing the German People for Hard Marks with Fabricated Corpses* (Tacoma Park, Md., 1973), pp. 2, 29.
7. Butz, *The Hoax of the Twentieth Century* (Brighton, 1977 ed.), pp. 30, 36–37, 49, 58–59, 69–73, 100–105, 131, 173, 198, 203–5, 246–50.

8.   Robert Faurisson, *Mémoire en Défense, contre ceux qui m'accusent de falsifier l'histoire: La question des chambres à gaz* (Paris, 1980); *Le Matin*, 16 November 1978, interview with Faurisson; report of the trial in *Patterns of Prejudice*, vol. 15, no. 4 (October 1981), pp. 51–55. Faurisson was influenced by Rassinier: Paul Rassinier, *Debunking the Genocide Myth* (Torrance, Calif., 1978).

9.   Wilhelm Staeglich, *Der Auschwitz-Mythos. Legende oder Wirklichkeit* (Tübingen, 1979); Armin Pfahl-Traghber, "Die Apologeten der "Auschwitz-Lüge"—Bedeutung und Entwicklung der Holocaust-Leugnung im Rechtsextremismus," *Jahrbuch Extremismus und Demokratie*, Vol. 8 (1996), pp. 75–101, esp. pp. 86–87. Hermann Graml, "Alte und neue Apologeten Hitlers," in Wolfgang Benz (ed.), *Rechtsextremismus in Deutschland: Voraussetzungen, Zusammenhänge, Wirkungen* (Frankfurt am Main, 1994), pp. 63–92, here 81–83.

10. Roger Eatwell, "How to Revise History (and Influence People?), Neo-Fascist Style," in Luciano Cheles, Ronnie Ferguson, and Michalina Vaughan, (eds.) *The Far Right in Western and Eastern Europe* (London, 1995), pp. 309–26, here p. 311. The element of diversity in Holocaust denial was also noted by Kenneth S. Stern, *Holocaust Denial* (New York, 1993), pp. 8–9.

11. Pierre Vidal-Naquet, *Assassins of Memory: Essays on the Denial of the Holocaust* (New York, 1992), pp. 18–23 (originally published in 1980).

12. (Yisrael Gutman), "Die Auschwitz-Lüge," in Jäckel et al. (eds.), *Enzyklopädie*, vol. I, pp. 121–27, here pp. 121–24.

13. Pfahl-Traghber, "Die Apologeten," pp. 75–77, esp. pp. 75–77.

14. Pierre Vidal-Naquet and Limor Yagil, *Holocaust Denial in France: Analysis of a Unique Phenomenon* (Tel Aviv, 1995).

15. Gill Seidel, *The Holocaust Denial: Antisemitism, Racism and the New Right* (Leeds, 1986).

16. Dokumentationsarchiv des österreichischen Widerstandes/Bundesministerium für Unterricht und Kunst, *Amoklauf gegen die Wirklichkeit. NS-Verbrechen und "revisionistische" Geschichtsschreibung* (Vienna, 1991); similarly (a–c only), the recent study by Michael Shermer and Alex Grobman, *Denying History: Who Says the Holocaust Never Happened and Why Do They Say It?* (Berkeley, 2000).

17. Reply to Defence of Second Defendant, p. 11.

18. Ibid., pp. 10–11.

19. Ibid., p. 4.

20. Irving, *Hitler's War*, 1977 ed., pp. xiv–xv.

21. Vidal-Naquet, *Assassins*, pp. 89, 124; Seidel, *The Holocaust Denial*, p. 121.

22. Stern, *Holocaust Denial*, p. 31.

23. Lipstadt, *Denying*, pp. 157–58; Shermer and Groban, *Denying*, pp. 65–67.

24. "David Irving's 1988 Testimony at the Trial of Ernst Zündel," on Irving's website http://www.fpp.co.uk: "Documents on the Auschwitz controversy,", pp. 30, 82–83, 138.

25. Videotape 207: NDR (North German Radio) 3, documentary, "Juden wurden nicht vergast," German verion of a Danish program by Jens Olaf Jersild, screened on 9 May 1993, at 38 min. 25 secs.; also videotape 189: speech presented in Calgary, 29 September 1991.

26. Audiocassette 89: Terry Lane, ABC 3LO Radio, interview with Irving, 18 March 1986.

27. "David Irving's 1988 Testimony," p. 12.

28. Videotape 223: Irving interviewed on Australian Channel 7, 1 October 1996, 3 mins. 25 secs.

29. "David Irving's 1988 Testimony," pp. 16, 151, 93.

30. Irving, *Nuremberg: The Last Battle* (London, 1996), p. 352 n. 13.

31. Videotape 200: "The Search for Truth in History," cited in Nigel Jackson, *The Case for David Irving* (Sidgwick, Australia, 1992), p. 88. Jackson described Irving as "one of the greatest historians ever to have written in English" (p. 95); videotape 190: Latvian Hall, Toronto, 8 November 1990—"50,000 people were killed in Auschwitz . . . the number is too high . . . nearly all of the deaths were due to disease" (from 55 mins. 30 secs.); audiocassette 108: speech presented to the Free Speech League, Victoria, British Columbia, 27 October 1990, no. 507)—40,000 killed at Auschwitz in three years; videotape 200: "The Search for Truth in History" (1993)—100,000 deaths from all causes, "25,000 people murdered in Auschwitz in three years" (from 1 hr. 13 mins. 15 secs.). The variation in the figures was typical of Irving's indifference to statistical accuracy.

32. Videotape 200: "The Search for Truth in History," 1993, at 1 hr. 12 mins.

33. Videotape 190: Irving at Latvian Hall, Toronto, 8 November 1992, from 1 hr. 7 mins. 15 secs.

34. Irving, "Battleship Auschwitz," *JHR*, vol. 10, no. 4.

35. See Irving, "Auschwitz and the Typhus Plague in Poland. More Preview Pages from David Irving's New Biography, *Churchill's War*, Vol.

II," posted on Irving's Focal Point website, seen 12 February 1999: see also F. H. Hinsley et al., *British Intelligence in the Second World War: Its Influence on Strategy and Operations* (Cambridge, 1979–84), vol. 2, appendix, p. 673: "The returns from Auschwitz, the largest of the camps with 20,000 prisoners, mentioned illness as the main cause of death, but included references to shootings and hangings. There were no references in the decrypts to gassing."

36. Richard Breitman, *Official Secrets: What the Nazis Planned, What the British and Americans Knew* (London, 1998), p. 115.

37. Discovery document 1,350. (also doc. 1,349). Hinsley added that he thought it highly unlikely that the original transcripts had been retained.

38. Irving, *Nuremberg: The Last Battle* (London, 1996), p. 341 n. 12.

39. Ibid., p. 62.

40. Reply to Defence of Second Defendant, pp. 5–6.

41. Irving, *Nuremberg*, pp. 24–25, 353.

42. Videotape 200: 1 hr. 15 mins. 40 secs.; also Videotape 184: Leuchter Report Press Conference, 23 June 1989, at 19 mins. 40 secs.

43. Rassinier, *Debunking*, p. 214; Butz, *The Hoax*, p. 242.

44. "David Irving on the Eichmann and Goebbels Papers: Speech at Los Angeles, California, October 11, 1992" (11th Conference of the Institute for Historical Review, transcript on Irving's Focal Point website).

45. David Irving, "Revelations from Goebbels's Diary," *JHR*, vol. 15, no. 1 (1995), 2–17, here p. 15.

46. "David Irving's 1988 Testimony," pp. 86, 132, 141.

47. "David Irving on the Eichmann and Goebbels Papers" (opening sentence of section: "Eichmann on Höss").

48. "David Irving on Freedom of Speech," 28 October, 1992.

49. "Speech by David Irving to a Packed Hall in the Primrose Hotel, Toronto, November 1, 1992." Transcript from Irving's Focal Point website.

50. Videotape 206: "*Holmes Show,*" New Zealand television, 4 June 1993, at 6 mins. 25 secs.

51. Jackson, *The Case for David Irving*, p. 89.

52. See, for example, Gilbert, *The Holocaust*; Marrus, *The Holocaust in History*; Hilberg, *The Destruction of the European Jews*, etc.

53. Ron Casey interview with David Irving, 27 July 1995, Station 2GB, *Media Monitors* (Sydney etc.), Broadcast transcript S36962003.

54. Audiocassette 86, Irving, "Censorship of History," lecture in Runnymede, Australia, 18 March 1986, 270–291.

55. Wolfgang Sofsky, *Die Ordnung des Terrors. Das Konzentrationslager,*

2nd ed. (Frankfurt am Main, 1997), pp. 237–45; also videotape 180: Toronto 1989.

56.   Videotape 232: "Speech to the Canadian Association for Free Expression, Carlton Inn, Toronto," from 20 mins. 25 secs. to 20 mins. 55 secs.

57.   Audiocassette 93: Irving, "The Manipulation of History," Toronto, 1 November 1986, 528–32.

58.   Reply to Defence of Second Defendant, p. 3.

59.   Ibid., pp. 5–6.

60.   David Irving's 1988 testimony at the trial of Ernst Zündel, pp. 99–100.

61.   Audiocassette 114, Irving, "The Worldwide Anti-Irving Lobby and the Eichmann 'Memoir,'" speech at the 11th International Revisionist Conference, October 1992, 420–430.

62.   Reply to Defence of Second Defendant, pp. 5–6.

63.   Ibid.

64.   Gabriel Weimann and Conrad Winn, *Hate on Trial: The Zündel Affair, the Media, and Public Opinion in Canada* (New York, 1986); Shelly Shapiro (ed.), *Truth Prevails: Demolishing Holocaust Denial: The End of "The Leuchter Report"* (New York, 1990); David Irving, foreword to *Auschwitz: The End of the Line: The Leuchter Report* (London, 1989); Shermer and Grobman, *Denying History*, pp. 64–67, 123–67.

65.   Jackson, *The Case for David Irving*, pp. 75–79.

66.   Robert Faurisson, "The Problem of the Gas Chambers," *JHR*, Summer 1980; Robert Faurisson, foreword to *The Leuchter Report: The End of a Myth: An Engineering Report on the Alleged Execution Gas Chambers at Auschwitz, Birkenau, and Majdanek, Poland* (American edition, 1988).

67.   Expert witness reports by Professor Robert Jan Van Pelt, Professor Christopher Browning, and Professor Peter Longerich; see also Shelly Shapiro (ed.), *Truth Prevails: Demolishing Holocaust Denial: The End of "The Leuchter Report"* (New York, 1990).

68.   TS 24/1, pp. 74–75.

69.   Only one witness at Nuremberg claimed to have seen bodies in the gas chambers; they may have been moved there temporarily from the adjacent crematorium, which was used for executions (Barbara Distel and Ruth Jakusch [eds.], *Concentration Camp Dachau 1933–1945* [Munich, 1989]).

70.   Videotape 186: Irving in Moers, 5 March 1990, at 4 mins. 45 secs.

71.   David Irving, "Revelations from Goebbels's Diary," *JHR*, vol. 15, no. 1 (1995), pp. 2–17, here p. 15.

72.   BBC2: "Journey to the Far Right" (20 March 1999).

73.   Videotape 184: Leuchter Report Press Conference, 23 June 1989, at 57 mins. 30 secs.

74.   Videotape 186: Irving in Moers, 5 March 1990, from 31 mins. 30 secs. and again at 1 hr. 17 mins. 45 secs.

75.   Videotape 190, "German reunificaiton and other topics," Latvian Hall, Toronto, 8 November 1990, at 1 hr. 1 min. 50 secs.

76.   Reply to Defence of Second Defendant, p. 3.

77.   Audiocassette 88: Irving press conference, Brisbane, 20 March 1986, 445–58. In the phrase "this is what they find very repugnant," 'they' presumably, as usual in Irving's speeches, referred to the Jews, or to historians working in some sense or some capacity on their behalf.

78.   Audiocassette 99: Irving speech in Toronto, August 1988 (private house), side 1, 727–54.

79.   For these statements, see "David Irving's 1988 testimony," pp. 45–46, 88.

80.   Ibid., pp. 3, 71; for Eichmann's 1961 statement, see Noakes and Pridham (eds.), *Nazism*, doc. 850, p. 1,135.

81.   Ibid., pp. 95–98.

82.   Rassinier, *Debunking*, p. 288.

83.   App, *The Six Million Swindle*, pp. 7–8, repeating arguments first advanced in App, *Morgenthau Era Letters*, 2nd ed. (Tacoma Park, Md., 1975), p. 101 (first ed., 1965).

84.   Irving, *The Search for Truth in History*, as summarized by Jackson, *The Case for David Irving*, p. 79; Discovery document, doc. 1,211: "Auschwitz—the end of the line"; Irving, "Deutsche Historiker—Lügner und Feiglinge, Rede vor der deutschen Presse in Berlin am 3. Oktober 1989," *Historische Tatsachen*, vol. 42 (1990), pp. 37–40; Irving, "Battleship Auschwitz," *JHR*, vol. 10, no. 4, 1990; Discovery document, doc. 1,697: Irving to Slater, 15 November 1993.

85.   Videotape 200: Irving, "The Search for Truth in History," 1993, at 1 hr. 14 mins. 55 secs. The document was supplied to Irving by a researcher working for Ernst Zündel (audiocassette 99: Irving in Toronto, 13 August 1988, 465–660).

86.   David Irving, "Auschwitz, and the Typhus Plague in Poland. More Preview Pages from David Irving's New Biography, Churchill's War, vol. ii. A Sneak Preview," posted on Irving's Internet site, checked 12 February 1999.

87.   PRO, FO 371/30917, C 7853, telegram no. 2831, Berne to Foreign Office, quoted in Martin Gilbert, *Auschwitz and the Allies*, (London, 1981)p. 57.

88.   Ibid., p. 58.

89.   PRO FO 371/30917, D. Allen, minute, 10 September 1942, quoted in Gilbert, *Auschwitz and the Allies*, p. 60.

90.   PRO, FO 371/3455, Roger Allen, minute, 27 August 1943.

91.   PRO, FO 371/3455, Cavendish-Bentinck, minute, 27 August 1943.

92.   PRO, FO 371/3455, Telegram, Foreign Office to Washington, 27 August 1943.

93.   PRO, FO 371/3455, Department of State Confidential Release, 28 August 1943.

94.   Reply to Defence of Second Defendant, pp. 5, 6, and 7.

95.   Jackson, *The Case for David Irving*, pp. 83, 86.

96.   *CODE*, no. 5 1990, p. 55. *CODE* (*Conföderation organisch denkender Europäer*, "Confederation of organically-thinking Europeans').

97.   "David Irving's 1988 testimony," pp. 136–37.

98.   Noakes and Pridham, *Nazism*, vol. 3, pp. 1,155–1,156, gave a maximum figure of 70.

99.   Videotape 190: "German reunification and other topics," Latvian Hall, Toronto, 8 November 1990, at 45 mins. 30 secs. To 48 mins. 35 secs.

100.   Videotape 189: Irving speech at Travelport Airport Inn, Calgary, Alberta, 29 Sept. 1991.

101.   Videotape 190: Irving Speech at the Bayerischer Hof, Milton, Ontario, 5 October 1991, at 2 hrs. 19 mins. 19 secs. To 2 hrs. 20 mins. 40 secs. Irving's reference was to an accident in which Senator Edward Kennedy's car had plunged off a bridge at Chapppaquidick Island, Massachusettes into a river below; the senator had escaped, but a young woman seated in the back had died.

102.   Videotape 220 (Tampa, Florida, 6 October 1995); and Videotape 186 (Moers, 5 March 1990).

103.   Videotape 220: "David Irving, Historian, in Tampa, Florida," 6 October 1995, from 22 mins. 40 secs.

104.   Videotape 225: "Cover Story" on Australian television program "Sunday," 4 March 1997, at 2 mins. 15 secs..

105.   Seidel, *The Holocaust Denial*, p. 39.

106.   Videotape 200: "The Search for Truth in History—Banned!", 1993, at 20 mins.

107.   Videotape 190: Irving Speech at the Bayerischer Hof, Milton, Ontario, 5 October 1991, from 2 hrs. 28 mins. 30 secs.

108.   "History's Cache and Carry," *The Guardian*, 7 July 1992.

109.   Rassinier, *Debunking*, p. 309.

110.   App, *The Six Million Swindle*, p. 2.

111.   Lipstadt, *Denying the Holocaust*, p. 57; Y. Gutman et al. (eds.), *Encyclopedia of the Holocaust* (New York, 1990), pp. 1,255–1,259.

112.   "Speech by David Irving to a packed hall in the Primrose Hotel, Toronto, November 1, 1992." Transcript on Irving's Focal Point website.

113.   Videotape 226: unedited material from *This Week*, 28 November 1991, 1 hr. 30 mins. 15 secs. To 1 hr. 31 mins. 15 secs.

114.   Jackson, *The Case for David Irving*, p. 85.

115.   Transcript of first half of David Irving's talk to the Clarendon Club in London, 19 September 1992 (Focal Point website); also audio-cassette 159 (same speech), "self-appointed, ugly, greasy, nasty, per-verted representatives of that community (i.e. Jews) in Britain."

116.   Videotape 190: Irving Speech at the Bayerischer Hof, Milton, Ontario, 5 October 1991, at 2 hrs. 44 mins.

117.   Speech at the Clarendon Club, Town Hall, Bromley, 29 May 1992, at 43 mins. 20 secs.

118.   Extract from Irving's "A Radical's Diary," 13–14 April 1998, on Irving's Focal Point website.

119.   See App, *A Straight Look*, p. 18, for alleged Jewish control of the media; Butz, *Hoax*, p. 87, for an alleged Jewish world conspiracy to persuade the world of the reality of the Holocaust.

120.   Videotape 190: Irving Speech at the Bayerischer Hof, Milton, Ontario, 5 October 1991, from 2 hrs. 10 mins. 30 secs.

121.   Audiocassette 127: "Irving in Oakland, California (Berkeley Free Speech Coalition)," 10 September 1996, 403–8.

122.   Videotape 220: "David Irving, Historian, in Tampa, Florida;" 6 October 1995, from c. 23 mins.

123.   Videotape 190: "German reunificaiton and other topics," Latvain Hall, Toronto, 8 November 1990, at 19 mins. 19 secs.

124.   Videotape 225: "Cover Story" on Australian television program "Sunday," 4 March 1997, Irving interviewed in Key West, Florida (33 mins. 10 secs.). Audiocassette 90: Irving in Christchurch, New Zealand, 26 March 1986; Magnus Brechtken, *"Madagascar für die Juden": Antisemitische Idee und politische Praxis* (Munich, 1997); Peter Longerich, *Politik der Vernichtung: Eine Gesamtdarstellung der nationalsozialistischen Judenverfolgung* (Munich, 1998), pp. 273–89.

125.   Printed in *Spotlight*, magazine of the Liberty Lobby, Washington D.C.; Lipstadt, *Denying*, pp. 150–51.

126.   Friedrich Paul Berg, "The Diesel Gas Chambers: Myth Within a Myth," *JHR*, vol. 5, no. 1 (Spring 1984), pp. 15–46.

127.   Carlo Mattogno, "The Myth of the Extermination of the Jews," *JHR*, vol. 8 (1988), pp. 133–72, 261–302.

128.   Carl O. Nordling, "How Many Jews Died in the German Concentration Camps?," *JHR*, vol. 11, no. 3 (1991), pp. 335–44.

129.   Friedrich Paul Berg, "Typhus and the Jews," *JHR*, vol. 8 (1988), pp. 433–81, here p. 462.

130.   Enrique Aynat, "Neither Trace Nor Proof: The Seven Auschwitz 'Gassing' Sites," *JHR*, vol. 11, no. 2 (1991), pp. 177–206.

131.   *JHR*, vol. 12, no. 4 (1992–93).

132.   E.g., vol. 11, nos. 1 and 2 (1991), vol. 10, no. 3 (1990), etc.

133.   Michael A. Hoffmann II, "The Psychology and Epistemology of 'Holocaust' Newspeak," *JHR*, vol. 6, no. 4 (1985–86) pp. 267–78, here p. 478.

134.   Irving, "A Radical's Diary," *Focal Point*, 8 March 1982, p. 13.

135.   See N. Fielding, *The National Front* (London, 1980), for the general background. Irving's note in a version of his diary entry published in *Focal Point* in 1982, that the Institute for Historical Review was run at that time by a man calling himself Lewis Brandon, strongly suggested that he was aware of Brandon's true identity and background (Irving, "A Radical's Diary," p. 13).

136.   *Statement of Record and Letter of Apology to Mel Mermelstein*, signed by G. G. Baumen, Attorney for the Legion for the Survival of Freedom, the Institute for Historical Review, the Noontide Press, and Elisabeth Carto, and Mark F. von Esch, Attorney for the Liberty Lobby and Willis Carto, 24 July 1985.

137.   "Record and Mission of the Institute for Historical Review," *JHR*, vol. 15, no. 5 (1995), pp. 18–21, here p. 19.

138.   Letter to subscribers enclosed with August 1995 issue of the journal. See also Shermer and Grobman, *Denying History*, pp. 43–46, 72–74.

139.   Institute for Historical Review: Endorsements, February 1994 (website publication, on http://www.ihr.org/top/endorsements.html).

140.   Kate Taylor (ed.), *Holocaust Denial: The David Irving Trial and International Revisionism* (London, 2000), pp. 90–91.

141.   Mark Weber, "From the Editor," *JHR*, vol. 13, no. 1 (1993), p. 3.

142.   Ibid., vol. 10, no. 4 (1990–91), pp. 389–416, 417–38 (by Irving); vol. 9, no. 3 (1989), pp. 261–86 (also by Irving, on Churchill); vol. 13, no. 1 (1993), pp. 4–19 (three articles, one by, two about, Irving); vol. 13, no. 2 (1993), pp. 14–25 (by Irving), and vol. 15, no. 1 (1995), pp. 2–23 (two articles by Irving).

143.   The title of the leaflet is: *Who Reads the Journal of Historical Review?* Copy in the Wiener Library, London.

144.   *Journal of Historical Review*, vol. 13, no. 1, p. 1.

145.   Discovery Document 145: Irving to Weber, 4 June 1992, for an example.

146.   Audiocassette 158: "David Irving speaks to NPD audience in Munich, 12 May 1991."

147.   James Bacque, *Other Losses: An Investigation into the Mass Deaths of German Prisoners of War at the Hands of the French and Americans After World War II* (London, 1990), and Günter Bischof and Stephen E. Ambrose (eds.), *Eisenhower and the German PoWs: Facts against Falsehood* (London, 1992).

148.   Günter Bischof, Dewey A. Browder et al., "Fact or Fiction? The Historical Profession and James Bacque," roundtable discussion at the German Studies Association, Salt Lake City, 9 October 1998, reported in *Bulletin of the German Historical Institute Washington*, vol. 23 (Fall 1998), pp. 19–21.

149.   David Irving, "On Contemporary History," pp. 273–74; Robert Faurisson, "A Challenge to David Irving," *JHR*, vol. 5, nos. 2–4 (Winter 1984), pp. 288–305, here p. 305.

150.   See "David Irving on the Eichmann and Goebbels Papers," question-and-answer session. Irving referred to subsequent criticism from Faurisson as "occasional sniping" and chose to emphasize their shared "intellectual crusade." See Robert Faurisson, "On David Irving," *Adelaide Institute*, vol. 43 (August 1996), p. 1, and the letter from Irving to Faurisson, 29 January 1997, in Irving's supplementary Discovery list.

151.   Videotape 190: Irving Speech at the Bayerischer Hof, Milton, Ontario, 5 October 1991, at 1 hr. 20 mins.

152.   Irving, *Nürnberg: die letzte Schlacht* (Tübingen, 1996), pp. 313–21; Faurisson, "How the British Obtained the Confessions of Rudolf Höss," *JHR*, vol. 7, no. 4 (Winter 1986–87), pp. 389–403, both reporting, for example, that Höss, the commandant of Auschwitz, knew no English, although his memoirs proved in fact that he did.

153.   Videotape 220: "David Irving, Historian, in Tampa, Florida," 6 October 1995, at beginning of tape.

154.   David Irving, "Revelations from Goebbels's Diary," *Journal of Historical Review*, vol. 15, no. 1 (1995), pp. 2–17, here p. 15.

155.   Ron H. Rosenbaum, *Explaining Hitler. The Search for the Origins of His Evil* (London, 1998), p. 234.

156.   Ibid., p. 233.

157.   Ibid., p. 223; and Norman Stone, "Failing to Find the Führer," *The Sunday Times*, 12 July 1998.

158.   Videotape 189. See also the extensive discussions of Irving's denial in Shermer and Grobman, *Denying History*, esp. pp. 48–58, 203–8.

CHAPTER FIVE

1. Rudolf Förster, "Dresden," in Marlene P. Hiller, Eberhard Jäckel, and Jürgen Rohwer (eds.), *Städte im 2. Weltkrieg. Ein internationaler Vergleich* (Essen, 1991), pp. 299–315, here pp. 302–5.
2. C. Webster and N. Frankland, *The Strategic Air Offensive Against Germany*, 4 vols. (London, 1961); Richard Overy, *Why the Allies Won* (London, 1995), chapter 4.
3. Geoffrey Best, *Humanity in Warfare: The Modern History of the International Law of Armed Conflicts*, 2nd ed. (Bristol, 1983), pp. 262–85; Reiner Pommerin, "Zur Einsicht bomben? Die Zerstörung Dresdens in der Luftkrieg-Strategie des Zweiten Weltkriegs," in Reiner Pommerin (ed.), *Dresden unterem Hakenkreuz* (Cologne, 1998), pp. 227–45.
4. Overy, *Why the Allies Won*, pp. 106, 132; Best, *Humanity*, p. 268; Pommerin, "Zur Einsicht," pp. 241–43.
5. Michael S. Sherry, *The Rise of American Air Power: The Creation of Armageddon* (New Haven/London, 1987), pp. 260–61.
6. William Kimber ed.: *The Destruction of Dresden* (London, 1963) (two impressions); William Kimber ed.: *The Destruction of Dresden* (London, 1964) (third impression); Corgi ed.: *The Destruction of Dresden* (London, 1966) (revised and updated edition); Corgi ed.: *The Destruction of Dresden* (London, 1971) (reissue); Elmfield ed.: *The Destruction of Dresden* (Morely, 1974); Futura ed.: *The Destruction of Dresden,* (London, 1980); Papermac ed.: *The Destruction of Dresden* (London, 1985); Focal Point ed.: *Apocalypse 1945: The Destruction of Dresden* (London, 1995) ("thoroughly revised and expanded on the basis of material available since 1963"). German editions: Sigbert Mohn ed.: *Der Untergang Dresdens* (Gütersloh, 1964); Rowohlt Verlag ed.: *Der Untergang Dresdens* (Reinbeck, 1967); Heyne Allgemeine Reihe ed.: *Der Untergang Dresdens* 1977 (five editions by 1985); Ullstein ed.: *Der Untergang Dresdens* (Frankfurt am Main, 1985).
7. Corgi ed., 1966, pp. 200–201; Focal Point ed., pp. 208–9.
8. Corgi ed., 1966, pp. 212–13; Focal Point ed., pp. 223–24.
9. Georg Feydt, in *Ziviler Luftschutz*, 1953, quoted in Götz Bergander, *Dresden im Luftkrieg. Vorgeschichte—Zerstörung—Folgen* (Cologne, 1977, 2nd ed., 1985), p. 153.
10. Corgi ed., 1966, p. 225.
11. Discovery document 142, newspaper clipping from the *Daily Sketch*, 29 April 1963.
12. Irving's microfilmed Dresden materials (hereinafter DJ), DJ 10:

Voight to Irving, 6 September 1962, enclosing comments on Irving's draft.

13. Focal Point ed., p. 242.

14. Walter Weidauer, *Inferno Dresden: öber Lügen und Legenden um die Aktion 'Donnerschlag'* (East Berlin, 1965, 2nd ed. 1966), p. 131-2.

15. Max Seydewitz, *Zerstörung und Wiederaufbau von Dresden* (East Berlin, 1955). Seydewitz was Dresden's mayor at the time of publication.

16. Kimber ed., 1963, p. 207.

17. Corgi ed., 1966, p. 280.

18. Corgi ed., 1966, p. 280.

19. DJ 10, New information on death toll in Allied air raids on Dresden 1945, introduction, dated November 1964, p. 7. In 1995 Irving claimed that by 1965 he had seen two other copies of TB 47, one of which had been shown to the playwright Rolf Hochhuth. Although Irving claimed that the original had not been found, he also described Hochhuth's copy as a "typed original with several hand-written corrections." Hochhuth's copy was sent to him by Dankwart Guratzsch as a result of an article in the German illustrated *Der Stern*. Guratzsch had found it among the papers of his father, who in turn may have received it from one of his students, a Dresden policeman. Indeed, Guratzsch described his copy as "a typed copy, with many, partly hand-written, corrections." But what he sent Hochhuth was a copy typed by Guratzsch himself: DJ 10, Dankwart Guratzsch to Rolf Hochhuth, 3 July 1965; Rolf Hochhuth to Irving, 10 September 1965; DJ 35, "Further Information on Tagesbefehl Extracted from My Day Book."

20. DJ 10, "New Information," p. 7. Hahn was also named as Irving's source for the "forged' TB 47 in a letter from Weidauer. See DJ 35, Walter Weidauer to Irving, 21 November 1966. Given the scarcity of photocopying equipment in East Germany at this time, the likelihood was that Hahn transcribed Funfack's copy by hand. If he had photographed it, presumably he would have said so.

21. DJ 10, "New Information," p. 8.

22. Ibid.

23. Discovery document 154, Irving to Donald McLahlan, 26 November 1965.

24. Discovery document 155, Irving to Dr. Dieter Struss, 28 November 1965, comment written in pencil replacing in type "correctness of the information."

25. DJ 12, Irving to the provost of Coventry Cathedral, 6 December 1964.

26. Discovery document 159, Irving to Schuller, *Stern*, 27 January 1965.

27. Discovery document 165, Irving to Calabi, Arnoldo Mondadori Editore, 19 March 1965.

28. DJ 35, *Die Welt der Literatur,* 10 December 1964; similarly, DJ 12: Irving to the provost of Coventry Cathedral, 6 December 1964.

29. DJ 35, Max Funfack to Irving, 19 January 1965. Partially reproduced as a plate in Weidauer, *Inferno Dresden,* p. 133.

30. DJ 35, Dr. Dieter Struss, "Umstrittener Tagesbefehl," reader's letter in *Die Welt,* 12 February 1965, p. 10. The first German edition had appeared on 10 September 1964 under Sigbert Mohn's imprint, too early to include details of TB 47. See DJ 12, "Schlimmer als Hiroshima" in *Rheinische Post,* 9 September 1964.

31. DJ 35, Irving "Die Totenziffern von Dresden," reader's letter to *Die Welt,* 12 February 1965, p. 10.

32. DJ 12, draft, "Two Questions on Dresden" for *The Sunday Telegraph,* February 1965, 15 pp., p. 9; Irving's underlining.

33. Discovery document 167, Irving to Dr. Noble Frankland, 28 May 1965.

34. DJ 12 Draft, "Bombing Dresden' for *The Observer,* 7 March 1965; Reader's letter from Irving, "Death-roll in Dresden," *The Observer,* 14 March 1965.

35. Rolf-Dieter Müller and Gerd R. Ueberschär, *Kriegsende 1945: Die Zerstörung des Deutschen Reiches* (Frankfurt am Main, 1994), p. 39.

36. DJ 12, R. H. S. Crossman, "Apocalypse at Dresden," *Esquire,* November 1963, pp. 149–54, p. 152.

37. Weidauer, *Inferno,* pp. 111–12.

38. Document 67 in Erhard Klöss (ed.), *Der Luftkrieg über Deutschland 1939–1945. Deutsche Berichte und Pressestimmen des neutralen Auslands* (Munich, 1963). pp. 260–62.

39. Doc. 69, in ibid., p. 265.

40. Discovery document 164, Order of the Day, 22 March 1945, p. 4; Corgi ed. 1966, pp. 259–60, appendix IV.

41. R. A. C. Parker, *Struggle for Survival: The History of the Second World War* (Oxford and New York, 1989), p. 167.

42. Discovery document 155, Irving to Dieter Struss, 28 November 1964.

43. Corgi ed., 1966, pp. 221–22; Focal Point ed., pp. 234–36.

44. Focal Point ed., p. 235.

45. Corgi ed., 1966, pp. 222, 260.

46.   DJ 12, Irving to Corgi Books, 25 May 1965.

47.   DJ 12, "Required Alterations in the Dresden Book," undated, 21 pp.

48.   Corgi ed., 1966, p. 280. My italics.

49.   Doc. 157, Irving to Oberst Teske, 1 December 1964.

50.   DJ 10, Bundesarchiv to Irving, 13 January 1965; DJ 35, Boberach (Bundesarchiv) to Irving, 13 May 1966.

51.   DJ 12, copy of Bundesarchiv to Irving, 13 January 1965, with pen marginalia, stamped as received 15 March 1965.

52.   DJ 10, interview with Major Nölke by *Stern* reporter.

53.   DJ 35, Virchow to Sakowsky, 4 February 1965.

54.   DJ 35, *Stern Hausmitteilung*, Gerd Baatz to Sakowski, 6 February 1965, received by Irving 15 March 1965.

55.   DJ 10, Irving to Werner Bühlmann, 24 June 1965.

56.   DJ 10, Werner Bühlmann to Irving, undated, received 21 July 1965.

57.   Heyne ed., 1985, appendix 5, "Aktennotiz zu einem Interview mit Frau Eva Grosse, München, Johanisplatz 14, am 10. Juli 1965 von 21.30 bis 22.30 Uhr in ihrer Wohnung," pp. 295–97.

58.   Heyne ed., 1985, p. 295.

59.   Ibid., p. 297.

60.   Ibid., p. 296. My italics.

61.   Corgi ed., 1966, p. 259. My italics.

62.   Focal Point ed., p. 240.

63.   DJ 35, Max Funfack to Irving, 19 January 1965.

64.   Doc. 160, Irving to Croix-Rouge, Comité International, Geneva, 27.1.65.

65.   DJ 35, P. Vibert (International Committee of the Red Cross) to Irving, 4 and 17 February 1965.

66.   DJ 35, idem to Irving, 17 February 1965.

67.   Corgi ed., 1966, p. 225.

68.   DJ 35, Max Funfack to Irving, 19 January 1965.

69.   Focal Point ed., p. 266.

70.   DJ 35, P. Vibert (International Committee of the Red Cross) to Irving, 17 February 1965; Irving to Walter Kleiner, 20 February 1965.

71.   Focal Point ed., p. 298 n. 29.

72.   DJ 35, Max Funfack to Irving, 19 March 1965.

73.   Ibid.

74.   DJ 35, Theo Miller to Irving, 7 February 1965.

75.   DJ 35, Theo Miller to Irving, 25 February 1965.

76.   Ibid.

77.   DJ 35, Theo Miller to Irving, 26 February 1965.

78.   The full title of this document was *Der Höhere SS- und Polizeiführer Elbe an den Gauen Halle-Merseburg, Sachsen und im Wehrkreis*

IV—*Befehlshaber der Ordnungspolizei, Schlussmeldung über die vier Luftangriffe auf den LS-Ort Dresden am 13., 14. und 15. Februar 1945*, signed [Police Colonel Wolfgang] Thierig, Eilenberg, 15 March 1945.

79. Weidauer, *Inferno*, p. 134.

80. Kimber ed., p. 223.

81. Bergander, *Dresden*, pp. 164–6.

82. DJ 35, Walter Lange to Irving, 5 April 1966; Irving to Walter Lange, 12 April 1966.

83. DJ 35, Walter Lange to Irving, 27 May 1966.

84. Focal Point ed., p. 299, nns. 36 and 37.

85. DJ 35, Boberach to Irving, 13 May 1966.

86. Bergander, *Dresden*, p. 164.

87. Ibid., p. 165.

88. DJ 35, Irving to Boberach, 16 May 1966.

89. DJ 35, "The Dresden Air Raids—A Correction," second draft, 29 June 1966; record of telephone conversation or message, 30 June 1966.

90. Doc. 180, Irving to *The Times*, 7 July 1966.

91. DJ 35, Irving to *The Sunday Telegraph*, 7 July 1966.

92. Dresden Updated Materials, Melden E. Smith Jr., "Dresden Revisited: New Perspectives on a Lingering Controversy," presented to the 1978 Missouri Valley History Conference, p. 5.

93. Doc. 182, Irving to Amy Howlett, 28.8.1966; doc. 183, list of alterations in the text of *The Destruction of Dresden*; doc. 1870, Irving to Calabi, Arnoldo Mondadori Editori, 28.8.1966.

94. Doc. 185, Irving to Alan Earney, 14 September 1966; doc. 187, Irving to Alan Earney, 16 September 1966.

95. DJ 35, record of telephone conversation with John Moorehead of the *Evening Standard*, 10:10 A.M., 7 July 1966.

96. DJ 35, Irving to R. H. Haydon, 11 July 1966.

97. DJ 35, Irving to Rudolf Lusar, 11 August 1966.

98. Doc. 184, Calabi to Irving, 9 September 1966. She simply wrote that she could "quite understand" Irving not wanting his letter to *The Times* to be reprinted.

99. Rowohlt ed., 1967, pp. 210–11, 247–48.

100. Bergander, *Dresden*, p. 161. There would have been no motive on Ehrlich's part for removing the zero, and since his copies were made in the police station, any tampering with the text of the original would immediately have come to light. The figure of 25,000 explained the comment in the report that rumors 'far exceeded' the reality.

101.   Heyne ed., 1985 (and therefore 1977), p. 223.
102.   Focal Point ed., pp. 239–40.
103.   Discovery document 1833, Irving to the Dresden City Museum, 10.3.1997.
104.   Discovery document 1063, Irving to the *Süddeutsche Zeitung*, 15 February 1985.
105.   Focal Point ed., p. 45.
106.   Ibid., p. 63.
107.   Ibid., p. 244.
108.   Ibid., pp. 243, 244.
109.   Corgi ed., 1966, vii; Corgi ed., 1971, p. 7.
110.   Corgi ed., 1966, p. 83; Focal Point ed., p. 82.
111.   Focal Point ed., p. 188; Corgi ed., 1966, p. 185.
112.   Corgi ed., 1966, p. 106.
113.   Ibid., p. 272.
114.   Focal Point ed., p. 104.
115.   Ibid., p. 176 and p. 290 n. 12; Heyne ed., 1985, appendix 3, p. 277.
116.   Feydt, quoted in Bergander, *Dresden*, p. 153.
117.   Bergander, *Dresden*, p. 154.
118.   Ibid., pp. 155–7.
119.   Friedrich Reichert, "Verbrannt bis zur Unkenntlichkeit," in Dresden City Museum (ed.), *Verbrannt bis zur Unkenntlichkeit: Die Zerstörung Dresdens 1945* (Altenburg, 1994), p. 55. Förster also gave the same figure, but allowed for a number of evacuees from the Rhineland, p. 309.
120.   Heyne ed., 1985, p. 289.
121.   Reichert, "Verbrannt bis zur Unkenntlichkeit," p. 58.
122.   Focal Point ed., p. 260.
123.   Corgi ed., 1966, p. 213; Focal Point ed., p. 224.
124.   Bergander, *Dresden*, pp. 165–66.
125.   Weidauer, *Inferno*, p. 126.
126.   The new material was discovered in the Stadtarchiv Dresden, *Marschall und Bestattungsamt, Nachtrag 1 and 5.*
127.   Corgi ed., 1966, pp. 214–15; Focal Point ed., pp. 225–26.
128.   Reichert, "Verbrannt bis zur Unkenntlichkeit," p. 58.
129.   Corgi ed., 1966, p. 216; Focal Point ed., pp. 227–28.
130.   Reichert, "Verbrannt bis zur Unkenntlichkeit," p. 58.
131.   Focal Point ed., p. xiii.
132.   Weidauer, *Inferno*, p. 120.
133.   Reichert, "Verbrannt bis zur Unkenntlichkeit," p. 58.
134.   Focal Point ed., pp. 272, xiii. My italics.
135.   Irving to Richard Crossman, 26 May 1963, PRO, FO 371/169329.

136.   Reichert, "Verbrannt bis zur Unkenntlichkeit," p. 61.
137.   Doc. 1340, obituary for William Kimber by Irving, 1 May 1991, published in *The Daily Telegraph*.
138.   Discovery document 1866.
139.   Discovery document 143.
140.   Focal Point ed., preface.
141.   Focal Point ed., p. xiv; doc. 1866, Kimber to Irving, 3 April 1963; doc. 143, Irving to William Kimber, 25 April 1963.
142.   Discovery document 143, Irving to William Kimber, 4 April 1963.
143.   Discovery document 147, Irving to Sydney Silverman, 2 June 1963.
144.   "German Reunification and other topics," speech at Latvian Hall, Toronto, 8 November 1990, transcript on Irving's website http://fpp. co.uk (see Videotape 190).
145.   U. Hohn, *Die Zerstörung deutscher Städte im Zweiten Weltkrieg* (Dortmund, 1991), p. 119 and p. 208 n. 586; H. Bardua, "Kriegsschäden in Baden-Württemberg 1939–1945," in Kommission für geschichtliche Landeskunde in Baden-Württemberg (ed.), *Historischer Atlas von Baden-Württemberg* (Stuttgart, 1975), p. 8; W. A. Boelcke, "Wirtschaft und Sozialsituationen," in O. Borst (ed.), *Das Dritte Reich in Baden und Württemberg* (Stuttgart, 1988), pp. 29–45, here p. 40.
146.   Focal Point ed., p. viii.
147.   For instance, his claim to *The Times* on 7 July 1966 that he had "no interest in promoting or perpetuating false legends"; Discovery document 180, Irving to *The Times,* 7 July 1966.
148.   Videotape 175: David Irving, "A Return to Honesty and Truth in History,' Elangani Hotel, Durban, South Africa, 5 March 1986.
149.   Videotape 226: unedited material from the "This Week" program, 28 November 1991.
150.   Videotape 184: Leuchter Report press conference, London, 23 June 1989. The titles read: "The Truth at Last, Six Million Lies, Focal Point Video."
151.   Videotape 200: Irving, "The Search for Truth in History—Banned!" 1993.
152.   Discovery document 1063, Irving to the *Süddeutsche Zeitung,* 15 February 1985.
153.   Discovery document 1064, Irving to *The Times,* 21.2.1985 (unpublished).

CHAPTER SIX

1.   David Robson, "A Game of Hide and Seek with Truth Behind the Barbed Wire," *Daily Express* (Early Edition), 18 March 2000, p. 11;

Stephen Moss, "History's Verdict on Holocaust Upheld," *The Guardian,* (Early Edition) 12 April 2000, p. 5.

2.   Geoffrey Wheatcroft, "Lies and libel," *The Guardian* (Early Edition), 18 March 2000, p. 22.

3.   Neal Ascherson, "Last Battle of Hitler's Historians," *The Observer,* 16 January 2000, p. 20.

4.   Moss, "History's Verdict," p. 5, quoting Goldhagen.

5.   Peter Longerich, "Wider die deutsche Ignoranz," *Frankfurter Allgemeine Zeitung,* 19 April 2000.

6.   A. C. Grayling, "The Last Word on History," *The Guardian Saturday Review,* 15 January 2000, p. 12.

7.   Anne Sebba, "Irrational Debates," *The Times Higher Education Supplement,* 7 January 2000, p. 16.

8.   Werner Birkenmaier, "Historie und Holocaust," *Stuttgarter Zeitung,* 13 March 2000.

9.   Ascherson, "Last Battle," p. 20.

10. Rachel Donnelly, "Irving Tells Court He Expects to Be Arrested in Britain," *The Irish Times* (Dublin, Main Edition), 14 January 2000, p. 1; also Simon Rocker, "Trial of Concentration Offers Many Pauses for Thought," *Jewish Chronicle,* 21 January 2000, p. 10.

11. Rocker, "Trial of Concentration Offers Many Pauses for Thought," p. 10.

12. Cal McCrystal, "Court No. 73 Comes to Auschwitz," *London Evening Standard,* 11 February 2000, pp. 30–31.

13. Ralf Dahrendorf, "Der Verstand triumphiert," *Die Zeit,* 19 April 2000.

14. *A Radical's Diary,* 10 February 2000, fpp.co.uk/online/.

15. "Arrogant Irving 'Has an Inferiority Complex.' The Best Broadcasts: from Radio 4," *The Guardian* (The Editor), 21 April 2000, p. 18.

16. "Irving's Last Stand," *The Economist,* 15–21 January 2000, p. 34.

17. "Irving Faces Extradition to Germany," *Metro London,* 14 January 2000, p. 11; "Germans Want to Extradite Me—Irving," *The Birmingham Post,* 14 January 2000, p. 7, etc.

18. Neal Ascherson, "In Dubio Pro Hitler," *Süddeutsche Zeitung,* 29 January 2000.

19. Ralf Sottscheck, "Verhandelt wird der Holocaust: Gerichtlich wehrt sich David Irving dagegen, ein"gefährlicher Holocaust-Verleugner" genannt zu werden. Längst ist er dabei selbst beklagter," *Die Tageszeitung* (Berlin), 16 March 2000.

20. Jenny Booth, "Humiliation for Holocaust Sceptic," *The Scotsman,* 12 April 2000, p. 4.

21. Dan Jacobson, "The Downfall of David Irving," *The Times Literary Supplement,* 21 April 2000, pp. 12–13.

22.   TS 10/2, p. 103.

23.   Jonathan Freedland, "Court 73—Where History Is on Trial," *The Guardian* (Early Edition), 5 February 2000, p. 3.

24.   James Dalrymple, "He Says Auschwitz Is a Myth, But He Has Never Set Foot in the Place, Never Seen the Evidence," *The Independent* (Early Edition), 12 April 2000, p. 5.

25.   Freedland, "Court 73—Where History Is on Trial," p. 3.

26.   Simon Rocker, "Quietly Floored by the Don," *Jewish Chronicle*, 14 April 2000, p. 37.

27.   Kate Taylor (ed.), *Holocaust Denial: The David Irving Trial and International Revisionism* (London, 2000), pp. 30–32.

28.   Neal Ascherson, "Last Battle of Hitler's Historians," *The Observer* (Early Edition), 16 January 2000, p. 20.

29.   Philipp Blom, "Rückkehr zur Realität," *Berliner Zeitung*, 12 April 2000.

30.   James Dalrymple, "The Curse of Revisionism," *The Independent* (Weekend Review), 29 January 2000, p. 4; similarly, Dan Jacobson, "The Downfall of David Irving," *The Times Literary Supplement*, 21 April 2000, pp. 12–13.

31.   Jacobson, "The Downfall," pp. 12–13.

32.   John Keegan, "The Trial of David Irving—and My Part in His Downfall," *The Daily Telegraph*, (Early Edition) 12 April 2000, p. 28.

33.   Robert Treichler, "Herrn Irvings Attacke," *Profil* (Vienna), 17 January 2000.

34.   Eva Menasse, "Entführung ins Detail," *Frankfurter Allgemeine Zeitung*, 20 January 2000.

35.   TS 17/2, p. 21.

36.   TS 16/2, pp. 72–73. For further expressions of the judge's impatience with Irving's irrelevant questions, see also TS 10/2, p. 53; TS 15/2, p. 22; TS 15/2, p. 77, TS 15/2, p. 82; TS 15/2 pp. 133; TS 16/2, p. 119.

37.   TS 17/2, p. 24.

38.   TS 15/2, p. 45.

39.   Ibid., pp. 178–79.

40.   TS 16/2, p. 134.

41.   TS 15/2, pp. 84–85; Irving, *Nuremberg*, pp. 51, 113, 127, 149–50, 241.

42.   TS 21/2, pp. 183–84.

43.   TS 15/2, p. 149.

44.   Ibid., p. 152.

45.   Ibid., p. 191.

46.   E.g., TS 16/2, p. 142, one example of many.

47. TS 16/2, p. 144, followed shortly afterwards by a formal ruling that Irving had to move on (p. 145).
48. TS 11/1, p. 16.
49. TS 10/2, pp. 156–57.
50. TS 11/1, p. 89.
51. Gerald Posner, "The World According to David Irving," *The Observer* (Early Edition), 19 March 2000, p. 3.
52. TS 7/2, p. 31.
53. TS 15/2, pp. 201–7; TS 31/1, p. 61.
54. TS 20/1, p. 103.
55. TS 16/2, pp. 17–23.
56. Ibid., pp. 50, 58.
57. Ibid., pp. 44–45.
58. TS 31/1, pp. 106, 112.
59. TS 12/1, pp. 162–63.
60. Ibid., pp. 285–91; TS 13/1, pp. 7–10, 29–32.
61. TS 17/2, pp. 54–61.
62. Irving, *Hitler's War*, 1977 ed., p. 332.
63. IfZ, Archiv F 37/2, also in Witte et al. (eds.), *Der Dienstkalender*, p. 280.
64. Irving, *Hitler's War*, 1991, p. 427.
65. TS 17/2, pp. 66–72.
66. TS 13/1, pp. 70–74.
67. Operational Situation Report USSR No. 156, 16.1.1942; reprinted in Y. Arad, S. Krakowski, and S. Spector (eds.), *The Einsatzgruppen Reports* (New York, 1989), pp. 279–83; IfZ Gh 02 47/3, Urteil des Schwurgerichts Hamburg in der Strafsache gegen J. und andere, vom 23.2.1973.
68. Irving, *Goebbels*, p. 645, n. 42, referring to ND-NO 3257.
69. Ibid., p. 379 and p. 645 n. 42; A. Ezergailis, *The Holocaust in Latvia 1941–1944* (Riga, 1996), p. 261.
70. TS 17/2, pp. 35–40.
71. TS 13/1, p. 87. TS 11/1, p. 46.
72. TS 13/1, p. 93.
73. GTB II/2, p. 498, entry for 13.12.1941.
74. TS 7/2, p. 84.
75. TS 13/1, pp. 162–82; TS 17/1, pp. 155–86.
76. Ibid., p. 170.
77. TS 17/2, pp. 167–72; TS 21/2, p. 154.
78. TS 18/1, pp. 50–51.
79. Ibid., p. 58.

80.   TS 8/2, pp. 74–81.

81.   TS 18/1, p.23.

82.   Ibid., p. 35.

83.   TS 19/1, p. 121; also TS 20/1, pp. 79–80.

84.   TS 15/2, pp. 128–29.

85.   Shermer and Grobman, *Denying History*, p. 55 (with photograph).

86.   TS 12/1, pp. 239–41.

87.   Taylor (ed.), *Holocaust Denial*, p. 25.

88.   TS 12/1, p. 232.

89.   TS 17/1, pp. 110–16.

90.   TS 18/1, p. 10.

91.   Ibid., pp. 126–27.

92.   *The Irving Judgment* (London, 2000) pp. 167–68, 344–45.

93.   TS 24/1, pp. 14, 25.

94.   *Diary of Anne Frank: The Critical Edition* (New York, 1989).

95.   TS 15/2, pp. 61–82; Harwood, *Did Six Million Really Die?* pp. 109–11; Butz, *Hoax*, p. 37; Faurisson, "Le Journal d'Anne Frank est-il authentique?" in S. Thion (ed.), *Vérité historique ou vérité politique?* (Paris, 1980).

96.   TS 15/2, pp. 95–98.

97.   TS 15/2, pp. 98–99.

98.   Ibid., p. 5.

99.   TS 2/1, pp. 80–81.

100.   Ibid., pp. 77, 95–98.

101.   Irving, Closing Statement, p. 1; TS 15/3, p. 50. The transcript differs from the typed version distributed by Irving at the trial, since Irving extemporized in numerous places, departing slightly from the text, and, more important, cut out a number of passages at the behest of the judge.

102.   Irving, Closing Statement, p. 2; TS 15/3, p. 52.

103.   Irving, Closing Statement, pp. 10–15; TS 15/3, pp. 66–72.

104.   TS 15/3, pp. 117, 131, 184, 209.

105.   Ibid., p. 162.

106.   Ibid., p. 194 ("I am clearly heard to say 'You must not,' because they are shouting the 'Siegheil' slogans, Mein Führer, and things like 'you must not always be thinking of the past' "); the prepared text merely refers to "the offscreen chanting of slogans'—Closing Statement, p. 91.

107.   Emma Klein, "Holocaust Whitewash," *The Tablet*, 15 April 2000, p. 508; Rocker, "Quietly Floored," p. 37.

108.   Rela Mintz Geffen, "Friend of Deborah Exits the Court Believing

Irving Is One to Beware," *Jewish Telegraphic Agency*, 21 March 2000.

CHAPTER SEVEN

1. Eva Menasse, "Wer nicht gegen mich ist, der ist für mich," *Frankfurter Allgemeine Zeitung*, 2 February 2000; *A Radical's Diary*, http://www.fpp.co.uk, 15/2, 15 Feb. 2000.
2. *A Radical's Diary*, 31/1, 31 Jan. 2000.
3. Irving, Closing Statement, p. 3; TS 15/3, pp. 53–54.
4. Clare Dyer, "Judging history," *The Guardian*, 17 April 2000, p. 10.
5. *The Irving Judgment*, pp. 335–39.
6. Ibid., pp. 298–307, 324–25.
7. Ibid., pp. 338–44.
8. Ibid., pp. 344–46.
9. Ibid., pp. 326, 329–30.
10. Ibid., pp. 346–47.
11. Vikram Dodd, "Irving: Consigned to History as a Racist Liar," *The Guardian* (Early Edition), 12 April 2000, p. 1.
12. Neal Ascherson, "The Battle May Be Over—But the War Goes On," *The Observer*, 16 April 2000, p. 19.
13. Michael Horsnell, "False Witness," *The Times*, section 2, 12 April 2000, pp. 3–5.
14. Paul Cheston, " 'Nazi' Author Loses His £2m Libel Battle," *London Evening Standard*, 11 April 2000, p. 5; Ian Burrell, "How History Will Judge David Irving," *The Independent* (Early Edition), 12 April 2000, p. 1; Dodd, "Irving," p. 1.
15. Gillian Glover, "Hitler's Part in My Downfall—or How I Lost a Courtroom War," *The Scotsman*, 18 April 2000, p. 14.
16. Vikram Dodd, "Beaten Irving Vows to Fight Attempts to Seize Home," *The Guardian*, 15 April 2000.
17. "Beef Tripe: David Irving," *Evening Standard*, 14 April 2000, p. 15.
18. Mark Bateman, "Why It Was Worth Taking On Irving," *The Times* (Law), 18 April 2000, p. 11.
19. Horsnell, "False Witness," p. 3.
20. Werner Birkenmaier, "Wahrheit vor Gericht," *Stuttgarter Zeitung*, 12 April 2000.
21. Dodd, "Irving," p. 1; Neil Tweedie, "Advice from Hitler Sends Ally on Road to Defeat," *Daily Telegraph* (Early Edition), 12 April 2000, pp. 4–5.
22. Piachra Gibbons, "Author with No Publisher and Few Funds

Landed with £2.5m Bill," *The Guardian* (Early Edition), 12 April 2000, p. 5.

23. Nick Fielding, "Hunt for Irving's Backers as Lawyers Seek £2m Costs," *The Sunday Times* (Early Edition), 16 April 2000, p. 11.

24. Reinhart Häcker, "Niederlage für einen Unbelehrbaren," *Kölner Stadt-Anzeiger,* 12 April 2000.

25. Sebastian Borger, "Du sollst nicht leugnen," *Potsdamer Neueste Nachrichten,* 12 April 2000.

26. "Racist Historian Faces £2m Bill for Libel Defeat," *Daily Telegraph* (Early Edition), 12 April 2000, p. 1.

27. Dan Jacobson, "The Downfall of David Irving," *The Times Literary Supplement,* 21 April 2000, pp. 12–13.

28. Lipstadt's allegation that the German historian Ernst Nolte had taken from Irving the claim that Hitler's "internment' of Jews was justified because they were at war with Germany was false: Irving took over the idea from Nolte.

29. "The Right Impression," *Jewish Telegraph* (Leeds), 19 April 2000, p. 4.

30. John Waters, "The Greatest Threat to Truth Comes from Denial," *The Irish Times,* 17 April 2000, p. 16.

31. "Jewish Leaders Criticise BBC over Irving," *The Herald* (Glasgow), 19 April 2000, p. 14.

32. *The Irving Judgment,* p. 293.

33. Ibid., p. 317.

34. Ibid., p. 327.

35. "A Radical's Diary," 11–17 April 2000, http://www.fpp.co.uk.

36. Glover, "Hitler's Part," p. 14.

37. Alex O'Connell, Michael Horsnell, and Linus Gergoriardis, "Irving's Cash Backers Stay in the Shadows," *The Times* (Early Edition), 12 April 2000, p. 6.

38. Andrew Roberts, "Irving's Greatest Triumph," *The Sunday Telegraph* (Early Edition), 16 April 2000, p. 32.

39. "Penguin Picks Up Moral Points in Libel Trial," *PR Week,* 21 April 2000, p. 6.

40. "Lest We Forget," *Daily Record* (Scotland), 13 April 2000, p. 13.

41. Lord Weidenfeld, "Irvings Furor," *Die Welt* (Berlin), 17 April 2000.

42. "Letter from London," "Extracted from the February Smith's Report," by Bradley Smith, on http://www.fpp.co.uk. ("What Revisionists Say About the Irving Trial").

43. Robert Mendick, "Loophole Lets BNP onto Town Council," *Independent on Sunday* (Early Edition), 16 April 2000, p. 13.

44. Ernst Zündel, "Extract from His Newsletter," and "Those Who

Choose to Be Their Own Lawyer, Choose a Fool," by Germar Rudolf, in "What Revisionists Say About the Irving Trial."

45. Robert Faurisson, "David Irving, at the Moment," 19 January 2000, in ibid.

46. Duncan Campbell, "Irving Turns to US Fans to Fund His Legal Costs," *The Guardian*, 31 May 2000.

47. Leader column, *The Guardian*, 12 April 2000; similarly, David Cesarani, "The Denial Was Always There," *The Sunday Times* (News Review), 16 April 2000, p. 7.

48. "Victory for a Truth Which Must Not Be Forgotten," *The Scotsman*, 12 April 2000, p. 17.

49. Tom Bower, "A Brilliant Historian Ruined by a Fatal Flaw." *Daily Mail* (Early Edition), 12 April 2000, pp. 6–7.

50. Conor Cruise O'Brien, "This Man Claims This Simply Never Happened," *Irish Independent* (Dublin), 15 January 2000, p. 6.

51. Peter Simple, "History," *The Daily Telegraph* (Early Edition), 21 April 2000, p. 28.

52. Stuart Nicolson, "Beliefs Turned Historian into International Pariah," *The Scotsman*, 12 January 2000, p. 2.

53. Tony Judt, "Wahrheit oder Integrität," *Süddeutsche Zeitung*, 14 April 2000.

54. John Erickson, "A Case of 'Forensic' Madness," *The Scotsman*, 12 April 2000, p. 4.

55. TS 7/2, p. 4.

56. Ibid., pp. 8–9.

57. John Keegan, "The Trial of David Irving—and My Part in His Downfall," *The Daily Telegraph* (Early Edition), 12 April 2000, p. 28.

58. Craig, *The Germans,* p. 72.

59. Trevor-Roper, "Hitler."

60. Sydnor, "The Selling"; Lukács, *The Hitler of History.*

61. Brendan Glacken, "It's Never That Simple," *The Irish Times*, 17 April 2000, p. 16.

62. TS 20/1, pp. 27, 40.

63. Ibid., pp. 40–41.

64. Donald Cameron Watt, "History Still Needs Its David Irvings," *London Evening Standard*, 11 April 2000, p. 13. Watt used the same comparison in conversation with the Austrian journalist Eva Menasse after his appearance in court (Eva Menasse, "Nennt mich pervers," *Frankfurter Allgemeine Zeitung*, 24 January 2000).

65. TS 11/1, p. 26.

66. Petra Steinberger, "Der Fälscher," *Süddeutsche Zeitung*, 12 April

        2000; Klaus Grimberg, "Ein Signal," *Neue Osnabrücker Zeitung*, 12
        April 2000.
67.   TS 20/1, p. 49.
68.   Ibid., pp. 42–43.
69.   Watt, "History," p. 13. In fact, only one historian was employed on
        this task, namely myself, and my report dealt with other works of Irv-
        ing besides his books on Hitler.
70.   N. Robinson, "The Irving Debate Simmers On," *The Guardian*, 13
        April 2000, p. 23.
71.   Anne McElvoy, "Unfortunately, Holocaust Denial Will Not End
        Here," *The Independent* (Review), 12 April 2000, p. 3.
72.   For a brief discussion, with further references, see Richard J. Evans,
        In Defence of History (London, 1997), pp. 116–24.
73.   Jackson, *The Case for David Irving*, p. 30.
74.   Thomas L. Haskell, "Objectivity Is Not Neutrality: Rhetoric and
        Practice in Peter Novick's *That Noble Dream*," *History and Theory*,
        vol. 29 (1990), pp. 129–57, here p. 132.
75.   Quoted in ibid., p. 121.
76.   Jäckel, "Noch einmal," p. 164.
77.   John Lukács, "The Price of Defending Hitler," *Newsweek*, 24 April
        2000, p. 4.
78.   Ascherson, "The Battle," p. 19.
79.   Howard Jacobson, "Just Because a Lot of People Agree on Some-
        thing Doesn't Mean They're Right," *The Independent* (Review), 15
        April 2000, p. 5.
80.   "Monitor," *The Independent* (Friday Review), 14 April 2000, p. 2.
81.   Peter Simple, "History," p. 28.
82.   Magnus Linklater, "This Is the Real Price of David Irving's Lies:
        Now Even the Most Honest Holocaust Scholar Risks Being
        Smeared," *The Times*, 13 April 2000, p. 20; endorsed by reader's let-
        ter from Roger Moorhouse, "Holocaust research," *The Times* (Early
        Edition), 22 April 2000, p. 23.
83.   Jürgen Krönig, "Ehrgeiz und Lügen," *Die Zeit*, 5 April 2000. Krönig's
        article contained many distortions in Irving's favor. He quoted the 1977
        edition of *Hitler's War* without apparently realizing that Irving's views
        on the Holocaust had changed by the time he revised the book in 1991;
        he mentioned Irving's admissions of error in court without apparently
        realizing the damage they did to his case; he cited Hugh Trevor-Roper's
        praise of Irving's energy as a researcher without mentioning the fact
        that the Oxford historian went on to say that he did not regard Irving
        as a historian at all, because he used the documents he collected to bol-
        ster preconceived and ideologically motivated arguments; and he cited

without comment Donald Cameron Watt's ignorant remark that the works of other historians would probably not be able to withstand the kind of scrutiny to which Irving's work had been subjected.

84.   "Don't Silence Irving," *Manchester Evening News*, 18 April 2000, p. 9.

85.   N. Robinson, in "Irving: The Debate Simmers On," *The Guardian*, 13 April 2000, p. 23.

86.   Bill Abbotts, in "Irving: The Debate Simmers On," *The Guardian*, 13 April 2000, p. 23.

87.   Linklater, "This Is the Real Price," p. 20.

88.   Ibid.

89.   Dieter Ebeling, "Hitlers williger Anwalt," *Berliner Morgenpost*, 3 March 2000.

90.   Glacken, "It's Never," p. 16.

91.   Martin Mears, "You're Free to Say Anything I Want," *The Times* (Legal), 15 February 2000, p. 12.

92.   David Robson, "The Liar Exposed at Last," *Daily Express*, 12 April 2000, p. 11.

93.   David Cesarani, "Irving Exposed as a Liar with No Interest in Pursuit of Truth," *The Irish Times*, 12 April 2000, p. 16.

94.   Horsnell, "False Witness," p. 3.

95.   Jost Nolte, "Irvings Waterloo," *Berliner Morgenpost*, 12 April 2000.

96.   Thomas Kielinger, "Das Sagbare und das Unsägliche," *Die Welt*, 18 April 2000.

97.   Anthony Julius and James Libson, "Losing Was Unthinkable. The Rest Is History," *The Independent* (Tuesday Review), 18 April 2000, p. 11.

98.   Horsnell, "False Witness," p. 5.

99.   "History and Bunk," *The Times* (Early Edition), leader, 12 April 2000, p. 23.

100.   "The Bad History Man," *Daily Telegraph* (Early Edition), 12 April 2000, p. 29. The *Telegraph* leader was in error, however, when it went on to say that Irving's defeat had no implications for free speech. Free speech, after all, had been upheld.

101.   Leader, *Daily Express*, 12 April 2000, p. 10 ("Deserved Defeat for Racist Who Denied Nazi History").

102.   Ian Burrell, "How History Will Judge David Irving," *The Independent* (Early Edition), 12 April 2000, p. 1.

103.   Kielinger, "Das Sagbare."

104.   "The Bad History Man," p. 29.

105.   McElvoy, "Unfortunately," p. 3.

106.   Julius and Libson, "Losing," p. 11.

107.   Mark Bateman, "Why It Was Worth Taking on Irving," *The Times* (Law), 18 April 2000, p. 11.

108.   Leader, *The Independent,* 12 January 2000, p. 3.

109.   Geoffrey Wheatcroft, "Lies and Libel," *The Guardian* (Early Edition), 18 March 2000, p. 22.

110.   "The Cost of Free Speech—England's Libel Laws Are Still Rotten," *The Guardian* leader (Early Edition), 13 April 2000, p. 23; similar condemnation in the *Daily Post* (Wales), 12 April 2000, p. 6.

111.   Matt Rees, "Israelis Welcome the Court Decision," *The Scotsman,* 12 April 2000, p. 4.

112.   Jonathan Freedland, "Let's Close the Book," *The Guardian,* (Early Edition), 12 April 2000, p. 21.

113.   David Cesarani, "History on Trial," *The Guardian,* 18 January 2000, pp. 1–3.

114.   Tim Cole, *Images of the Holocaust: The Myth of the 'Shoah Business'* (London, 1999).

115.   "Survivors Welcome Verdict," *Eastern Daily Press,* 12 April 2000, p. 8.

116.   Katrina Tweedie, " 'This man should have spent five minutes in Auschwitz,' " *The Scotsman,* 12 April 2000, p. 4.

117.   "Holocaust Seminar," *London Jewish News,* 17 March 2000, p. 5.

118.   Eve-Ann Prentice, "You Could Smell the Bodies Burning," *The Times* (Early Edition), 18 January 2000, p. 34.

119.   *Jewish Chronicle,* 14 April 2000.

120.   "The Bad History Man," *Daily Telegraph* leader (Early Edition), 12 April 2000, p. 29. The leader also reported Irving's "failure to persuade the court that he had been defamed" by Lipstadt's book. In fact, the defense admitted from the outset that the remarks made about Irving in the book were defamatory, and sought—successfully, as it turned out—to justify them on the grounds that they were true.

121.   Jan Colley, Cathy Gordon, and John Aston, " 'Evil Racist' Irving Faces Libel Ruin," *The Birmingham Post,* 12 April 2000, p. 7.

122.   Horsnell, "False Witness," p. 5.

123.   Vikram Dodd, "Irving," p. 1.

124.   Lipstadt, *Denying,* p. xiii. Unerring in his ability to hit the wrong note, Donald Cameron Watt pushed this line of thought one stage further when he asked: "What happens when the witnesses are all dead, if the reality has not been thrashed out? The truth needs an Irving's challenge to keep it alive." (Watt, "History," p. 13). This assumed that the reality had not been 'thrashed out,' and ignored all the research that had been going on in the field for the past thirty years.

125.   Freedland, "Let's Close the Book," p. 21.
126.   Robert Treichler, "Herrn Irvings Attacke," *Profil* (Vienna), 17 January 2000.
127.   Eva Menasse, "David Irving hat verloren," *Frankfurter Allgemeine Zeitung*, 13 April 2000.
128.   Thomas Kielinger, "Die Geschichte bewusst verdreht," *Die Welt* (Berlin), 12 April 2000.
129.   McElvoy, "Unfortunately," p. 3.
130.   "Internationale Reaktionen auf David Irvings verlorenen Prozess," *Die Welt* (Berlin), 13 April 2000.
131.   James Dalrymple, "He Says Auschwitz Is a Myth, But He Has Never Set Foot in the Place, Never Seen the Evidence," *The Independent* (Early Edition), 12 April 2000, p. 5.
132.   "Truth's Sheer Weight," *The Guardian*, leader column, 12 April 2000.
133.   The Bad History Man," p. 29.

INDEX